SHONEN JUMP GRAPHIC NOVEL

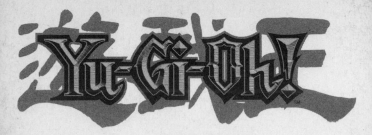

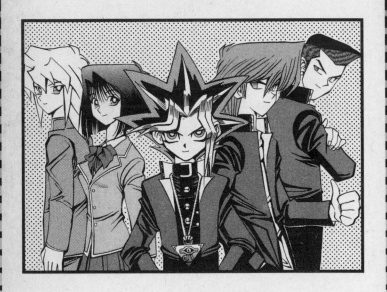

Vol. 7
MONSTER WORLD
STORY AND ART BY
KAZUKI TAKAHASHI

THE STORY SO FAR...

When he solved the ancient Egyptian Millennium Puzzle, shy 10th-grader Yugi became *Yu-Gi-Oh*, the King of Games! When Yugi met Bakura, a new transfer student, he discovered that he wasn't the only high school student with a Millennium Item. To make friends with Bakura, Yugi and his friends invited themselves over to play the tabletop role-playing game "Monster World." But little did they know that Bakura was the hapless host of the evil spirit of the Millennium Ring! Now, the players have walked into Bakura's trap, and if they lose, their souls will be trapped in the game... forever!

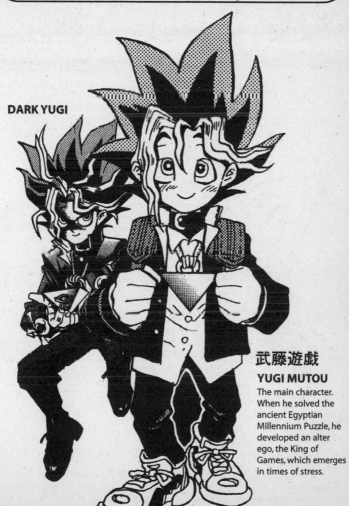

DARK YUGI

武藤遊戯

YUGI MUTOU

The main character.
When he solved the
ancient Egyptian
Millennium Puzzle, he
developed an alter
ego, the King of
Games, which emerges
in times of stress.

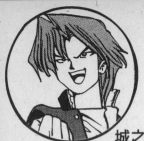

真崎杏子

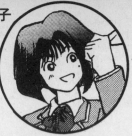

KATSUYA JONOUCHI
城之内克也

Yugi's classmate, a tough guy who gets in lots of fights. He used to think Yugi was a wimp, but now they are good friends. In the English anime he's known as "Joey Wheeler."

ANZU MAZAKI

Yugi's classmate and childhood friend. She fell in love with the charismatic voice of Yugi's alter ego, but doesn't know that they're the same person. Her first name means "Peach." In the English anime she's known as "Téa Gardner."

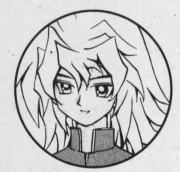

摸良　了

RYO BAKURA

Like Yugi, Bakura has two personalities: a shy, insecure high school student who loves RPGs, and a sadistic game master with supernatural powers.

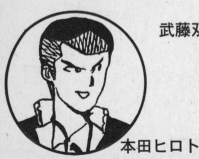

武藤双六

本田ヒロト

HIROTO HONDA

Yugi's classmate, a friend of Jonouchi. In the English anime he's known as "Tristan Taylor."

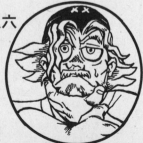

SUGOROKU MUTOU

Yugi's grandfather, the owner of the Kame ("Turtle") game store. His first name, "Sugoroku", is a Japanese game similar to backgammon.

Yu-Gi-Oh!

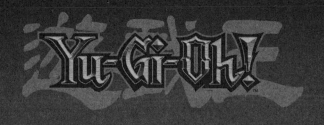

Vol. 7

CONTENTS

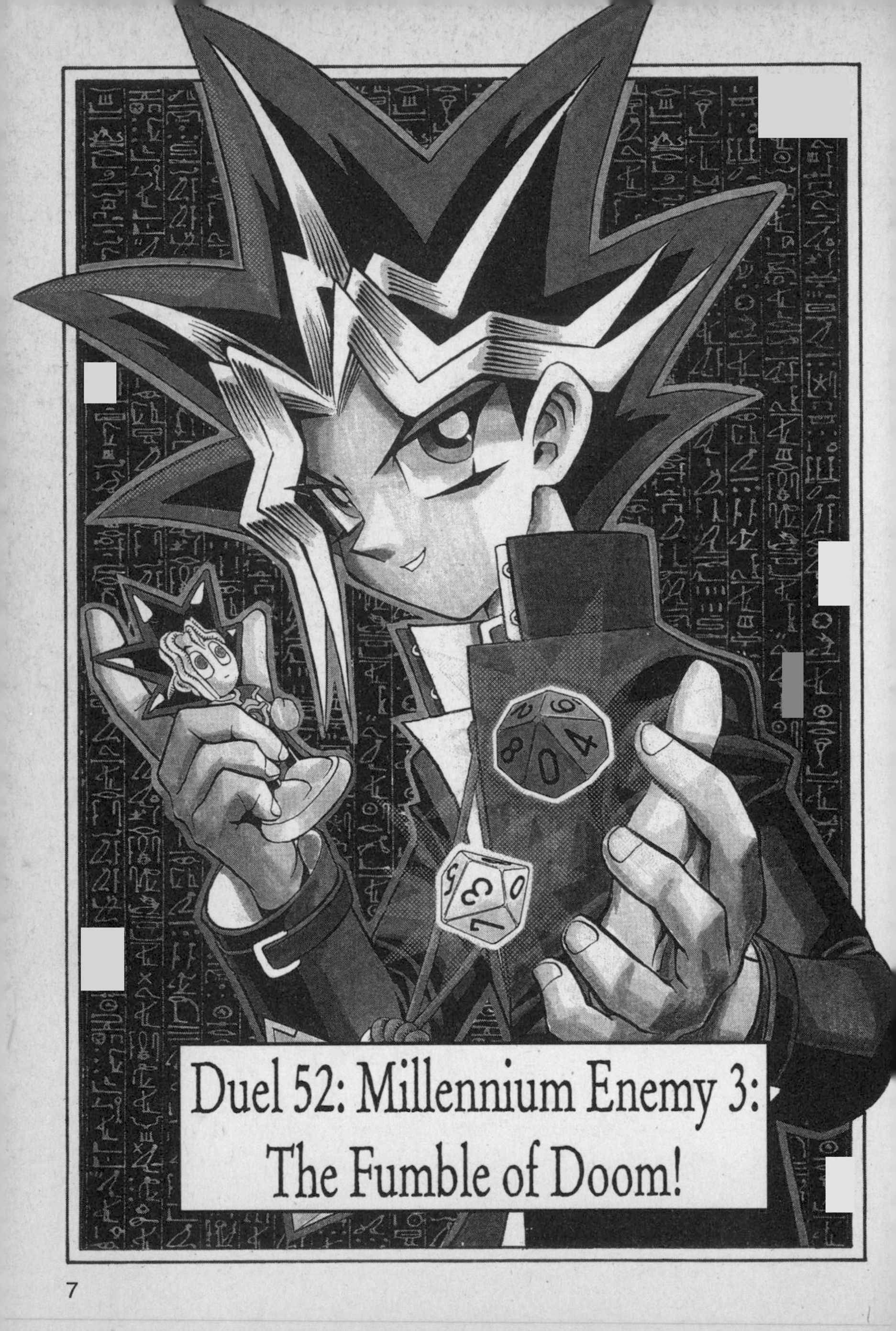
Duel 52: Millennium Enemy 3:
The Fumble of Doom!

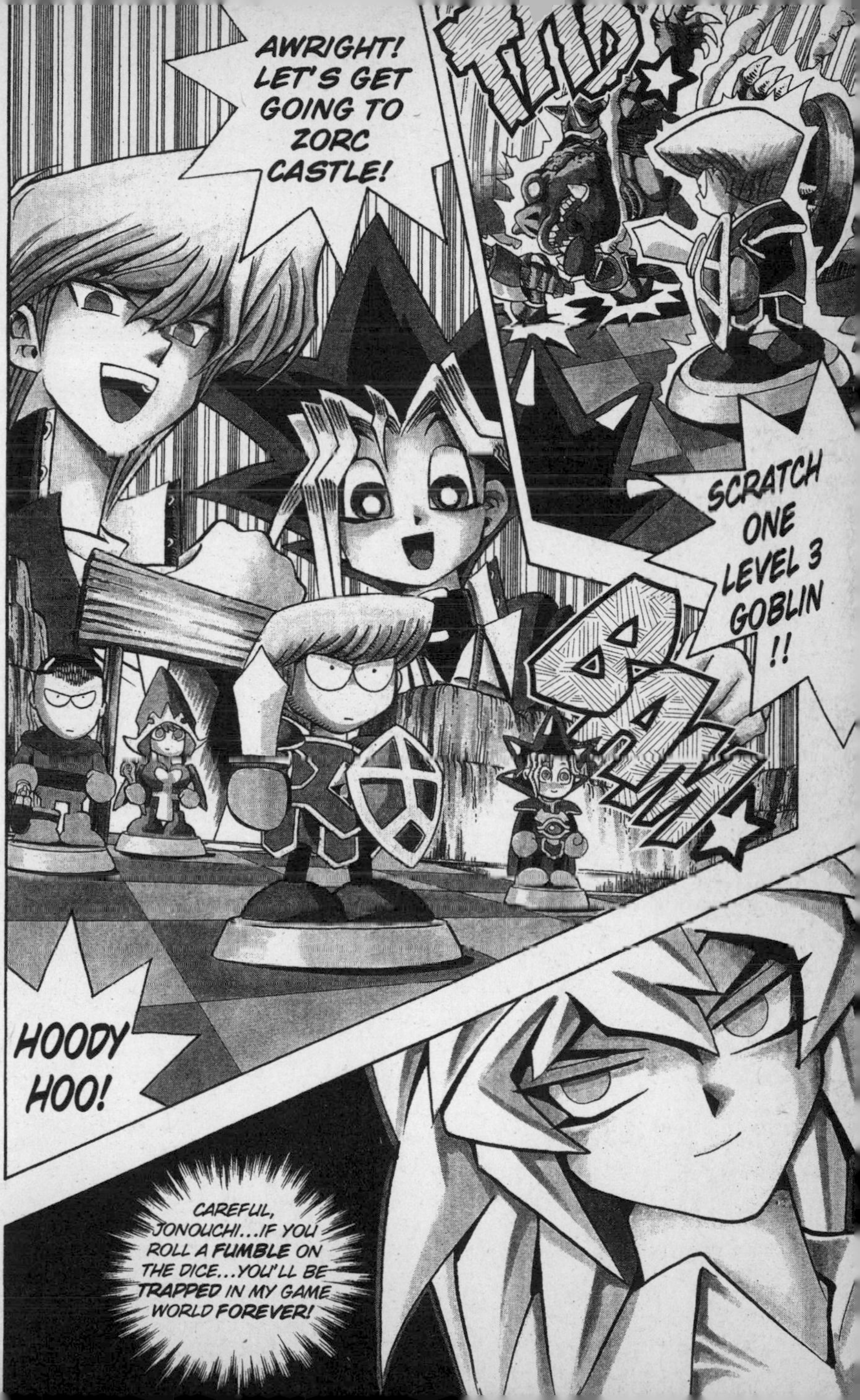
SCRATCH ONE LEVEL 3 GOBLIN !!
BAM
AWRIGHT! LET'S GET GOING TO ZORC CASTLE!
HOODY HOO!
CAREFUL, JONOUCHI...IF YOU ROLL A **FUMBLE** ON THE DICE...YOU'LL BE **TRAPPED** IN MY GAME WORLD **FOREVER!**

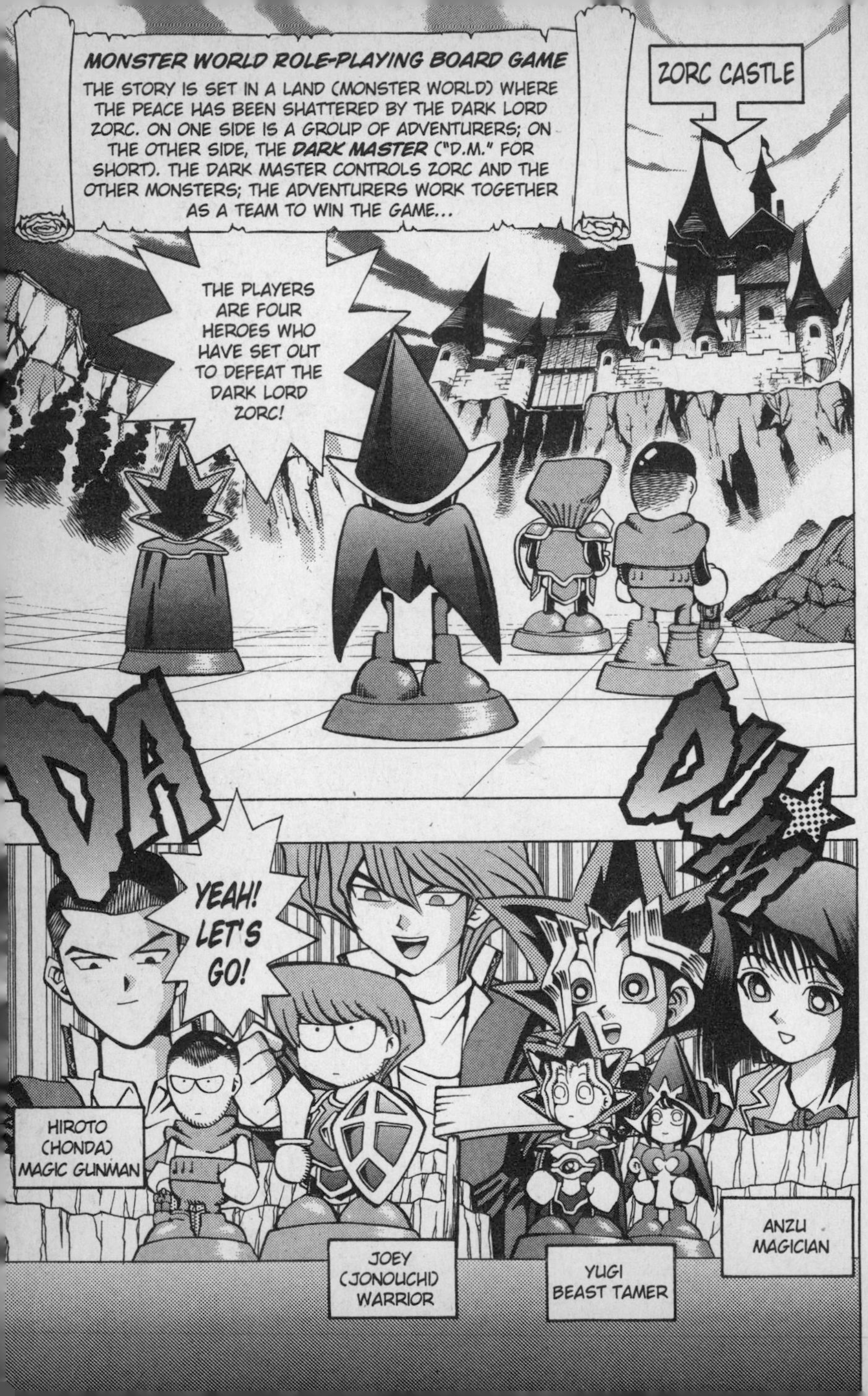
ZORC CASTLE
MONSTER WORLD ROLE-PLAYING BOARD GAME
THE STORY IS SET IN A LAND (MONSTER WORLD) WHERE THE PEACE HAS BEEN SHATTERED BY THE DARK LORD ZORC. ON ONE SIDE IS A GROUP OF ADVENTURERS; ON THE OTHER SIDE, THE DARK MASTER ("D.M." FOR SHORT). THE DARK MASTER CONTROLS ZORC AND THE OTHER MONSTERS; THE ADVENTURERS WORK TOGETHER AS A TEAM TO WIN THE GAME...
THE PLAYERS ARE FOUR HEROES WHO HAVE SET OUT TO DEFEAT THE DARK LORD ZORC!
DA DA!
YEAH! LET'S GO!
ANZU MAGICIAN
YUGI BEAST TAMER
JOEY (JONOUCHI) WARRIOR
HIROTO (HONDA) MAGIC GUNMAN

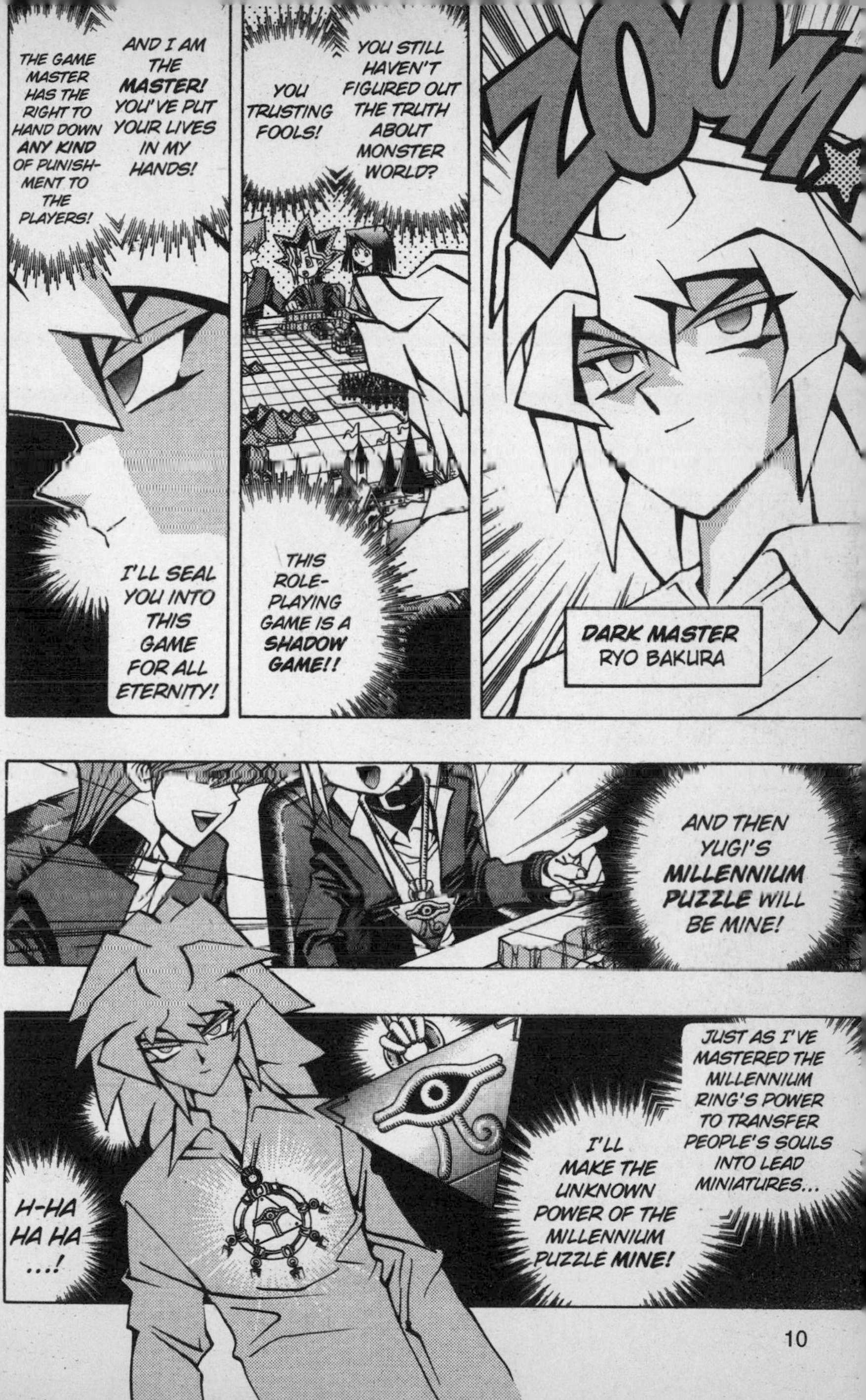
ZOOM
DARK MASTER RYO BAKURA
YOU STILL HAVEN'T FIGURED OUT THE TRUTH ABOUT MONSTER WORLD?
YOU TRUSTING FOOLS!
THIS ROLE-PLAYING GAME IS A SHADOW GAME!!
AND I AM THE MASTER! YOU'VE PUT YOUR LIVES IN MY HANDS!
THE GAME MASTER HAS THE RIGHT TO HAND DOWN ANY KIND OF PUNISHMENT TO THE PLAYERS!
I'LL SEAL YOU INTO THIS GAME FOR ALL ETERNITY!
AND THEN YUGI'S MILLENNIUM PUZZLE WILL BE MINE!
JUST AS I'VE MASTERED THE MILLENNIUM RING'S POWER TO TRANSFER PEOPLE'S SOULS INTO LEAD MINIATURES...
I'LL MAKE THE UNKNOWN POWER OF THE MILLENNIUM PUZZLE MINE!
H-HA HA HA ...!

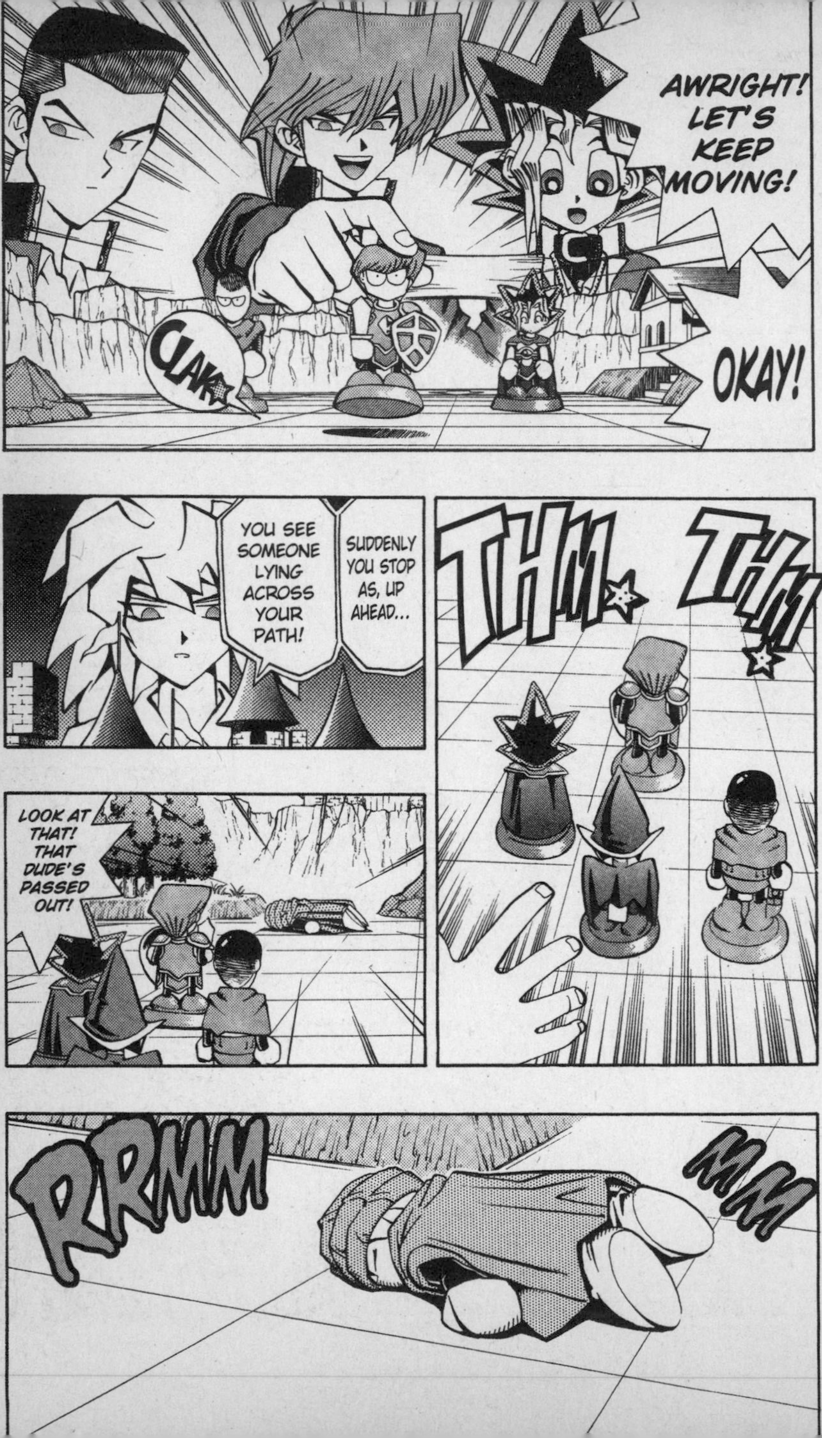
AWRIGHT! LET'S KEEP MOVING!
OKAY!
CLAK
THM
THM
SUDDENLY YOU STOP AS, UP AHEAD...
YOU SEE SOMEONE LYING ACROSS YOUR PATH!
LOOK AT THAT! THAT DUDE'S PASSED OUT!
RRMM
MM

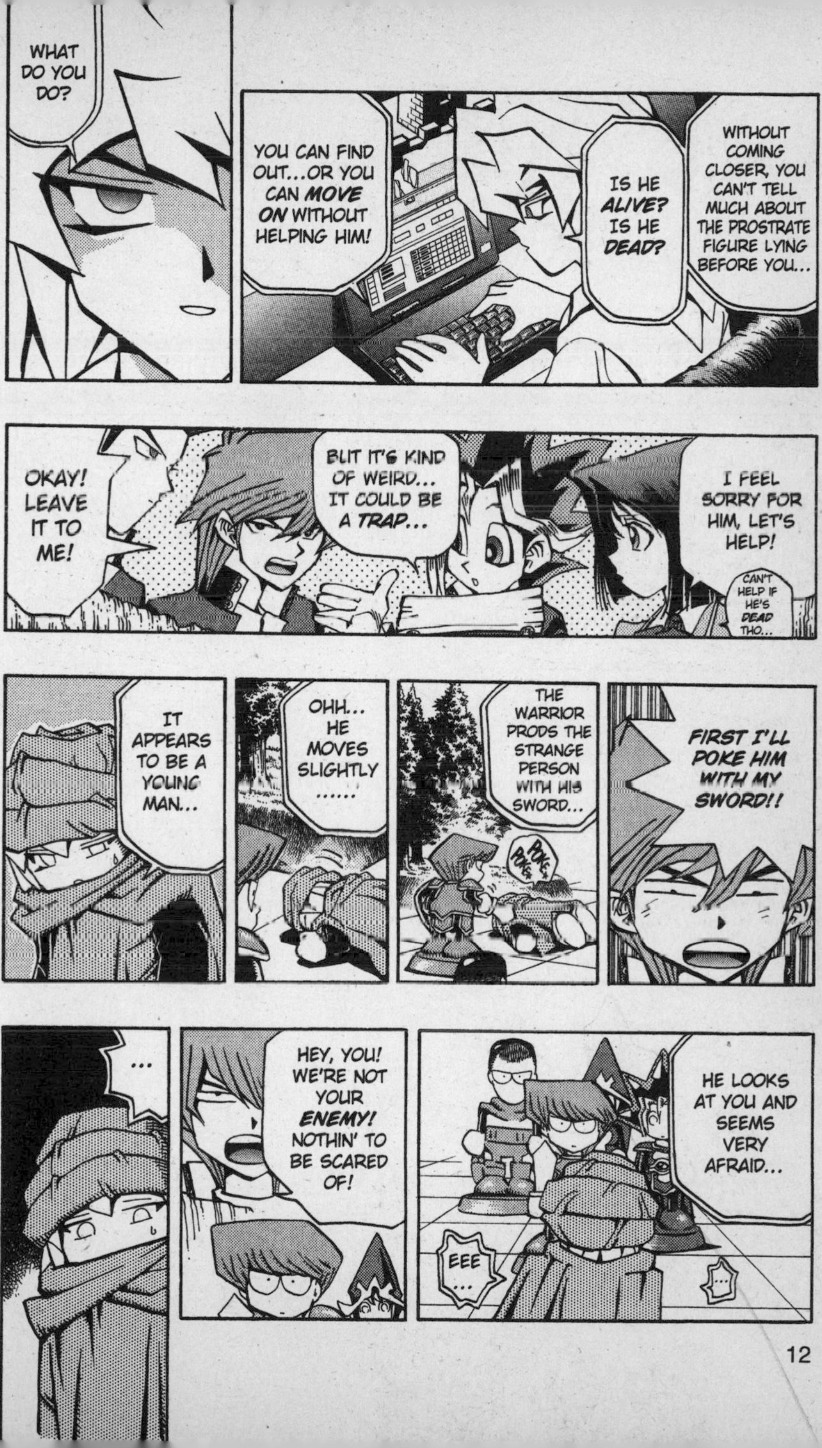
WITHOUT COMING CLOSER, YOU CAN'T TELL MUCH ABOUT THE PROSTRATE FIGURE LYING BEFORE YOU...
IS HE ALIVE? IS HE DEAD?
YOU CAN FIND OUT...OR YOU CAN MOVE ON WITHOUT HELPING HIM!
WHAT DO YOU DO?
I FEEL SORRY FOR HIM, LET'S HELP!
CAN'T HELP IF HE'S DEAD THO...
BUT IT'S KIND OF WEIRD... IT COULD BE A TRAP...
OKAY! LEAVE IT TO ME!
FIRST I'LL POKE HIM WITH MY SWORD!!
THE WARRIOR PRODS THE STRANGE PERSON WITH HIS SWORD...
POKE POKE
OHH... HE MOVES SLIGHTLY ......
IT APPEARS TO BE A YOUNG MAN...
HE LOOKS AT YOU AND SEEMS VERY AFRAID...
...
EEE ...
HEY, YOU! WE'RE NOT YOUR ENEMY! NOTHIN' TO BE SCARED OF!
...

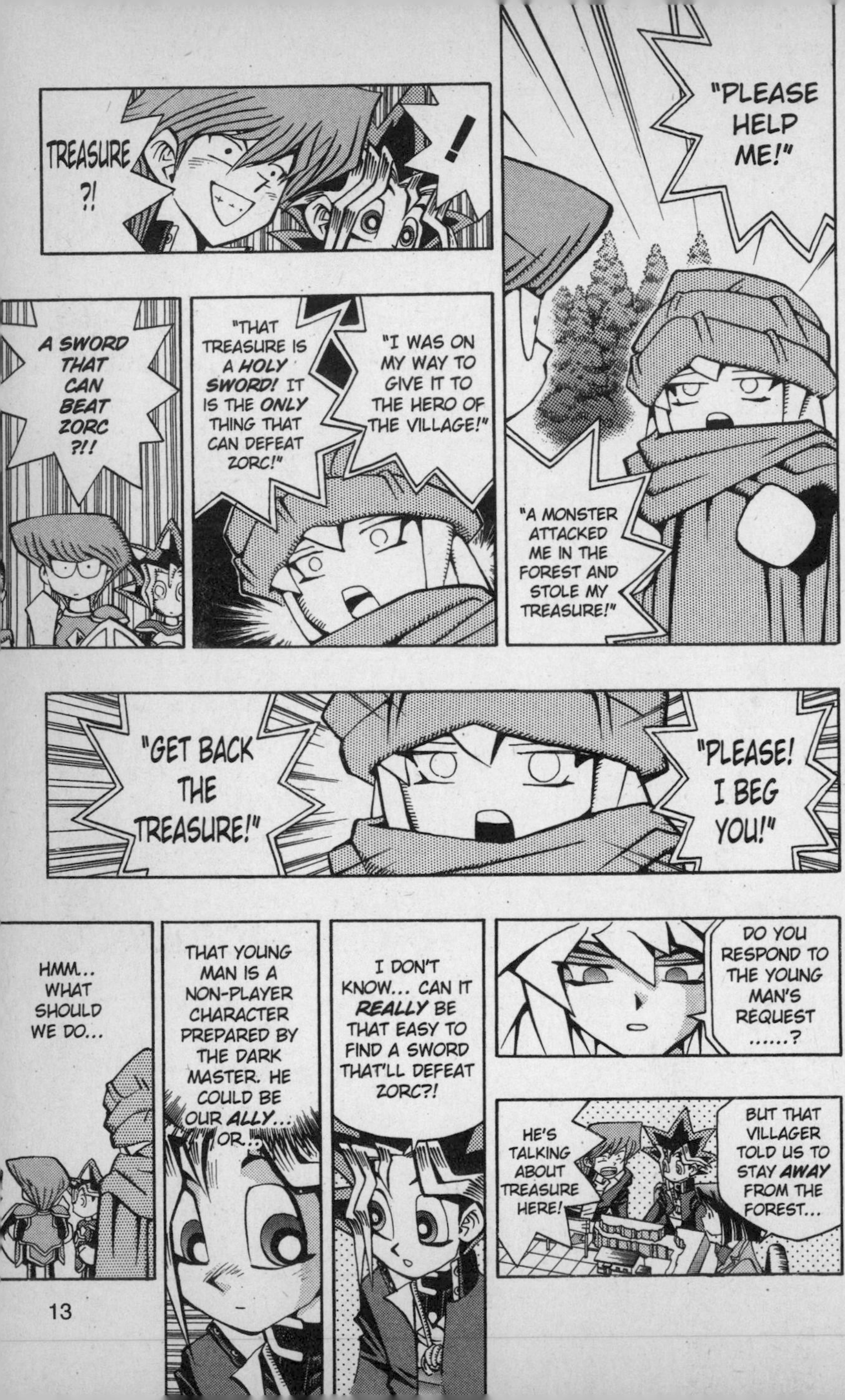
"PLEASE HELP ME!"
"A MONSTER ATTACKED ME IN THE FOREST AND STOLE MY TREASURE!"
TREASURE ?!
!
"I WAS ON MY WAY TO GIVE IT TO THE HERO OF THE VILLAGE!"
"THAT TREASURE IS A *HOLY SWORD!* IT IS THE *ONLY* THING THAT CAN DEFEAT ZORC!"
A SWORD THAT CAN BEAT ZORC ?!!
"PLEASE! I BEG YOU!"
"GET BACK THE TREASURE!"
DO YOU RESPOND TO THE YOUNG MAN'S REQUEST ......?
BUT THAT VILLAGER TOLD US TO STAY *AWAY* FROM THE FOREST...
HE'S TALKING ABOUT TREASURE HERE!
I DON'T KNOW... CAN IT *REALLY* BE THAT EASY TO FIND A SWORD THAT'LL DEFEAT ZORC?!
THAT YOUNG MAN IS A NON-PLAYER CHARACTER PREPARED BY THE DARK MASTER. HE COULD BE OUR *ALLY*... OR...
HMM... WHAT SHOULD WE DO...

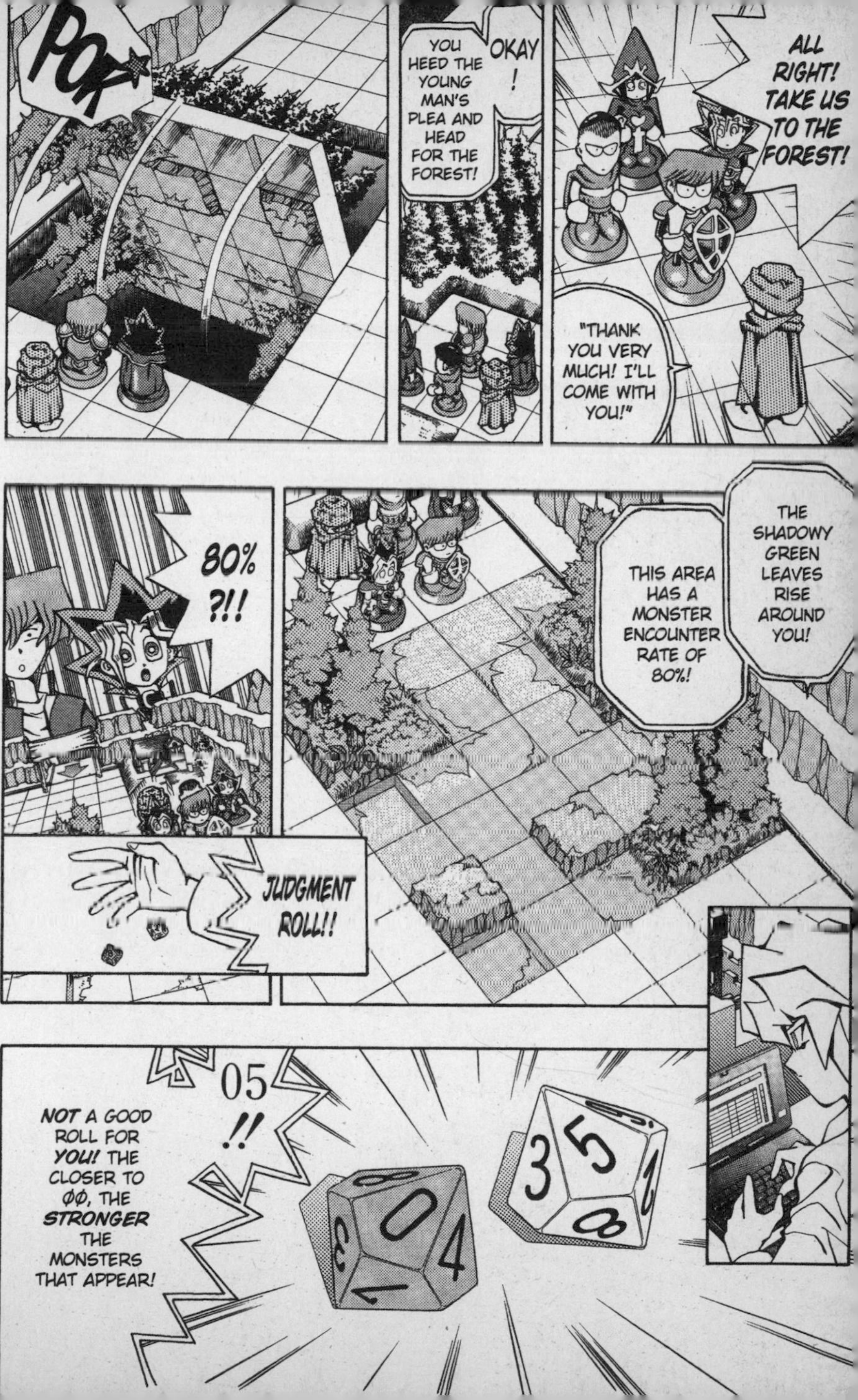
ALL RIGHT! TAKE US TO THE FOREST!
"THANK YOU VERY MUCH! I'LL COME WITH YOU!"
OKAY!
YOU HEED THE YOUNG MAN'S PLEA AND HEAD FOR THE FOREST!
POK
THE SHADOWY GREEN LEAVES RISE AROUND YOU!
THIS AREA HAS A MONSTER ENCOUNTER RATE OF 80%!
80% ?!!
JUDGMENT ROLL!!
05 !!
NOT A GOOD ROLL FOR YOU! THE CLOSER TO ØØ, THE STRONGER THE MONSTERS THAT APPEAR!

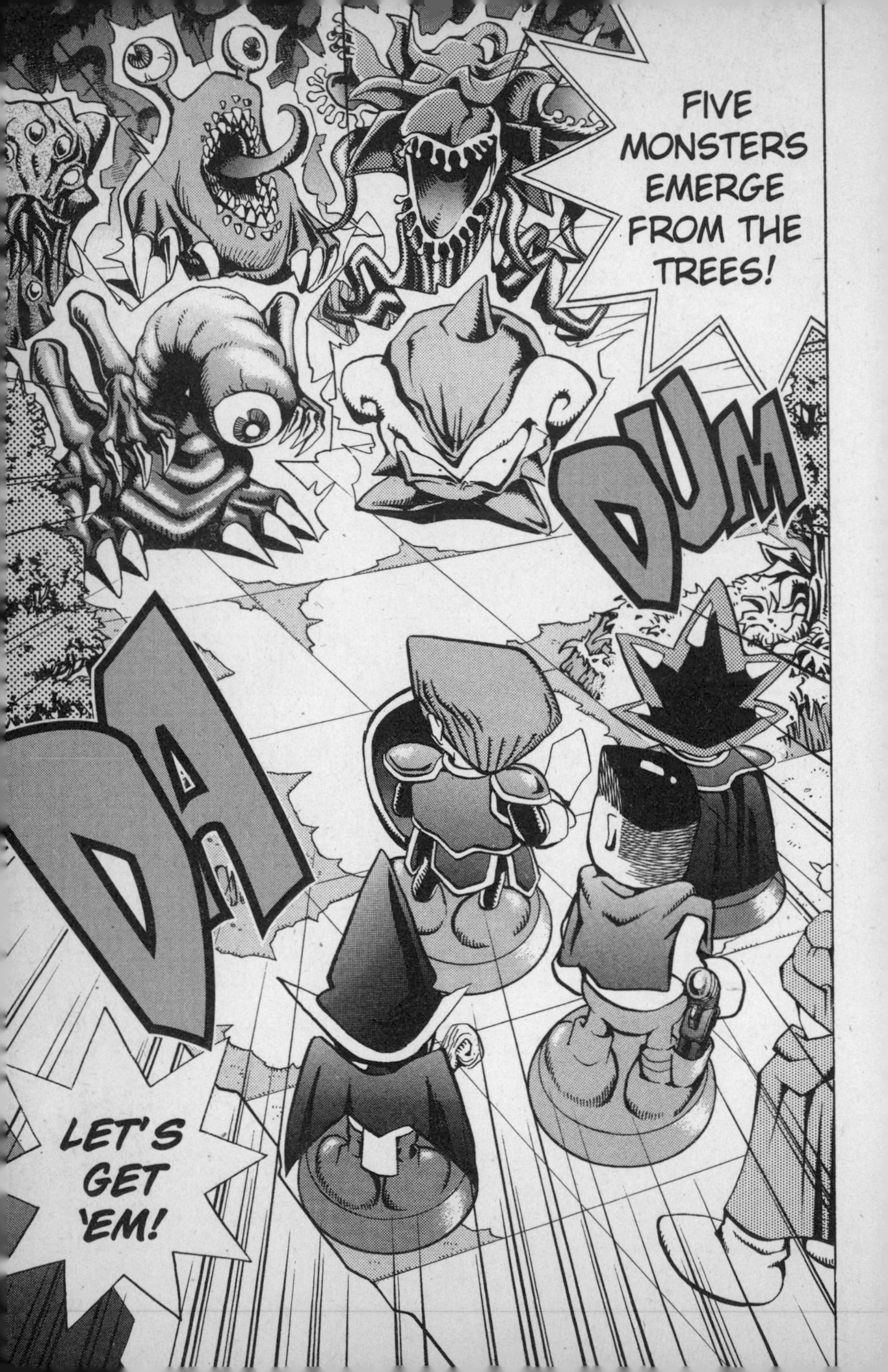
FIVE MONSTERS EMERGE FROM THE TREES!
DUM
DA
LET'S GET 'EM!

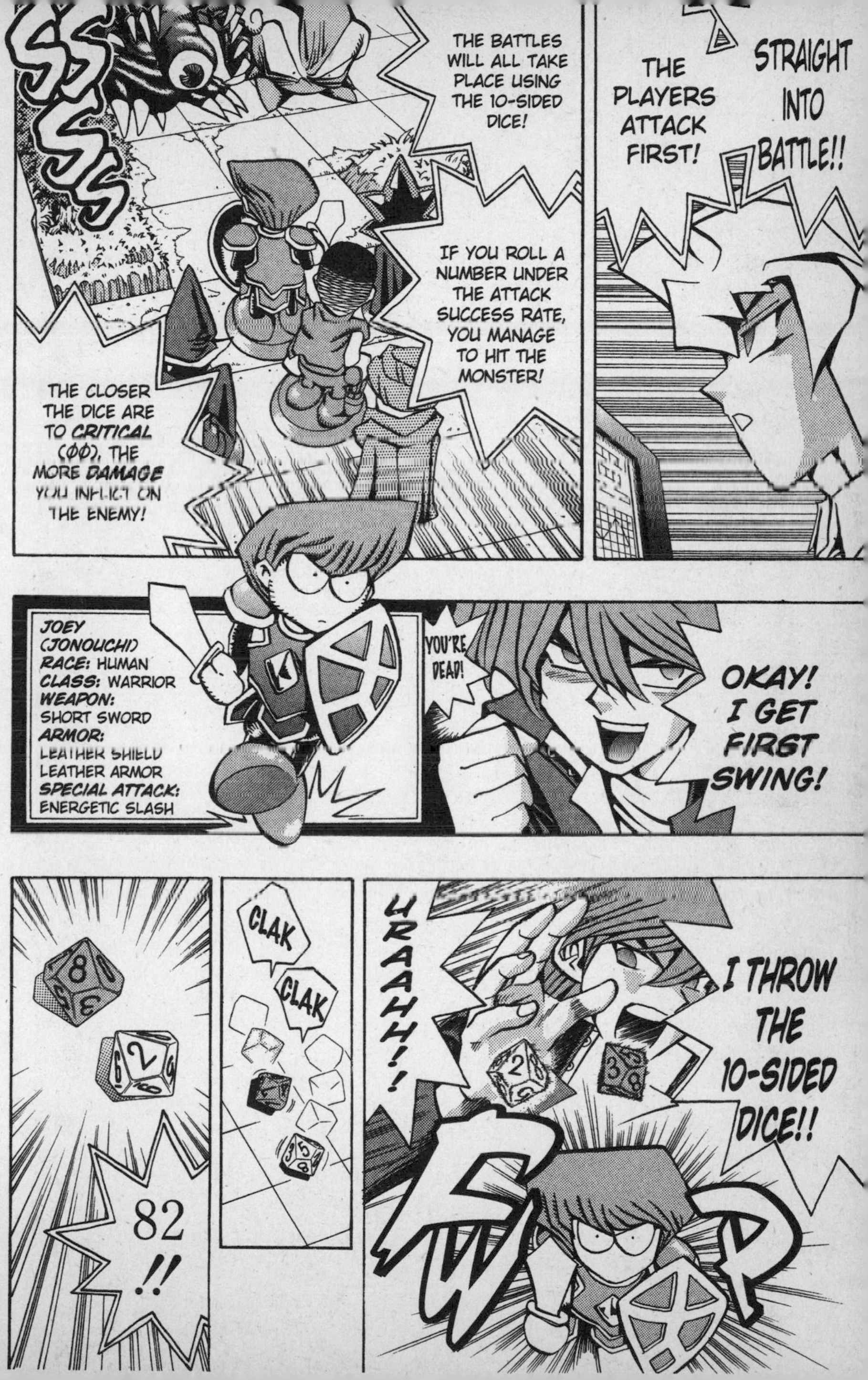
STRAIGHT INTO BATTLE!!
THE PLAYERS ATTACK FIRST!
THE BATTLES WILL ALL TAKE PLACE USING THE 10-SIDED DICE!
IF YOU ROLL A NUMBER UNDER THE ATTACK SUCCESS RATE, YOU MANAGE TO HIT THE MONSTER!
THE CLOSER THE DICE ARE TO CRITICAL (ØØ), THE MORE DAMAGE YOU INFLICT ON THE ENEMY!
OKAY! I GET FIRST SWING!
YOU'RE DEAD!
JOEY (JONOUCHI)
RACE: HUMAN
CLASS: WARRIOR
WEAPON: SHORT SWORD
ARMOR: LEATHER SHIELD LEATHER ARMOR
SPECIAL ATTACK: ENERGETIC SLASH
I THROW THE 10-SIDED DICE!!
URAAHH!!
CLAK
CLAK
82 !!

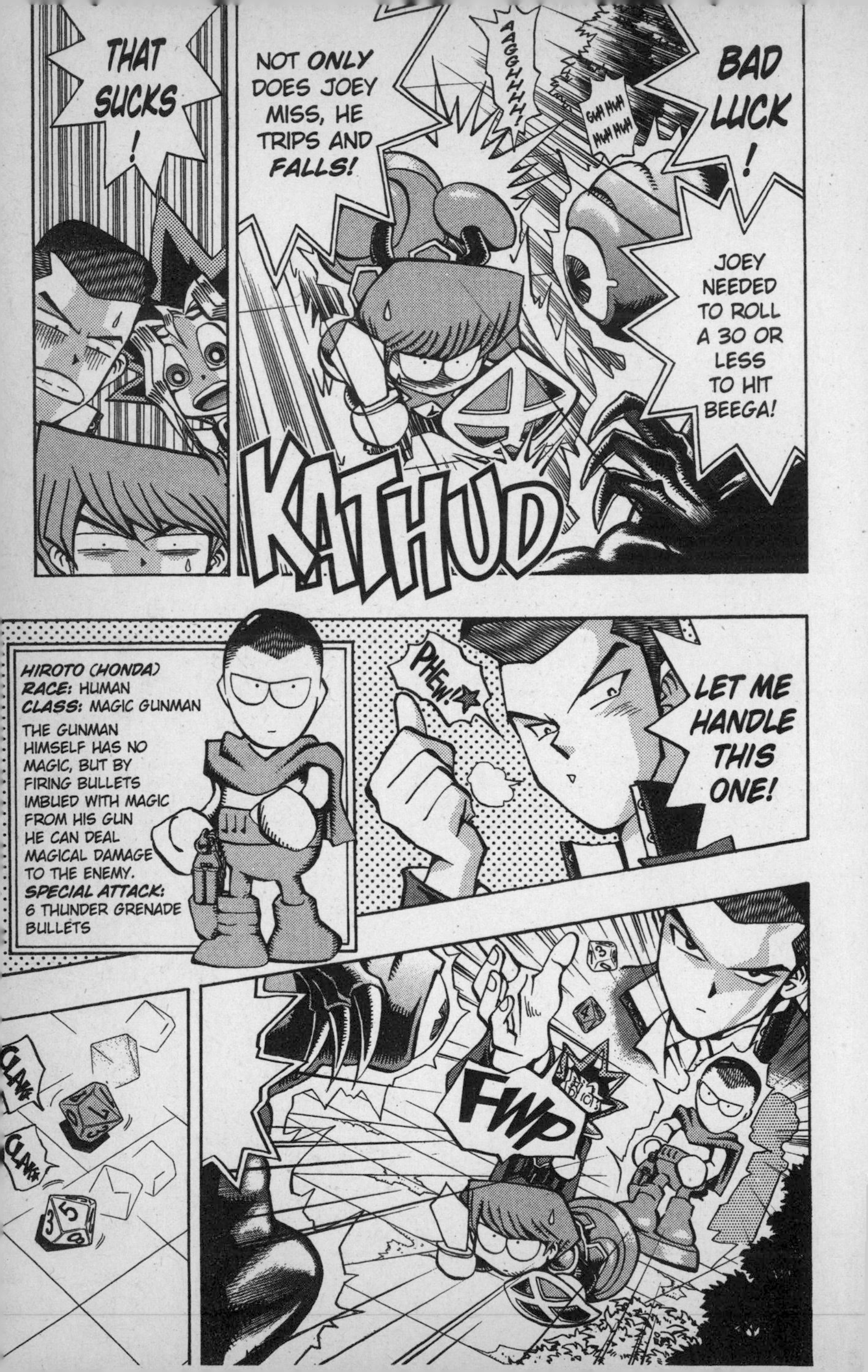
BAD LUCK!
AAGGHHHH!
GWAH HWAH HWAH HWAH
NOT ONLY DOES JOEY MISS, HE TRIPS AND FALLS!
JOEY NEEDED TO ROLL A 30 OR LESS TO HIT BEEGA!
KATHUD
THAT SUCKS!
PHEW!☆
LET ME HANDLE THIS ONE!
HIROTO (HONDA)
RACE: HUMAN
CLASS: MAGIC GUNMAN
THE GUNMAN HIMSELF HAS NO MAGIC, BUT BY FIRING BULLETS IMBUED WITH MAGIC FROM HIS GUN HE CAN DEAL MAGICAL DAMAGE TO THE ENEMY.
SPECIAL ATTACK: 6 THUNDER GRENADE BULLETS
FWP
CLANK
CLANK

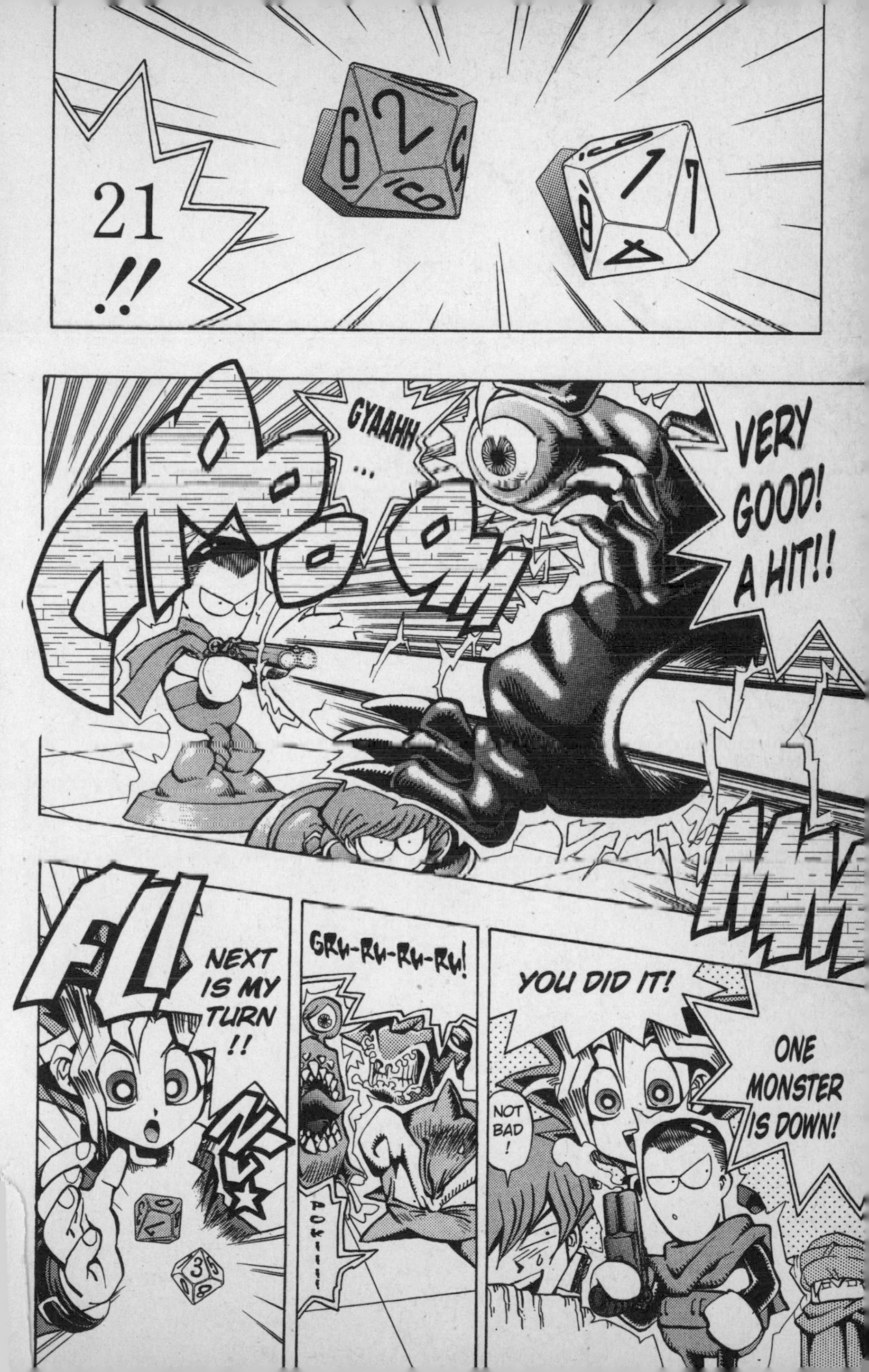
21 !!
GYAAHH...
VERY GOOD! A HIT!!
YOU DID IT!
ONE MONSTER IS DOWN!
NOT BAD!
GRU-RU-RU-RU!
NEXT IS MY TURN !!

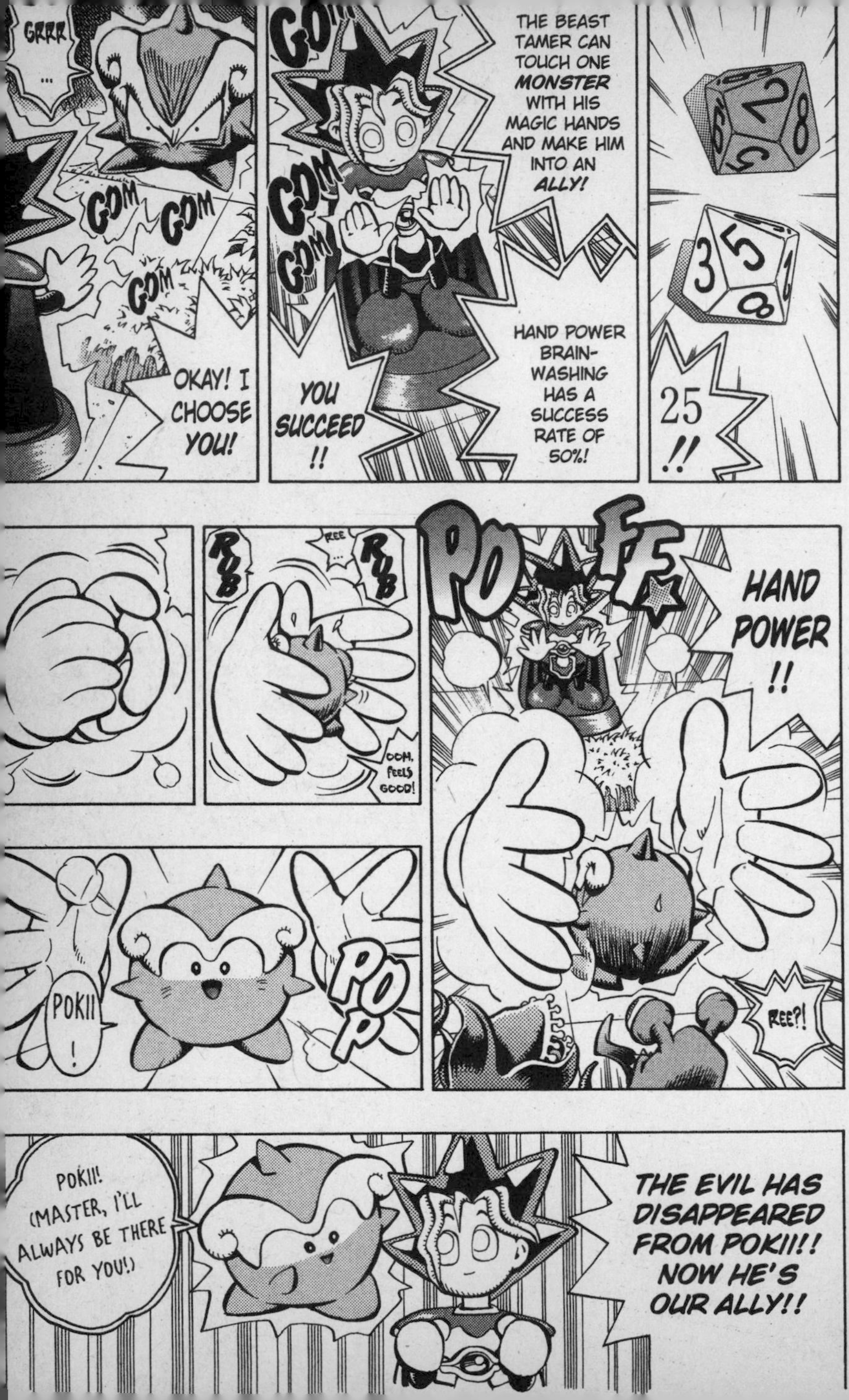
25
!!
THE BEAST TAMER CAN TOUCH ONE MONSTER WITH HIS MAGIC HANDS AND MAKE HIM INTO AN ALLY!
GOM GOM GOM
HAND POWER BRAIN-WASHING HAS A SUCCESS RATE OF 50%!
YOU SUCCEED !!
GRRR ...
GOM GOM
GOM
OKAY! I CHOOSE YOU!
HAND POWER !!
REE?!
RUB
REE ...
RUB
OOM, FEELS GOOD!
POP
POKII !
THE EVIL HAS DISAPPEARED FROM POKII!! NOW HE'S OUR ALLY!!
POKII! (MASTER, I'LL ALWAYS BE THERE FOR YOU!)

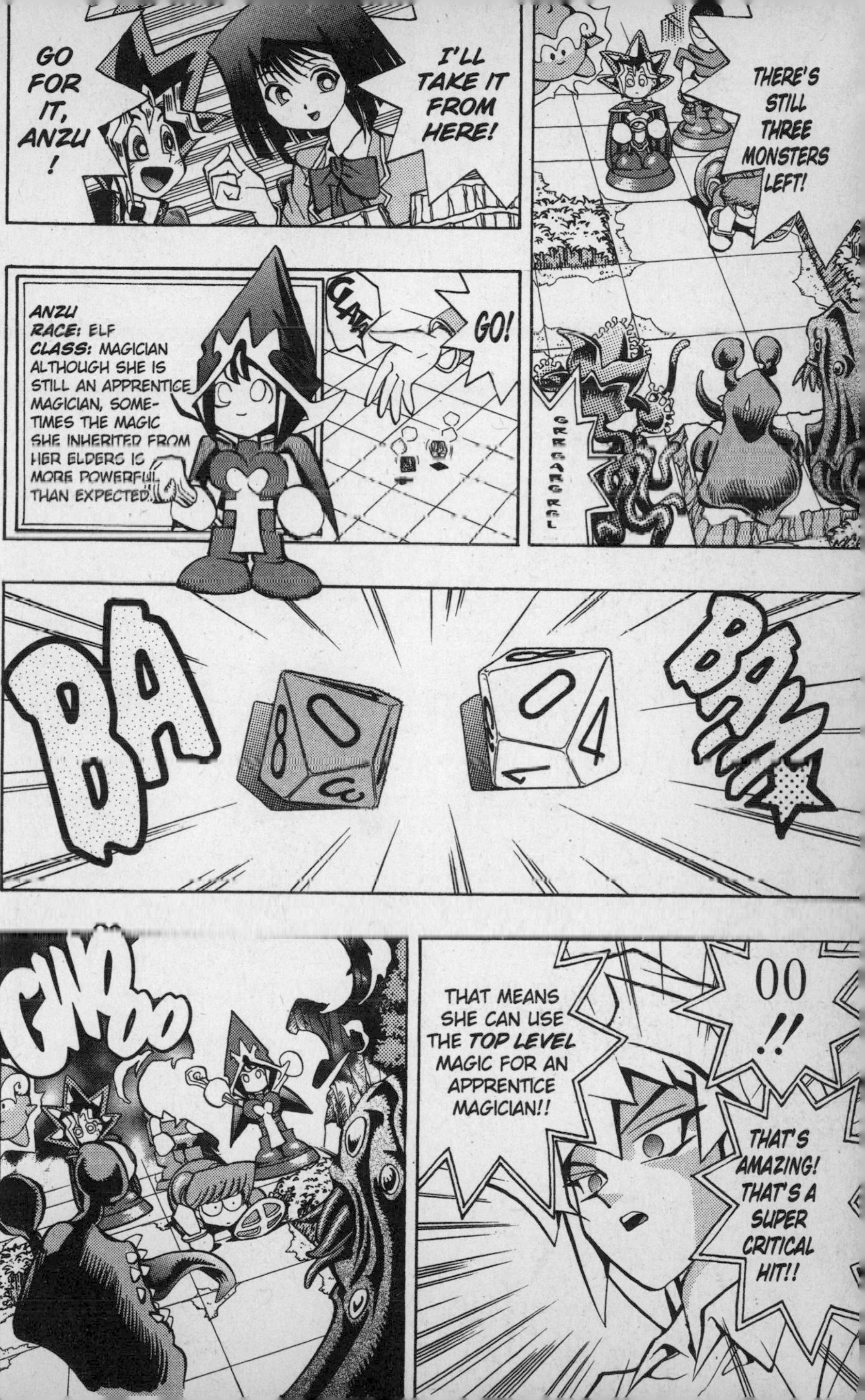
THERE'S STILL THREE MONSTERS LEFT!
GRR GARG RGL
I'LL TAKE IT FROM HERE!
GO FOR IT, ANZU!
GO!
CLATTA
ANZU
RACE: ELF
CLASS: MAGICIAN
ALTHOUGH SHE IS STILL AN APPRENTICE MAGICIAN, SOMETIMES THE MAGIC SHE INHERITED FROM HER ELDERS IS MORE POWERFUL THAN EXPECTED.
BAM
BA
00 !!
THAT'S AMAZING! THAT'S A SUPER CRITICAL HIT!!
THAT MEANS SHE CAN USE THE TOP LEVEL MAGIC FOR AN APPRENTICE MAGICIAN!!
GWOOO

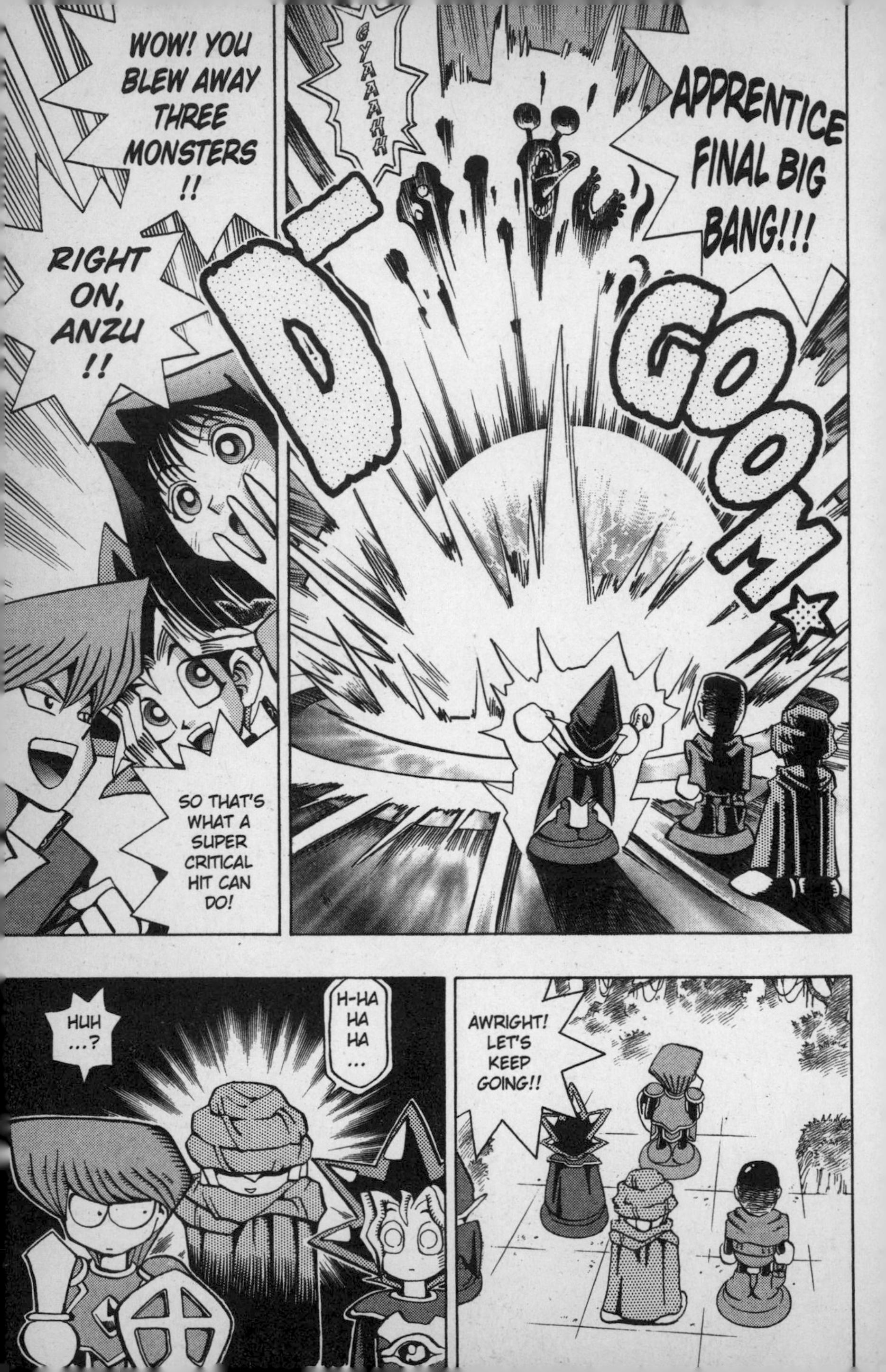
APPRENTICE FINAL BIG BANG!!!
GYAAAAHH
DOGOOM
WOW! YOU BLEW AWAY THREE MONSTERS!!
RIGHT ON, ANZU!!
SO THAT'S WHAT A SUPER CRITICAL HIT CAN DO!
AWRIGHT! LET'S KEEP GOING!!
H-HA HA HA...
HUH...?

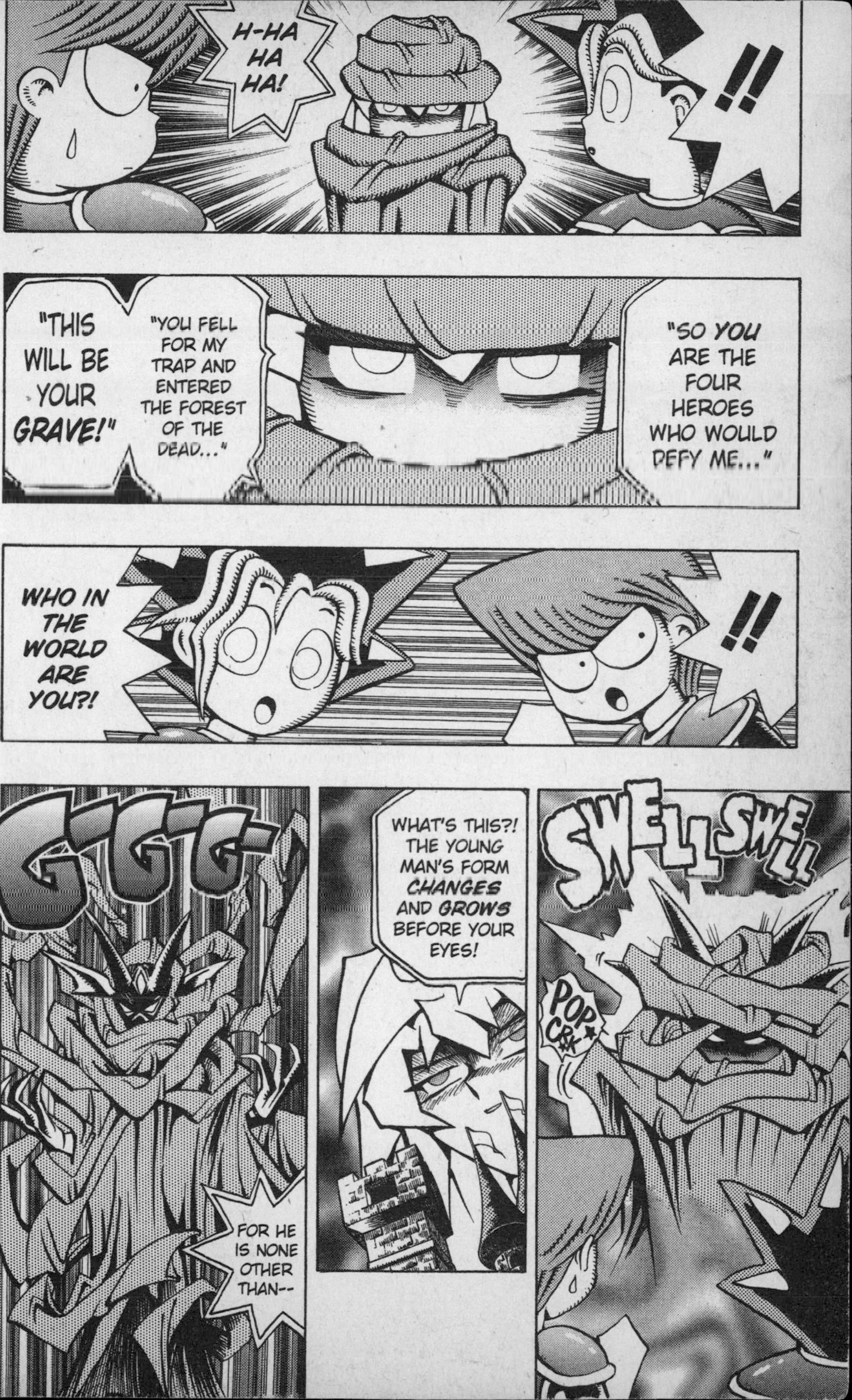
H-HA HA HA!
!!
"SO YOU ARE THE FOUR HEROES WHO WOULD DEFY ME..."
"YOU FELL FOR MY TRAP AND ENTERED THE FOREST OF THE DEAD..."
"THIS WILL BE YOUR GRAVE!"
!!
WHO IN THE WORLD ARE YOU?!
SWELL SWELL
POP
CRK
WHAT'S THIS?! THE YOUNG MAN'S FORM CHANGES AND GROWS BEFORE YOUR EYES!
G-G-G-
FOR HE IS NONE OTHER THAN--

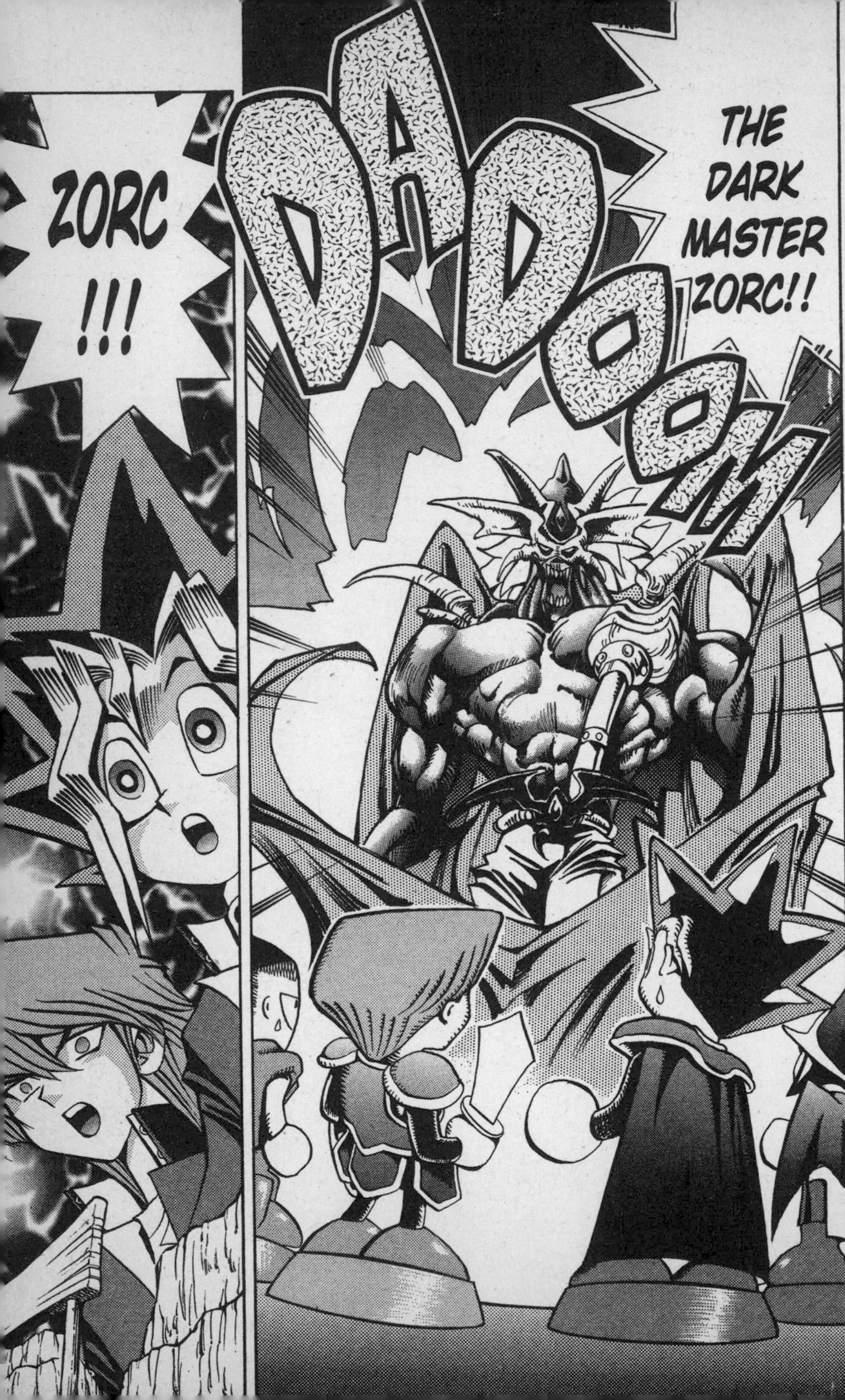
THE DARK MASTER ZORC!!
DADOOM
ZORC!!!

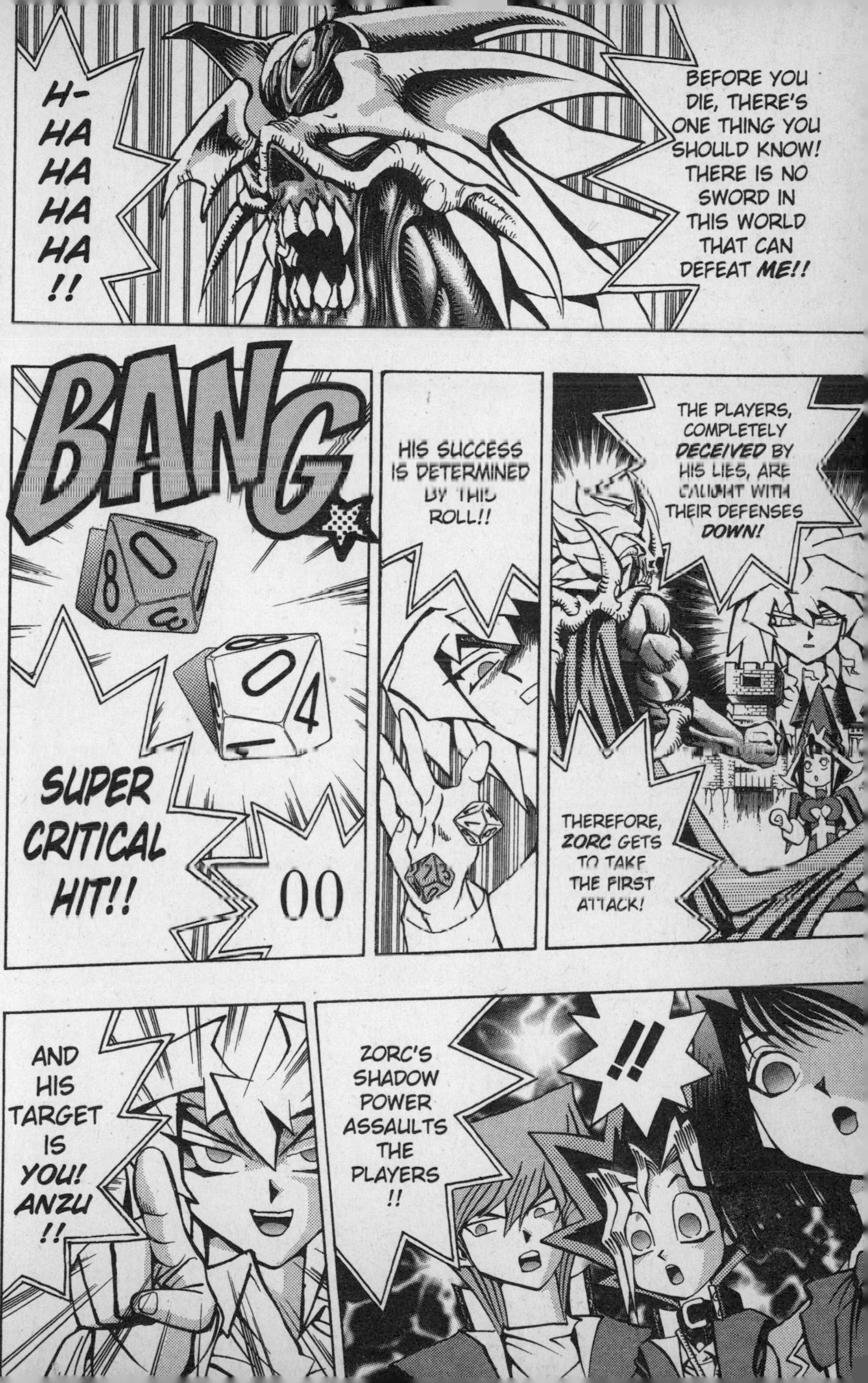
BEFORE YOU DIE, THERE'S ONE THING YOU SHOULD KNOW! THERE IS NO SWORD IN THIS WORLD THAT CAN DEFEAT ME!!
H-HAHAHAHA!!
THE PLAYERS, COMPLETELY DECEIVED BY HIS LIES, ARE CAUGHT WITH THEIR DEFENSES DOWN!
THEREFORE, ZORC GETS TO TAKE THE FIRST ATTACK!
HIS SUCCESS IS DETERMINED BY THIS ROLL!!
BANG
SUPER CRITICAL HIT!!
00
!!
ZORC'S SHADOW POWER ASSAULTS THE PLAYERS!!
AND HIS TARGET IS YOU! ANZU!!

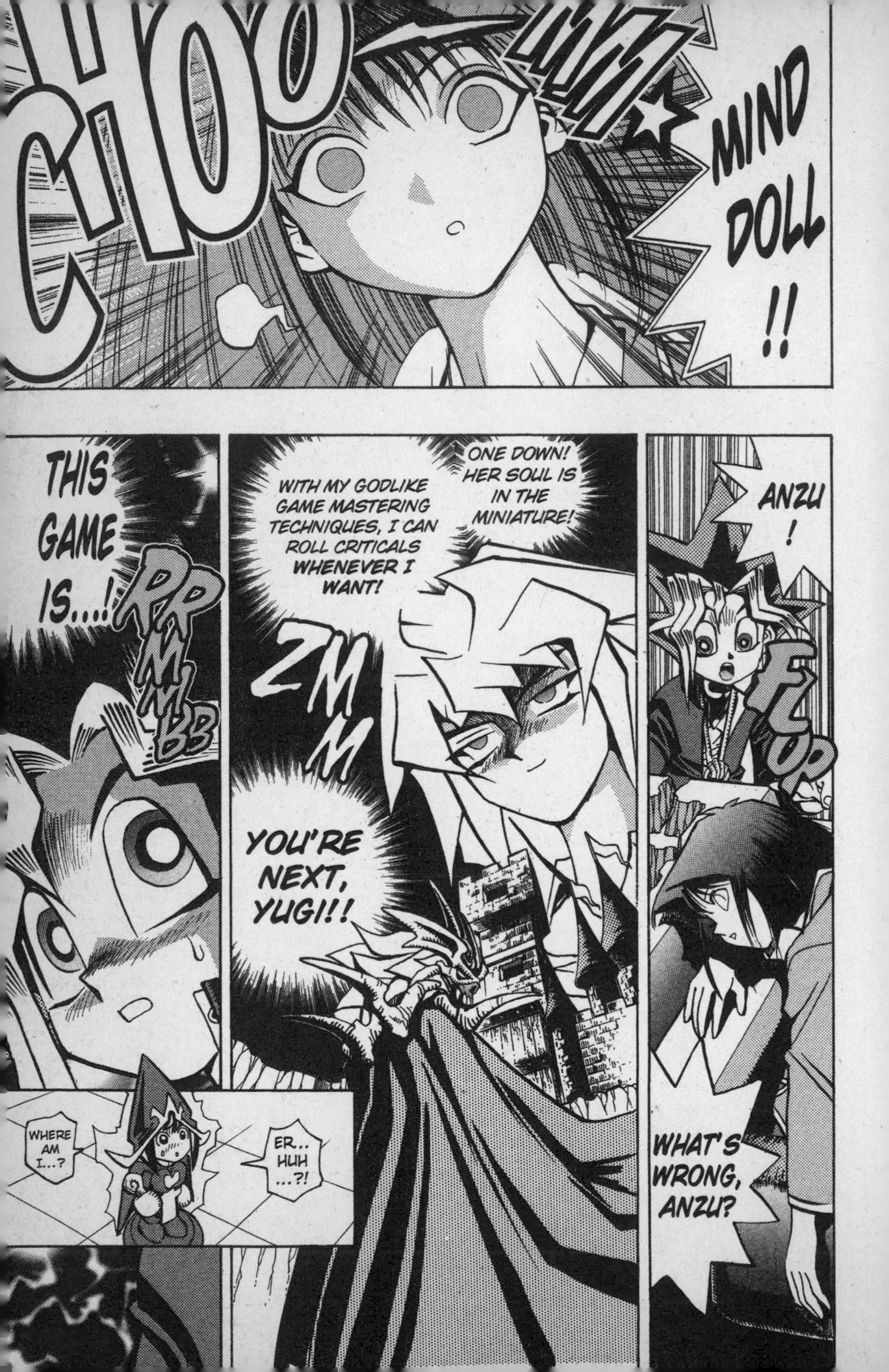
MIND DOLL !!
ANZU !
FLOP
WHAT'S WRONG, ANZU?
ONE DOWN! HER SOUL IS IN THE MINIATURE!
WITH MY GODLIKE GAME MASTERING TECHNIQUES, I CAN ROLL CRITICALS WHENEVER I WANT!
ZMMM
YOU'RE NEXT, YUGI!!
THIS GAME IS...!
ER.. HUH ...?!
WHERE AM I...?

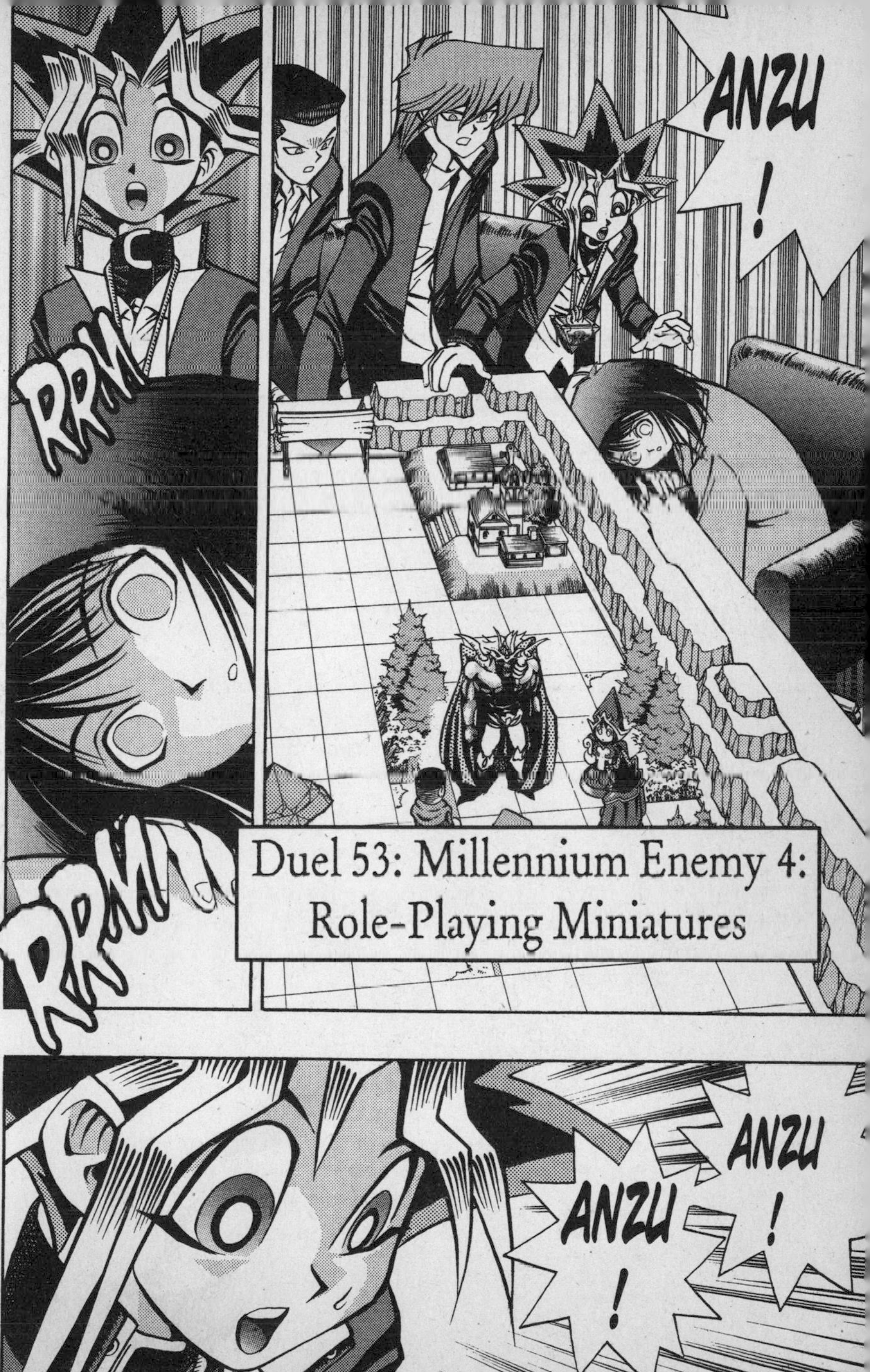
ANZU!
Duel 53: Millennium Enemy 4: Role-Playing Miniatures
RRM
RRM
ANZU!
ANZU!

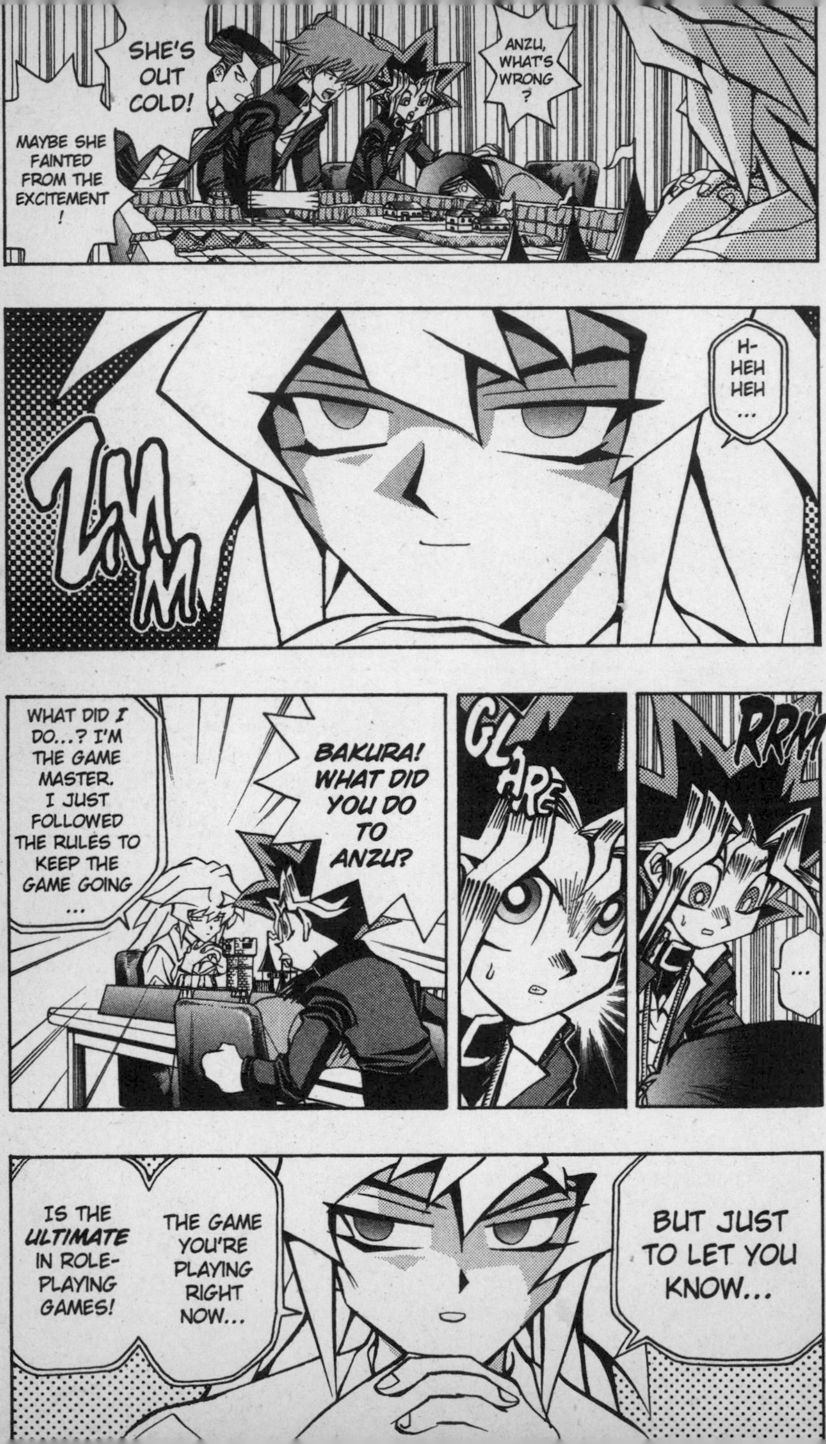
ANZU, WHAT'S WRONG?
SHE'S OUT COLD!
MAYBE SHE FAINTED FROM THE EXCITEMENT!
H-HEH HEH...
RRM
...
GLARE
BAKURA! WHAT DID YOU DO TO ANZU?
WHAT DID I DO...? I'M THE GAME MASTER. I JUST FOLLOWED THE RULES TO KEEP THE GAME GOING...
BUT JUST TO LET YOU KNOW...
THE GAME YOU'RE PLAYING RIGHT NOW...
IS THE ULTIMATE IN ROLE-PLAYING GAMES!

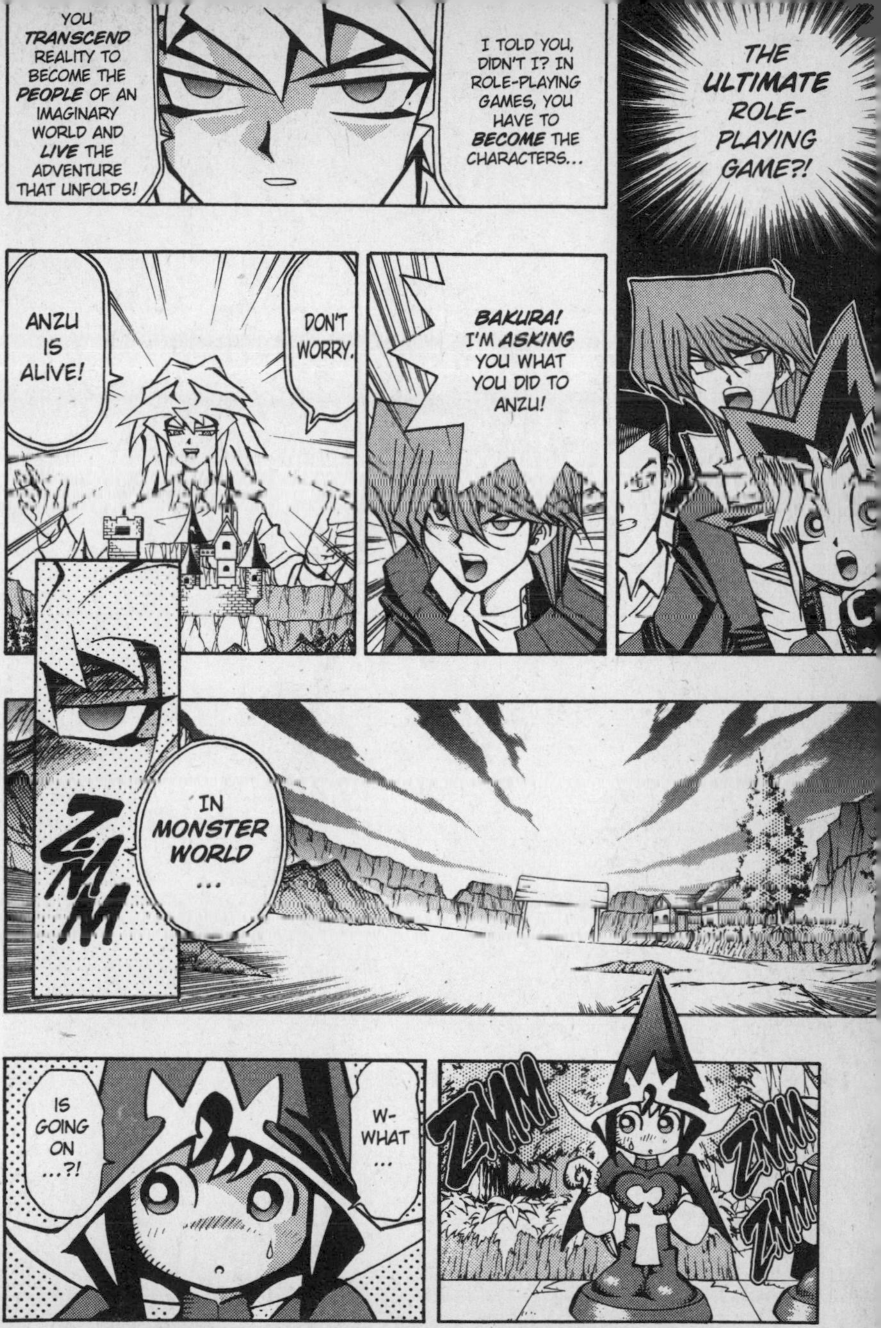
THE ULTIMATE ROLE-PLAYING GAME?!
I TOLD YOU, DIDN'T I? IN ROLE-PLAYING GAMES, YOU HAVE TO BECOME THE CHARACTERS...
YOU TRANSCEND REALITY TO BECOME THE PEOPLE OF AN IMAGINARY WORLD AND LIVE THE ADVENTURE THAT UNFOLDS!
BAKURA! I'M ASKING YOU WHAT YOU DID TO ANZU!
DON'T WORRY.
ANZU IS ALIVE!
IN MONSTER WORLD ...
ZMM
ZMM
ZMM
ZMM
W-WHAT ...
IS GOING ON ...?!

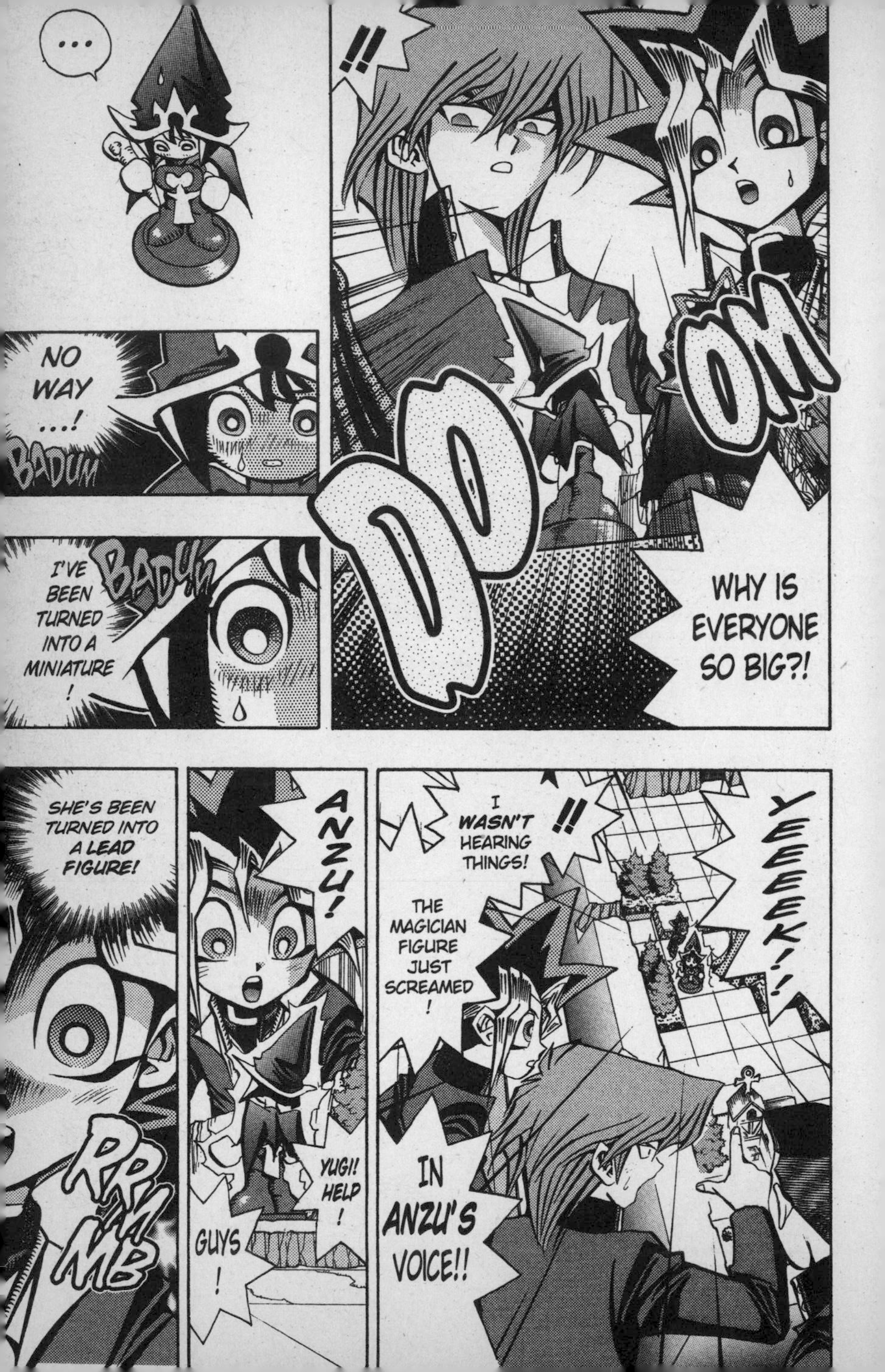
!!
DOOM
WHY IS EVERYONE SO BIG?!
...
NO WAY ...!
BADUM
I'VE BEEN TURNED INTO A MINIATURE!
BADUM
YEEEEK!!
!!
I WASN'T HEARING THINGS!
THE MAGICIAN FIGURE JUST SCREAMED!
IN ANZU'S VOICE!!
ANZU!
YUGI! HELP!
GUYS!
SHE'S BEEN TURNED INTO A LEAD FIGURE!
RRMMB

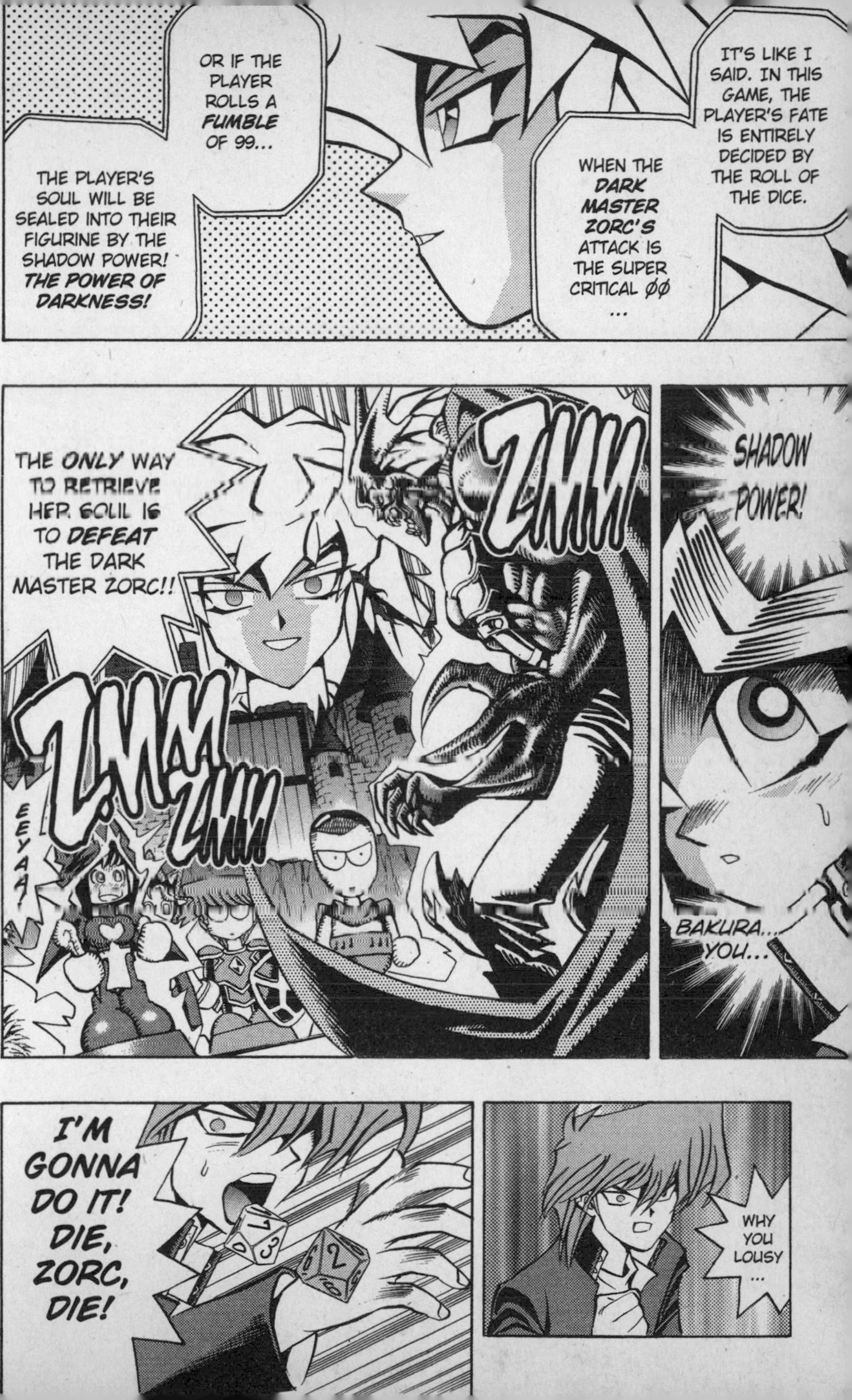
IT'S LIKE I SAID. IN THIS GAME, THE PLAYER'S FATE IS ENTIRELY DECIDED BY THE ROLL OF THE DICE.
WHEN THE DARK MASTER ZORC'S ATTACK IS THE SUPER CRITICAL ØØ ...
OR IF THE PLAYER ROLLS A FUMBLE OF 99...
THE PLAYER'S SOUL WILL BE SEALED INTO THEIR FIGURINE BY THE SHADOW POWER! THE POWER OF DARKNESS!
SHADOW POWER!
BAKURA... YOU...
THE ONLY WAY TO RETRIEVE HER SOUL IS TO DEFEAT THE DARK MASTER ZORC!!
ZMM
ZMM
ZMM
EEYAAA!
WHY YOU LOUSY ...
I'M GONNA DO IT! DIE, ZORC, DIE!

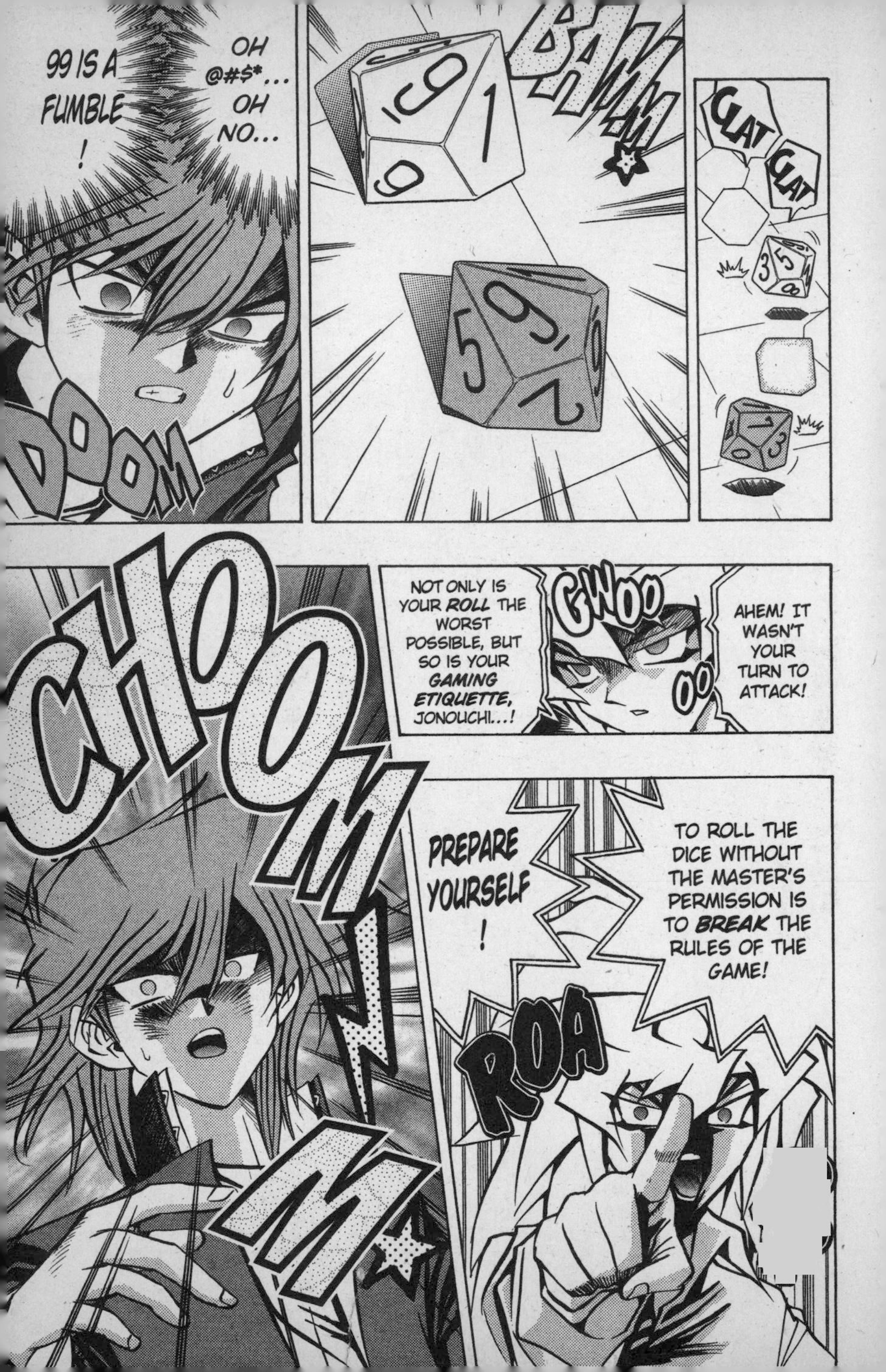
CLAT
CLAT
BAM
OH @#$*... OH NO...
99 IS A FUMBLE!
DOOM
AHEM! IT WASN'T YOUR TURN TO ATTACK!
GWOO
OO
NOT ONLY IS YOUR **ROLL** THE WORST POSSIBLE, BUT SO IS YOUR ***GAMING ETIQUETTE***, JONOUCHI...!
TO ROLL THE DICE WITHOUT THE MASTER'S PERMISSION IS TO ***BREAK*** THE RULES OF THE GAME!
PREPARE YOURSELF!
ROA
CHOOMM

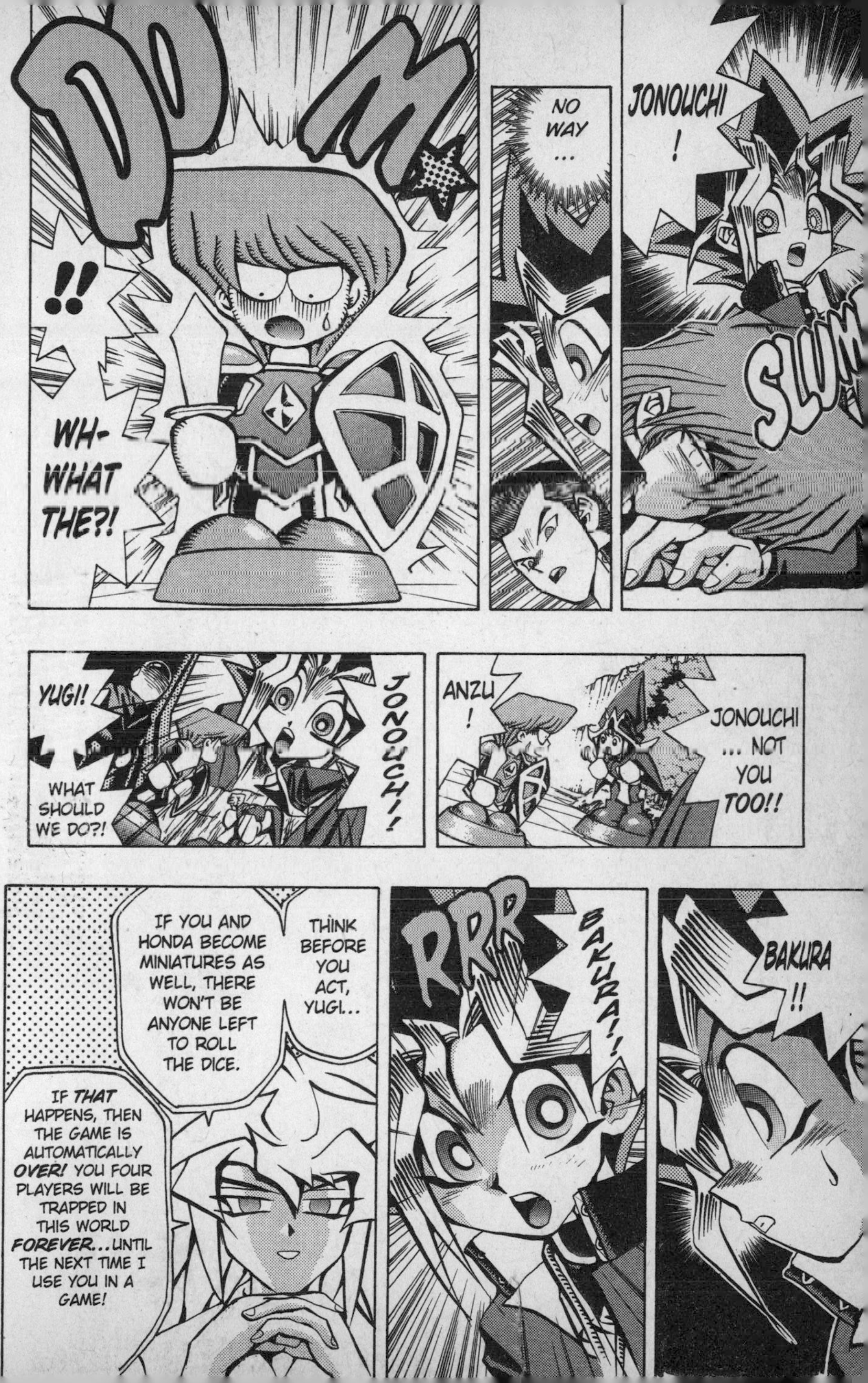
JONOUCHI !
SLUM
NO WAY ...
DOM
!!
WH- WHAT THE?!
ANZU !
JONOUCHI ... NOT YOU TOO!!
JONOUCHI!!
YUGI!
WHAT SHOULD WE DO?!
BAKURA !!
BAKURA!!
RRR
THINK BEFORE YOU ACT, YUGI...
IF YOU AND HONDA BECOME MINIATURES AS WELL, THERE WON'T BE ANYONE LEFT TO ROLL THE DICE.
IF *THAT* HAPPENS, THEN THE GAME IS AUTOMATICALLY ***OVER!*** YOU FOUR PLAYERS WILL BE TRAPPED IN THIS WORLD ***FOREVER...*** UNTIL THE NEXT TIME I USE YOU IN A GAME!

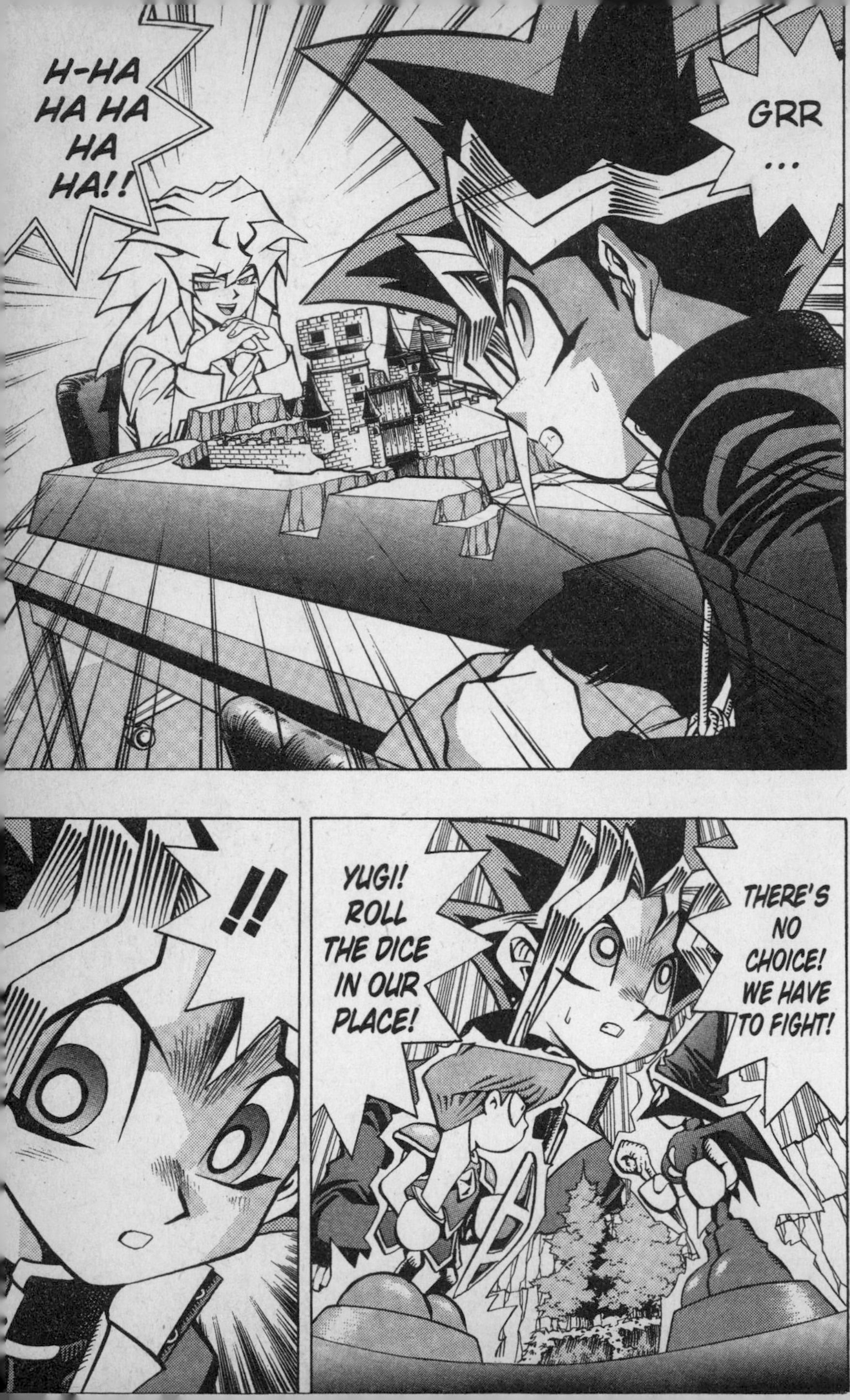
GRR ...
H-HA HA HA HA HA!!
THERE'S NO CHOICE! WE HAVE TO FIGHT!
YUGI! ROLL THE DICE IN OUR PLACE!
!!

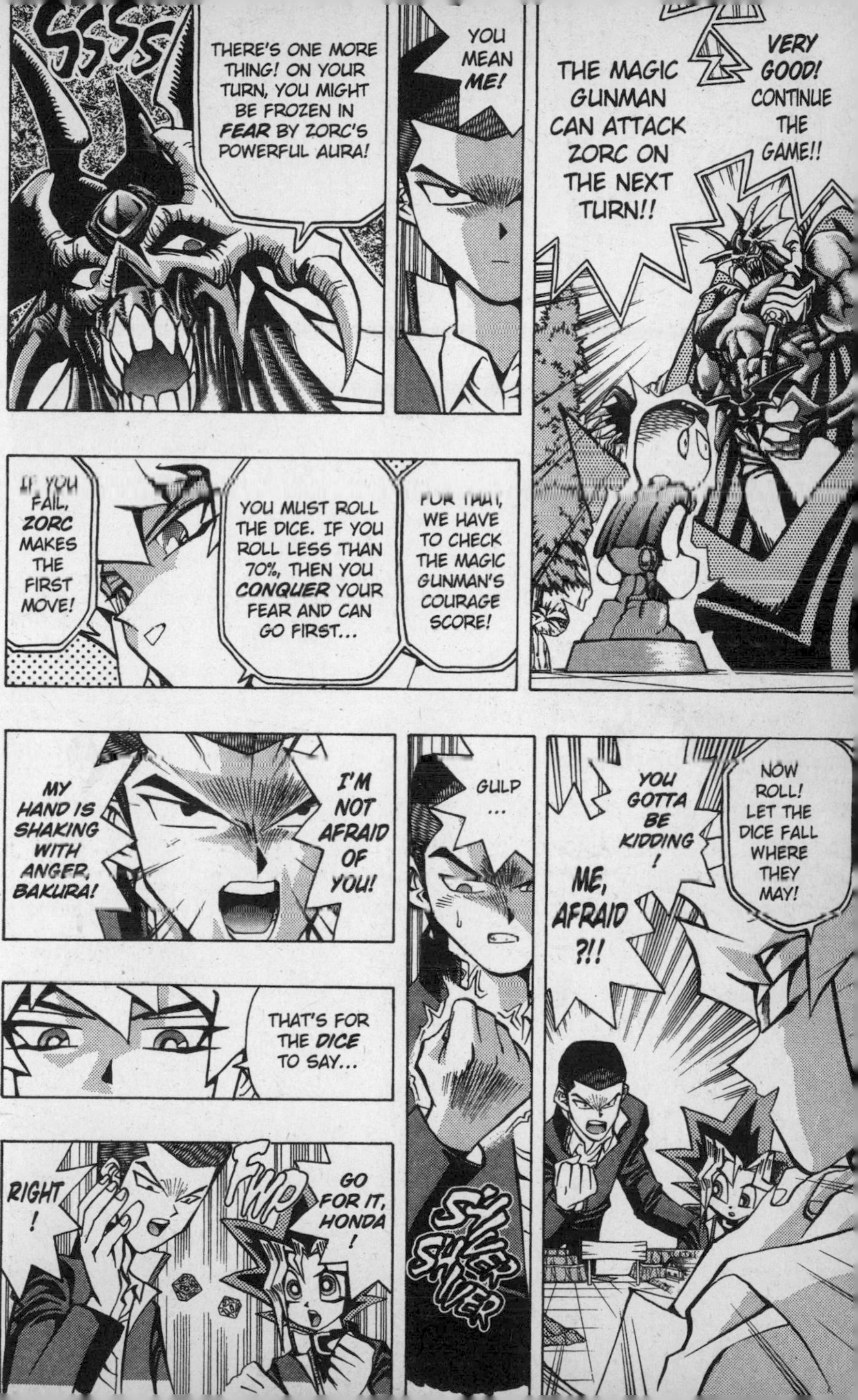
VERY GOOD! CONTINUE THE GAME!!
THE MAGIC GUNMAN CAN ATTACK ZORC ON THE NEXT TURN!!
YOU MEAN ME!
SSSSS
THERE'S ONE MORE THING! ON YOUR TURN, YOU MIGHT BE FROZEN IN FEAR BY ZORC'S POWERFUL AURA!
FOR THAT, WE HAVE TO CHECK THE MAGIC GUNMAN'S COURAGE SCORE!
YOU MUST ROLL THE DICE. IF YOU ROLL LESS THAN 70%, THEN YOU CONQUER YOUR FEAR AND CAN GO FIRST...
IF YOU FAIL, ZORC MAKES THE FIRST MOVE!
NOW ROLL! LET THE DICE FALL WHERE THEY MAY!
YOU GOTTA BE KIDDING!
ME, AFRAID?!!
GULP...
SHIVER SHIVER
I'M NOT AFRAID OF YOU!
MY HAND IS SHAKING WITH ANGER, BAKURA!
THAT'S FOR THE DICE TO SAY...
GO FOR IT, HONDA!
FWP
RIGHT!

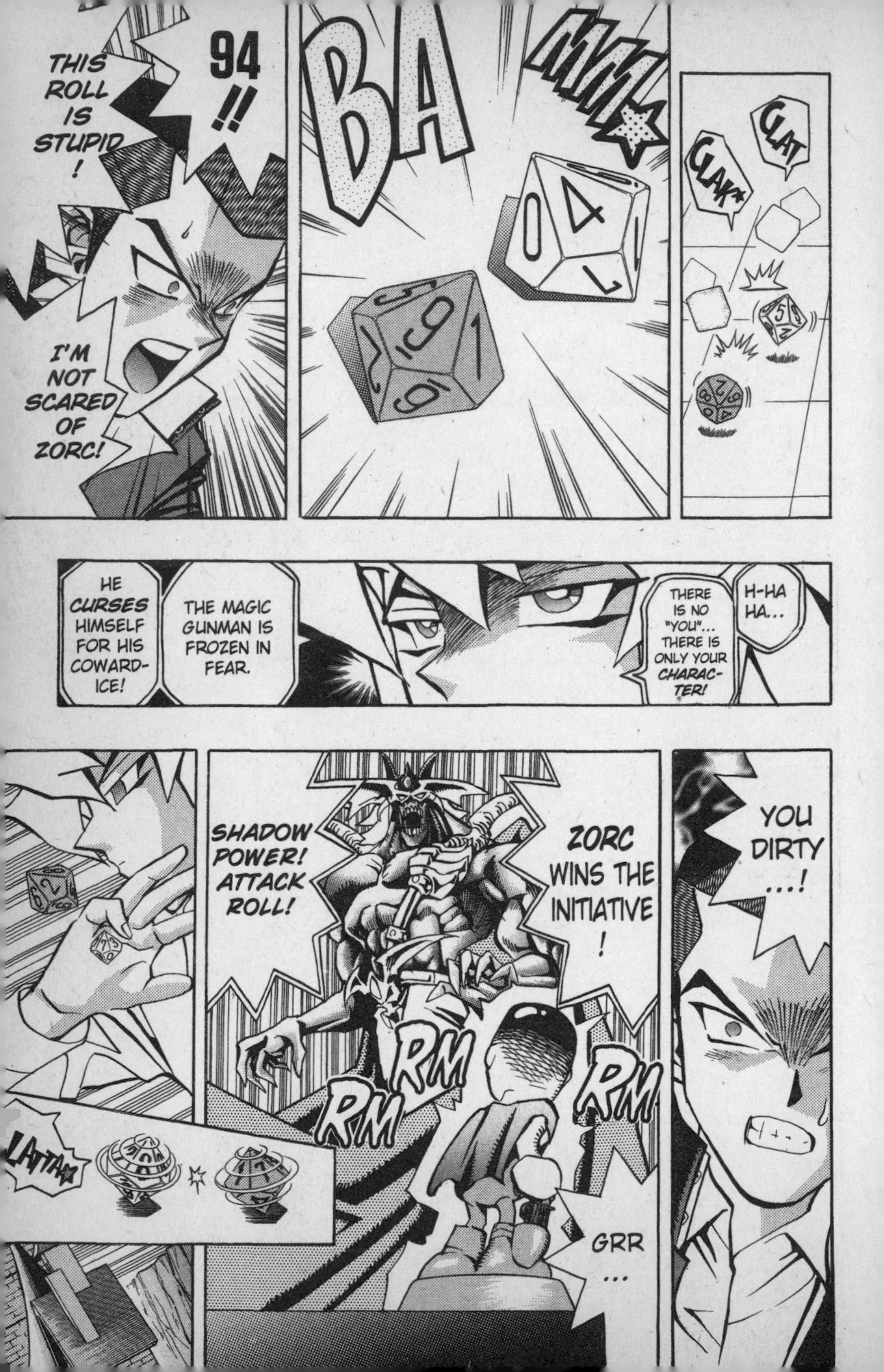
CLAT
CLAK
BAMM
94!!
THIS ROLL IS STUPID!
I'M NOT SCARED OF ZORC!
H-HA HA...
THERE IS NO "YOU"... THERE IS ONLY YOUR CHARACTER!
THE MAGIC GUNMAN IS FROZEN IN FEAR.
HE CURSES HIMSELF FOR HIS COWARDICE!
YOU DIRTY...!
ZORC WINS THE INITIATIVE!
SHADOW POWER! ATTACK ROLL!
RM RM RM
GRR...
LATTA

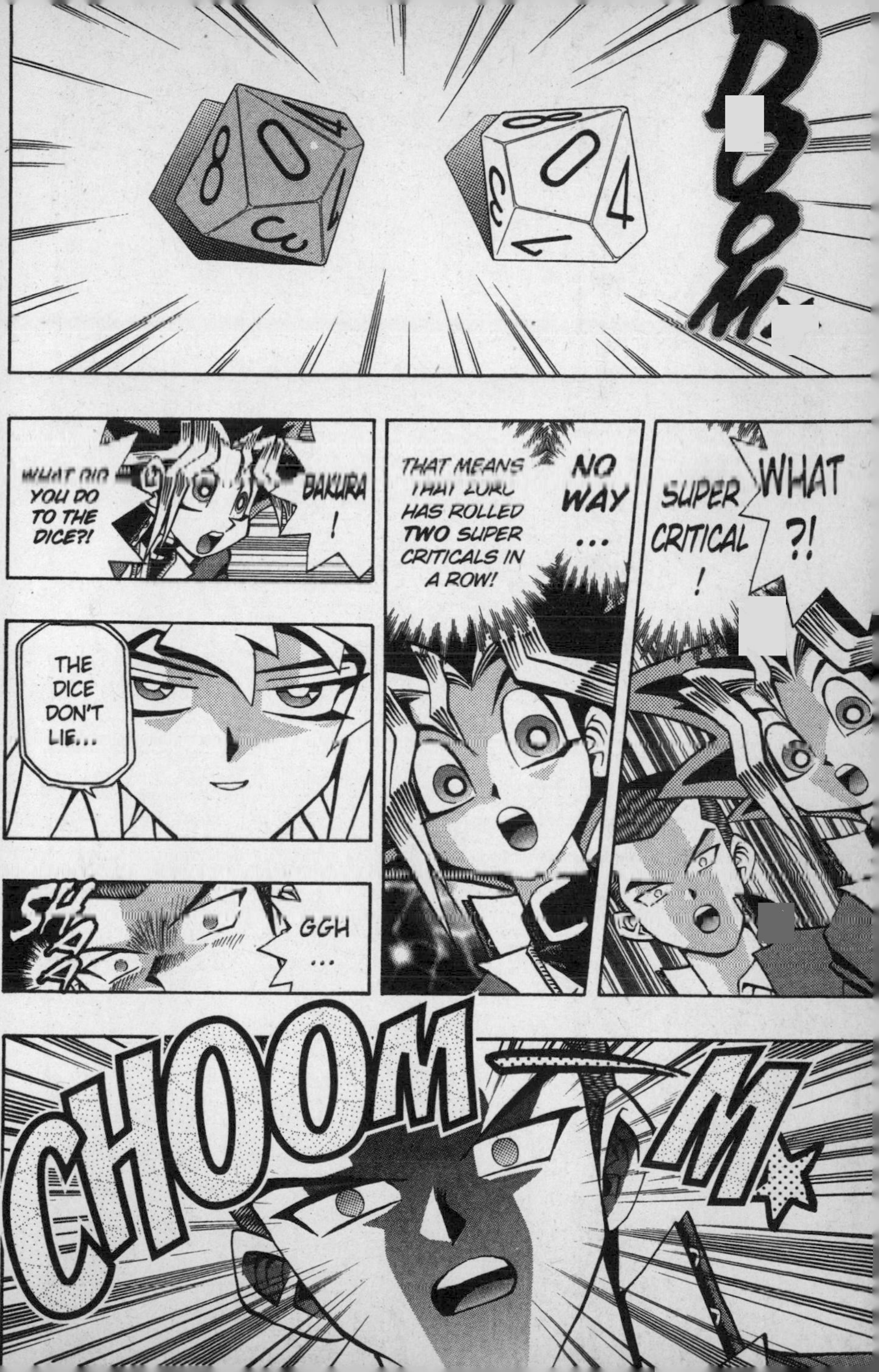
BOOM
WHAT ?!
SUPER CRITICAL !
NO WAY ...
THAT MEANS THAT ZORC HAS ROLLED TWO SUPER CRITICALS IN A ROW!
BAKURA !
WHAT DID YOU DO TO THE DICE?!
THE DICE DON'T LIE...
GGH ...
CHOOOM

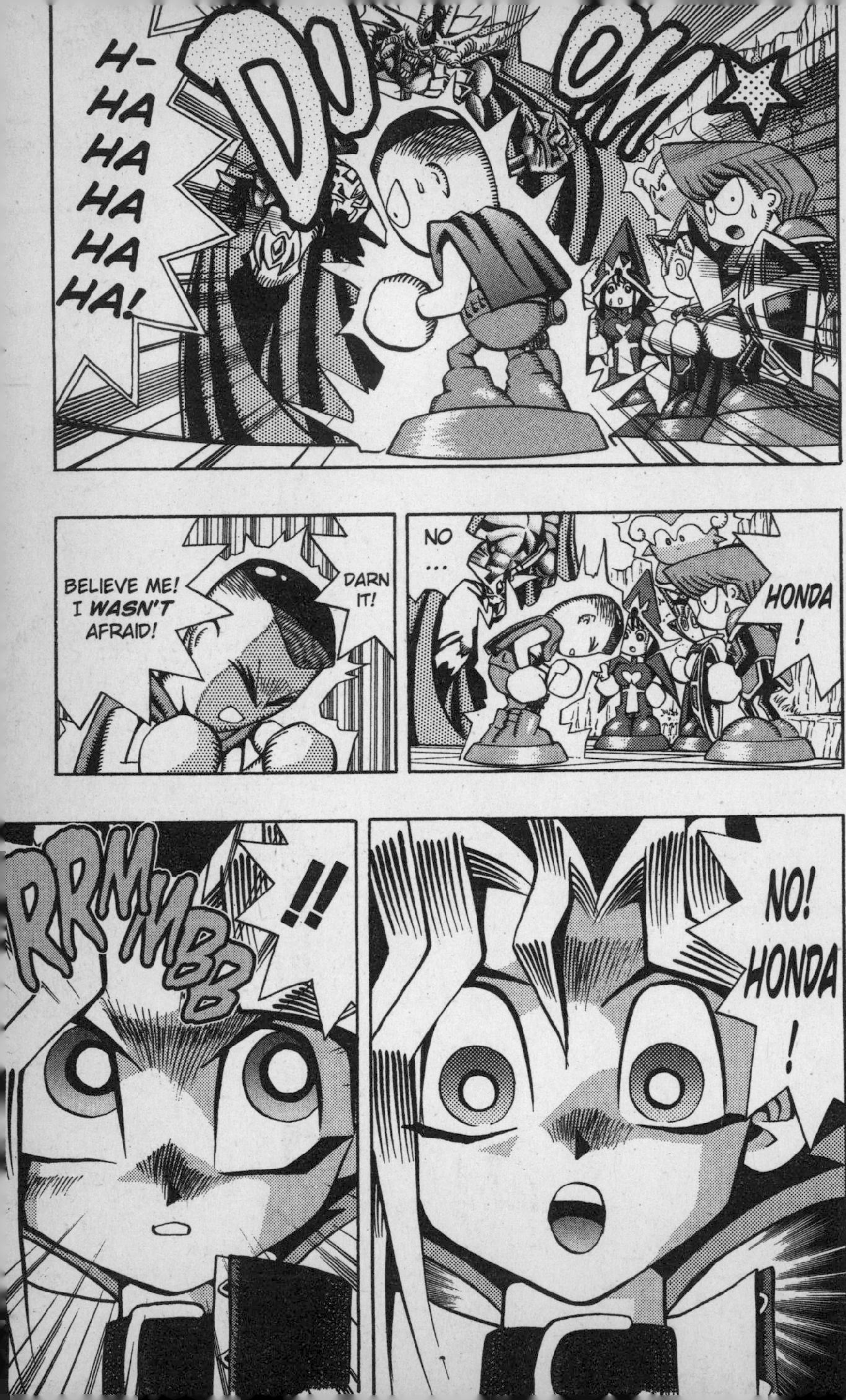
H- HA HA HA HA HA!
NO ...
HONDA !
DARN IT!
BELIEVE ME! I WASN'T AFRAID!
NO! HONDA !
RRMMBB
!!

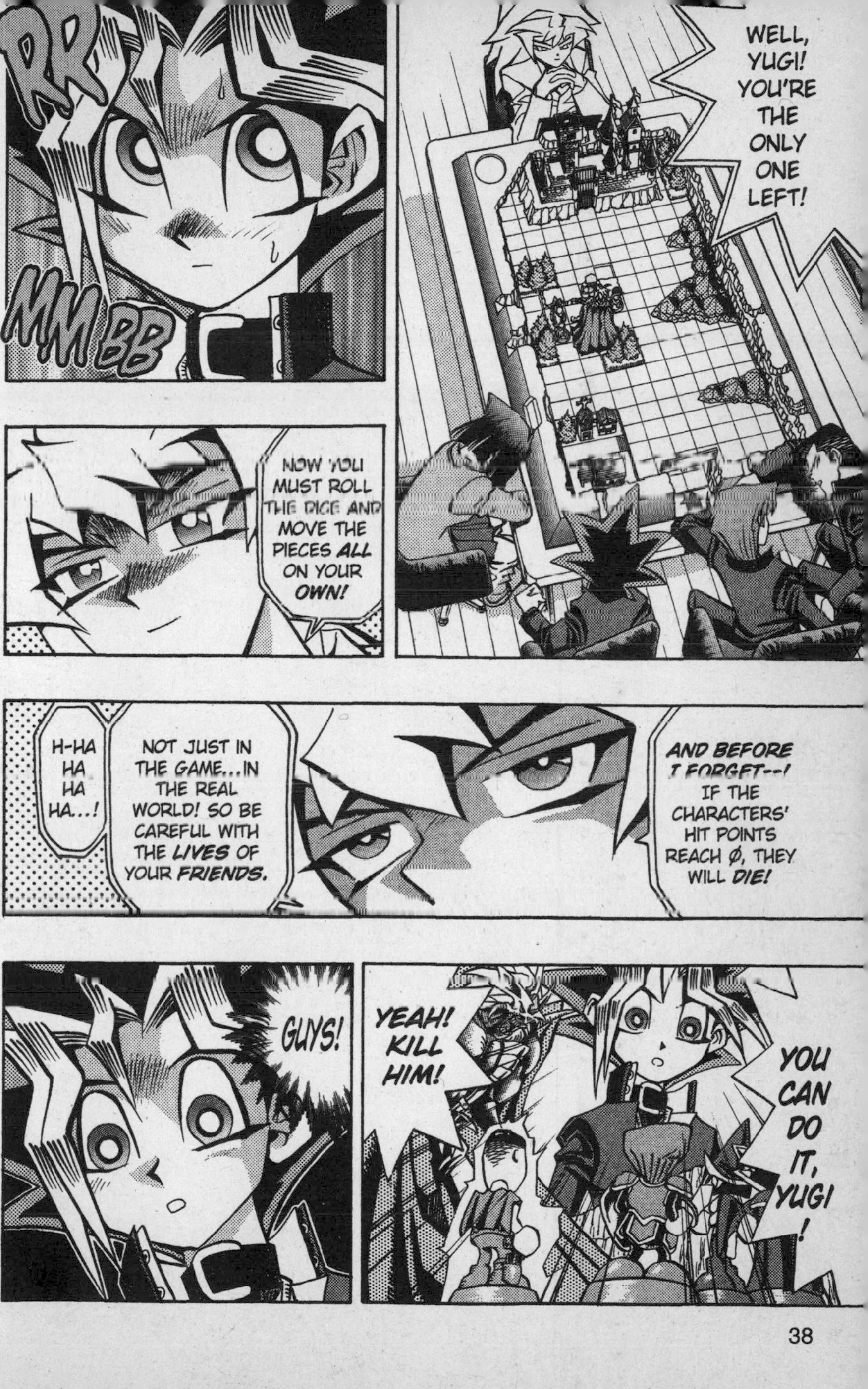
WELL, YUGI! YOU'RE THE ONLY ONE LEFT!
RRMMBB
NOW YOU MUST ROLL THE DICE AND MOVE THE PIECES ALL ON YOUR OWN!
AND BEFORE I FORGET--! IF THE CHARACTERS' HIT POINTS REACH Ø, THEY WILL DIE!
NOT JUST IN THE GAME...IN THE REAL WORLD! SO BE CAREFUL WITH THE LIVES OF YOUR FRIENDS.
H-HA HA HA HA...!
YOU CAN DO IT, YUGI!
YEAH! KILL HIM!
GUYS!

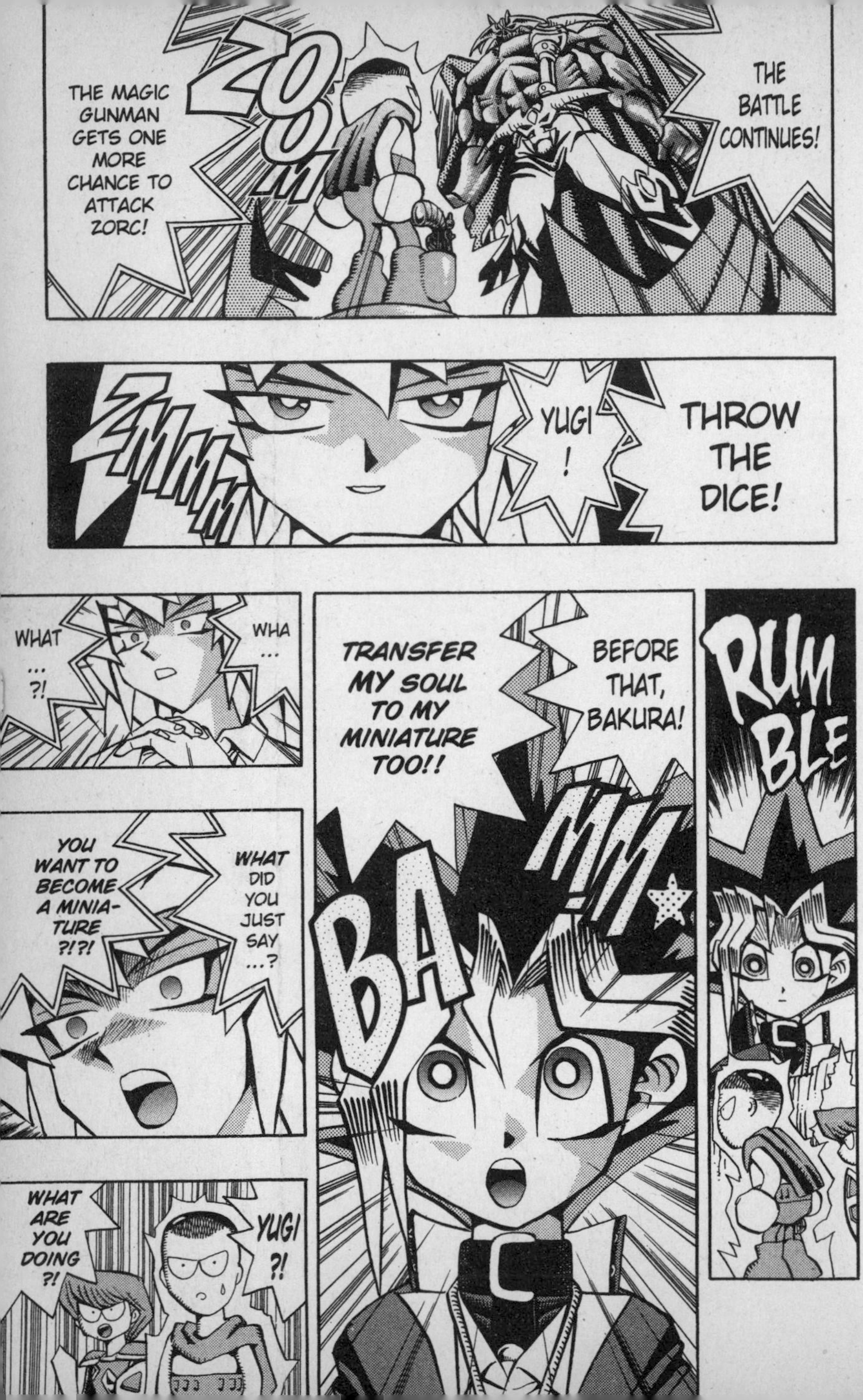
THE BATTLE CONTINUES!
ZOOM
THE MAGIC GUNMAN GETS ONE MORE CHANCE TO ATTACK ZORC!
THROW THE DICE!
YUGI!
ZMMM
RUMBLE
BEFORE THAT, BAKURA!
TRANSFER MY SOUL TO MY MINIATURE TOO!!
BAMM!
WHA...
WHAT...?!
WHAT DID YOU JUST SAY...?
YOU WANT TO BECOME A MINIATURE?!?!
YUGI?!
WHAT ARE YOU DOING?!

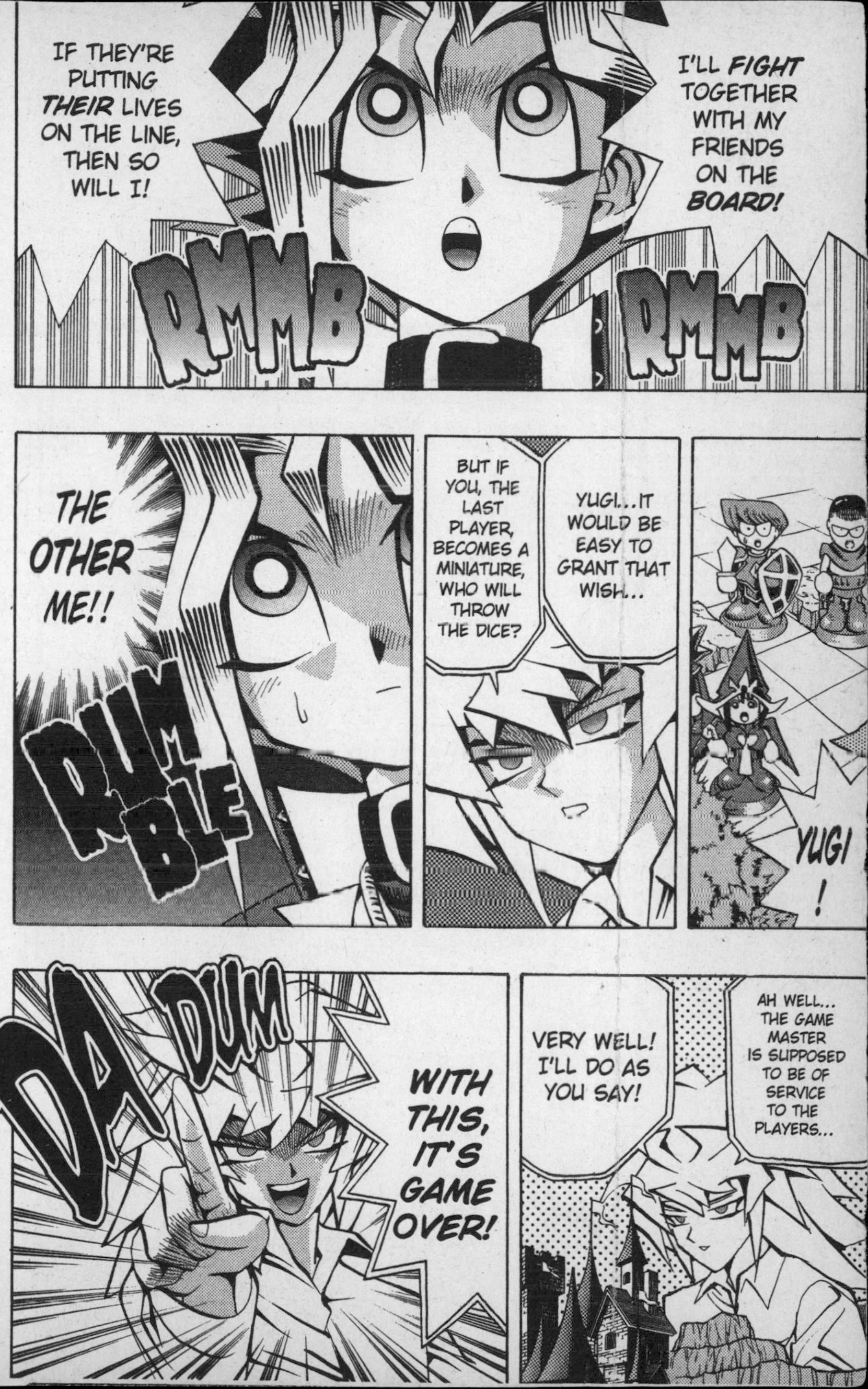
I'LL FIGHT TOGETHER WITH MY FRIENDS ON THE BOARD!
IF THEY'RE PUTTING THEIR LIVES ON THE LINE, THEN SO WILL I!
RMMB
RMMB
YUGI!
YUGI...IT WOULD BE EASY TO GRANT THAT WISH...
BUT IF YOU, THE LAST PLAYER, BECOMES A MINIATURE, WHO WILL THROW THE DICE?
THE OTHER ME!!
RUMBLE
AH WELL... THE GAME MASTER IS SUPPOSED TO BE OF SERVICE TO THE PLAYERS...
VERY WELL! I'LL DO AS YOU SAY!
DA DUM
WITH THIS, IT'S GAME OVER!

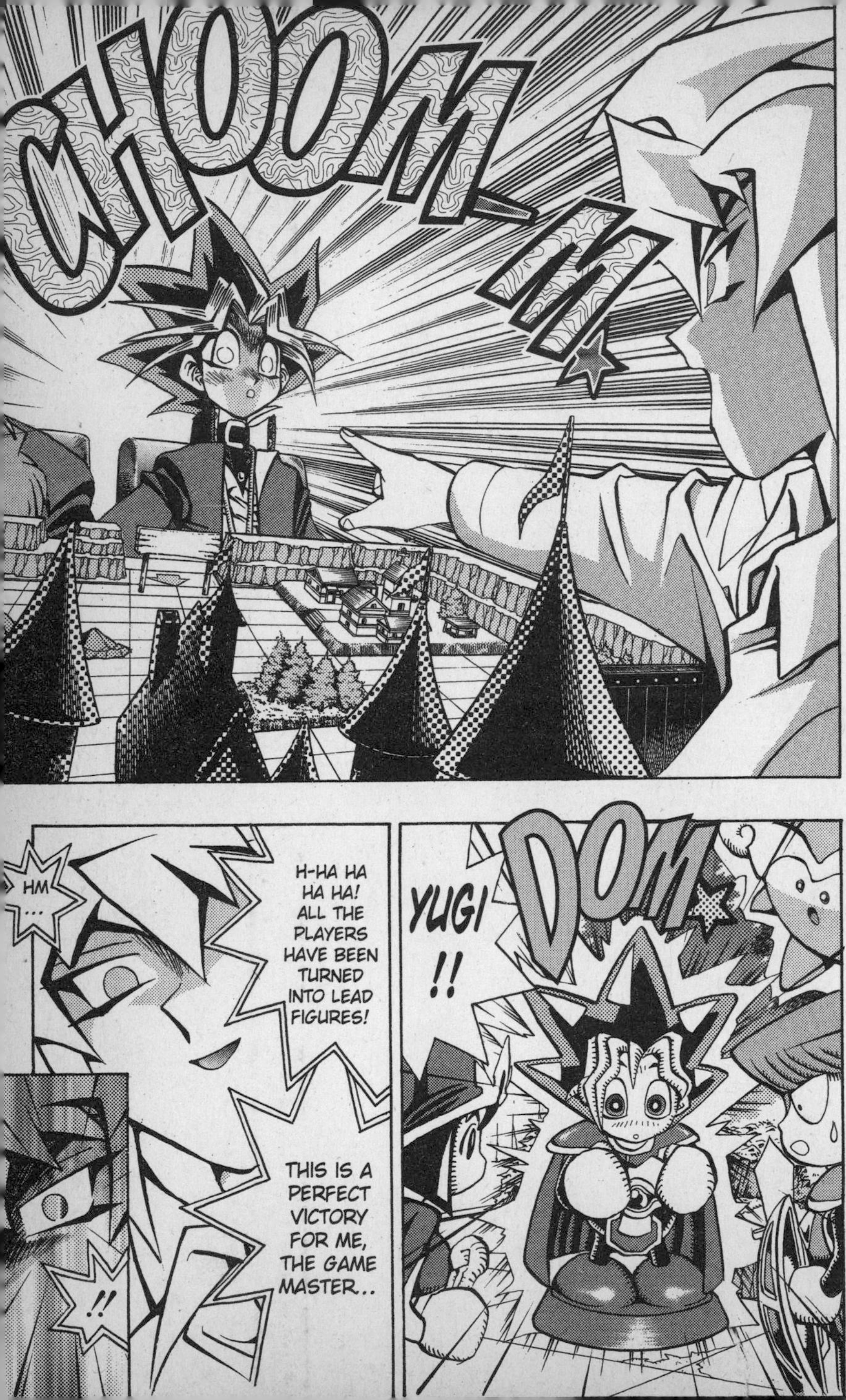
CHOOM-M
DOM
YUGI !!
HM ...
H-HA HA HA HA! ALL THE PLAYERS HAVE BEEN TURNED INTO LEAD FIGURES!
THIS IS A PERFECT VICTORY FOR ME, THE GAME MASTER...
!!

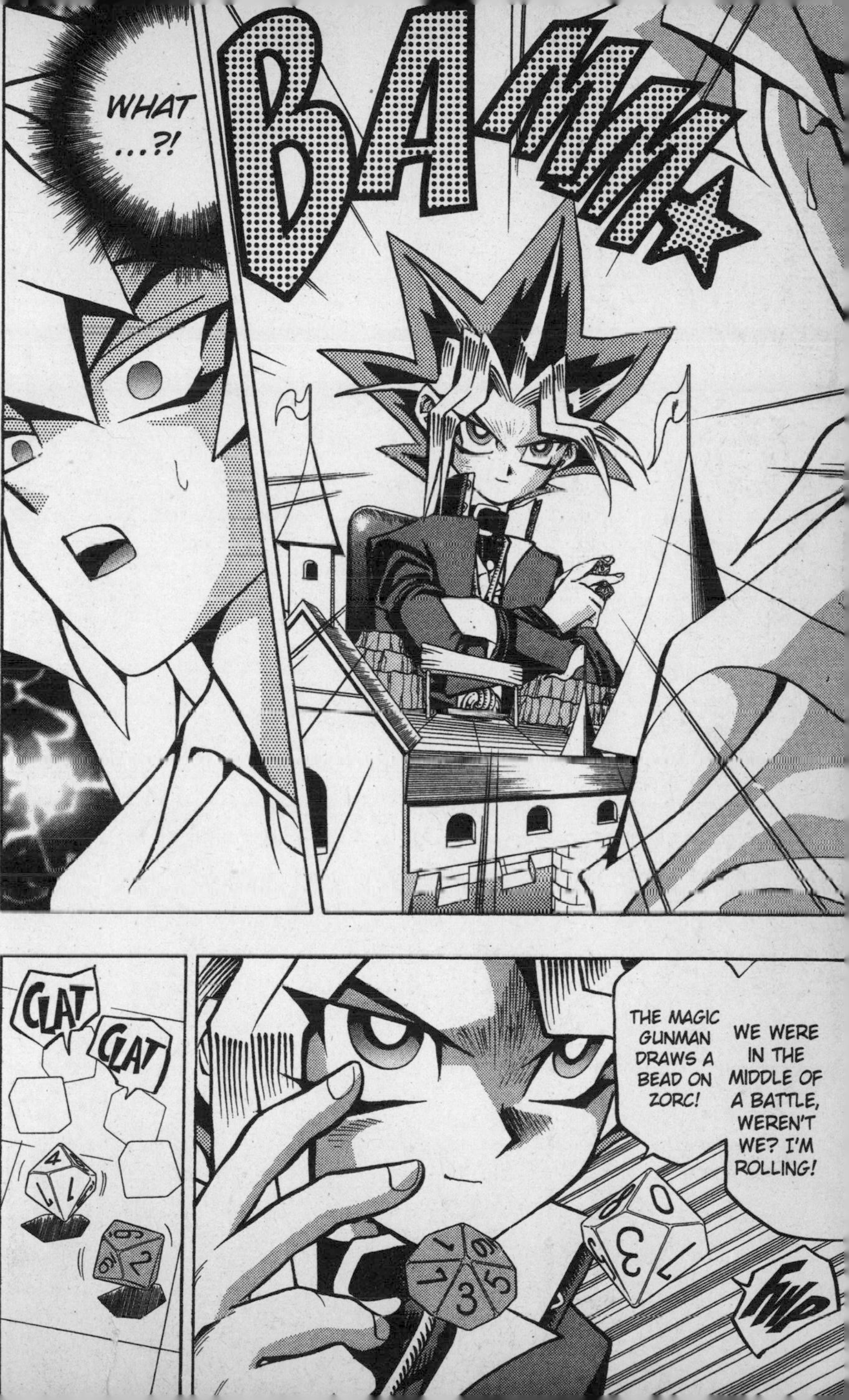
BAMM
WHAT ...?!
WE WERE IN THE MIDDLE OF A BATTLE, WEREN'T WE? I'M ROLLING!
THE MAGIC GUNMAN DRAWS A BEAD ON ZORC!
FWP
CLAT
CLAT

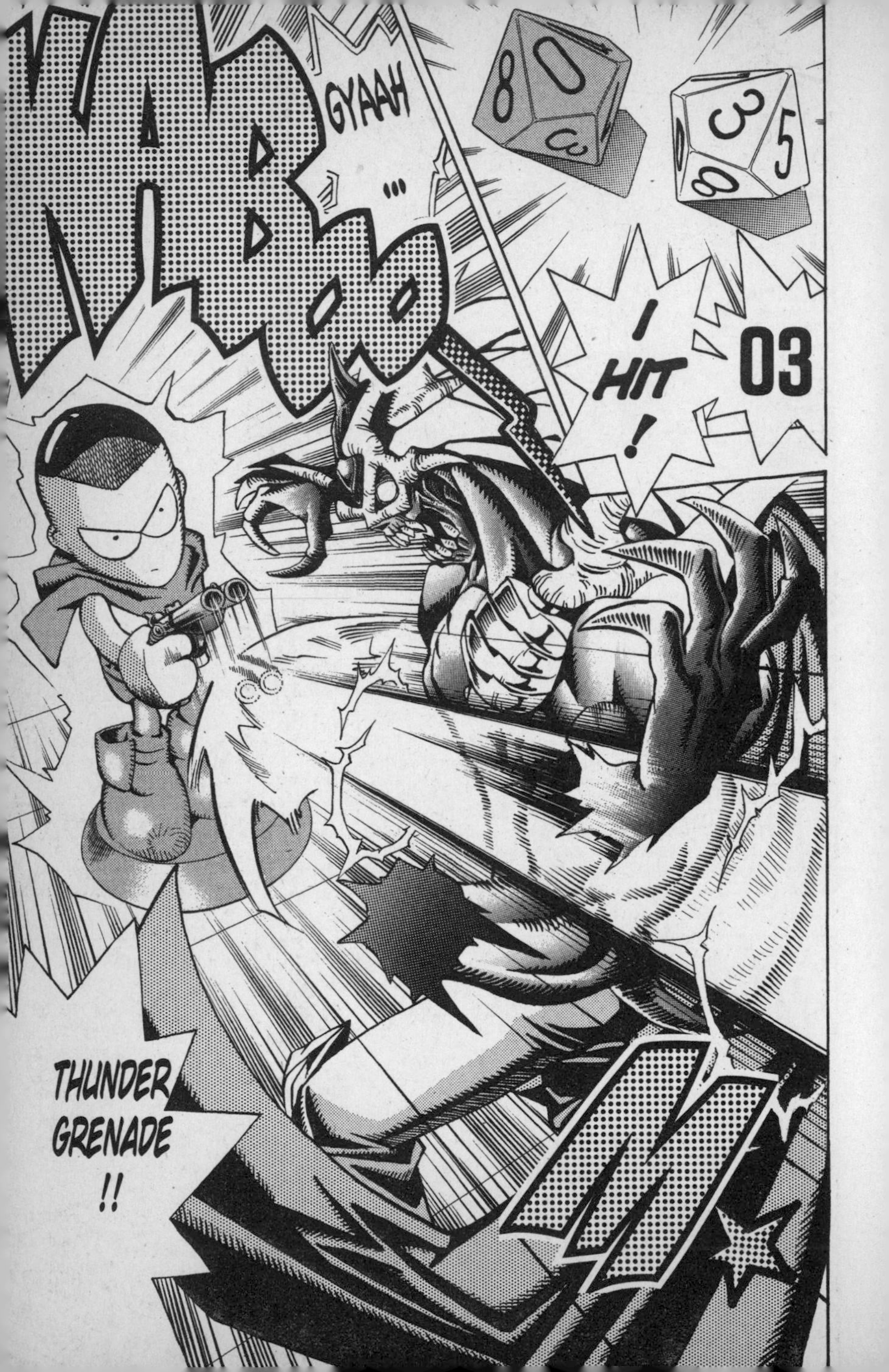
03
HIT !
GYAAH ...
THUNDER GRENADE !!

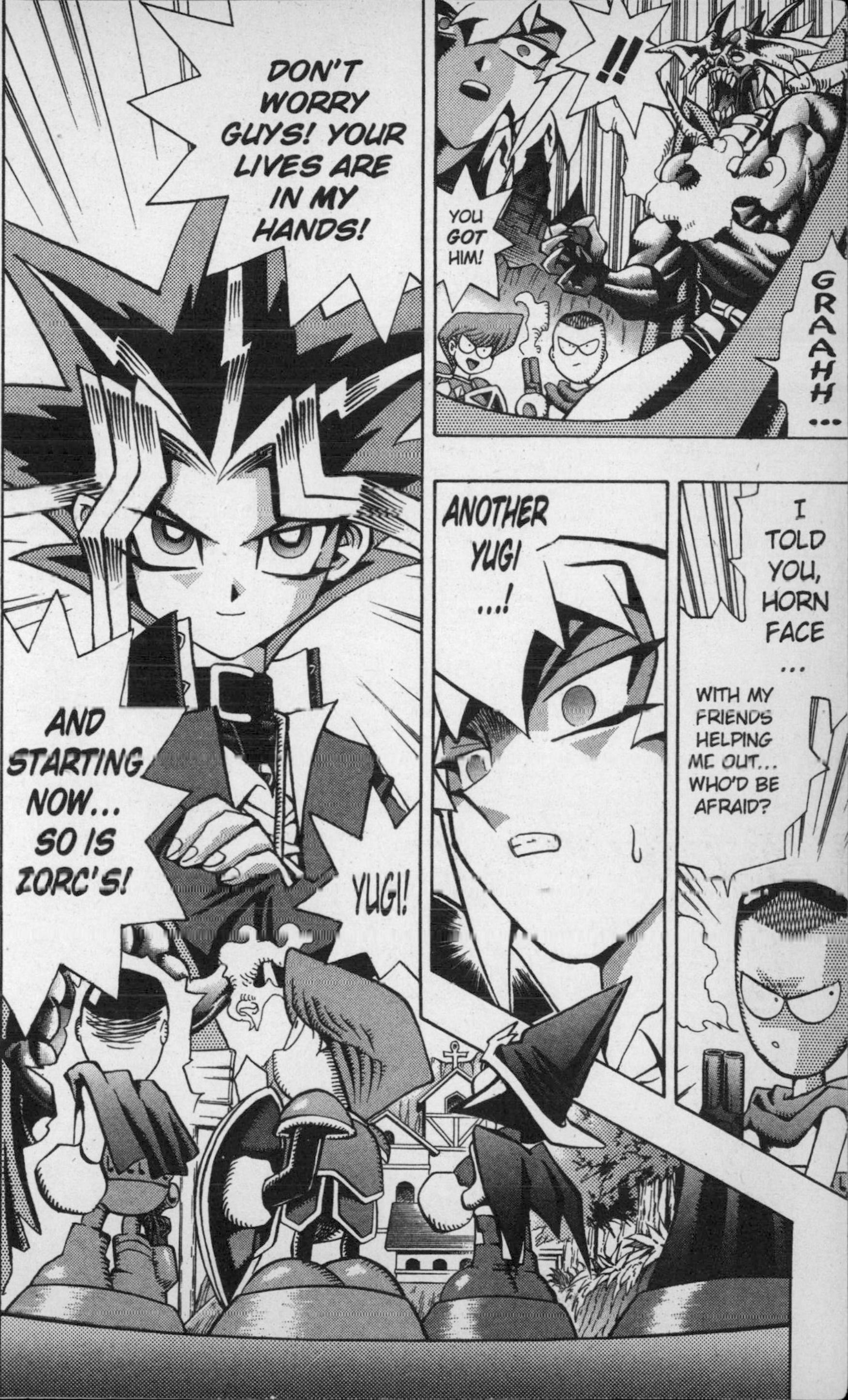
!!
GRAAHH...
YOU GOT HIM!
I TOLD YOU, HORN FACE...
WITH MY FRIENDS HELPING ME OUT... WHO'D BE AFRAID?
ANOTHER YUGI ...!
DON'T WORRY GUYS! YOUR LIVES ARE IN MY HANDS!
AND STARTING NOW... SO IS ZORC'S!
YUGI!

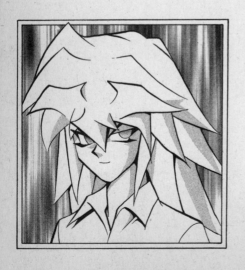

Duel 54: Millennium Enemy 5

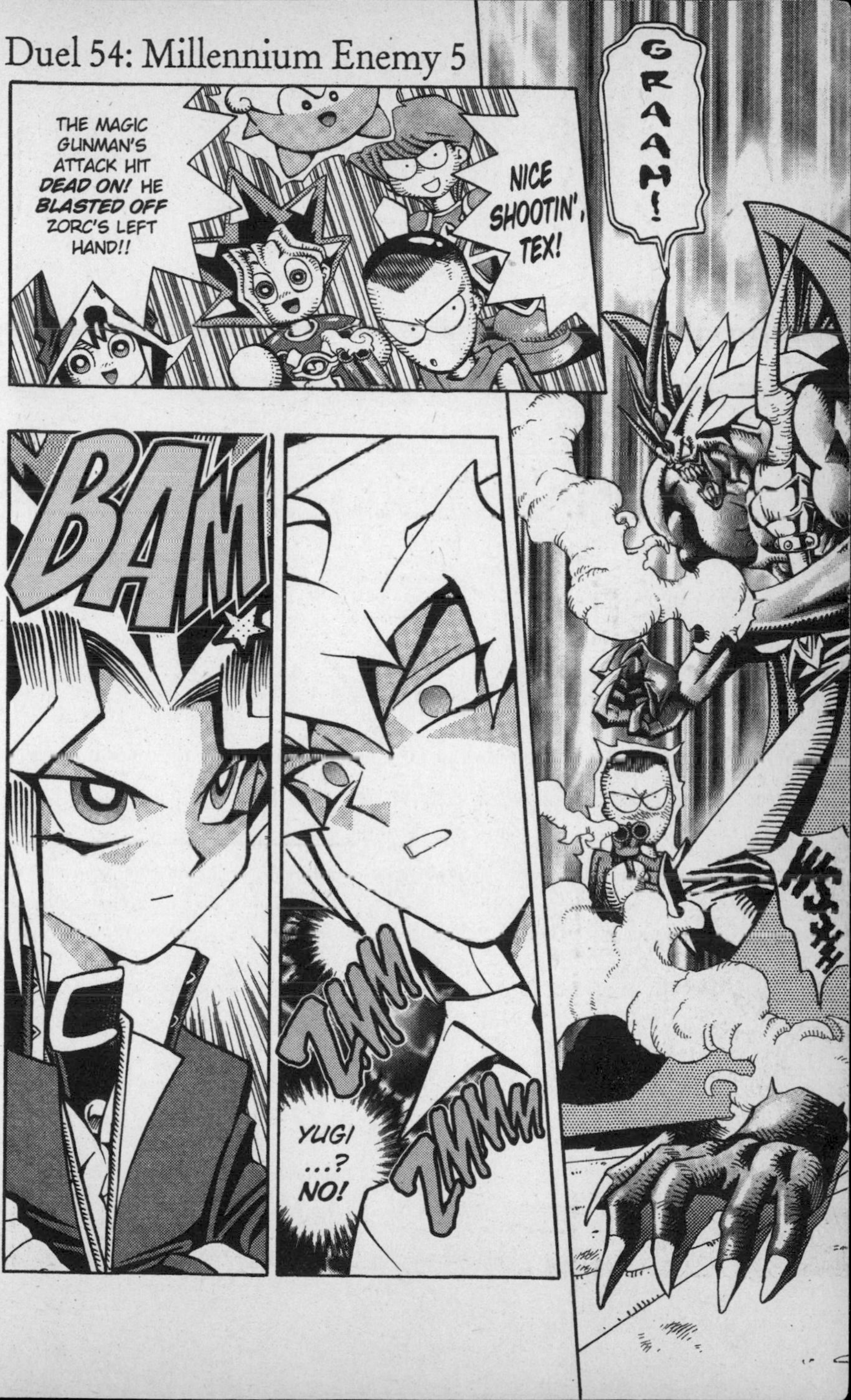
GRAAH!
NICE SHOOTIN', TEX!
THE MAGIC GUNMAN'S ATTACK HIT DEAD ON! HE BLASTED OFF ZORC'S LEFT HAND!!
ZMM
ZMMM
YUGI ...? NO!
BAM

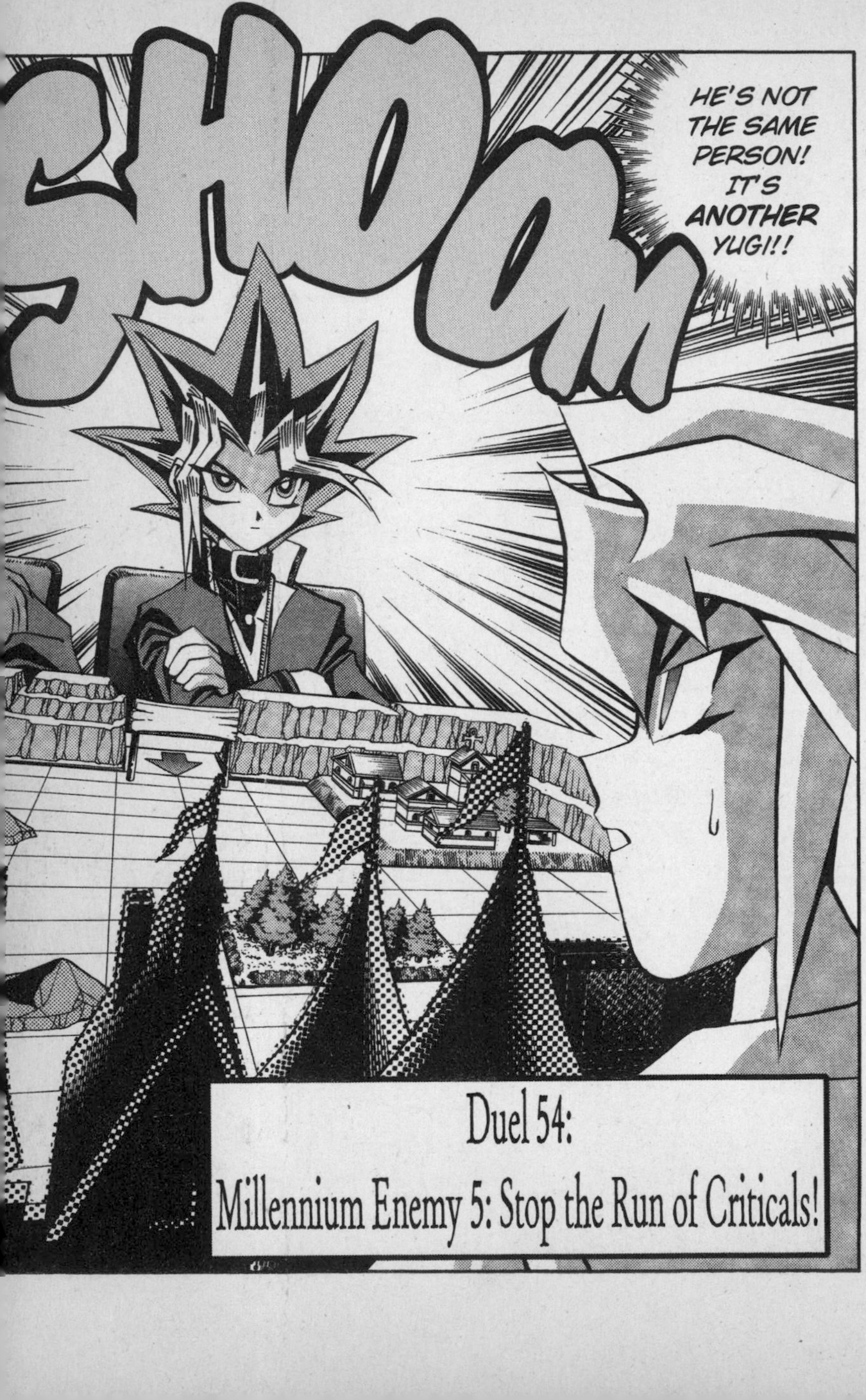
HE'S NOT THE SAME PERSON! IT'S ANOTHER YUGI!!
SHOOM

Duel 54:
Millennium Enemy 5: Stop the Run of Criticals!

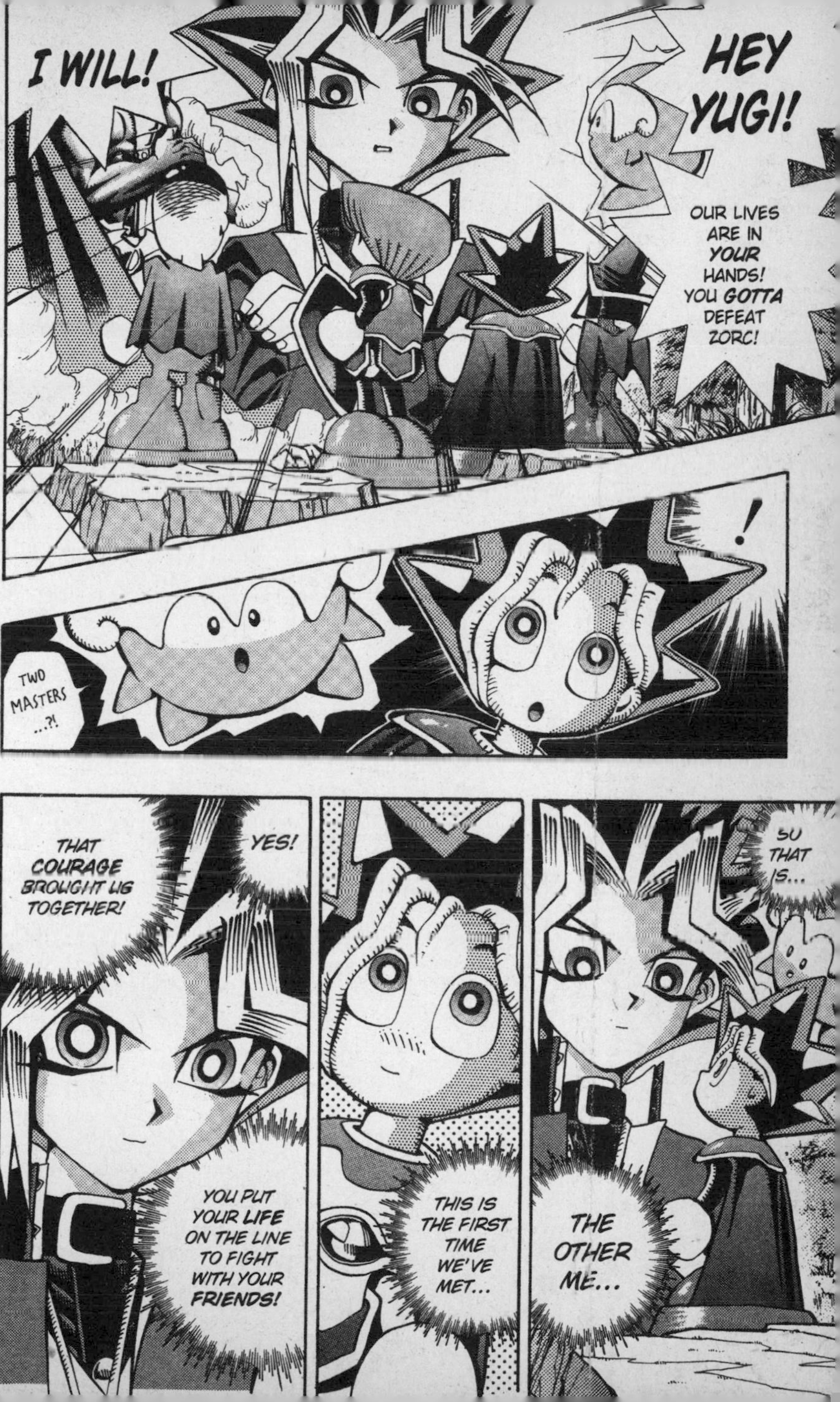
HEY YUGI!
OUR LIVES ARE IN YOUR HANDS! YOU GOTTA DEFEAT ZORC!
I WILL!
!
TWO MASTERS ...?!
SO THAT IS...
THE OTHER ME...
THIS IS THE FIRST TIME WE'VE MET...
YES!
THAT COURAGE BROUGHT US TOGETHER!
YOU PUT YOUR LIFE ON THE LINE TO FIGHT WITH YOUR FRIENDS!

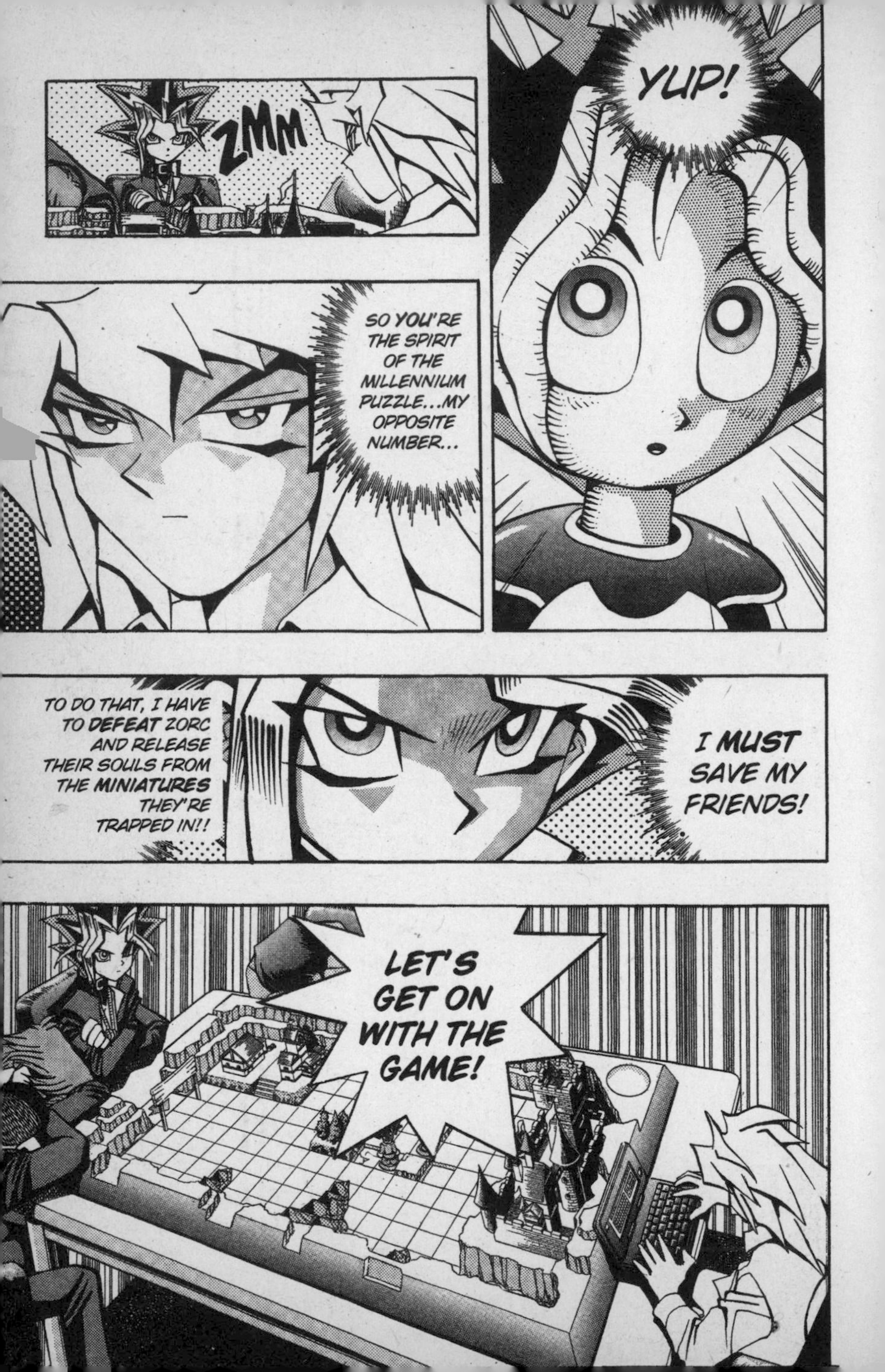
YUP!
ZMM
SO YOU'RE THE SPIRIT OF THE MILLENNIUM PUZZLE...MY OPPOSITE NUMBER...
I MUST SAVE MY FRIENDS!
TO DO THAT, I HAVE TO DEFEAT ZORC AND RELEASE THEIR SOULS FROM THE MINIATURES THEY'RE TRAPPED IN!!
LET'S GET ON WITH THE GAME!

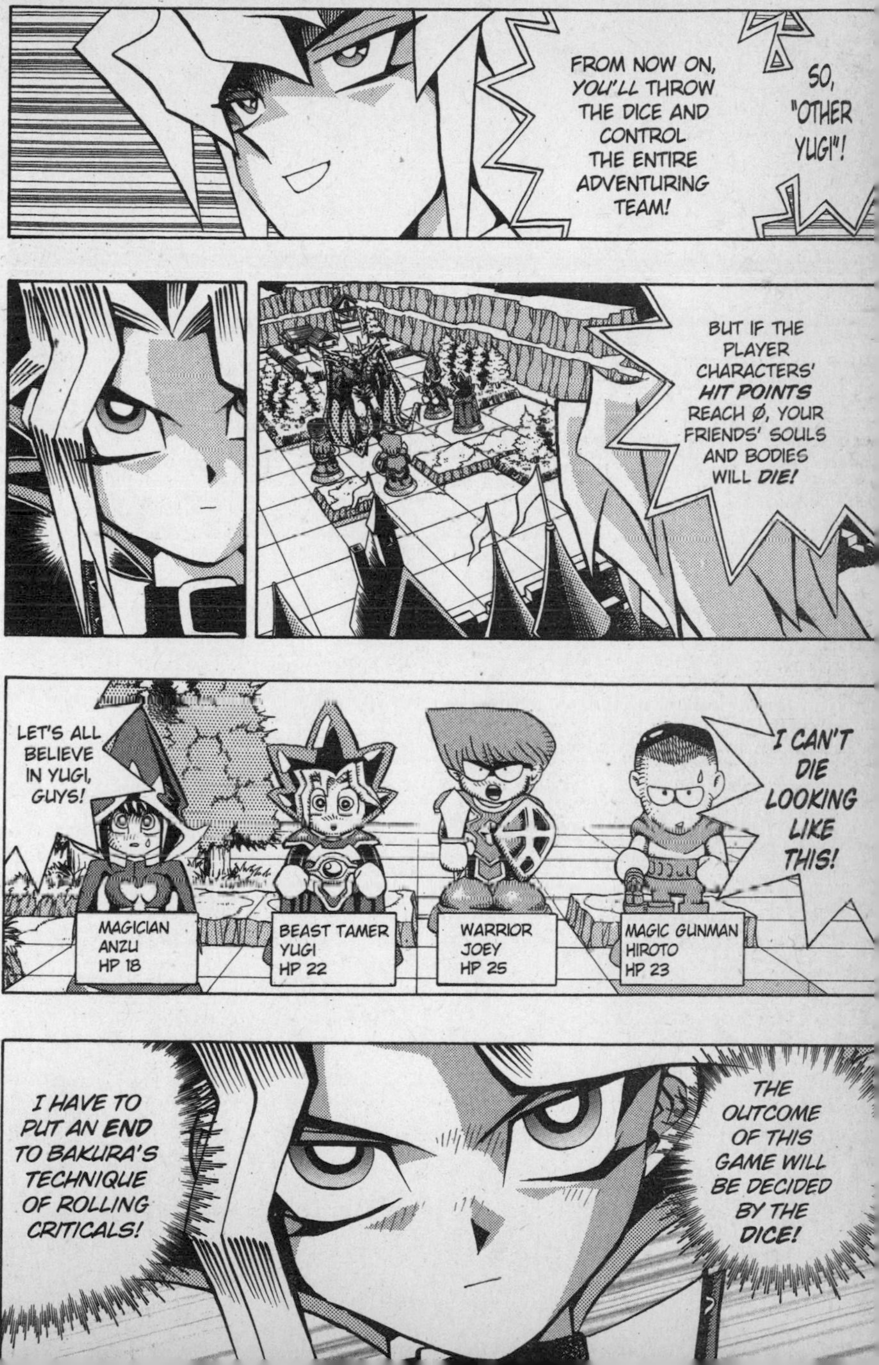

SO, "OTHER YUGI"!
FROM NOW ON, YOU'LL THROW THE DICE AND CONTROL THE ENTIRE ADVENTURING TEAM!
BUT IF THE PLAYER CHARACTERS' HIT POINTS REACH Ø, YOUR FRIENDS' SOULS AND BODIES WILL DIE!
I CAN'T DIE LOOKING LIKE THIS!
LET'S ALL BELIEVE IN YUGI, GUYS!
MAGIC GUNMAN HIROTO HP 23
WARRIOR JOEY HP 25
BEAST TAMER YUGI HP 22
MAGICIAN ANZU HP 18
THE OUTCOME OF THIS GAME WILL BE DECIDED BY THE DICE!
I HAVE TO PUT AN END TO BAKURA'S TECHNIQUE OF ROLLING CRITICALS!

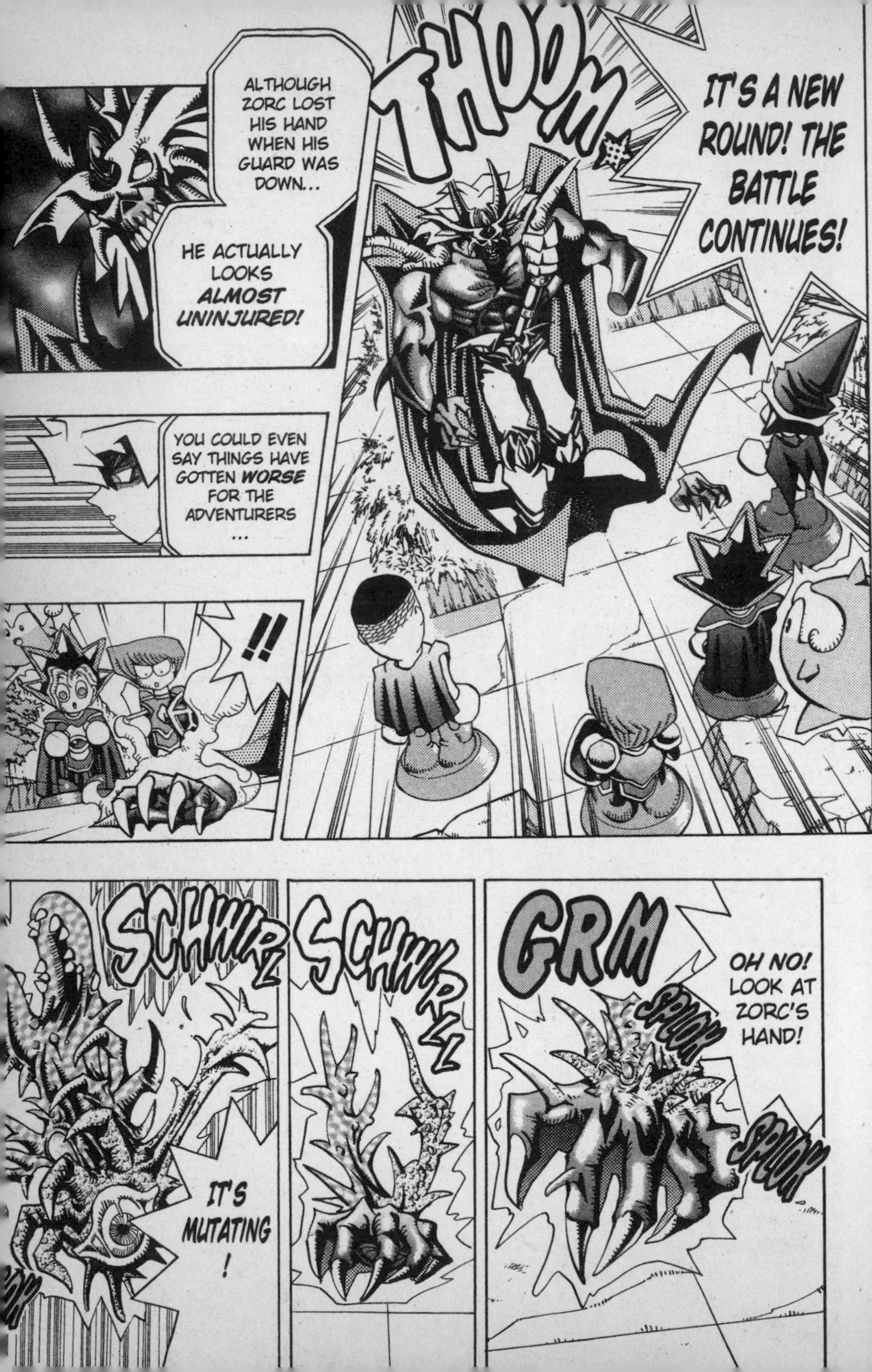
THOOM
IT'S A NEW ROUND! THE BATTLE CONTINUES!
ALTHOUGH ZORC LOST HIS HAND WHEN HIS GUARD WAS DOWN...
HE ACTUALLY LOOKS ALMOST UNINJURED!
YOU COULD EVEN SAY THINGS HAVE GOTTEN WORSE FOR THE ADVENTURERS ...
!!
GRM
OH NO! LOOK AT ZORC'S HAND!
SCHWIRL
SCHWIRL
IT'S MUTATING!

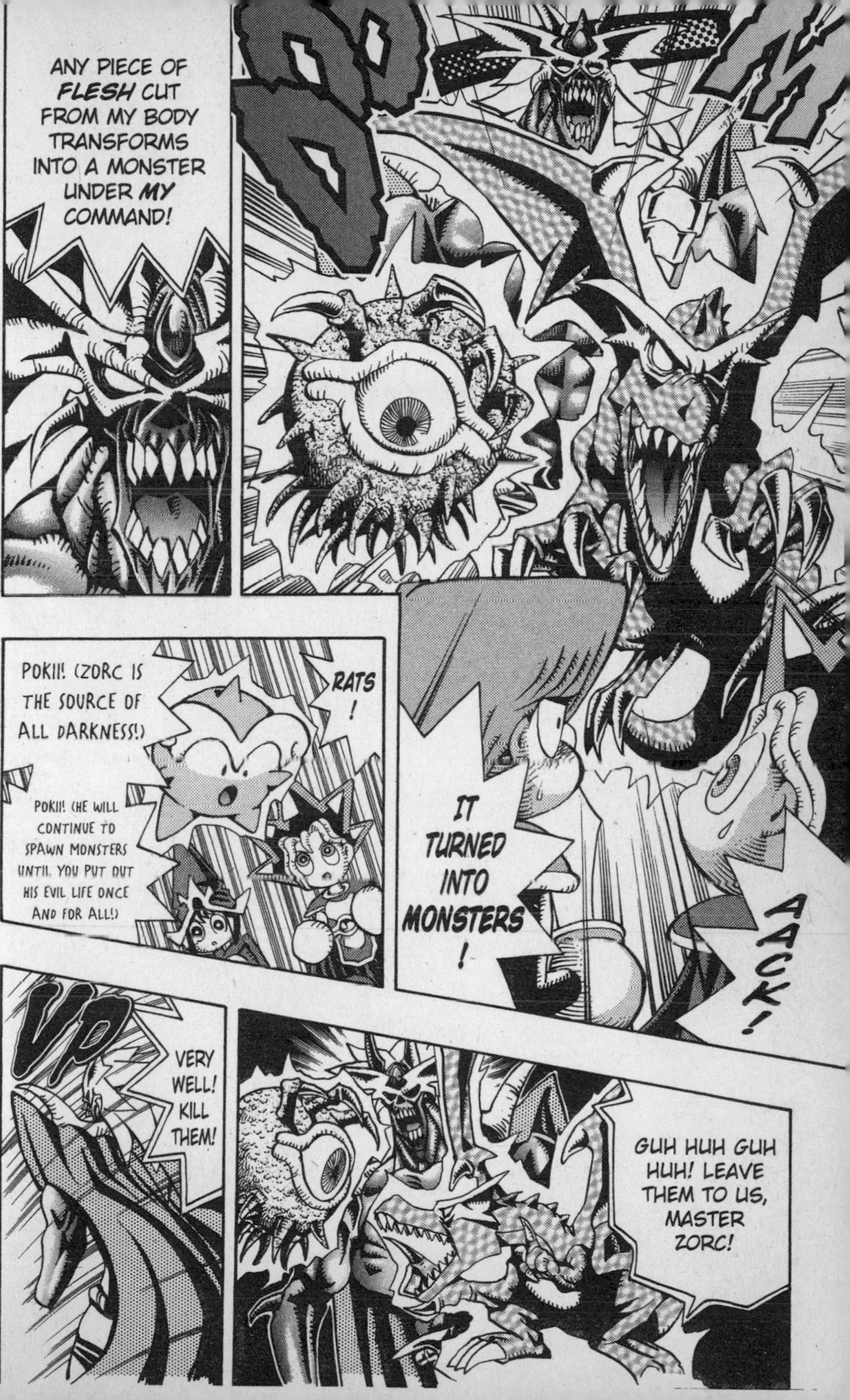
ANY PIECE OF FLESH CUT FROM MY BODY TRANSFORMS INTO A MONSTER UNDER MY COMMAND!
AACK!
IT TURNED INTO MONSTERS!
RATS!
POKII! (ZORC IS THE SOURCE OF ALL DARKNESS!)
POKII! (HE WILL CONTINUE TO SPAWN MONSTERS UNTIL YOU PUT OUT HIS EVIL LIFE ONCE AND FOR ALL!)
GUH HUH GUH HUH! LEAVE THEM TO US, MASTER ZORC!
VP
VERY WELL! KILL THEM!

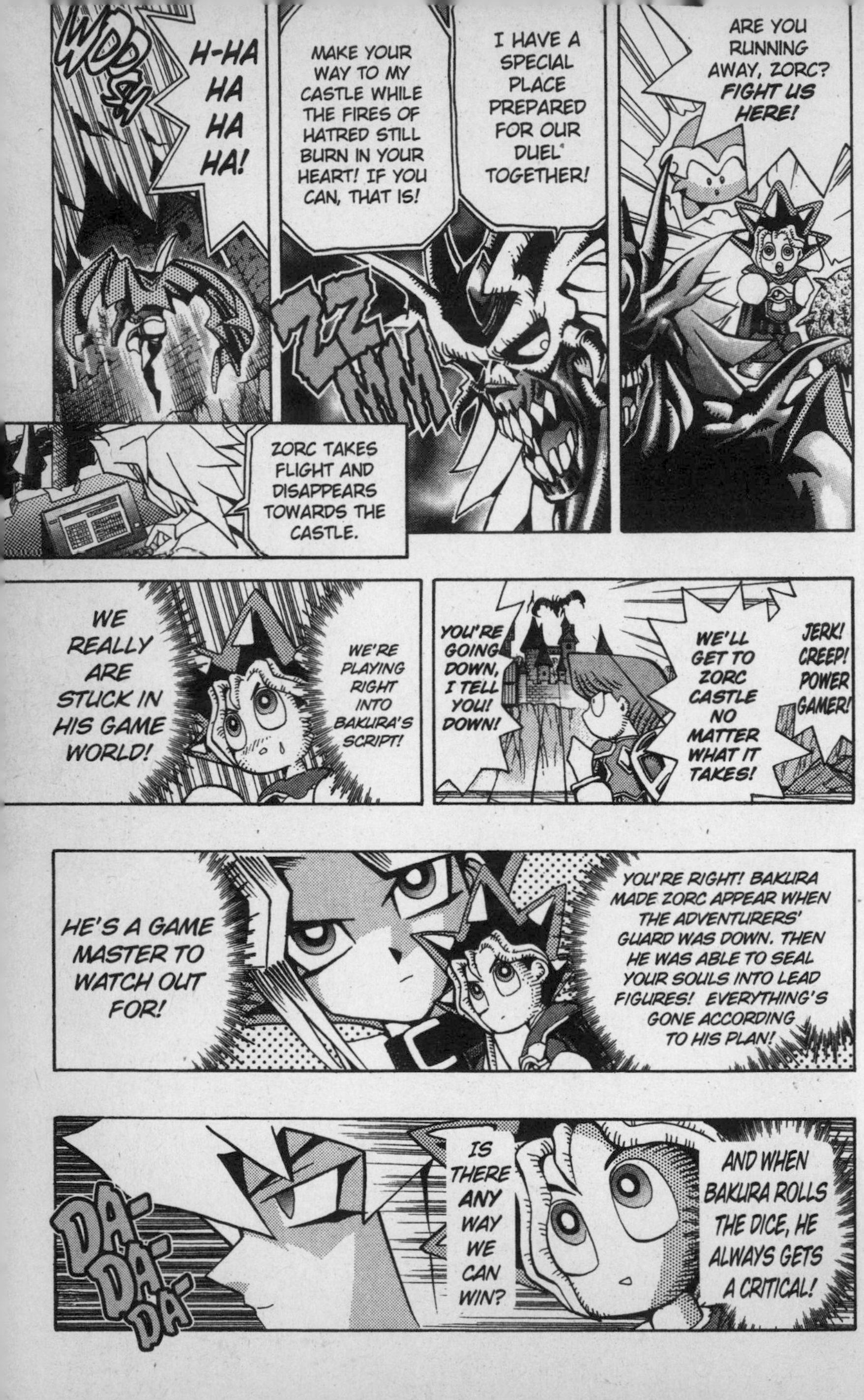
ARE YOU RUNNING AWAY, ZORC? FIGHT US HERE!
I HAVE A SPECIAL PLACE PREPARED FOR OUR DUEL TOGETHER!
MAKE YOUR WAY TO MY CASTLE WHILE THE FIRES OF HATRED STILL BURN IN YOUR HEART! IF YOU CAN, THAT IS!
WOOSH
H-HA HA HA HA!
ZORC TAKES FLIGHT AND DISAPPEARS TOWARDS THE CASTLE.
JERK! CREEP! POWER GAMER!
WE'LL GET TO ZORC CASTLE NO MATTER WHAT IT TAKES!
YOU'RE GOING DOWN, I TELL YOU! DOWN!
WE'RE PLAYING RIGHT INTO BAKURA'S SCRIPT!
WE REALLY ARE STUCK IN HIS GAME WORLD!
YOU'RE RIGHT! BAKURA MADE ZORC APPEAR WHEN THE ADVENTURERS' GUARD WAS DOWN. THEN HE WAS ABLE TO SEAL YOUR SOULS INTO LEAD FIGURES! EVERYTHING'S GONE ACCORDING TO HIS PLAN!
HE'S A GAME MASTER TO WATCH OUT FOR!
AND WHEN BAKURA ROLLS THE DICE, HE ALWAYS GETS A CRITICAL!
IS THERE ANY WAY WE CAN WIN?
DA-DA-DA-

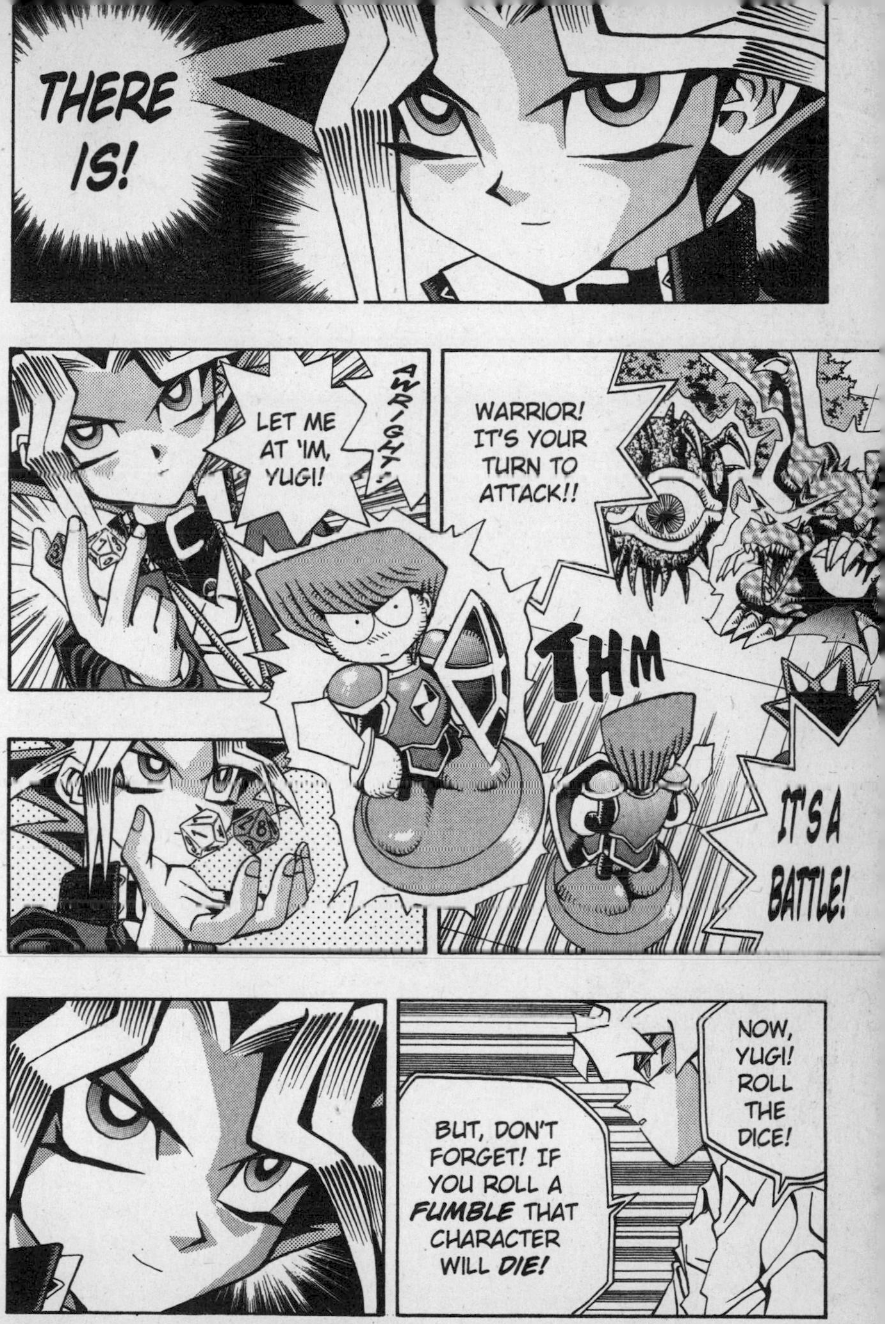

THERE IS!
WARRIOR! IT'S YOUR TURN TO ATTACK!!
THM
IT'S A BATTLE!
AWRIGHT!!
LET ME AT 'IM, YUGI!
NOW, YUGI! ROLL THE DICE!
BUT, DON'T FORGET! IF YOU ROLL A *FUMBLE* THAT CHARACTER WILL *DIE!*

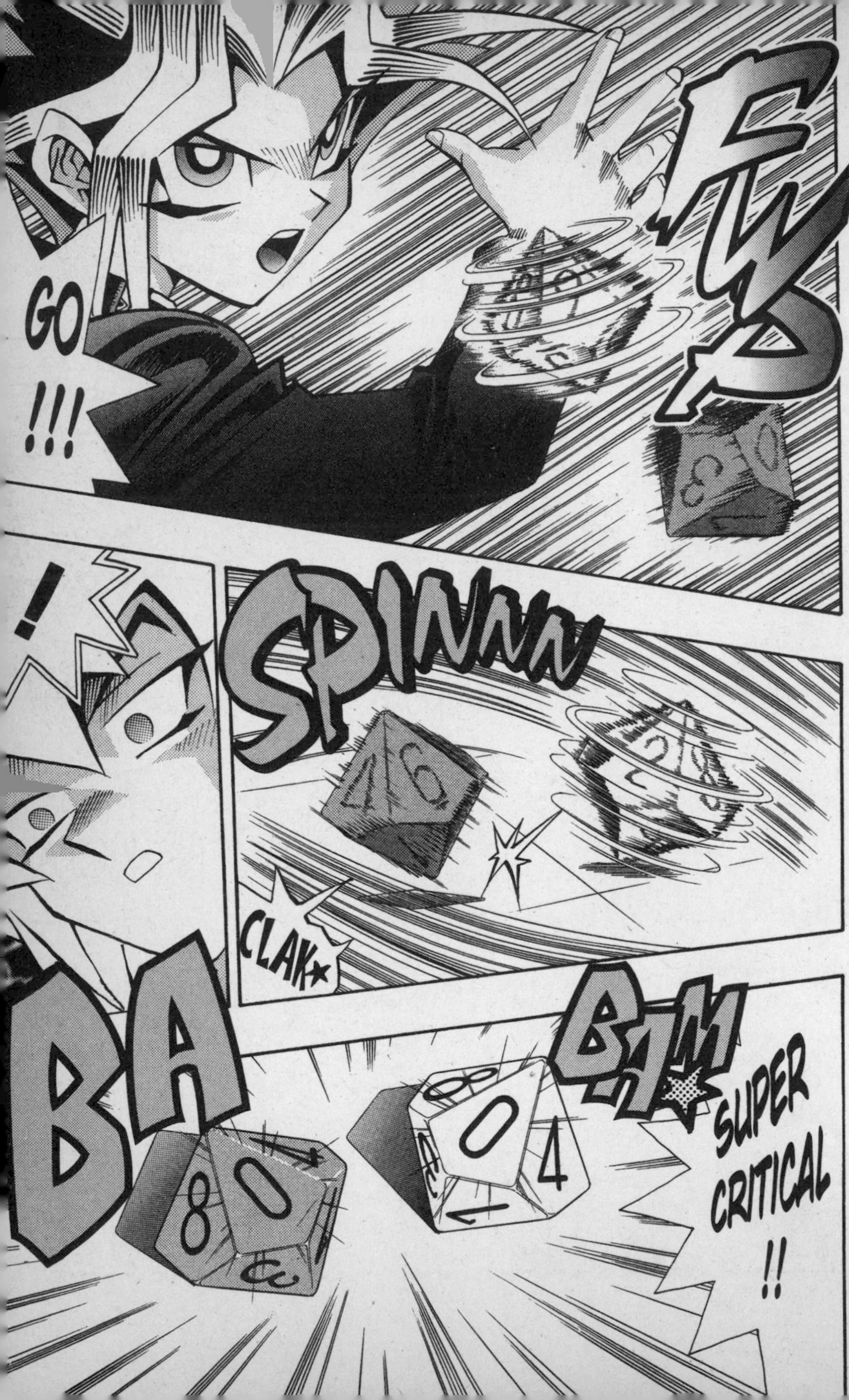
GO !!!
SPINNN
CLAK★
!
BAM
SUPER CRITICAL !!
BA

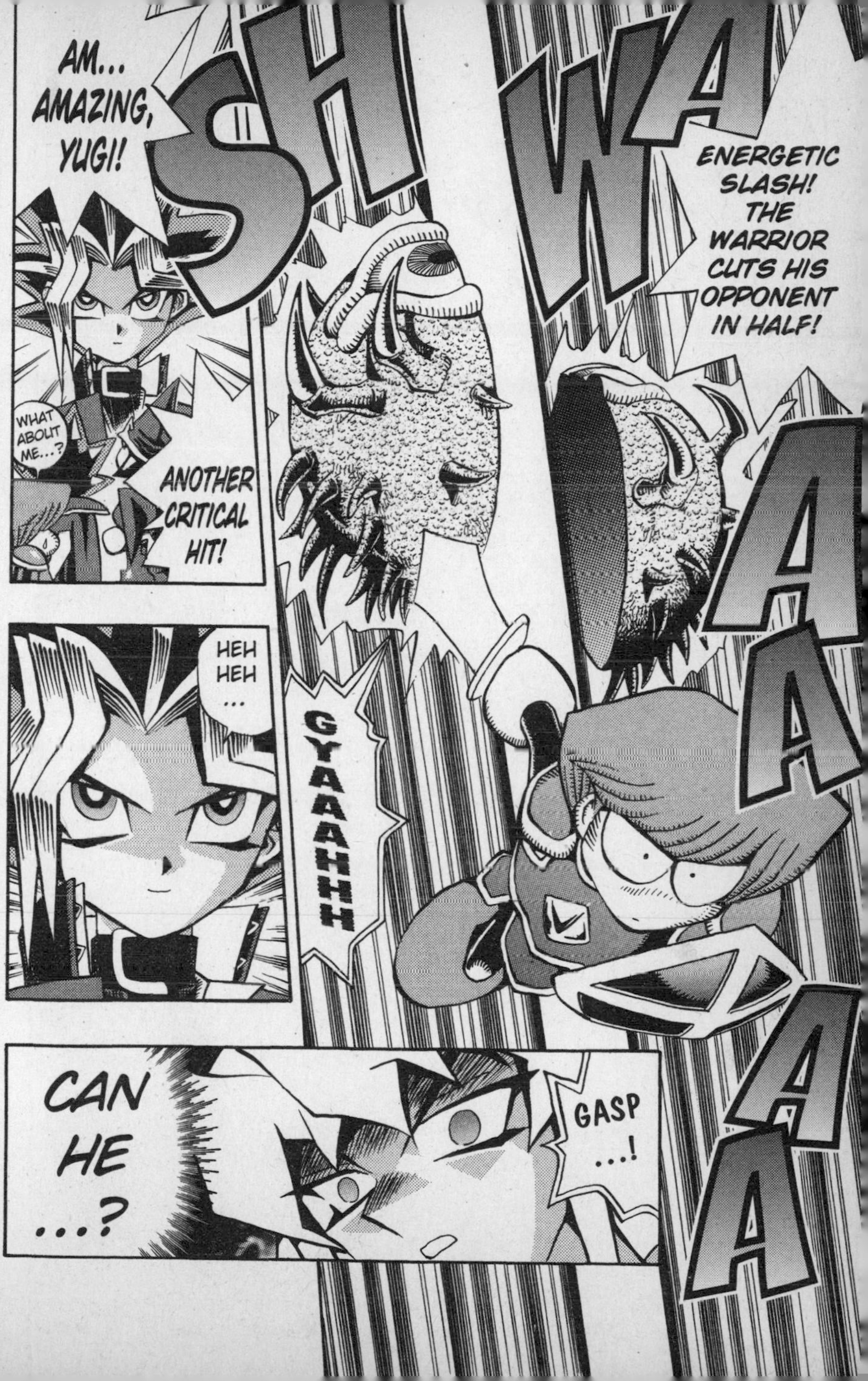
SHWAAAAA
ENERGETIC SLASH! THE WARRIOR CUTS HIS OPPONENT IN HALF!
GYAAAHHH
AM... AMAZING, YUGI!
WHAT ABOUT ME...?
ANOTHER CRITICAL HIT!
HEH HEH ...
GASP ...!
CAN HE ...?

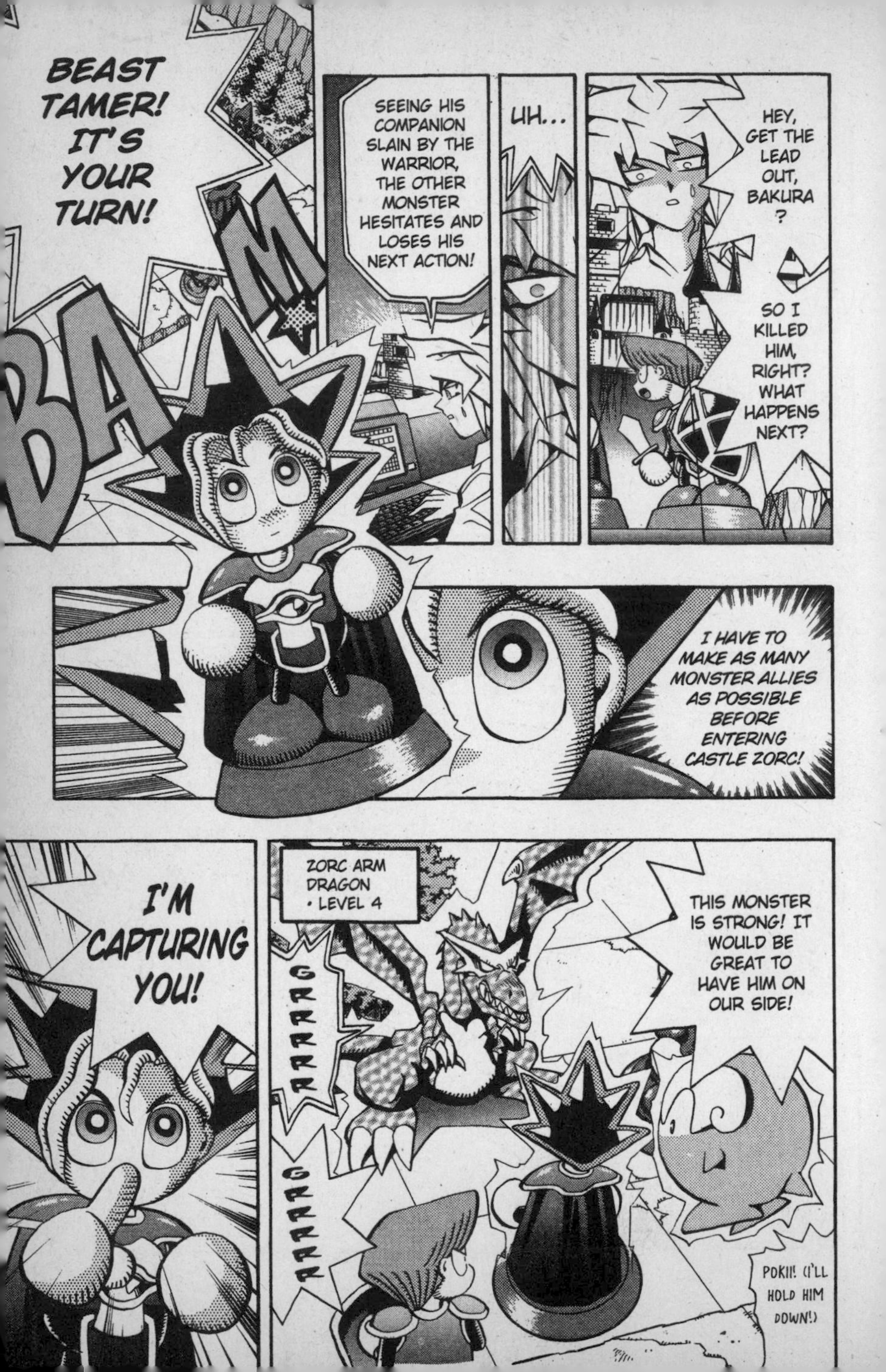
HEY, GET THE LEAD OUT, BAKURA?
SO I KILLED HIM, RIGHT? WHAT HAPPENS NEXT?
UH...
SEEING HIS COMPANION SLAIN BY THE WARRIOR, THE OTHER MONSTER HESITATES AND LOSES HIS NEXT ACTION!
BEAST TAMER! IT'S YOUR TURN!
BAM
I HAVE TO MAKE AS MANY MONSTER ALLIES AS POSSIBLE BEFORE ENTERING CASTLE ZORC!
THIS MONSTER IS STRONG! IT WOULD BE GREAT TO HAVE HIM ON OUR SIDE!
ZORC ARM DRAGON • LEVEL 4
GRRRRRR
GRRRRRR
POKII! (I'LL HOLD HIM DOWN!)
I'M CAPTURING YOU!

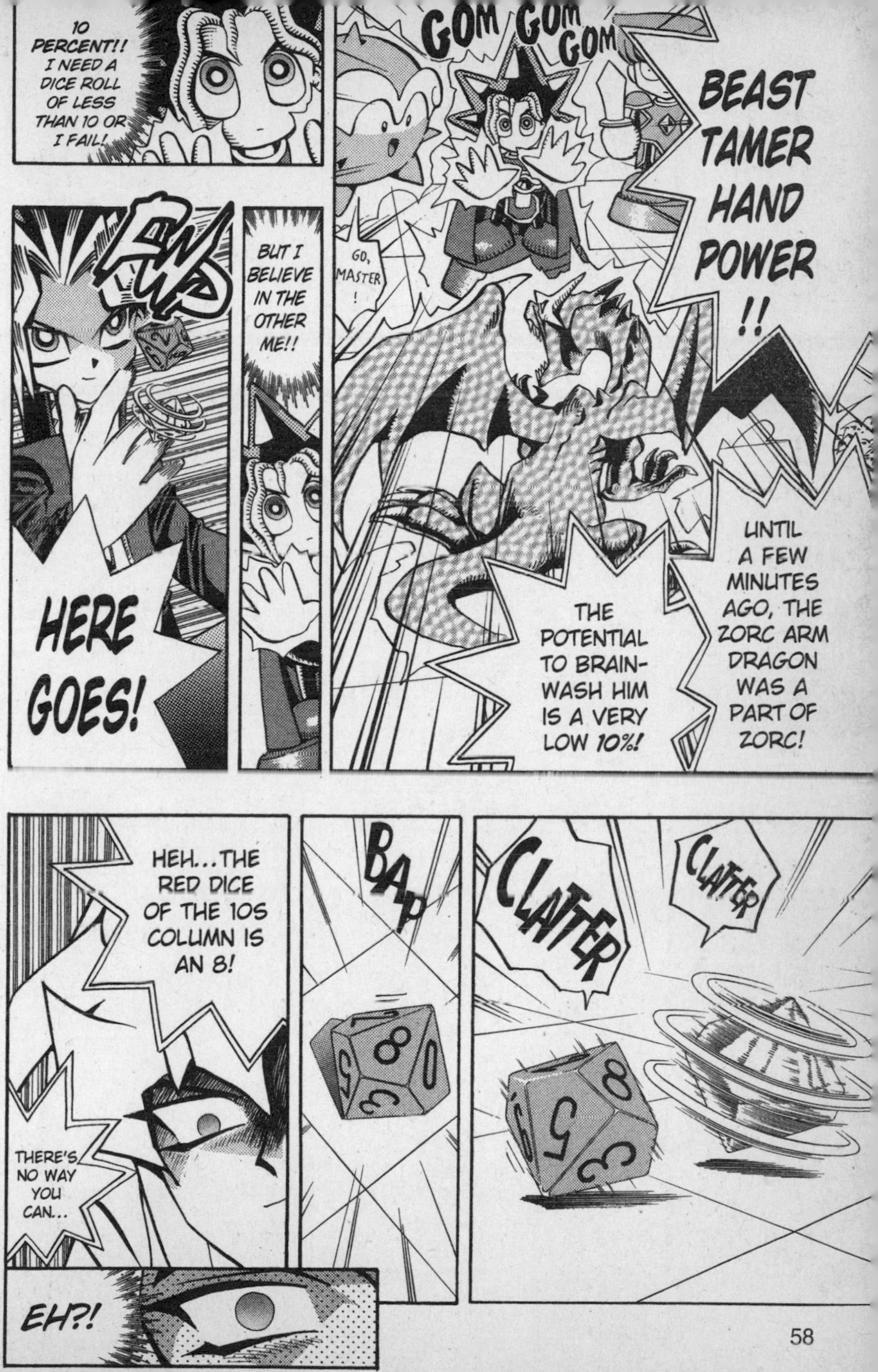
GOM GOM GOM
BEAST TAMER HAND POWER!!
GO, MASTER!
UNTIL A FEW MINUTES AGO, THE ZORC ARM DRAGON WAS A PART OF ZORC!
THE POTENTIAL TO BRAIN-WASH HIM IS A VERY LOW 10%!
10 PERCENT!! I NEED A DICE ROLL OF LESS THAN 10 OR I FAIL!
BUT I BELIEVE IN THE OTHER ME!!
FWAP
HERE GOES!
CLATTER
CLATTER
BAP
HEH...THE RED DICE OF THE 10S COLUMN IS AN 8!
THERE'S NO WAY YOU CAN...
EH?!

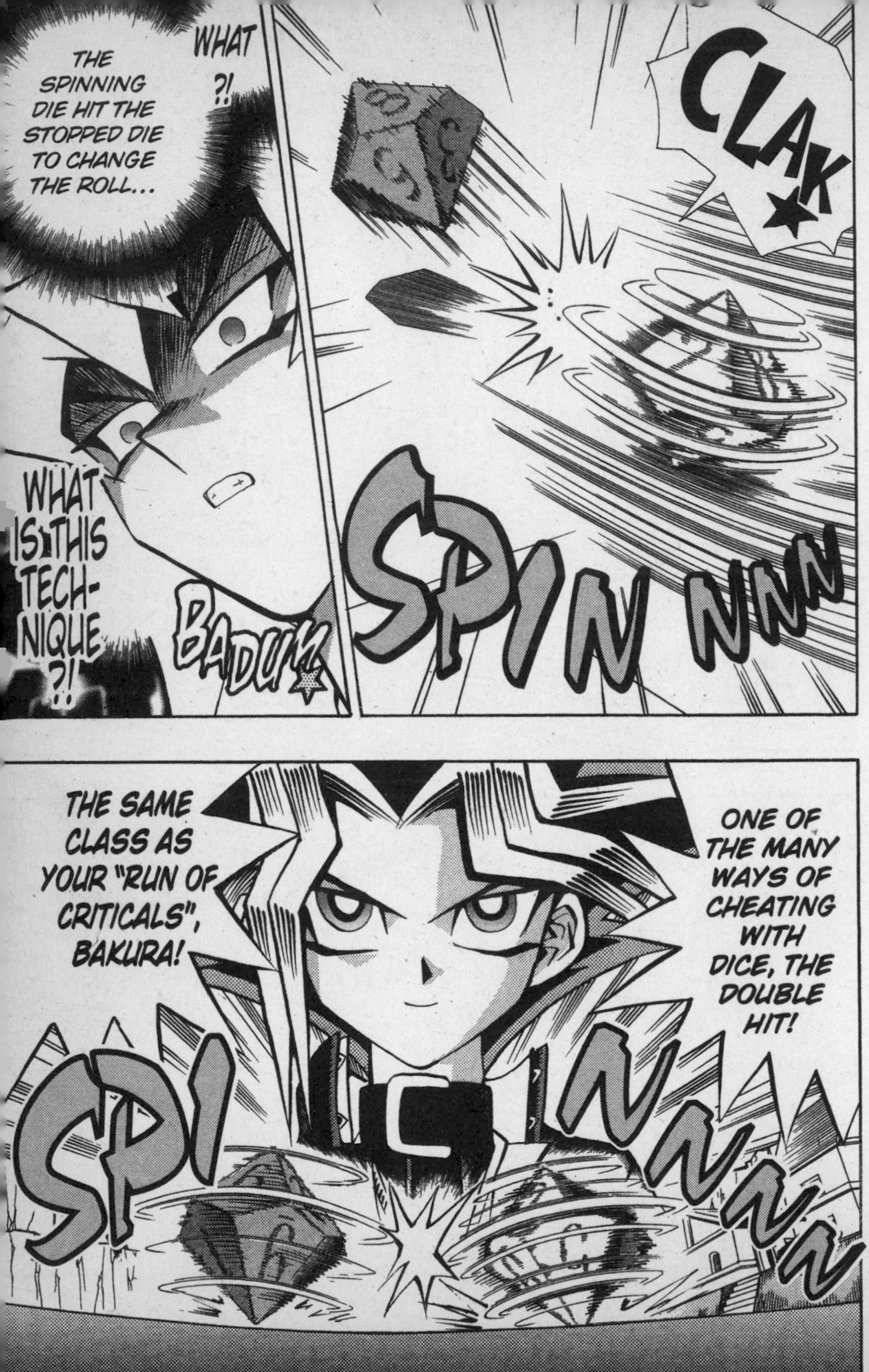
CLAK
SPINNNN
THE SPINNING DIE HIT THE STOPPED DIE TO CHANGE THE ROLL...
WHAT ?!
WHAT IS THIS TECHNIQUE ?!
BADUM
ONE OF THE MANY WAYS OF CHEATING WITH DICE, THE DOUBLE HIT!
THE SAME CLASS AS YOUR "RUN OF CRITICALS", BAKURA!
SPINNNNNNN

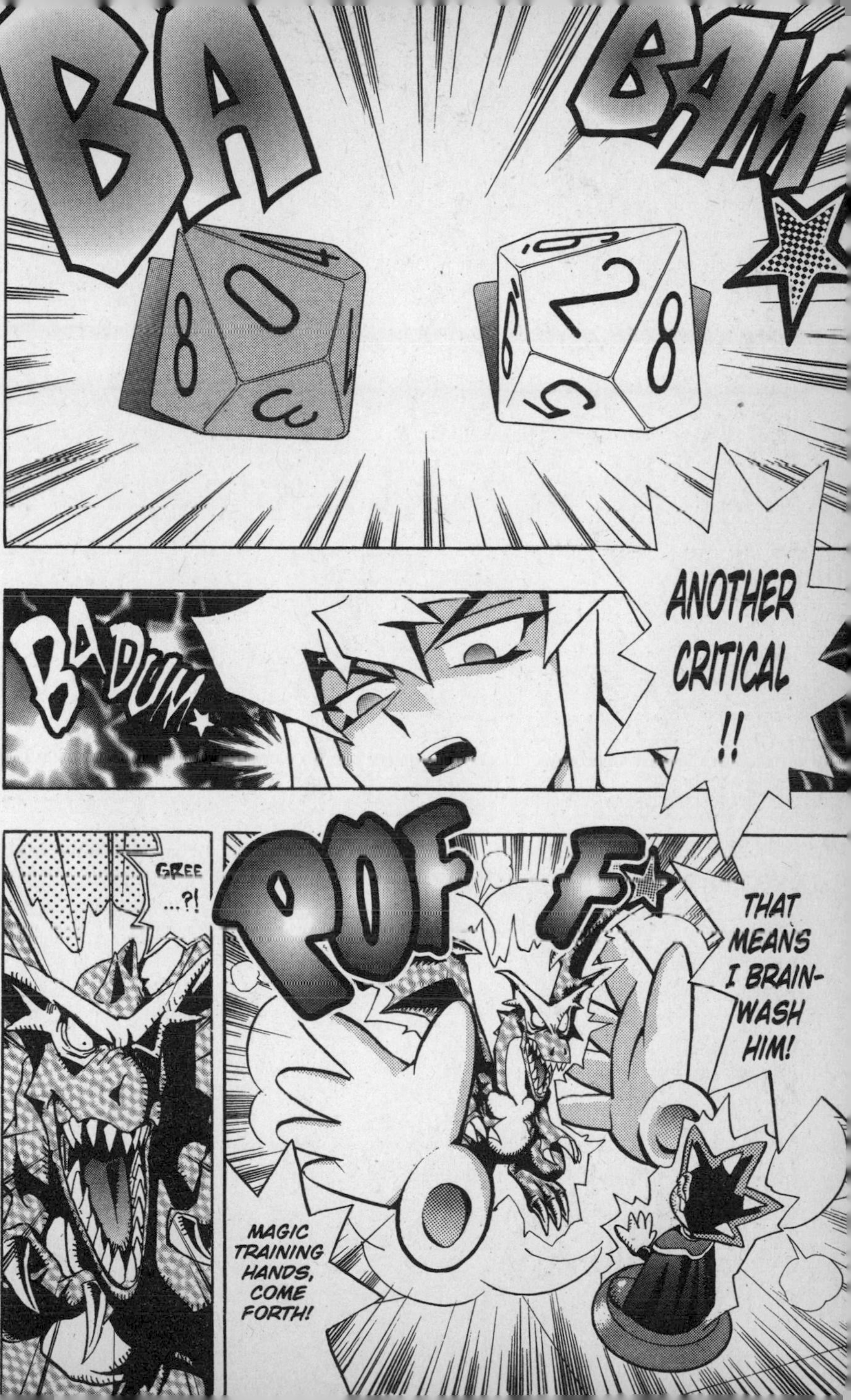
BA
BAM
BADUM
ANOTHER CRITICAL!!
POOF
THAT MEANS I BRAIN-WASH HIM!
MAGIC TRAINING HANDS, COME FORTH!
GREE ...?!

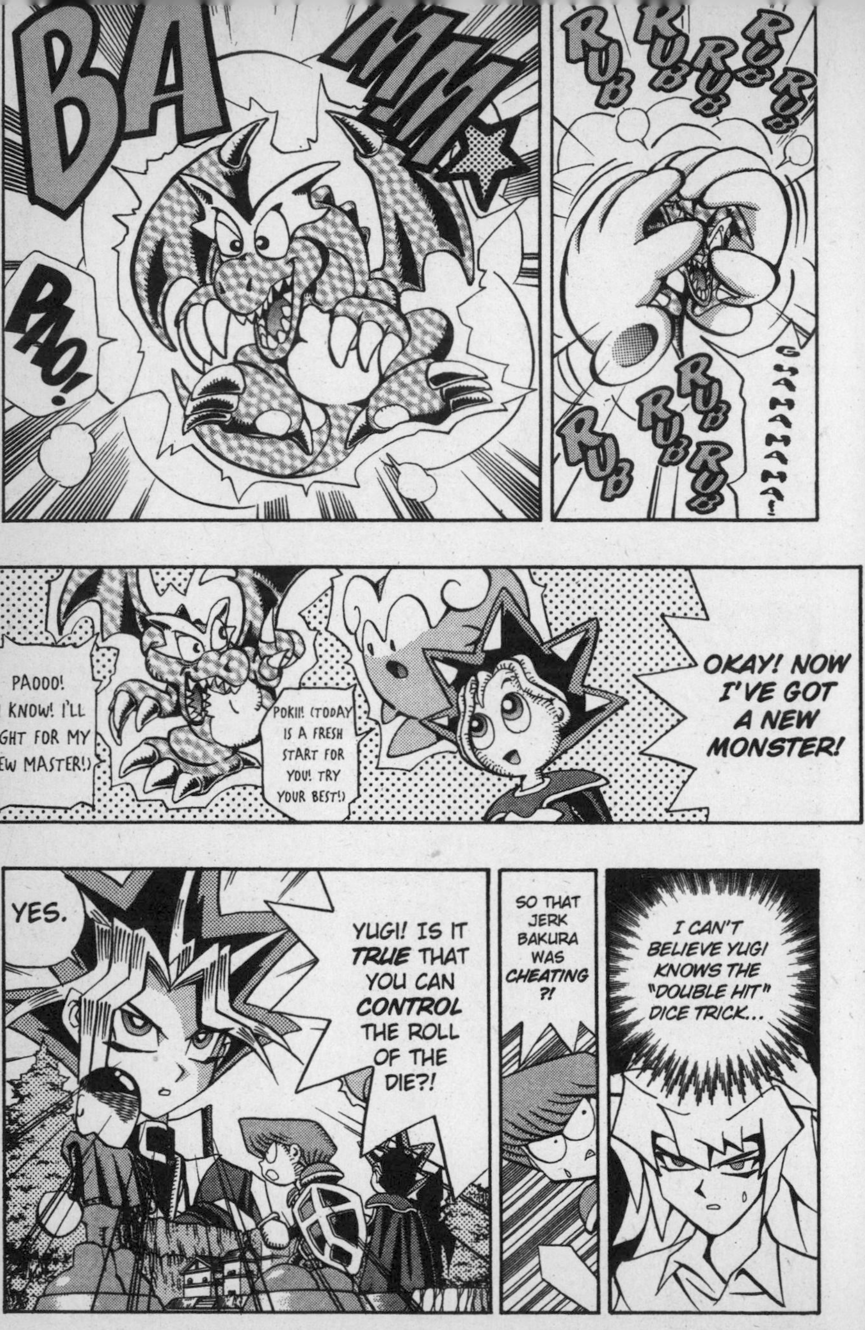
RUB RUB RUB RUB
GYAHAHAHA!
RUB RUB RUB RUB
BAMMM
PAO!
OKAY! NOW I'VE GOT A NEW MONSTER!
POKII! (TODAY IS A FRESH START FOR YOU! TRY YOUR BEST!)
PAOOO! (I KNOW! I'LL FIGHT FOR MY NEW MASTER!)
I CAN'T BELIEVE YUGI KNOWS THE "DOUBLE HIT" DICE TRICK...
SO THAT JERK BAKURA WAS CHEATING?!
YUGI! IS IT TRUE THAT YOU CAN CONTROL THE ROLL OF THE DIE?!
YES.

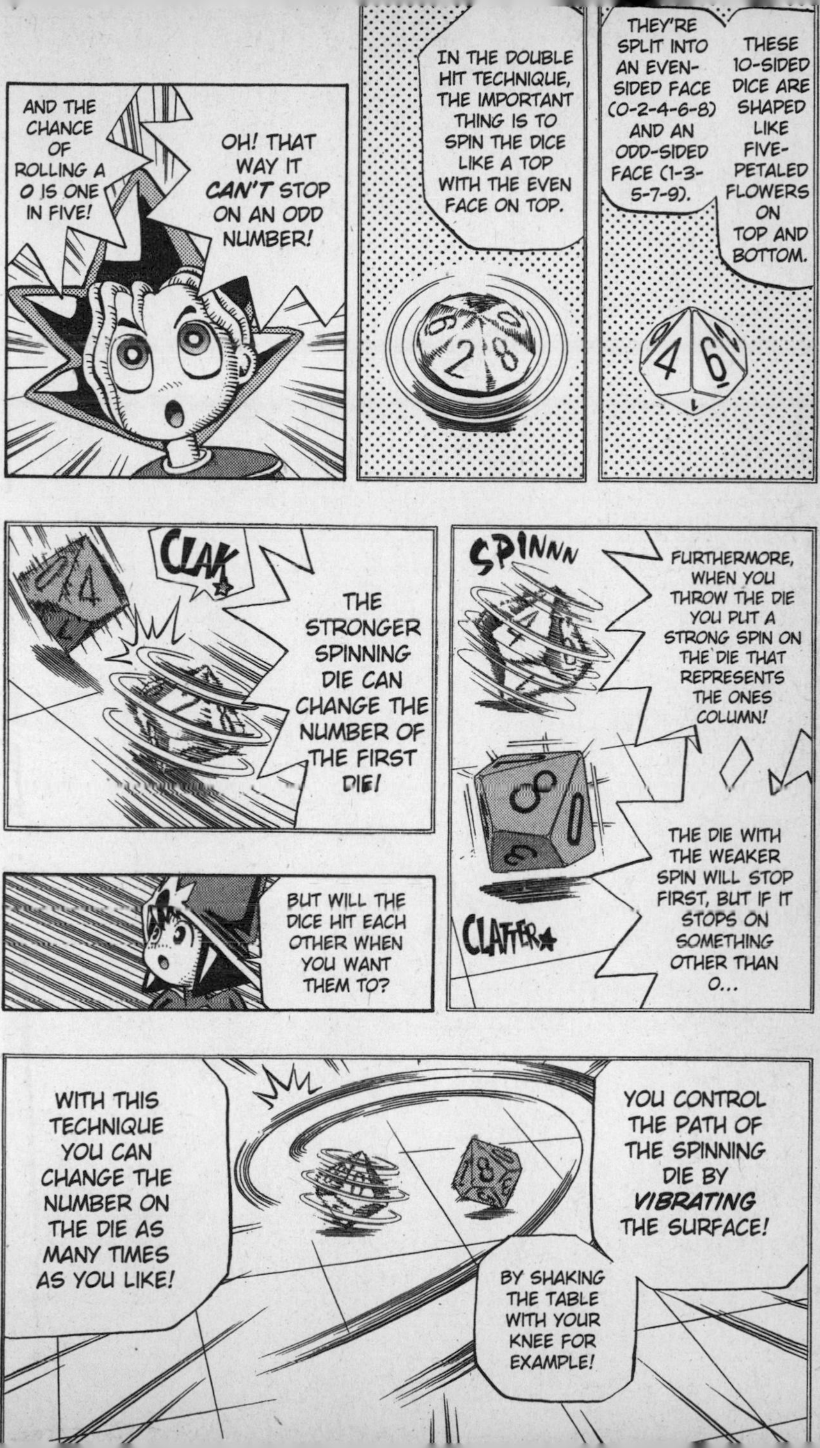
THESE 10-SIDED DICE ARE SHAPED LIKE FIVE-PETALED FLOWERS ON TOP AND BOTTOM.
THEY'RE SPLIT INTO AN EVEN-SIDED FACE (0-2-4-6-8) AND AN ODD-SIDED FACE (1-3-5-7-9).
IN THE DOUBLE HIT TECHNIQUE, THE IMPORTANT THING IS TO SPIN THE DICE LIKE A TOP WITH THE EVEN FACE ON TOP.
OH! THAT WAY IT *CAN'T* STOP ON AN ODD NUMBER!
AND THE CHANCE OF ROLLING A 0 IS ONE IN FIVE!
SPINNN
FURTHERMORE, WHEN YOU THROW THE DIE YOU PUT A STRONG SPIN ON THE DIE THAT REPRESENTS THE ONES COLUMN!
THE DIE WITH THE WEAKER SPIN WILL STOP FIRST, BUT IF IT STOPS ON SOMETHING OTHER THAN 0...
CLATTER
CLAK
THE STRONGER SPINNING DIE CAN CHANGE THE NUMBER OF THE FIRST DIE!
BUT WILL THE DICE HIT EACH OTHER WHEN YOU WANT THEM TO?
YOU CONTROL THE PATH OF THE SPINNING DIE BY *VIBRATING* THE SURFACE!
BY SHAKING THE TABLE WITH YOUR KNEE FOR EXAMPLE!
WITH THIS TECHNIQUE YOU CAN CHANGE THE NUMBER ON THE DIE AS MANY TIMES AS YOU LIKE!

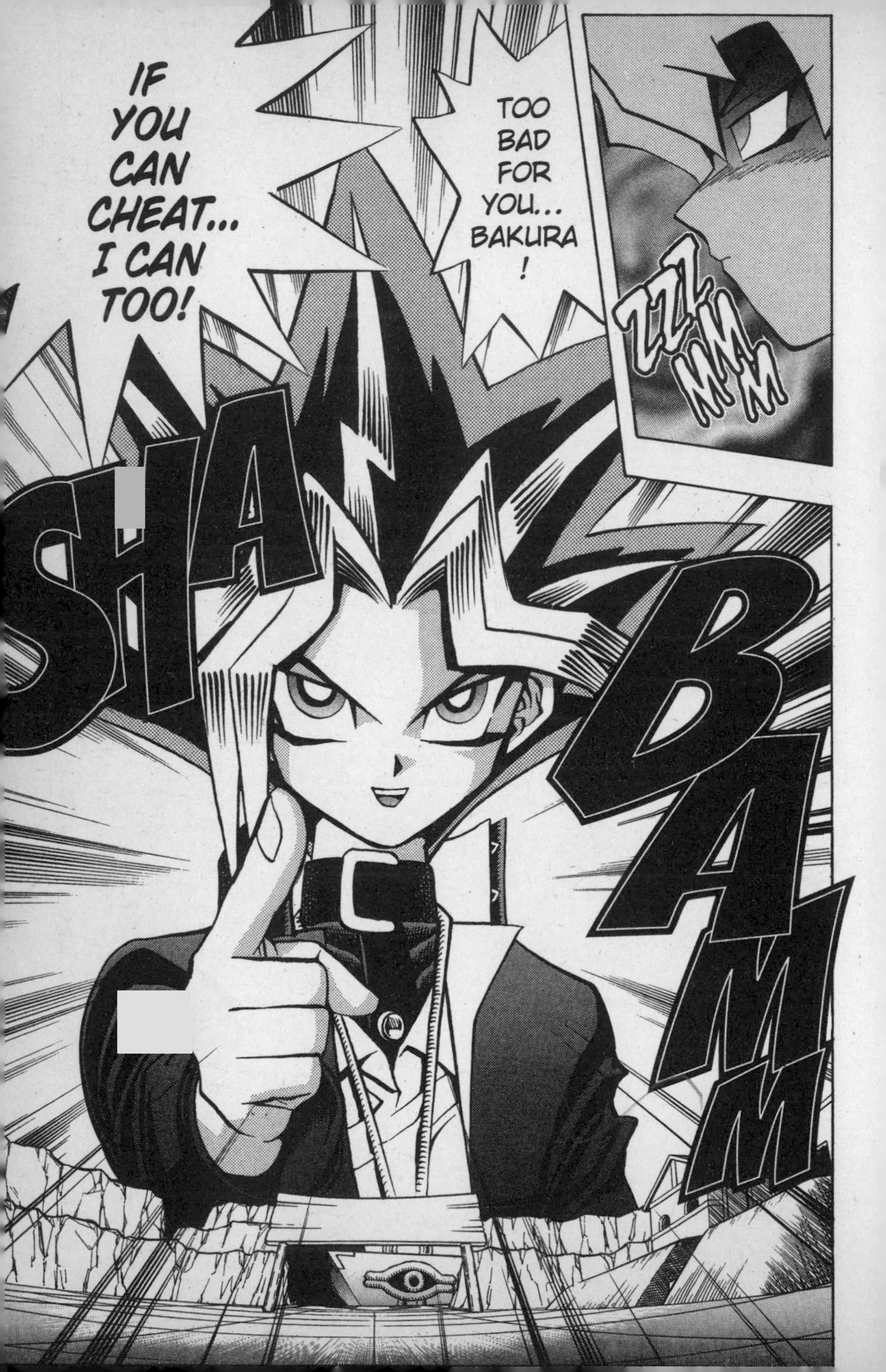
ZZZMMMM
TOO BAD FOR YOU... BAKURA!
IF YOU CAN CHEAT... I CAN TOO!
SHABAMM

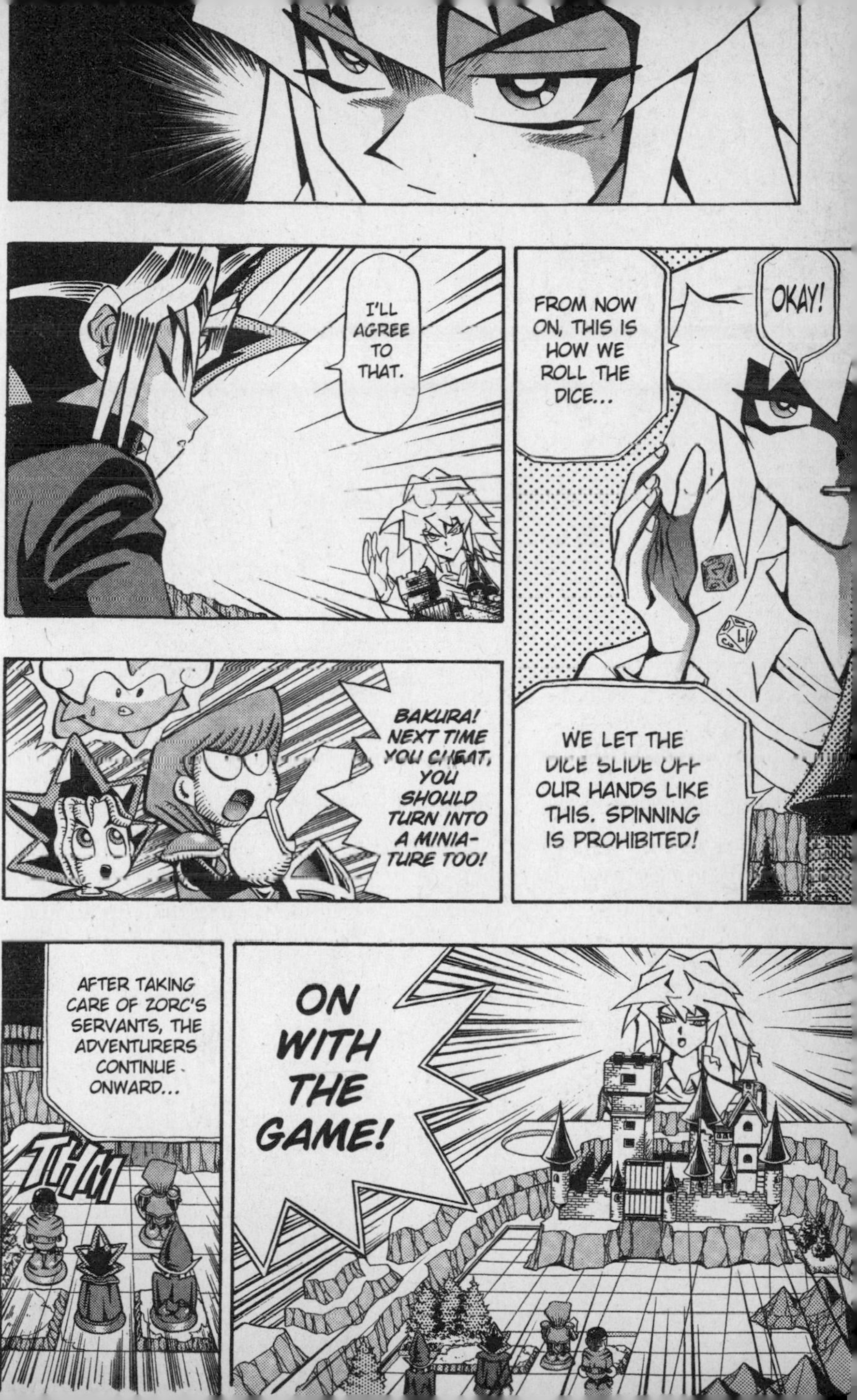
OKAY!
FROM NOW ON, THIS IS HOW WE ROLL THE DICE...
WE LET THE DICE SLIDE OFF OUR HANDS LIKE THIS. SPINNING IS PROHIBITED!
I'LL AGREE TO THAT.
BAKURA! NEXT TIME YOU CHEAT, YOU SHOULD TURN INTO A MINIA-TURE TOO!
ON WITH THE GAME!
AFTER TAKING CARE OF ZORC'S SERVANTS, THE ADVENTURERS CONTINUE ONWARD...
THM

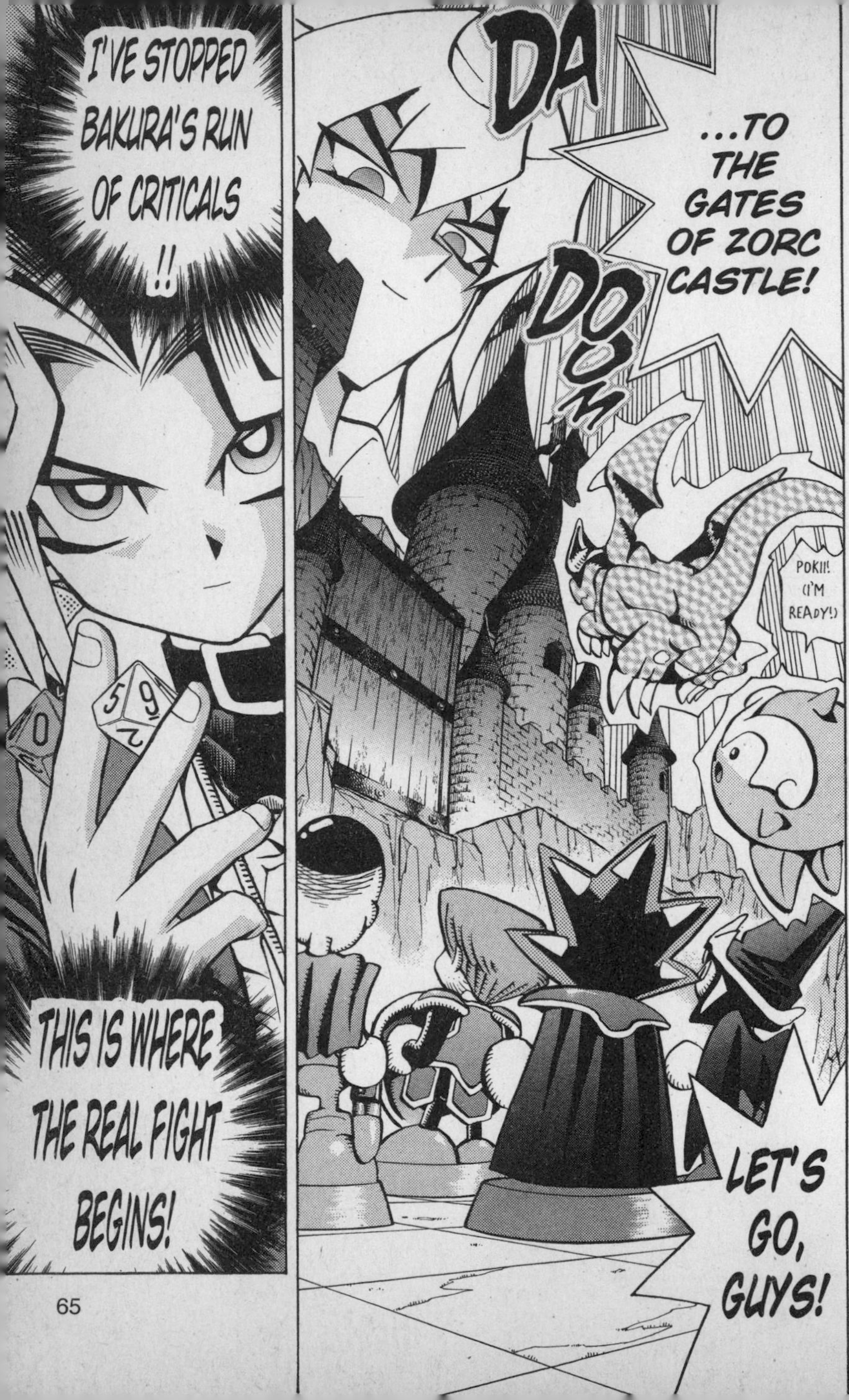
...TO THE GATES OF ZORC CASTLE!
DA DOOM
POKII! (I'M READY!)
LET'S GO, GUYS!
I'VE STOPPED BAKURA'S RUN OF CRITICALS !!
THIS IS WHERE THE REAL FIGHT BEGINS!

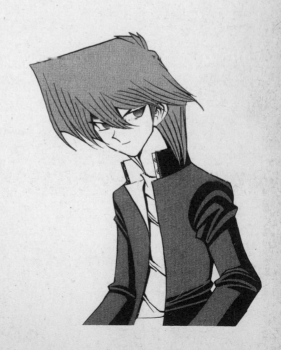

Duel 55: Millennium Enemy 6: The Traps of Zorc Castle

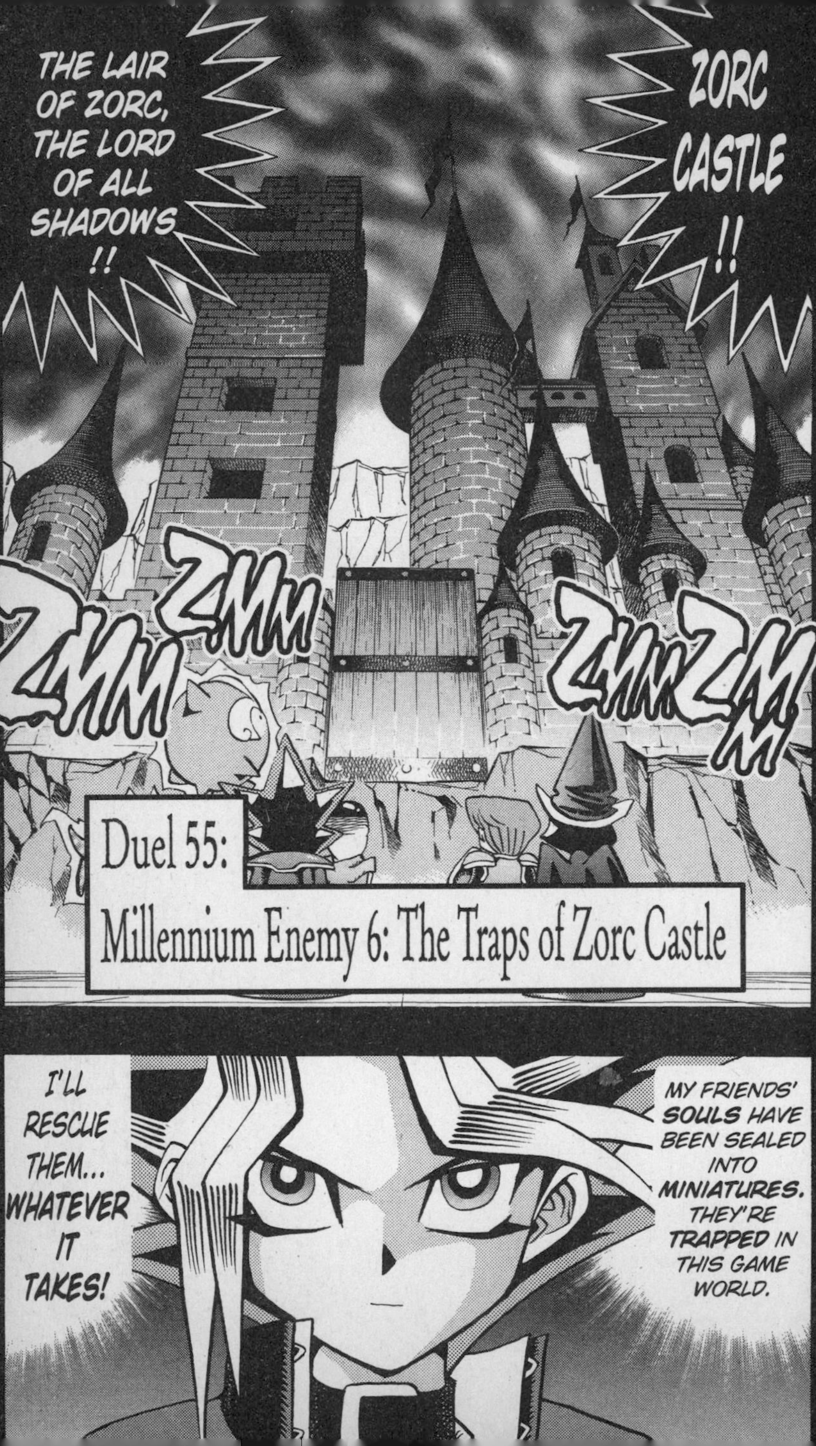
ZORC CASTLE !!
THE LAIR OF ZORC, THE LORD OF ALL SHADOWS !!
ZMM ZMM
ZMM ZMM
ZMM ZMM
MY FRIENDS' SOULS HAVE BEEN SEALED INTO MINIATURES. THEY'RE TRAPPED IN THIS GAME WORLD.
I'LL RESCUE THEM... WHATEVER IT TAKES!

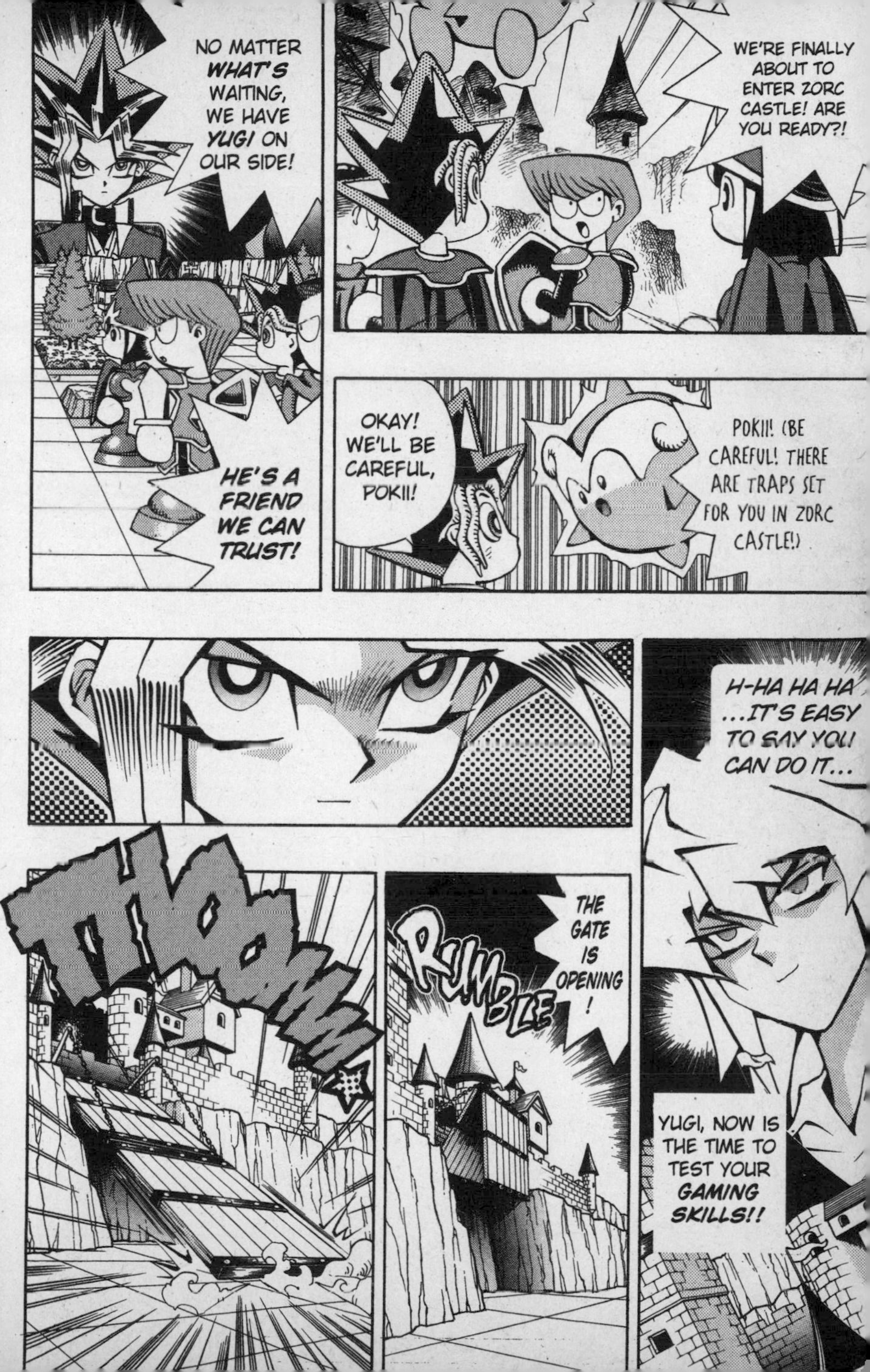
WE'RE FINALLY ABOUT TO ENTER ZORC CASTLE! ARE YOU READY?!
POKII! (BE CAREFUL! THERE ARE TRAPS SET FOR YOU IN ZORC CASTLE!)
OKAY! WE'LL BE CAREFUL, POKII!
NO MATTER WHAT'S WAITING, WE HAVE YUGI ON OUR SIDE!
HE'S A FRIEND WE CAN TRUST!
H-HA HA HA ...IT'S EASY TO SAY YOU CAN DO IT...
YUGI, NOW IS THE TIME TO TEST YOUR GAMING SKILLS!!
RUMBLE
THE GATE IS OPENING!

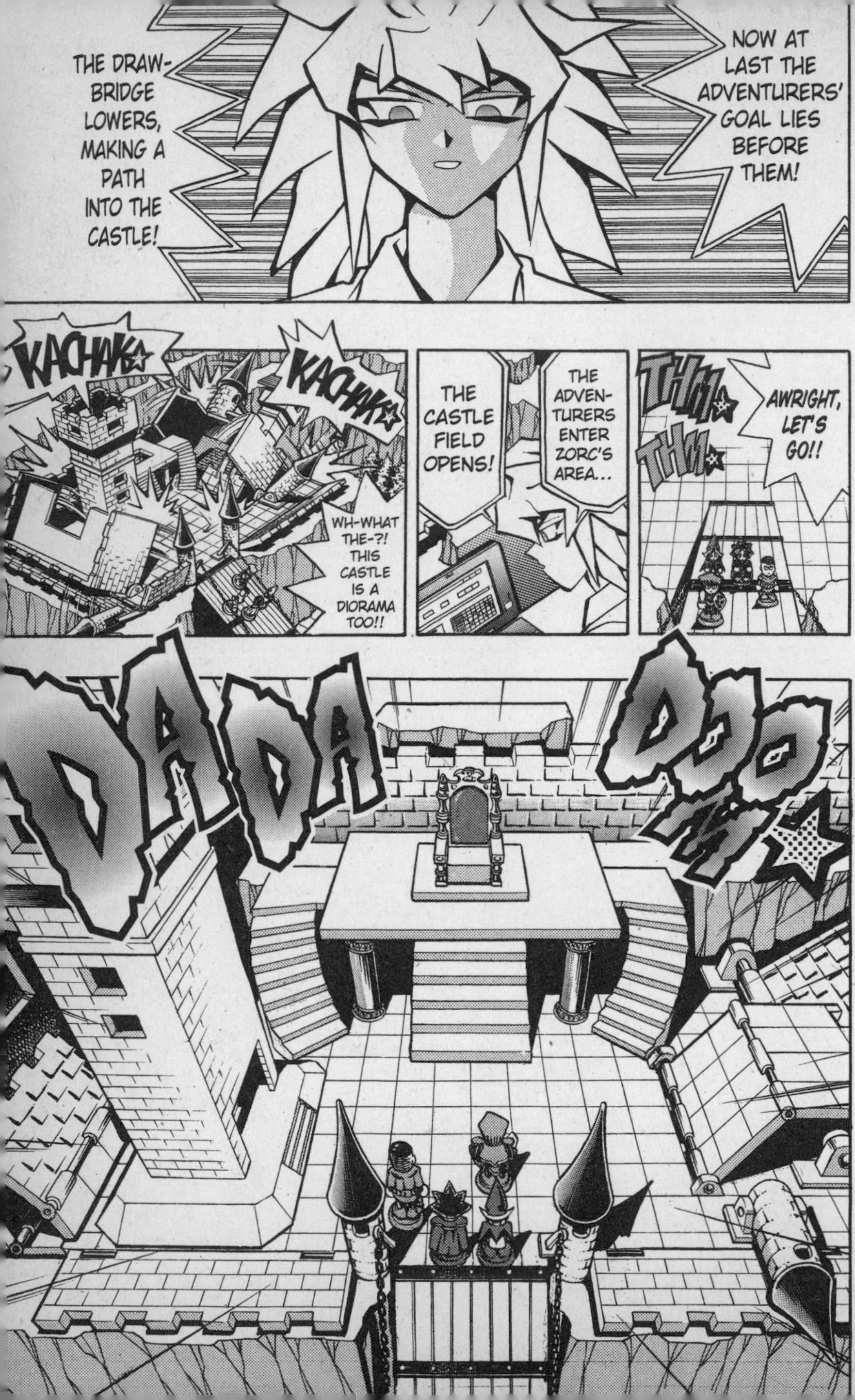
NOW AT LAST THE ADVENTURERS' GOAL LIES BEFORE THEM!
THE DRAW-BRIDGE LOWERS, MAKING A PATH INTO THE CASTLE!
AWRIGHT, LET'S GO!!
THM
THM
THE ADVENTURERS ENTER ZORC'S AREA...
THE CASTLE FIELD OPENS!
KACHAK
KACHAK
WH-WHAT THE-?! THIS CASTLE IS A DIORAMA TOO!!
DADA

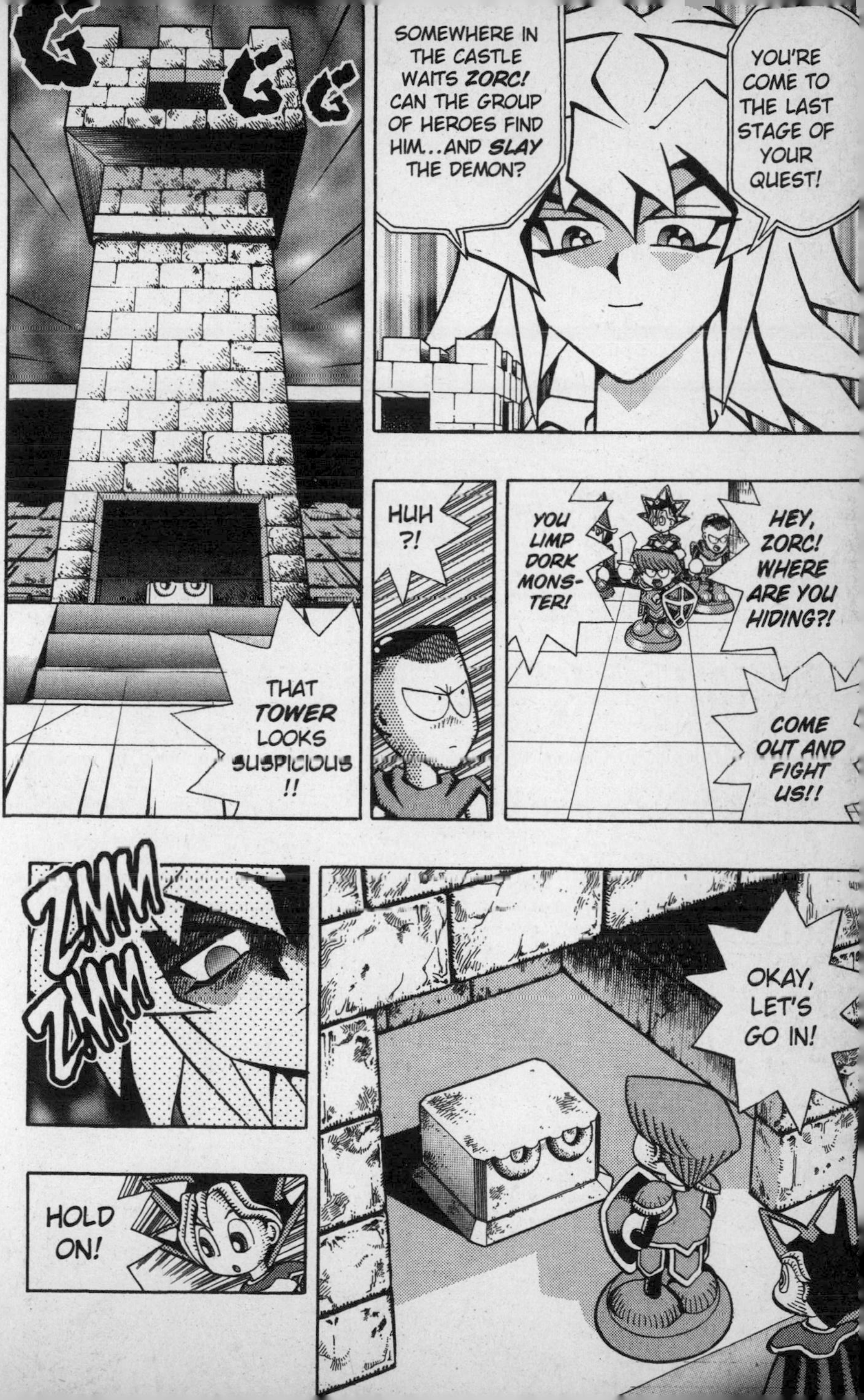
YOU'RE COME TO THE LAST STAGE OF YOUR QUEST!
SOMEWHERE IN THE CASTLE WAITS ZORC! CAN THE GROUP OF HEROES FIND HIM...AND SLAY THE DEMON?
HEY, ZORC! WHERE ARE YOU HIDING?!
YOU LIMP DORK MONSTER!
COME OUT AND FIGHT US!!
HUH ?!
G G G
THAT TOWER LOOKS SUSPICIOUS !!
OKAY, LET'S GO IN!
ZMM ZMM
HOLD ON!

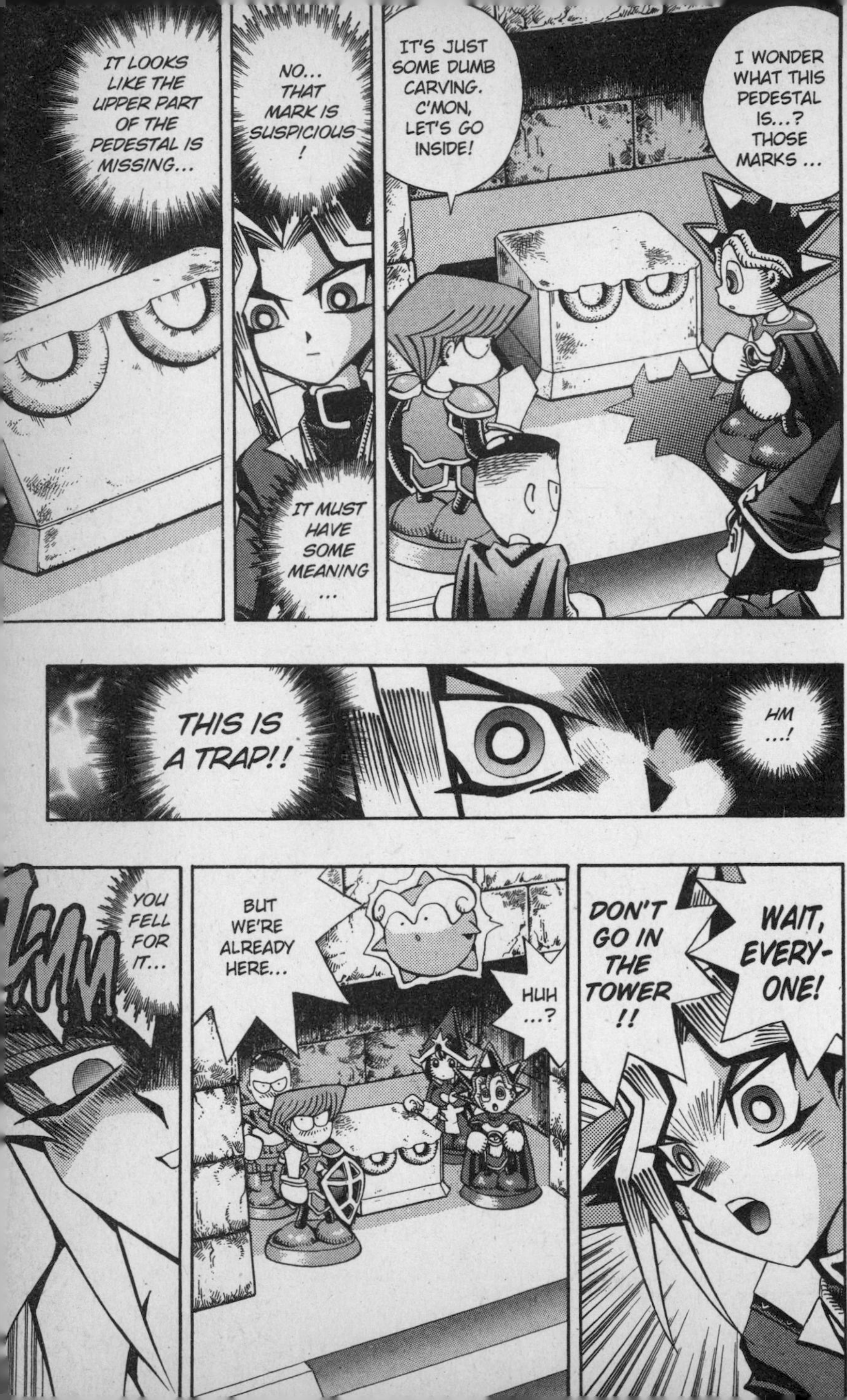
I WONDER WHAT THIS PEDESTAL IS...? THOSE MARKS ...
IT'S JUST SOME DUMB CARVING. C'MON, LET'S GO INSIDE!
NO... THAT MARK IS SUSPICIOUS !
IT MUST HAVE SOME MEANING ...
IT LOOKS LIKE THE UPPER PART OF THE PEDESTAL IS MISSING...
HM ...!
THIS IS A TRAP!!
WAIT, EVERY-ONE!
DON'T GO IN THE TOWER !!
HUH ...?
BUT WE'RE ALREADY HERE...
YOU FELL FOR IT...

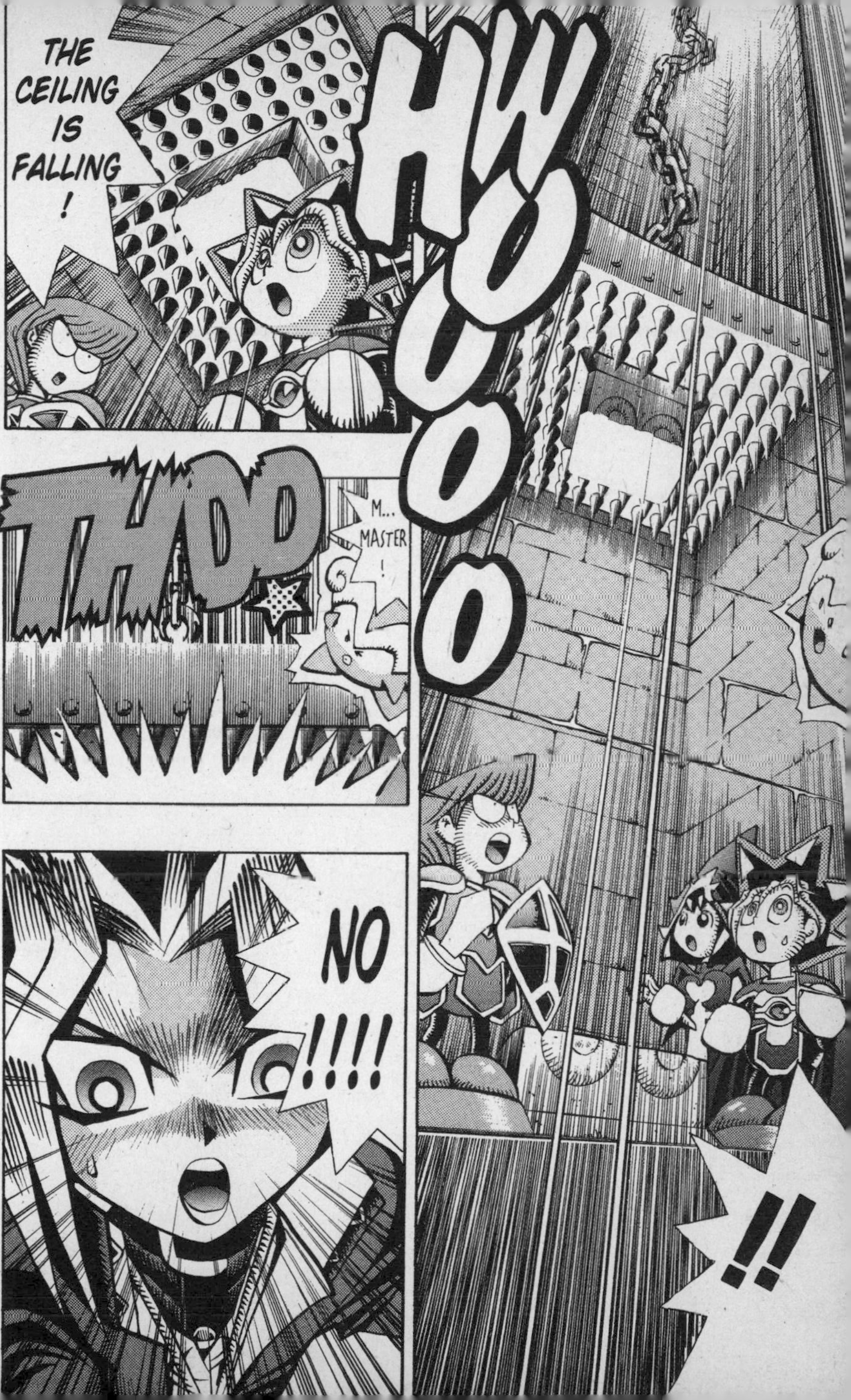
HWOOOOO
!!
THE CEILING IS FALLING!
M... MASTER!
NO!!!!

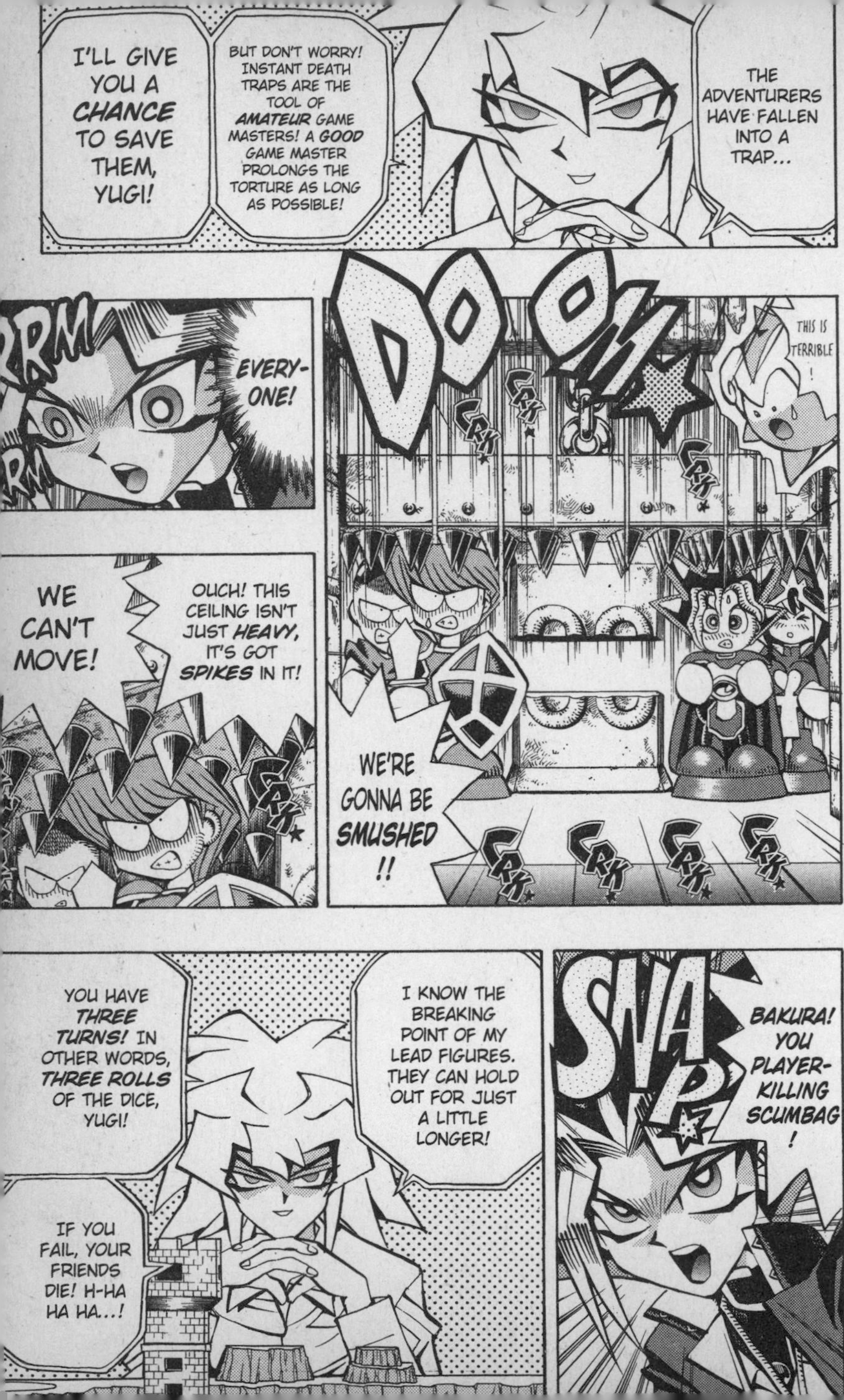
THE ADVENTURERS HAVE FALLEN INTO A TRAP...
BUT DON'T WORRY! INSTANT DEATH TRAPS ARE THE TOOL OF AMATEUR GAME MASTERS! A GOOD GAME MASTER PROLONGS THE TORTURE AS LONG AS POSSIBLE!
I'LL GIVE YOU A CHANCE TO SAVE THEM, YUGI!
DOOM
THIS IS TERRIBLE!
CRK
CRK
CRK
WE'RE GONNA BE SMUSHED!!
CRK CRK CRK CRK
RRM
EVERY-ONE!
OUCH! THIS CEILING ISN'T JUST HEAVY, IT'S GOT SPIKES IN IT!
WE CAN'T MOVE!
CRK
SNAP
BAKURA! YOU PLAYER-KILLING SCUMBAG!
I KNOW THE BREAKING POINT OF MY LEAD FIGURES. THEY CAN HOLD OUT FOR JUST A LITTLE LONGER!
YOU HAVE THREE TURNS! IN OTHER WORDS, THREE ROLLS OF THE DICE, YUGI!
IF YOU FAIL, YOUR FRIENDS DIE! H-HA HA HA...!

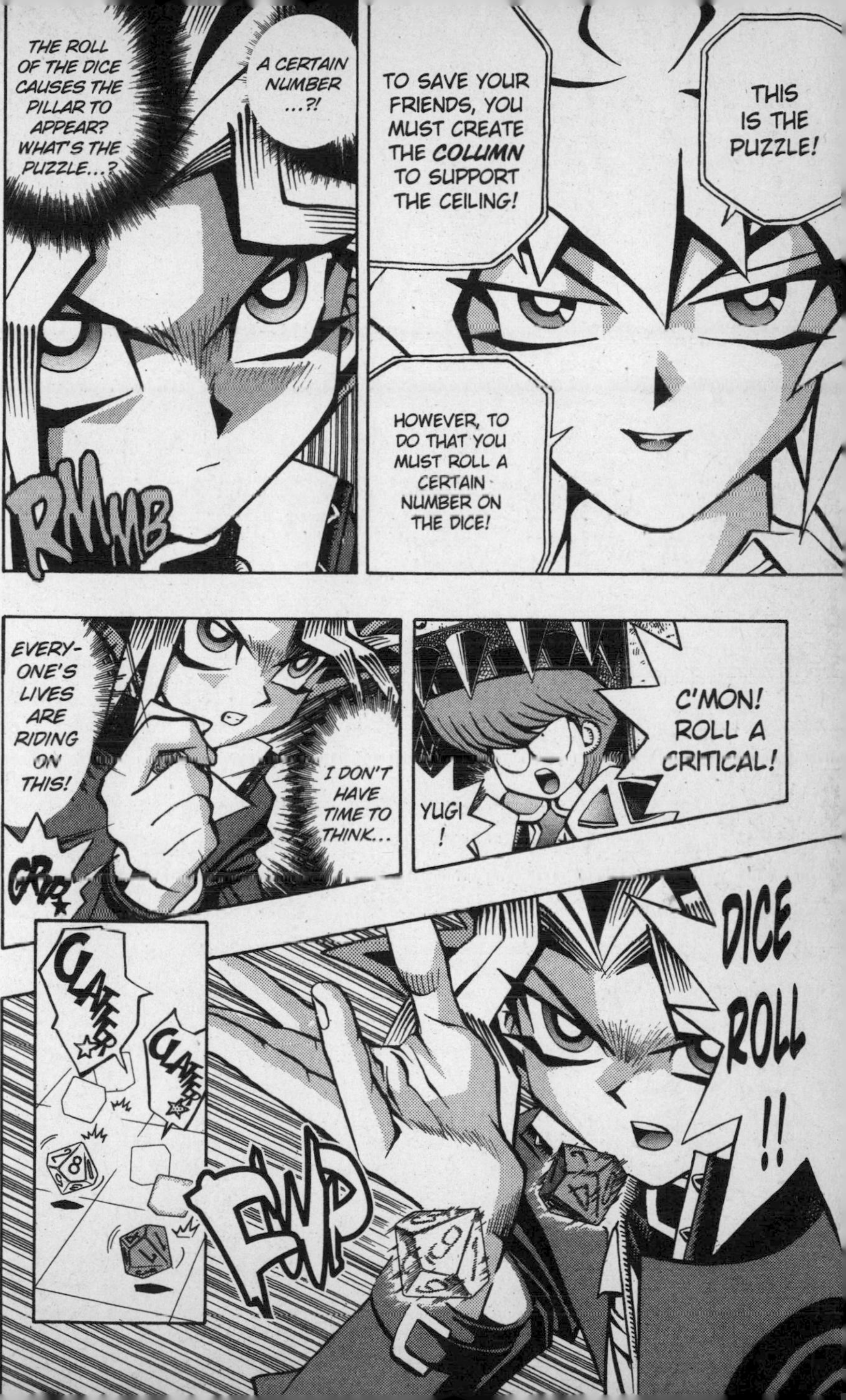
THIS IS THE PUZZLE!
TO SAVE YOUR FRIENDS, YOU MUST CREATE THE ***COLUMN*** TO SUPPORT THE CEILING!
HOWEVER, TO DO THAT YOU MUST ROLL A CERTAIN NUMBER ON THE DICE!
A CERTAIN NUMBER ...?!
THE ROLL OF THE DICE CAUSES THE PILLAR TO APPEAR? WHAT'S THE PUZZLE...?
RMMB
C'MON! ROLL A CRITICAL!
YUGI!
I DON'T HAVE TIME TO THINK...
EVERY-ONE'S LIVES ARE RIDING ON THIS!
GRIP
DICE ROLL!!
FWIP
CLATTER
CLATTER

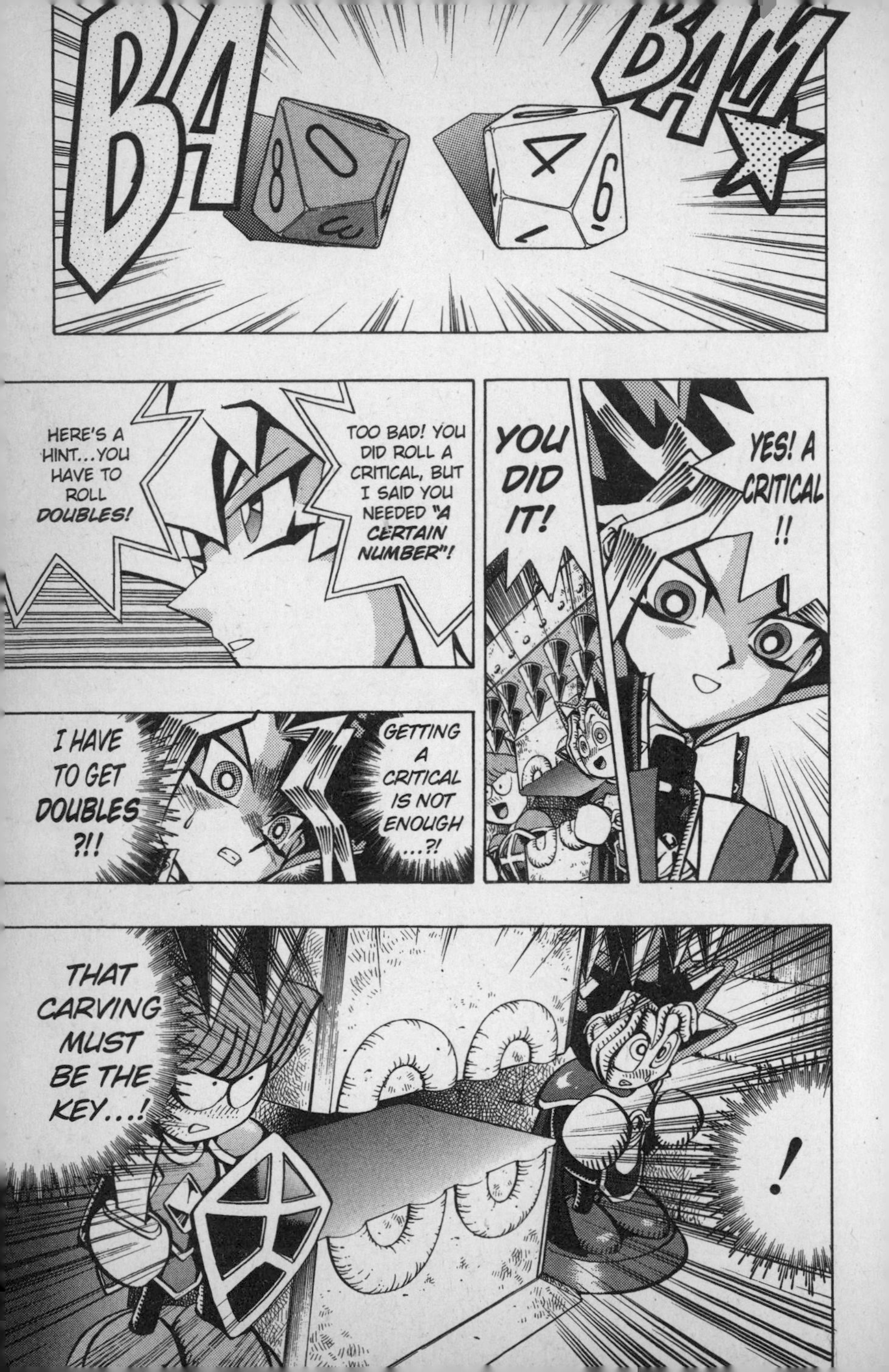
BA BAM
YES! A CRITICAL!!
YOU DID IT!
TOO BAD! YOU DID ROLL A CRITICAL, BUT I SAID YOU NEEDED "A CERTAIN NUMBER"!
HERE'S A HINT...YOU HAVE TO ROLL DOUBLES!
GETTING A CRITICAL IS NOT ENOUGH...?!
I HAVE TO GET DOUBLES?!!
!
THAT CARVING MUST BE THE KEY...!

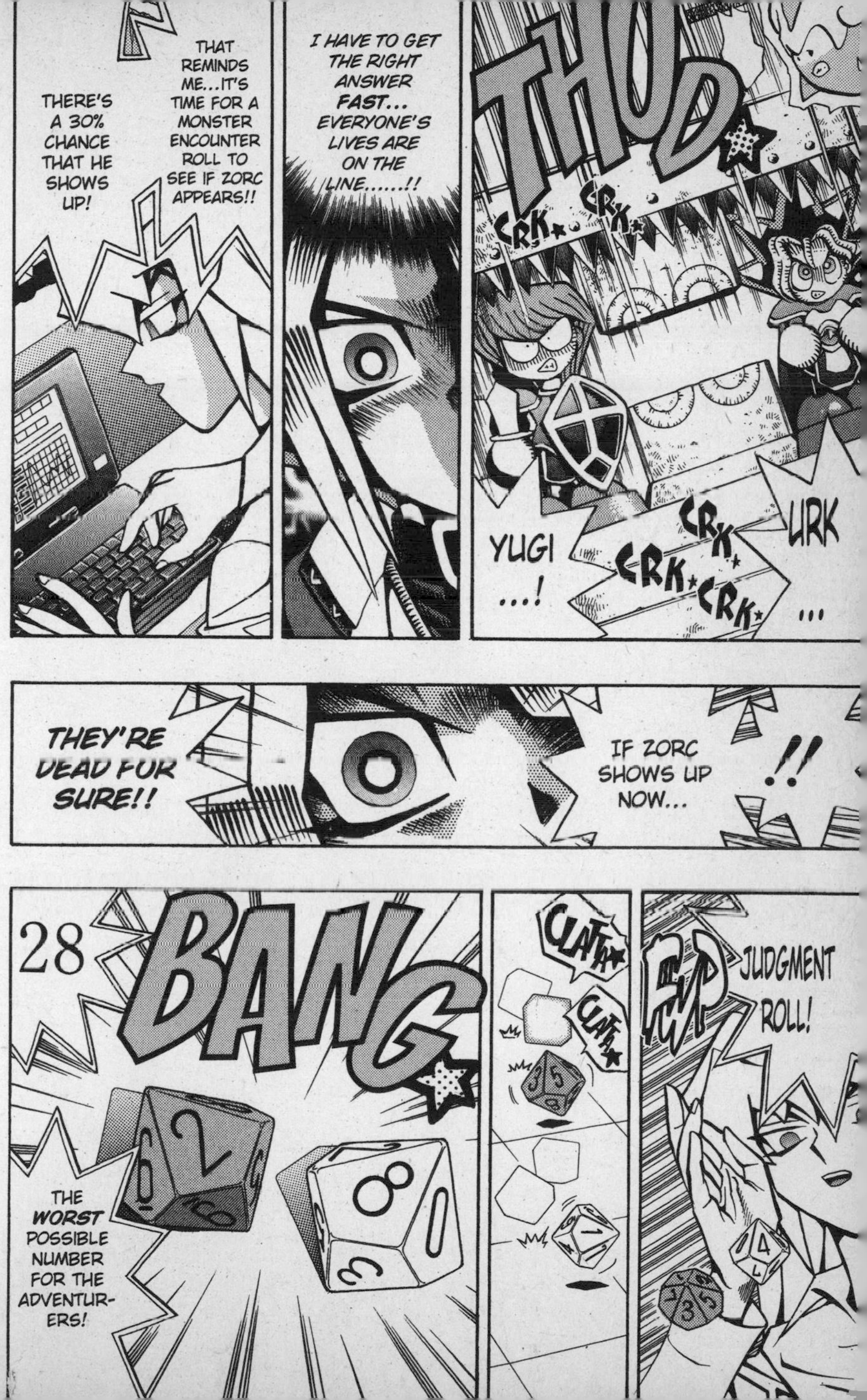
THUD
CRK CRK
URK
...
CRK CRK CRK
YUGI
...!
I HAVE TO GET THE RIGHT ANSWER FAST... EVERYONE'S LIVES ARE ON THE LINE......!!
THAT REMINDS ME...IT'S TIME FOR A MONSTER ENCOUNTER ROLL TO SEE IF ZORC APPEARS!!
THERE'S A 30% CHANCE THAT HE SHOWS UP!
!!
IF ZORC SHOWS UP NOW...
THEY'RE DEAD FOR SURE!!
JUDGMENT ROLL!
CLATTA
CLATTA
28
BANG
THE WORST POSSIBLE NUMBER FOR THE ADVENTURERS!

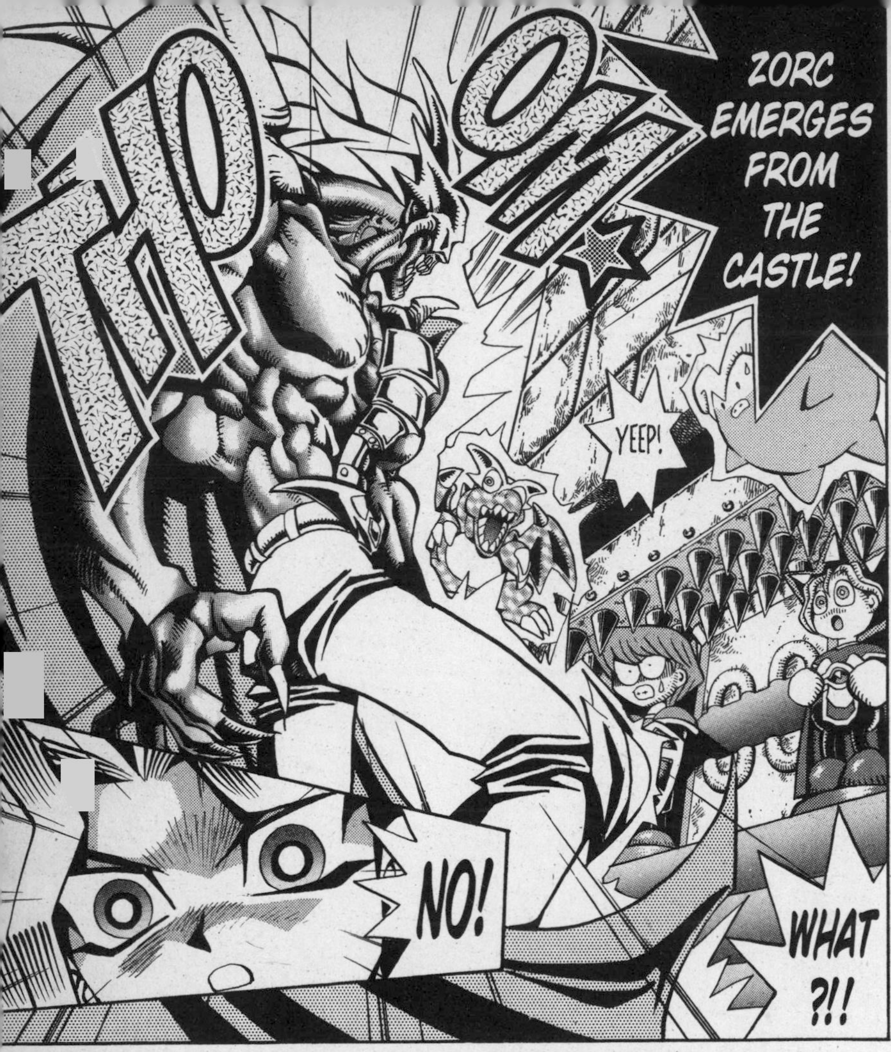
ZORC EMERGES FROM THE CASTLE!
THOOM
YEEP!
WHAT ?!!
NO!

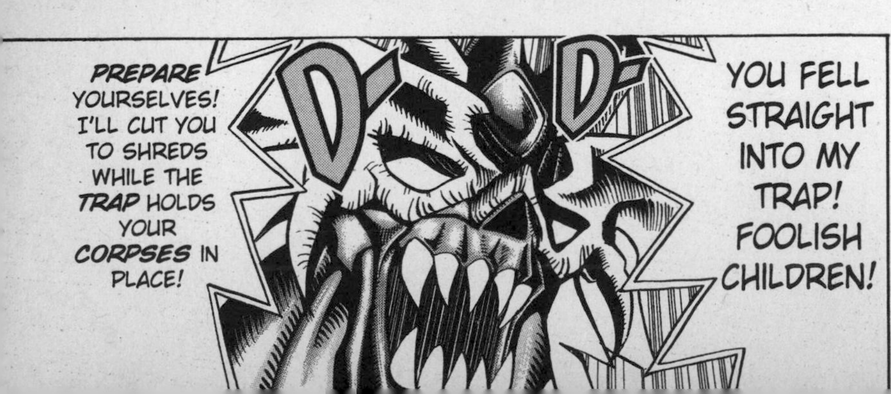
YOU FELL STRAIGHT INTO MY TRAP! FOOLISH CHILDREN!
D- D-
PREPARE YOURSELVES! I'LL CUT YOU TO SHREDS WHILE THE TRAP HOLDS YOUR CORPSES IN PLACE!

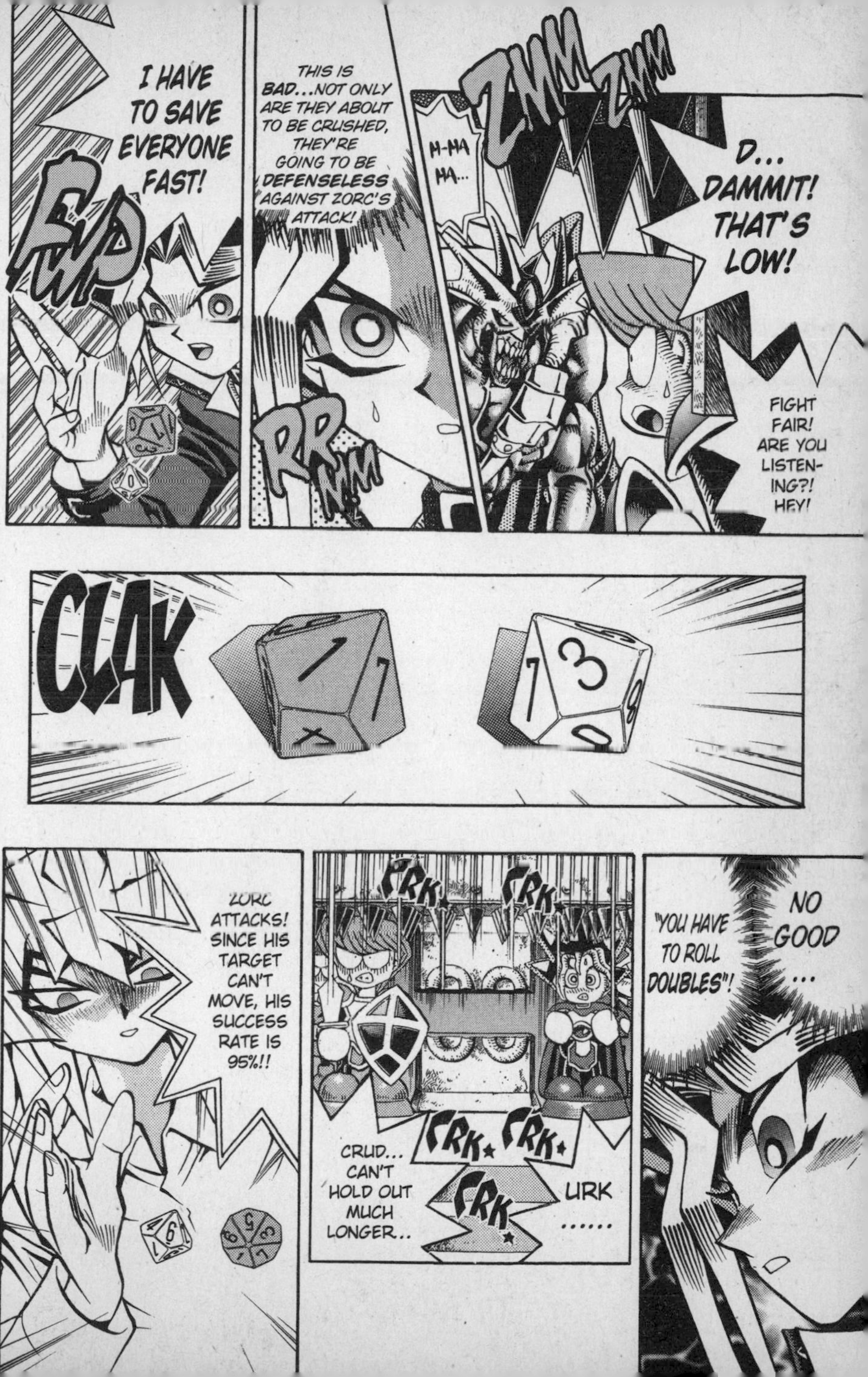
ZMM ZMM
D... DAMMIT! THAT'S LOW!
H-HA HA...
FIGHT FAIR! ARE YOU LISTEN-ING?! HEY!
THIS IS BAD...NOT ONLY ARE THEY ABOUT TO BE CRUSHED, THEY'RE GOING TO BE DEFENSELESS AGAINST ZORC'S ATTACK!
RRMM
I HAVE TO SAVE EVERYONE FAST!
FWP
CLAK
NO GOOD ...
"YOU HAVE TO ROLL DOUBLES"!
CRK CRK
CRK CRK
CRK
URK ......
CRUD... CAN'T HOLD OUT MUCH LONGER...
ZORC ATTACKS! SINCE HIS TARGET CAN'T MOVE, HIS SUCCESS RATE IS 95%!!

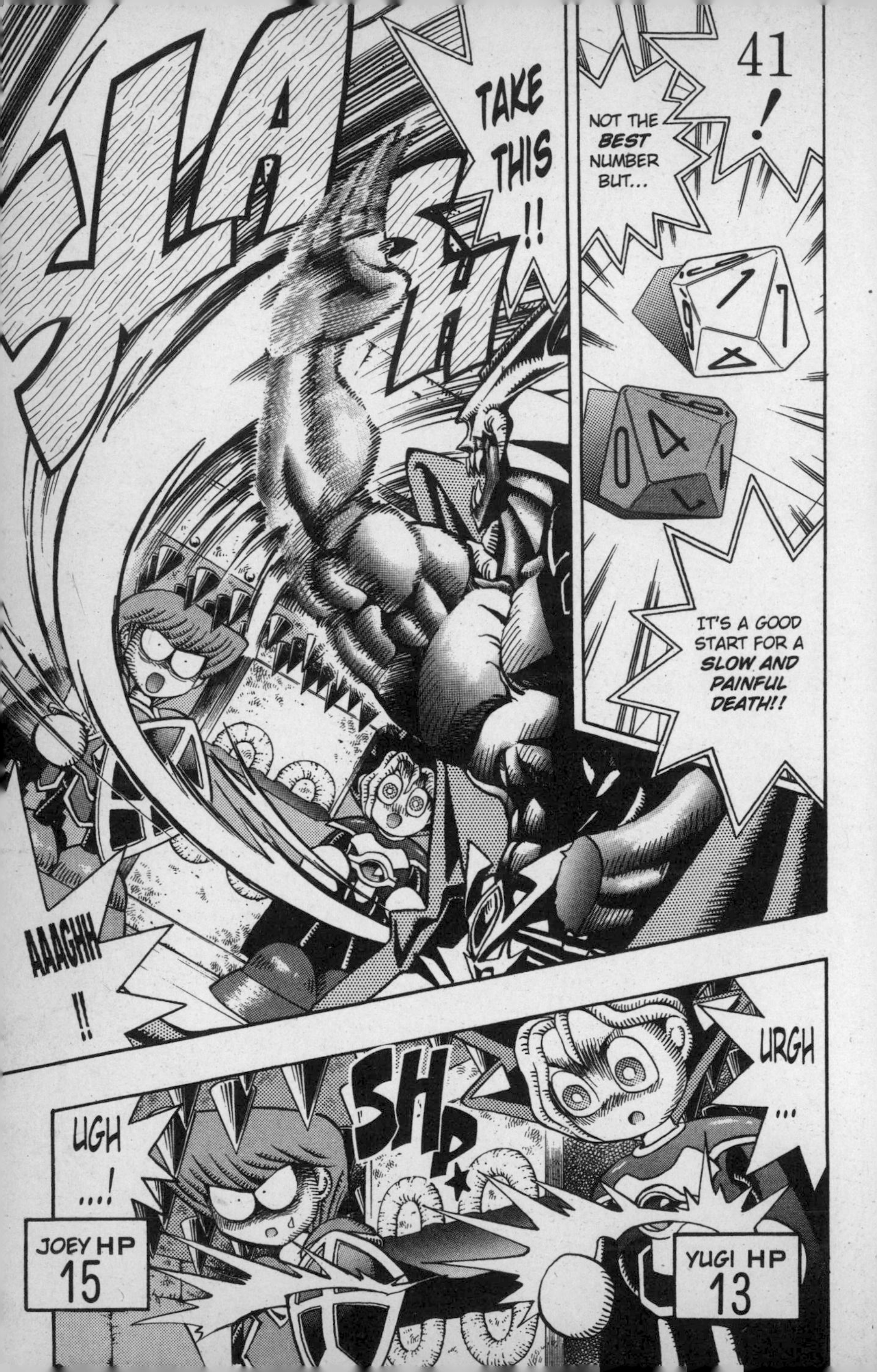
41
!
NOT THE BEST NUMBER BUT...
IT'S A GOOD START FOR A SLOW AND PAINFUL DEATH!!
TAKE THIS!!
AAAGHH!!
URGH...
SHP
UGH...!
YUGI HP 13
JOEY HP 15

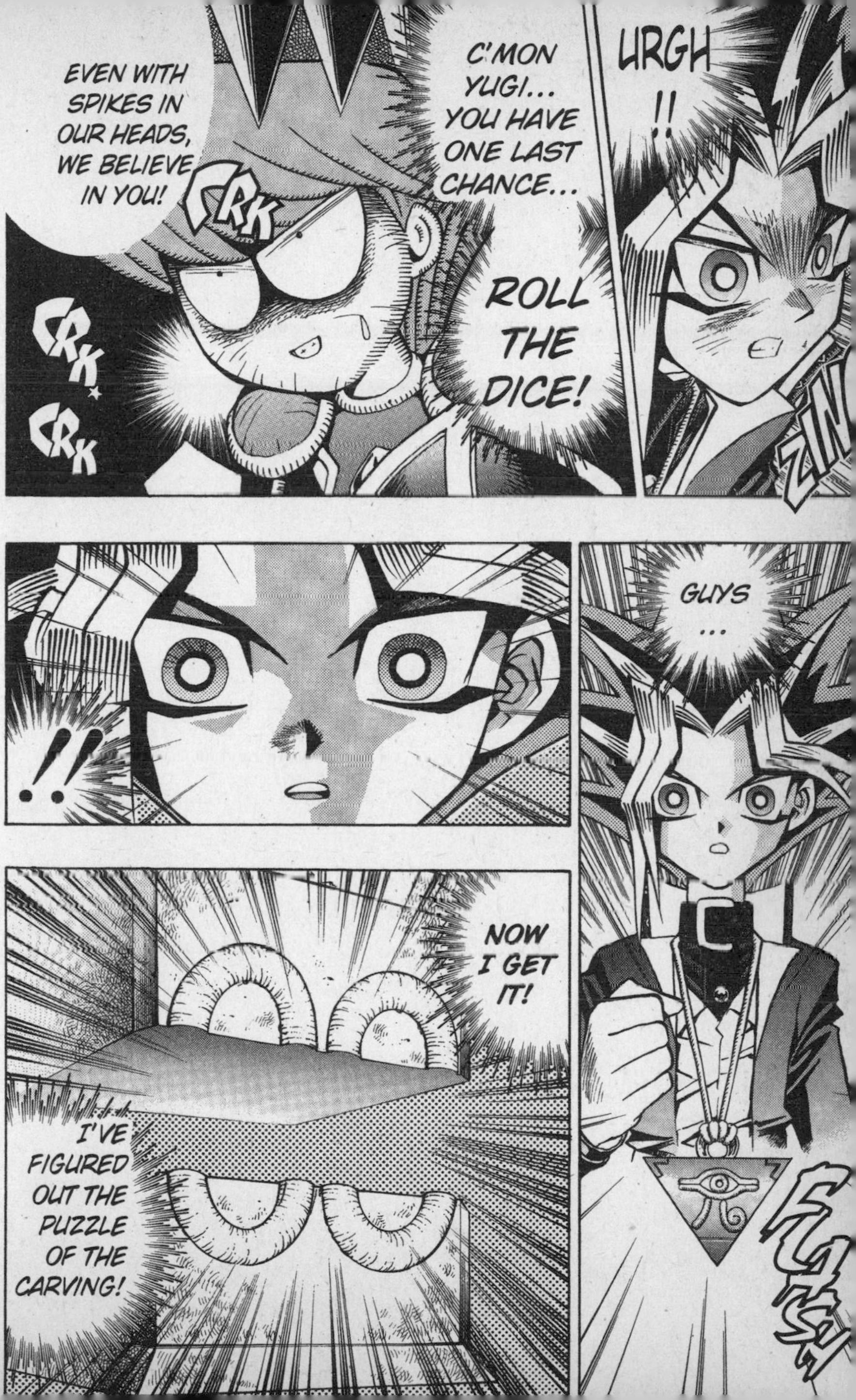
URGH !!
ZING
C'MON YUGI... YOU HAVE ONE LAST CHANCE...
EVEN WITH SPIKES IN OUR HEADS, WE BELIEVE IN YOU!
CRK
ROLL THE DICE!
CRK★ CRK
GUYS ...
FLASH
!!
NOW I GET IT!
I'VE FIGURED OUT THE PUZZLE OF THE CARVING!

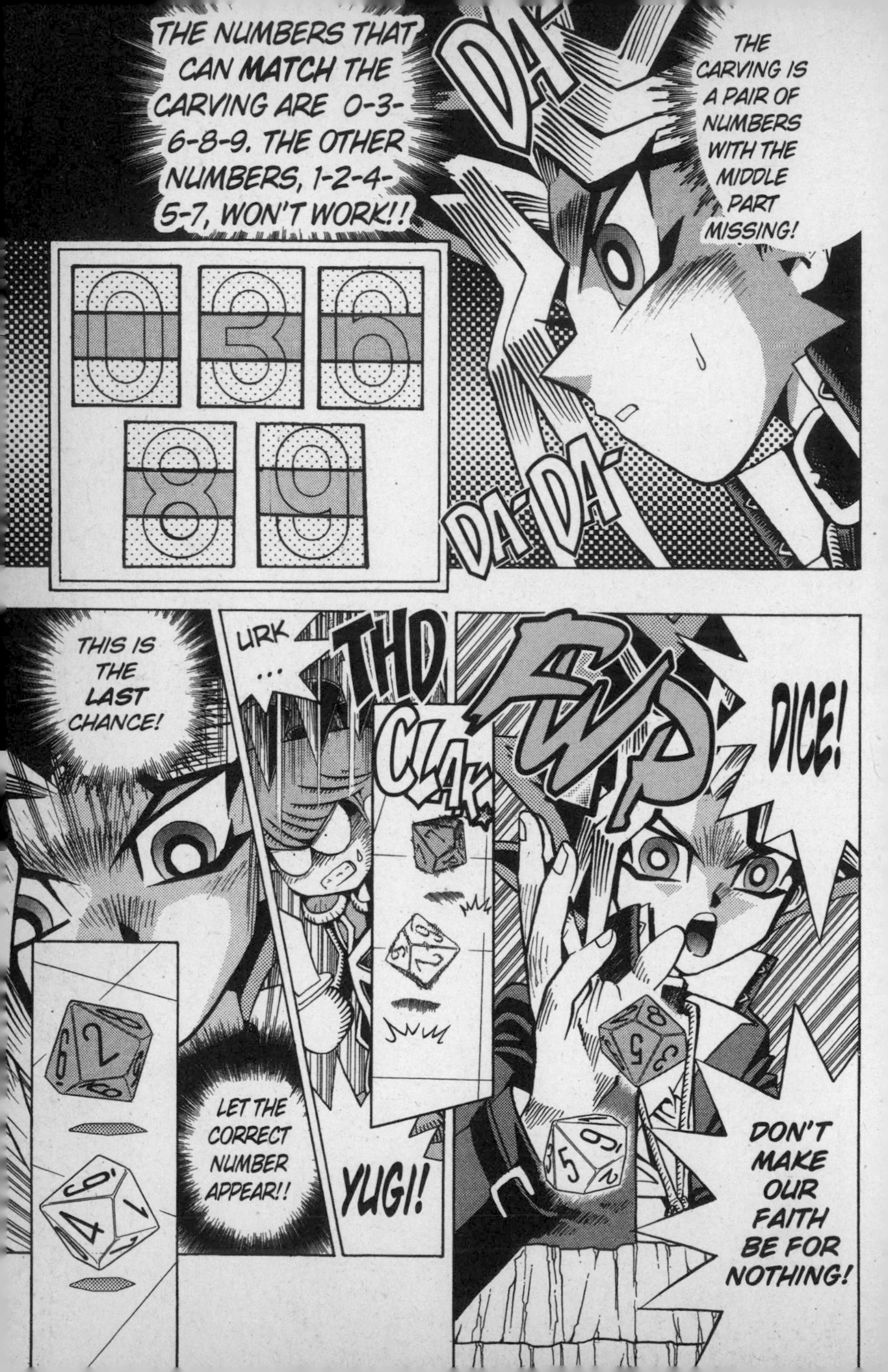
DA
THE CARVING IS A PAIR OF NUMBERS WITH THE MIDDLE PART MISSING!
DA-DA
THE NUMBERS THAT CAN MATCH THE CARVING ARE 0-3-6-8-9. THE OTHER NUMBERS, 1-2-4-5-7, WON'T WORK!!
DICE!
DON'T MAKE OUR FAITH BE FOR NOTHING!
URK ...
THD
CLAK
YUGI!
THIS IS THE LAST CHANCE!
LET THE CORRECT NUMBER APPEAR!!

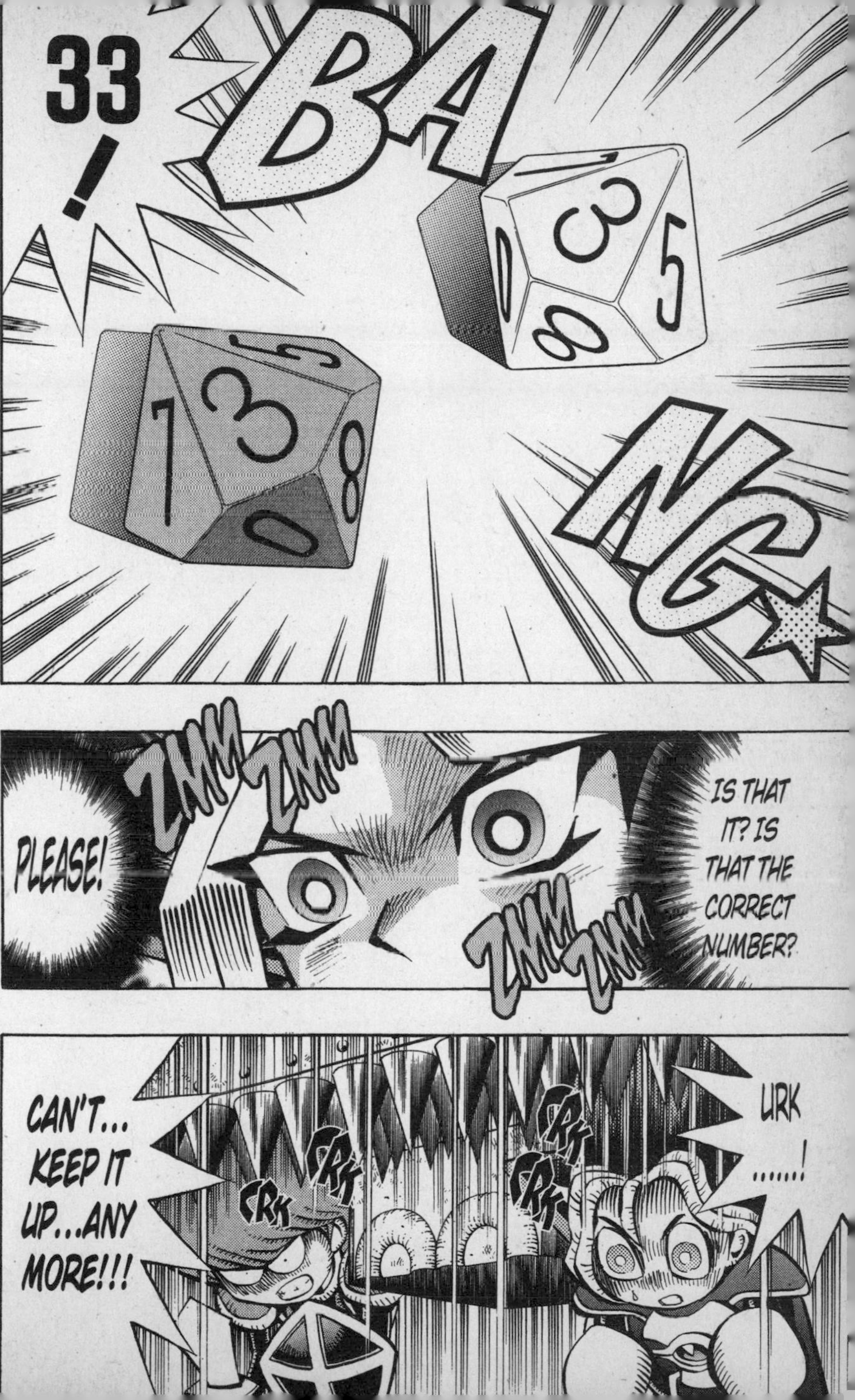
BANG☆
33!
IS THAT IT? IS THAT THE CORRECT NUMBER?
ZMM ZMM
ZMM ZMM
PLEASE!
URK ......!
CRK CRK
CRK CRK
CAN'T... KEEP IT UP...ANY MORE!!!

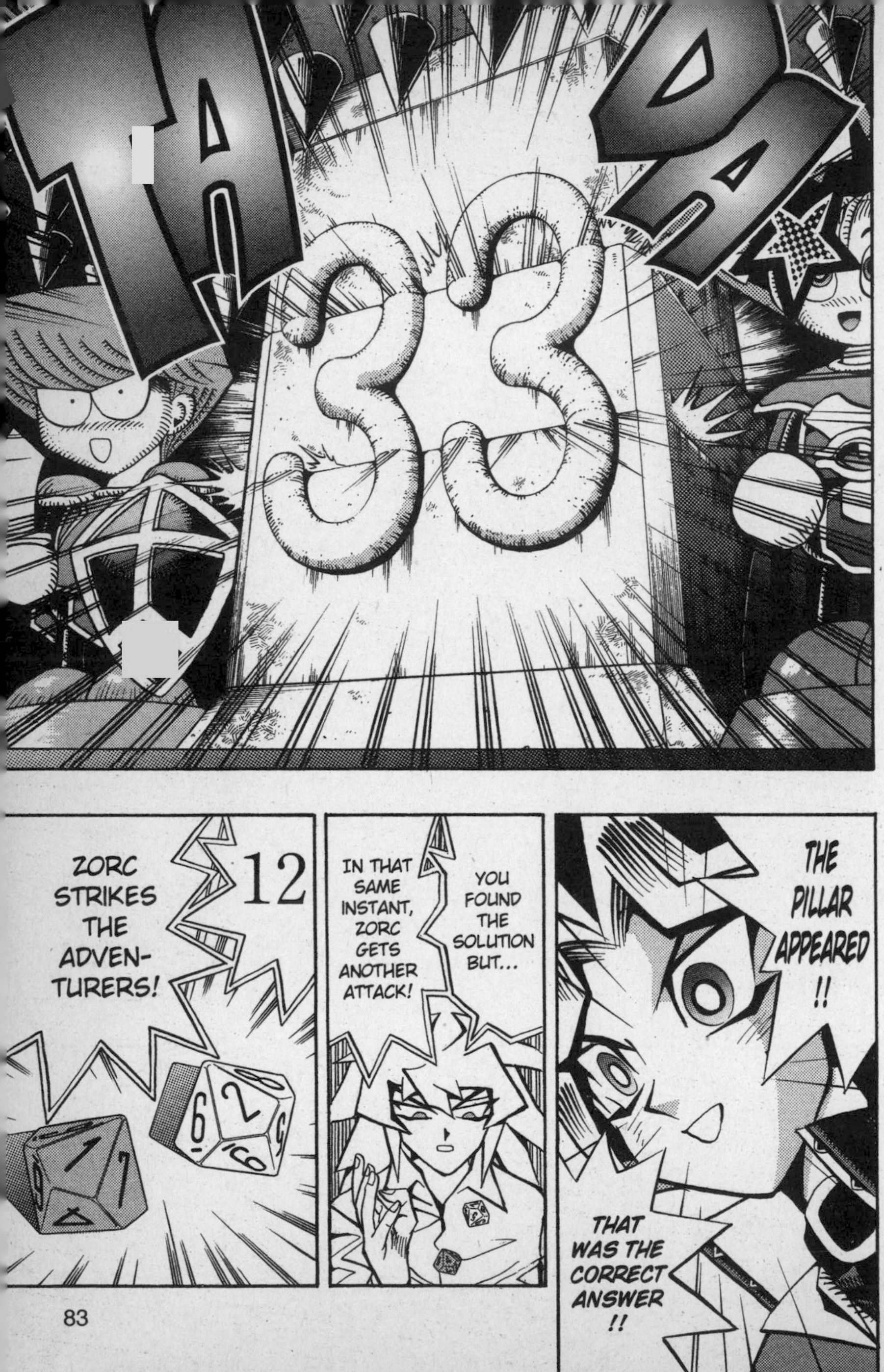
33
THE PILLAR APPEARED !!
THAT WAS THE CORRECT ANSWER !!
YOU FOUND THE SOLUTION BUT...
IN THAT SAME INSTANT, ZORC GETS ANOTHER ATTACK!
12
ZORC STRIKES THE ADVEN-TURERS!

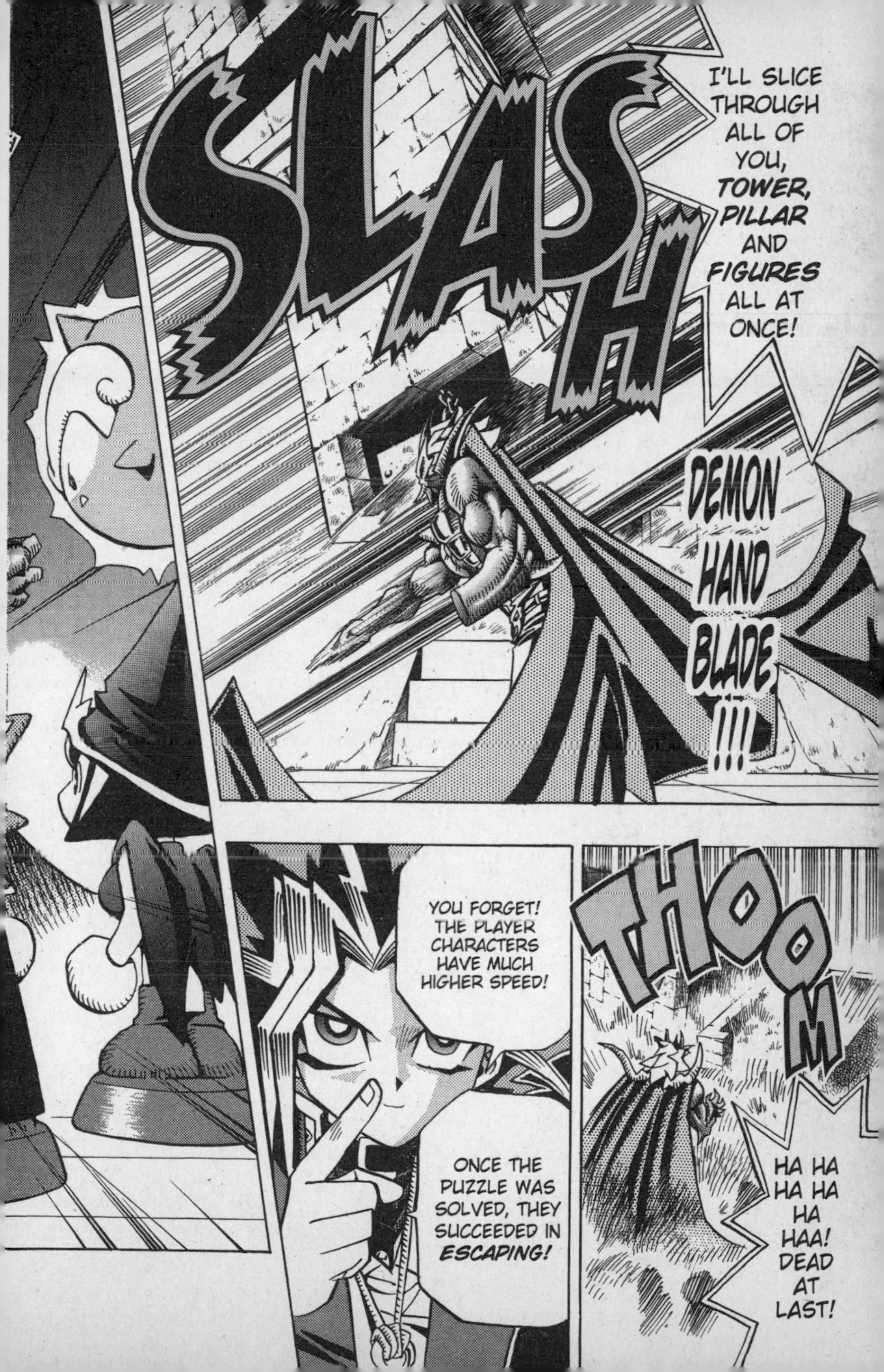
I'LL SLICE THROUGH ALL OF YOU, TOWER, PILLAR AND FIGURES ALL AT ONCE!
SLASH
DEMON HAND BLADE!!!
THOOOM
HA HA HA HA HA HAA! DEAD AT LAST!
YOU FORGET! THE PLAYER CHARACTERS HAVE MUCH HIGHER SPEED!
ONCE THE PUZZLE WAS SOLVED, THEY SUCCEEDED IN ESCAPING!

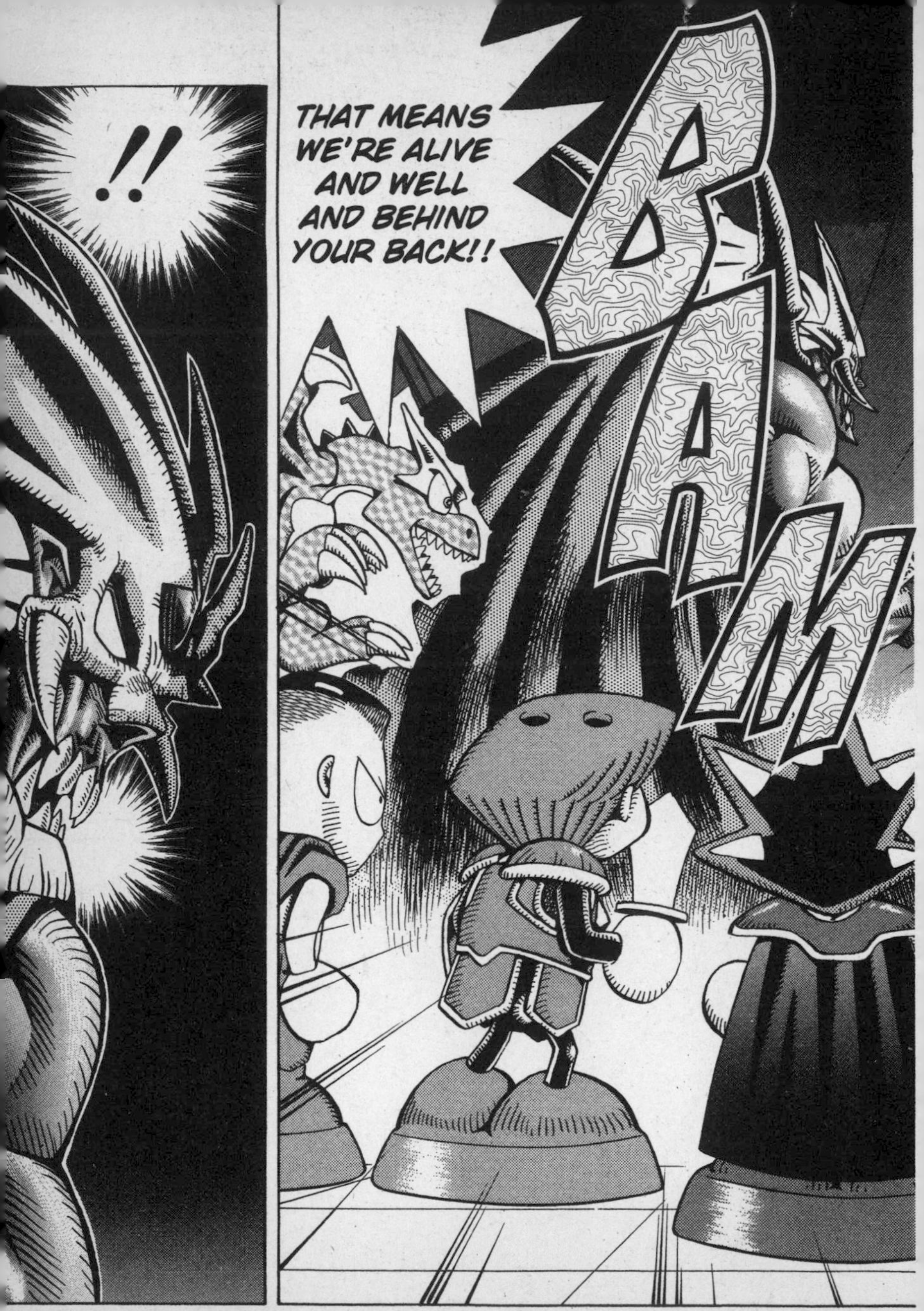
THAT MEANS WE'RE ALIVE AND WELL AND BEHIND YOUR BACK!!
BAM
!!

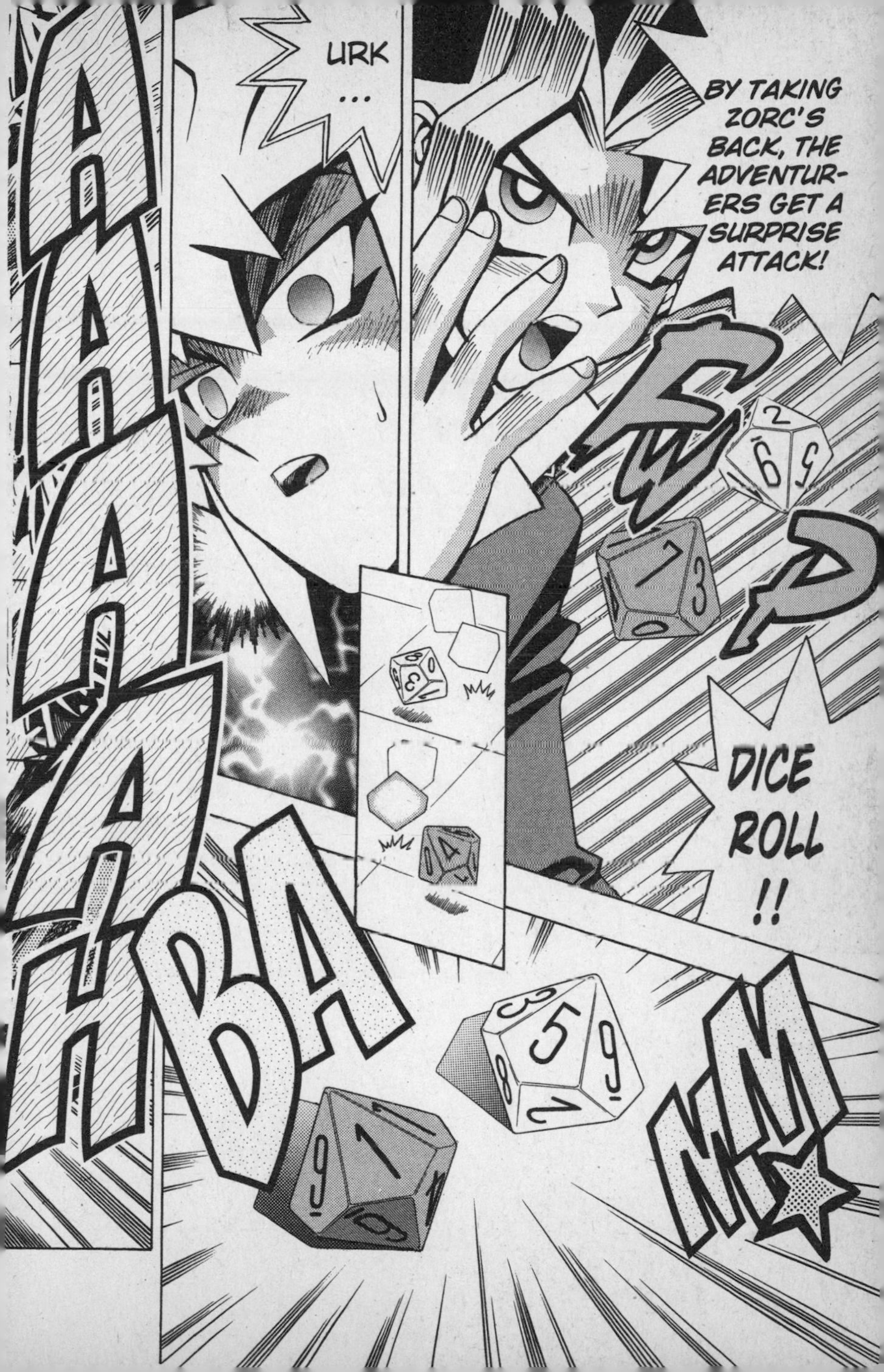
BY TAKING ZORC'S BACK, THE ADVENTURERS GET A SURPRISE ATTACK!
DICE ROLL !!
URK ...

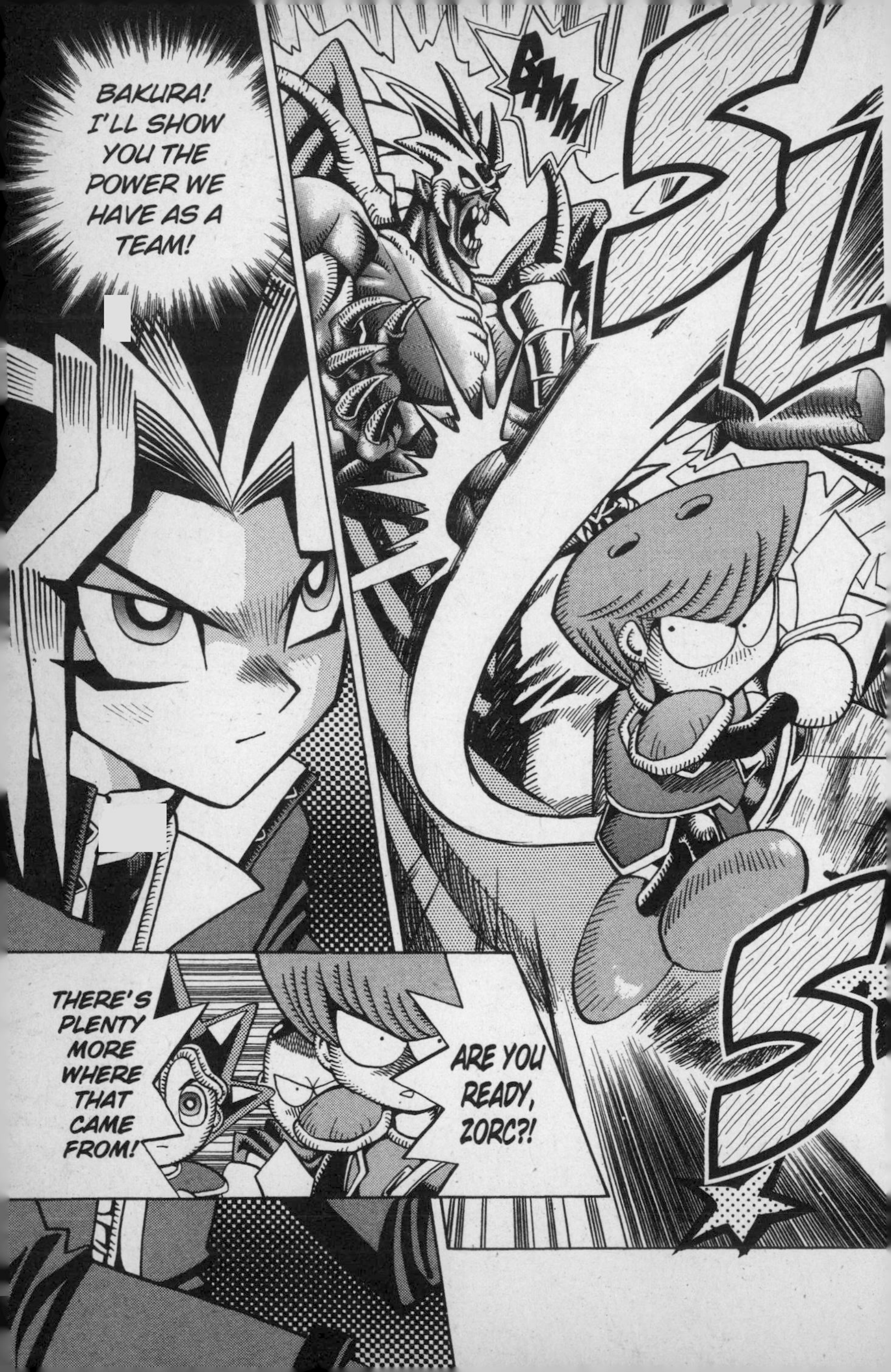
BAMM
BAKURA! I'LL SHOW YOU THE POWER WE HAVE AS A TEAM!
ARE YOU READY, ZORC?!
THERE'S PLENTY MORE WHERE THAT CAME FROM!

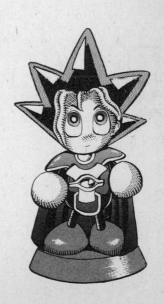

Duel 56: Millennium Enemy 7: I'll Fight Too!

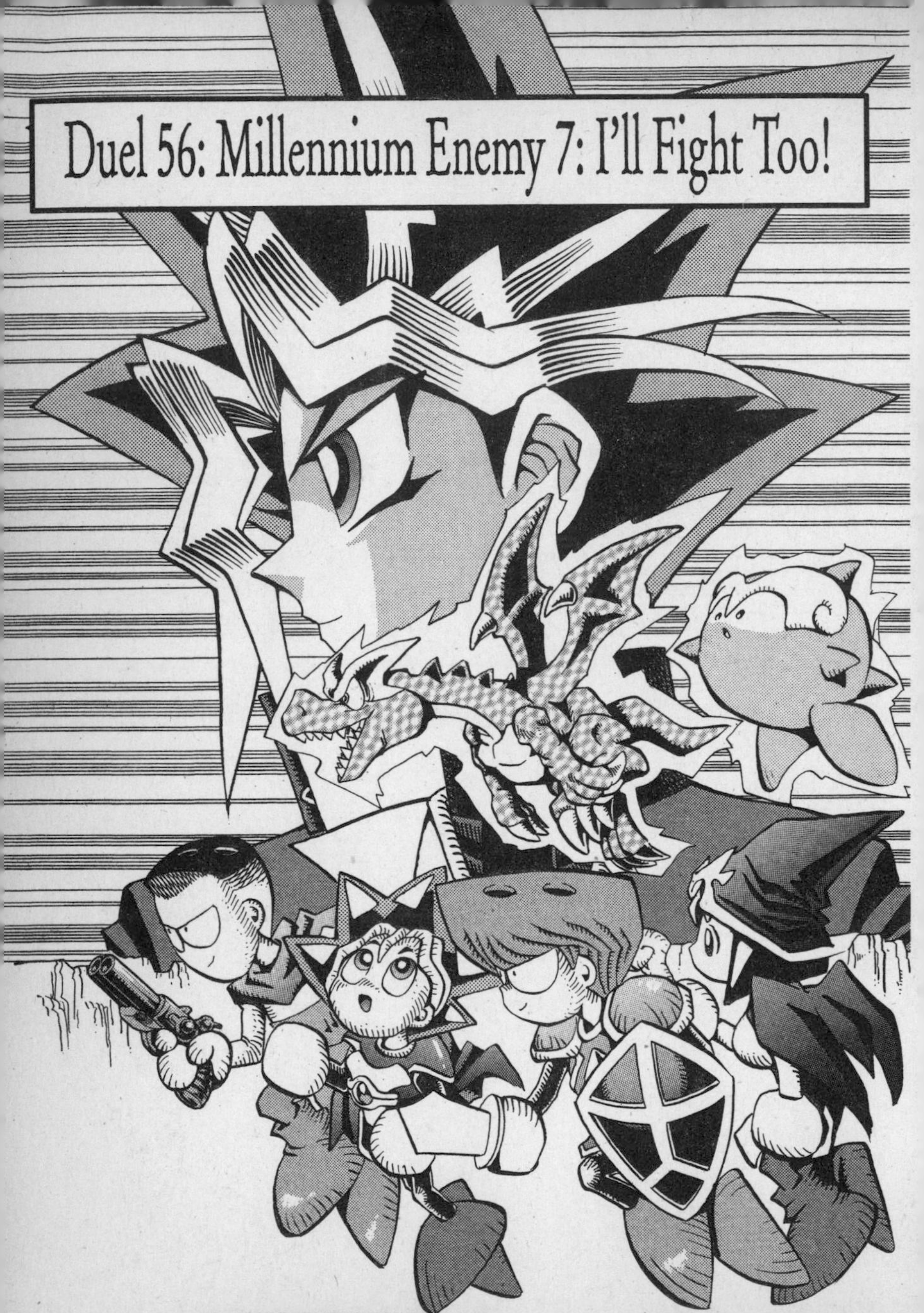

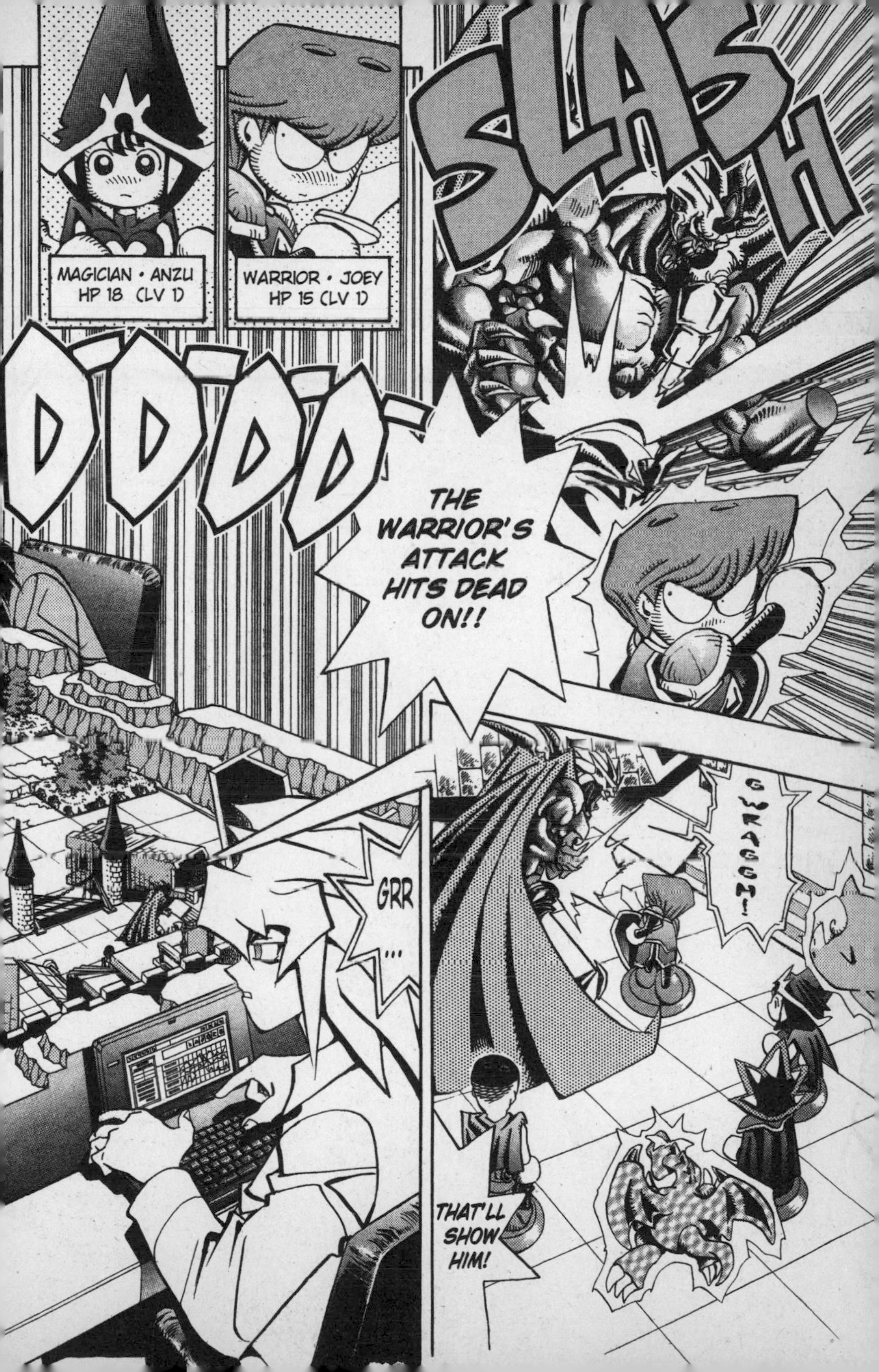
SLASH
WARRIOR • JOEY
HP 15 (LV 1)
MAGICIAN • ANZU
HP 18 (LV 1)
THE WARRIOR'S ATTACK HITS DEAD ON!!
DDDD
GWRAGGH!
THAT'LL SHOW HIM!
GRR...

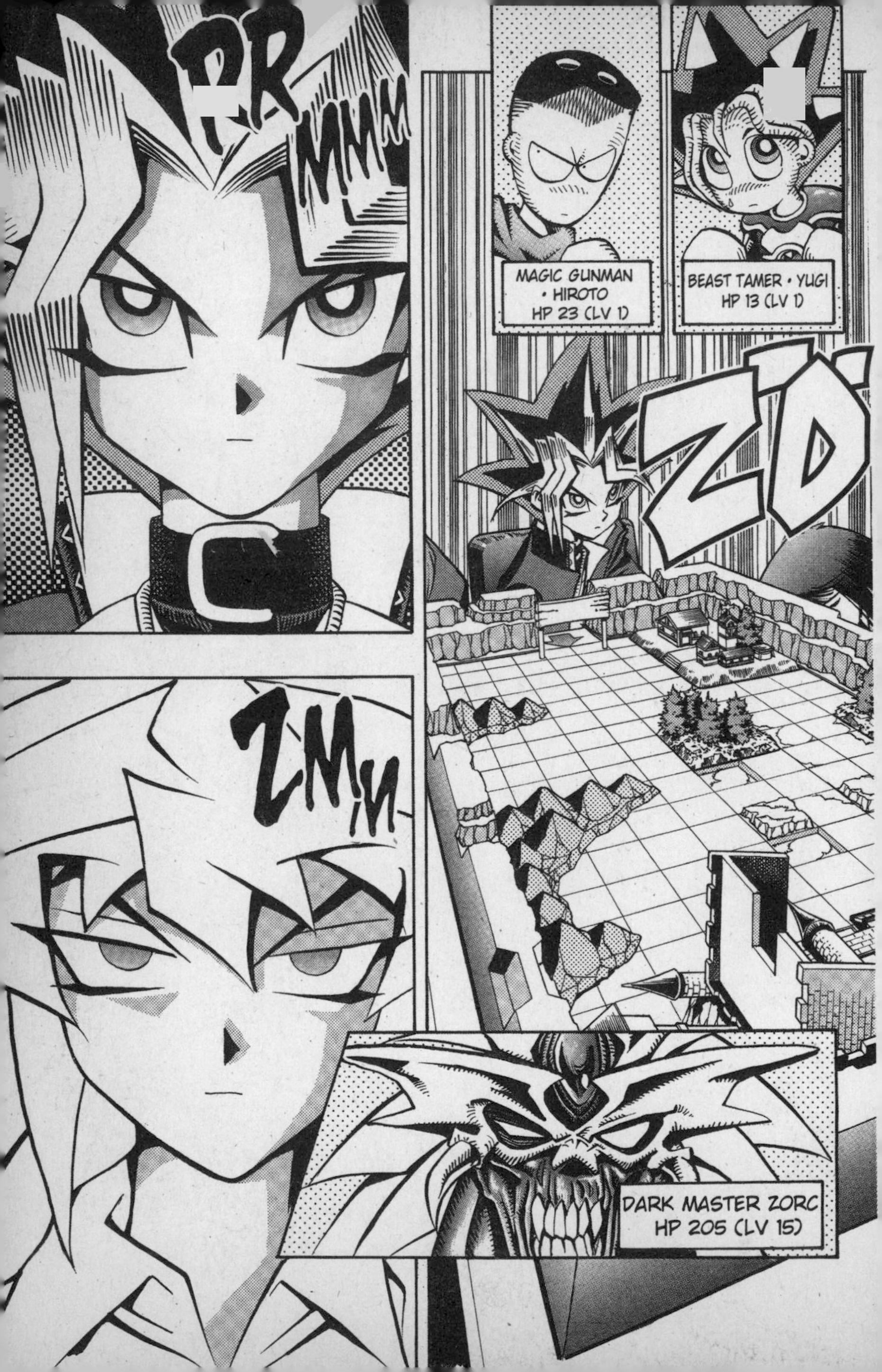
BEAST TAMER • YUGI
HP 13 (LV 1)
MAGIC GUNMAN • HIROTO
HP 23 (LV 1)
ZD
DARK MASTER ZORC
HP 205 (LV 15)
PRMMM
ZMN

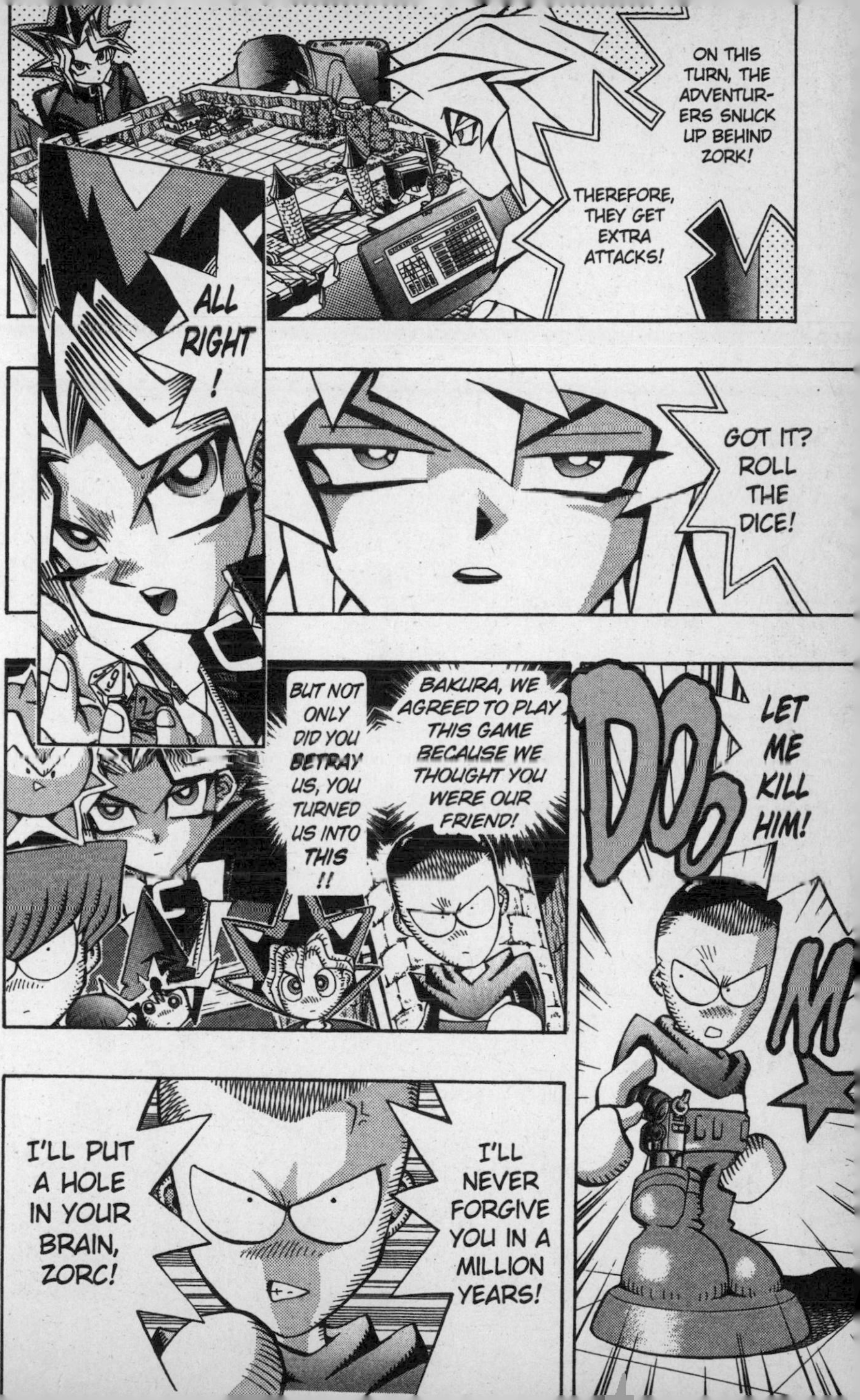

ON THIS TURN, THE ADVENTURERS SNUCK UP BEHIND ZORK!
THEREFORE, THEY GET EXTRA ATTACKS!
GOT IT? ROLL THE DICE!
ALL RIGHT!
DOOM
LET ME KILL HIM!
BAKURA, WE AGREED TO PLAY THIS GAME BECAUSE WE THOUGHT YOU WERE OUR FRIEND!
BUT NOT ONLY DID YOU BETRAY US, YOU TURNED US INTO THIS!!
I'LL NEVER FORGIVE YOU IN A MILLION YEARS!
I'LL PUT A HOLE IN YOUR BRAIN, ZORC!

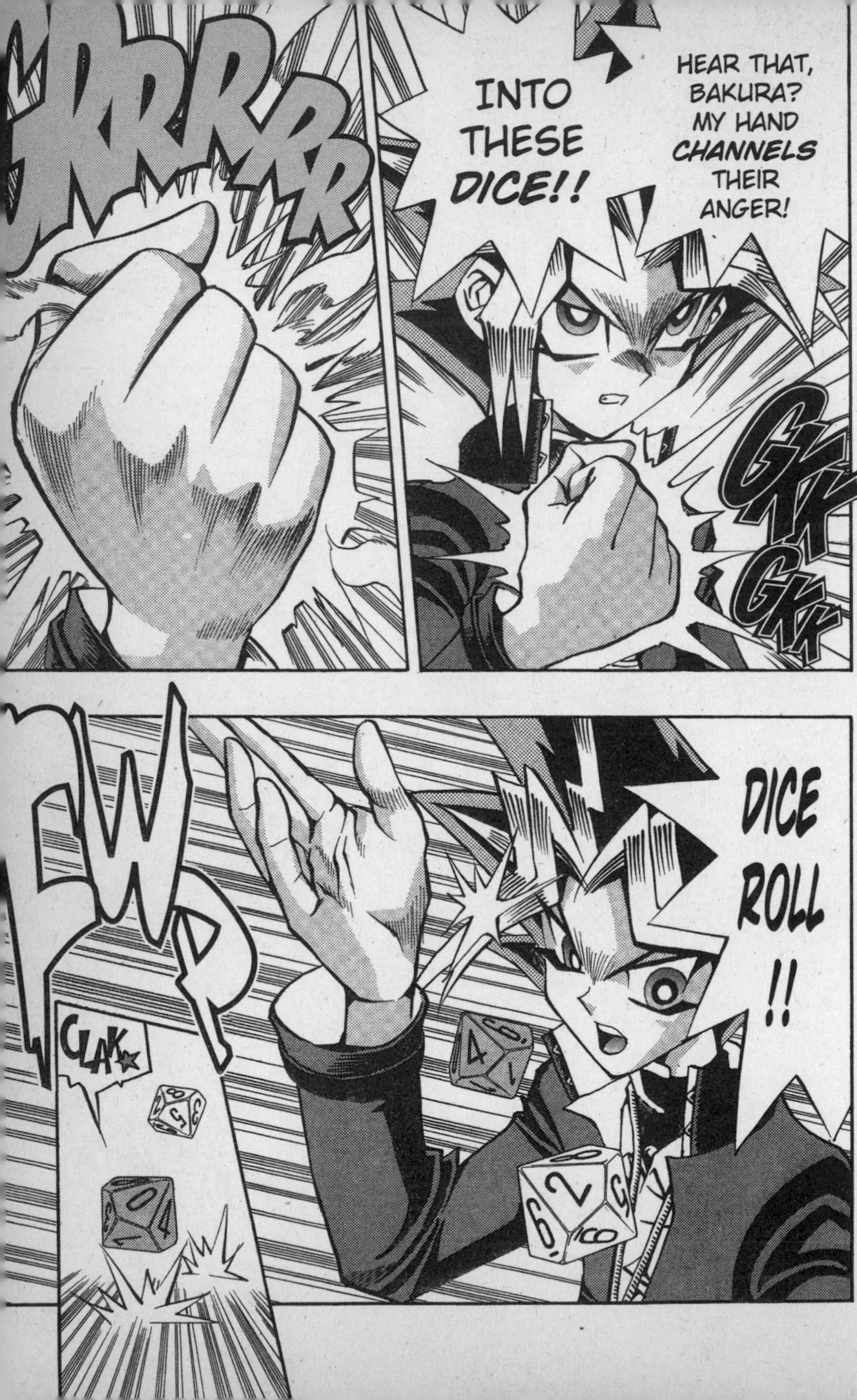
HEAR THAT, BAKURA? MY HAND CHANNELS THEIR ANGER!
INTO THESE DICE!!
GKK GKK
DICE ROLL !!
WHP
CLAK

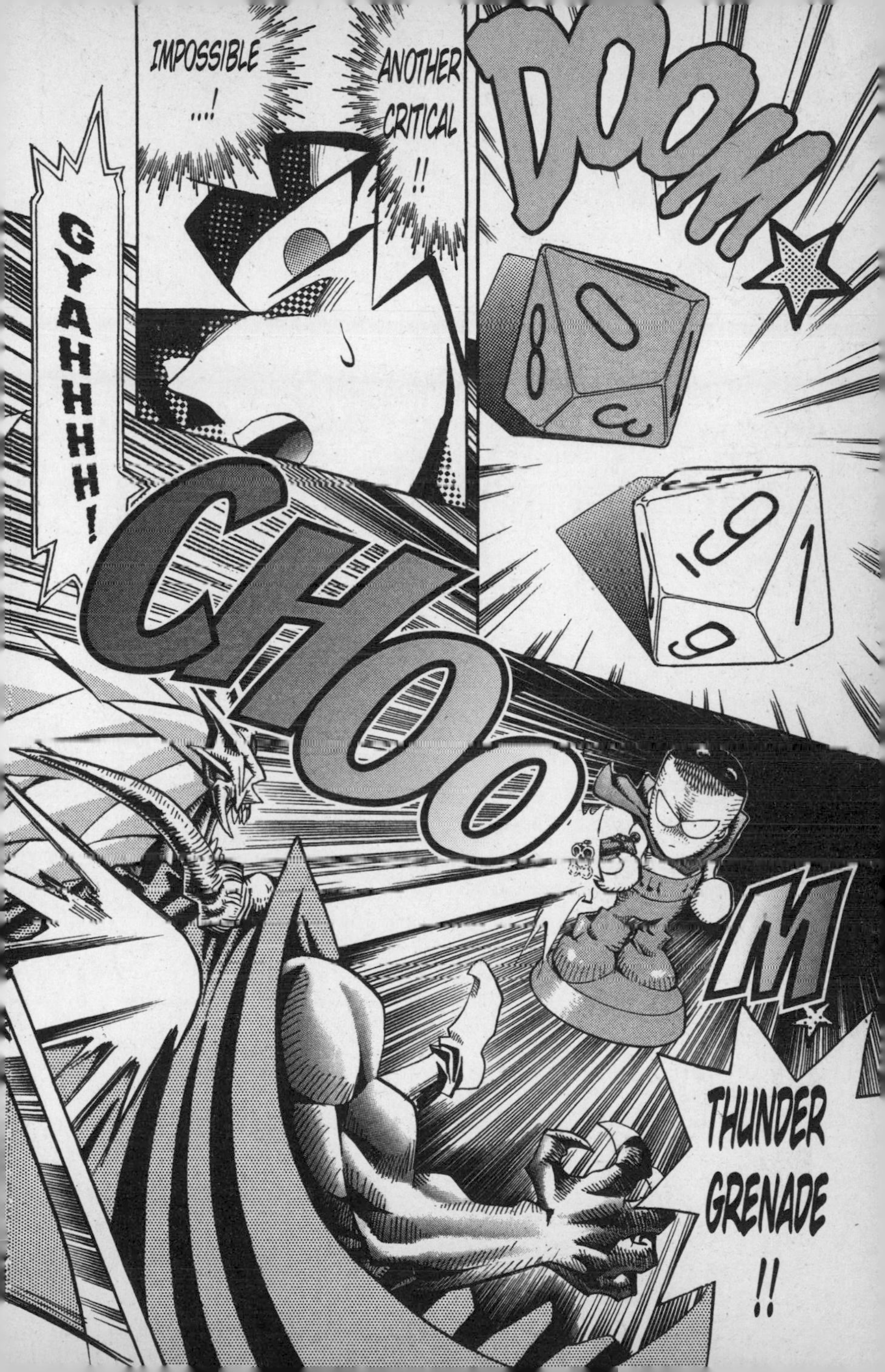
DOOM
ANOTHER CRITICAL !!
IMPOSSIBLE ...!
GYAHHHH!
CHOOOM
THUNDER GRENADE !!

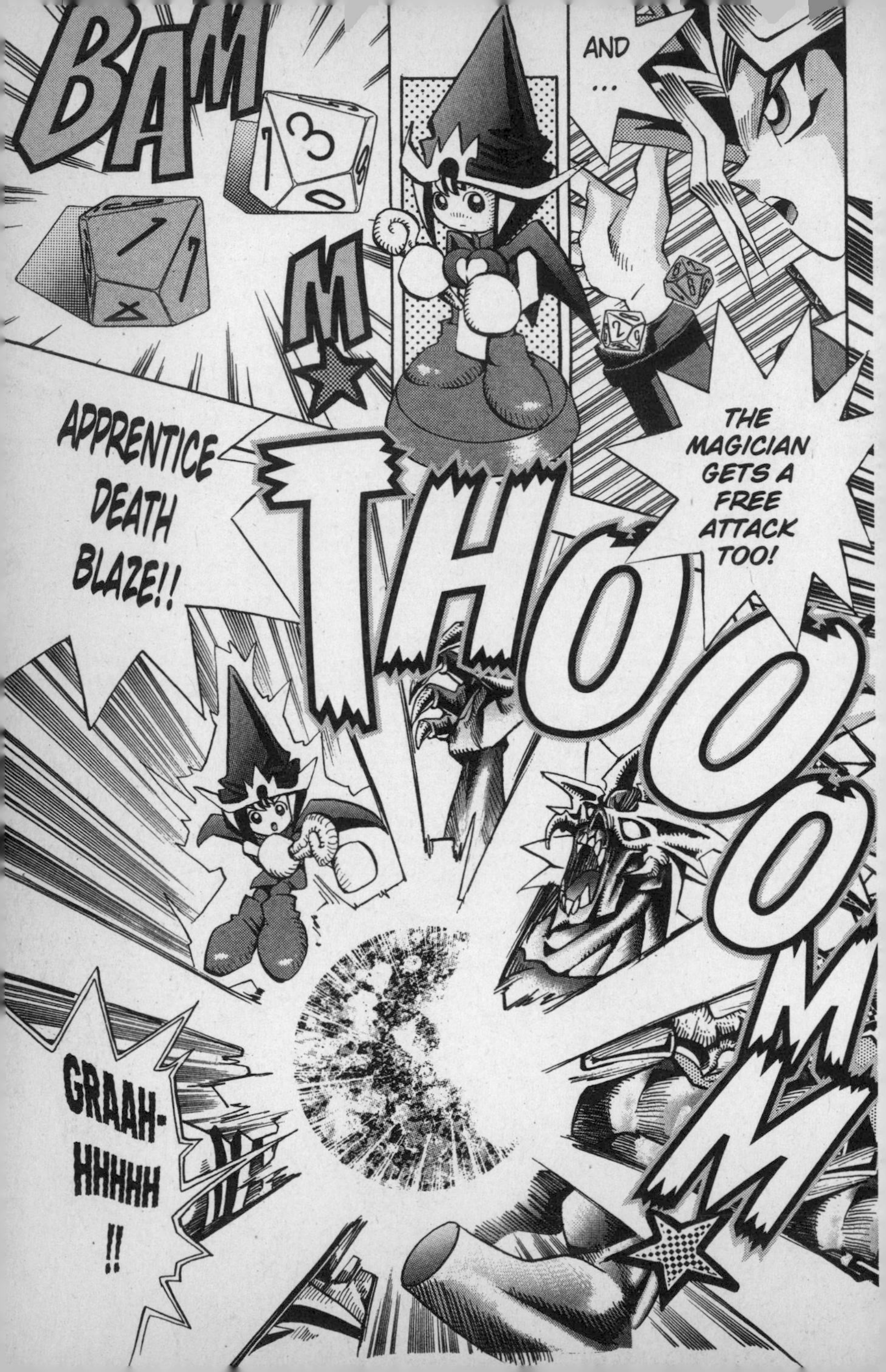
AND ...
M
BAM
THE MAGICIAN GETS A FREE ATTACK TOO!
THOOOOMM
APPRENTICE DEATH BLAZE!!
GRAAH-HHHHH!!

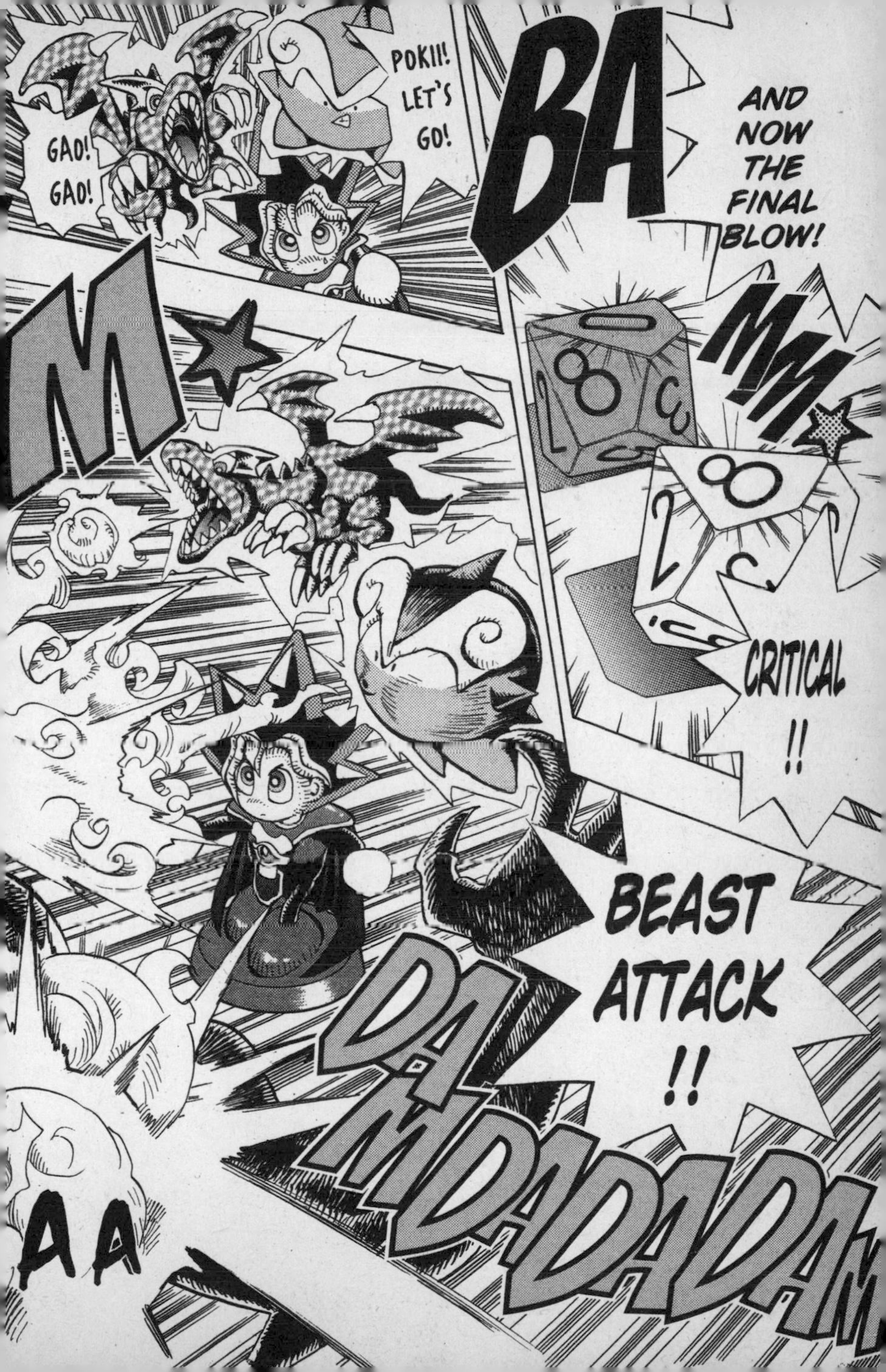
AND NOW THE FINAL BLOW!
BA
MM
CRITICAL !!
POKII! LET'S GO!
GAO! GAO!
M
BEAST ATTACK !!
DA
DADADADAM
AA

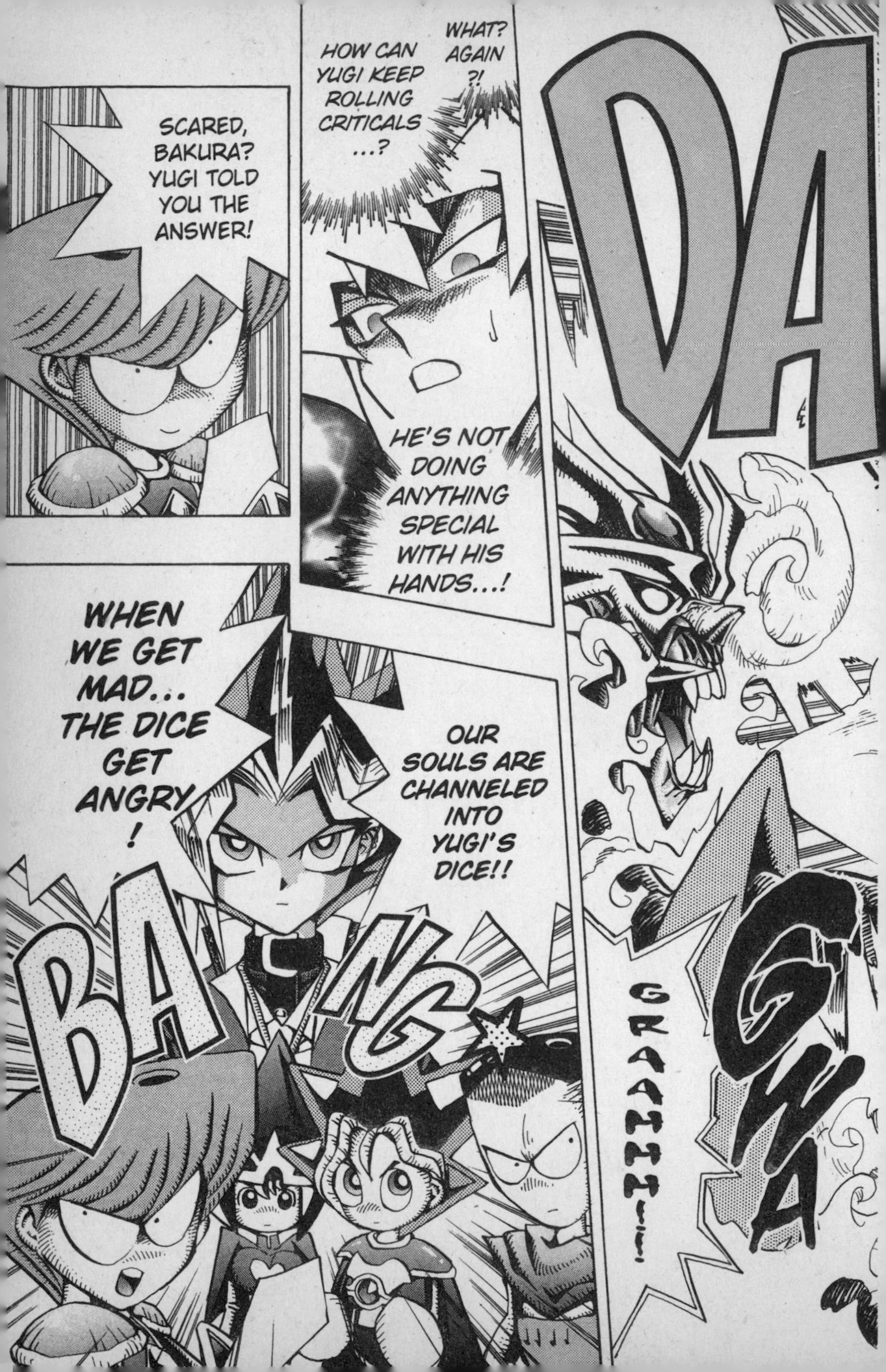
DA
GRAAHH...!
WHAT? AGAIN ?!
HOW CAN YUGI KEEP ROLLING CRITICALS ...?
HE'S NOT DOING ANYTHING SPECIAL WITH HIS HANDS...!
SCARED, BAKURA? YUGI TOLD YOU THE ANSWER!
WHEN WE GET MAD... THE DICE GET ANGRY !
OUR SOULS ARE CHANNELED INTO YUGI'S DICE!!
BANG

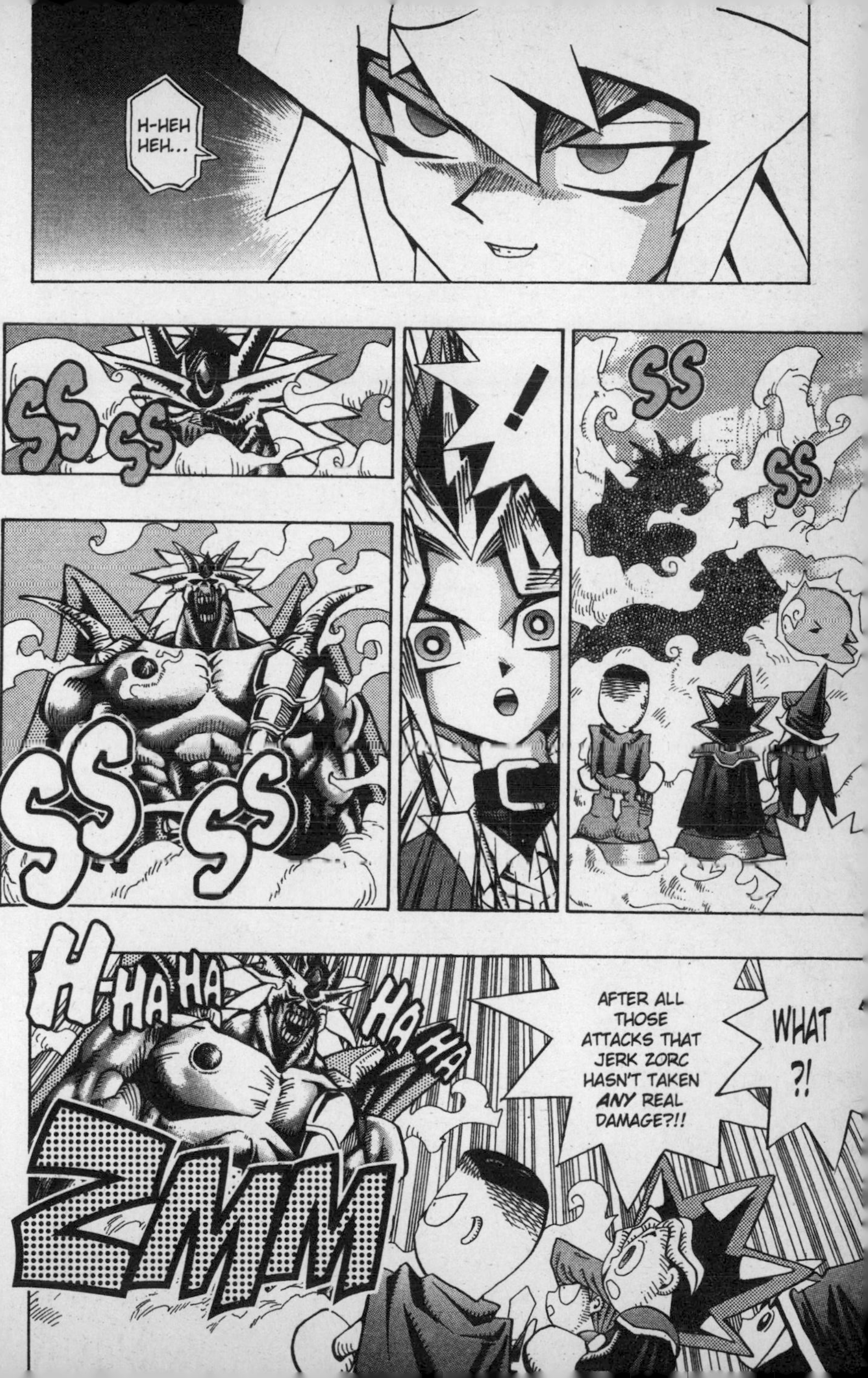
H-HEH HEH...
SS
SS
!
SS SS
SS-SS
WHAT ?!
AFTER ALL THOSE ATTACKS THAT JERK ZORC HASN'T TAKEN ANY REAL DAMAGE?!!
H-HA HA HA HA HA
ZMM

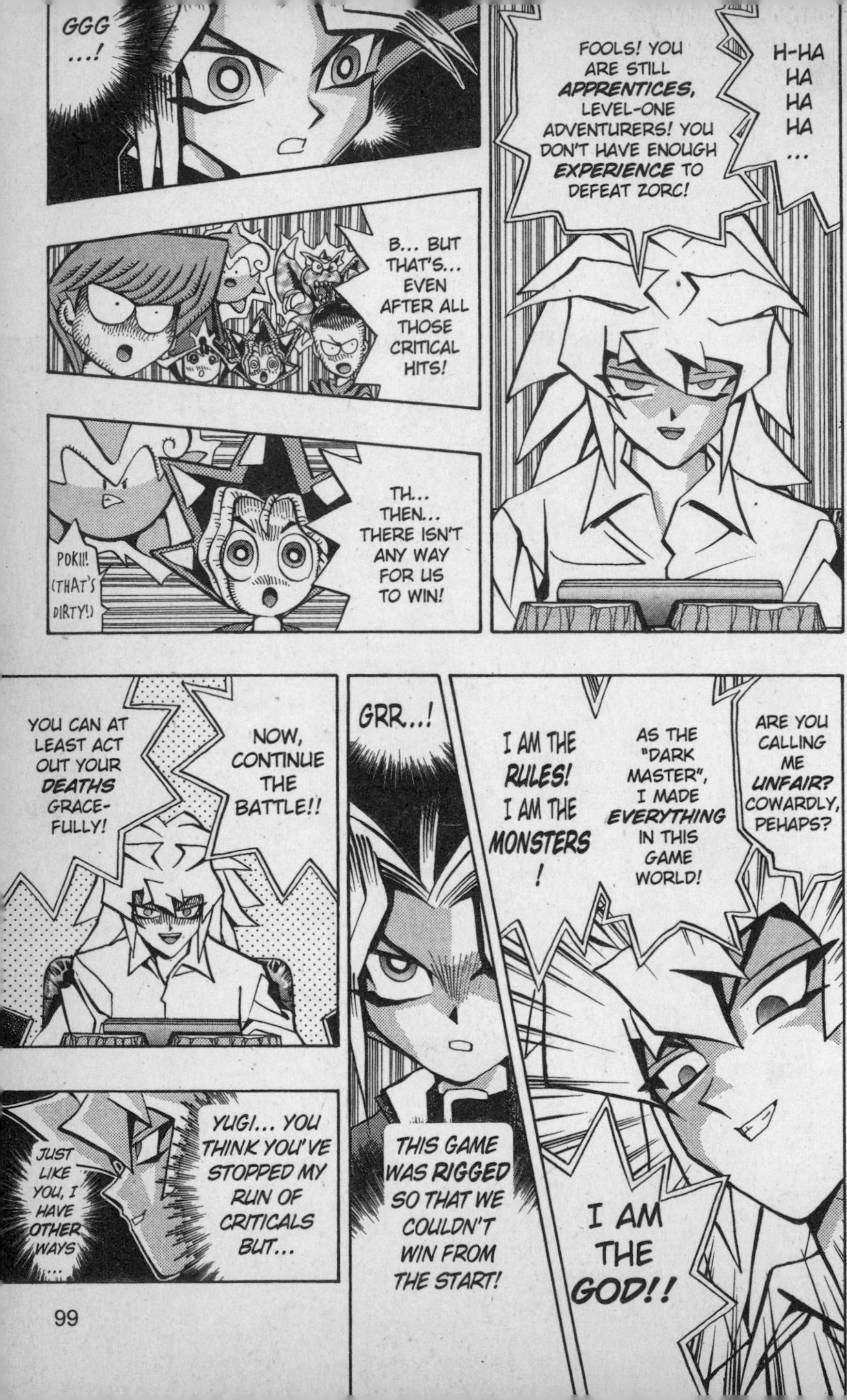

H-HA HA HA HA ...
FOOLS! YOU ARE STILL APPRENTICES, LEVEL-ONE ADVENTURERS! YOU DON'T HAVE ENOUGH EXPERIENCE TO DEFEAT ZORC!
GGG ...!
B... BUT THAT'S... EVEN AFTER ALL THOSE CRITICAL HITS!
TH... THEN... THERE ISN'T ANY WAY FOR US TO WIN!
POKII! (THAT'S DIRTY!)
ARE YOU CALLING ME UNFAIR? COWARDLY, PEHAPS?
AS THE "DARK MASTER", I MADE EVERYTHING IN THIS GAME WORLD!
I AM THE RULES! I AM THE MONSTERS!
I AM THE GOD!!
GRR...!
THIS GAME WAS RIGGED SO THAT WE COULDN'T WIN FROM THE START!
NOW, CONTINUE THE BATTLE!!
YOU CAN AT LEAST ACT OUT YOUR DEATHS GRACEFULLY!
YUGI... YOU THINK YOU'VE STOPPED MY RUN OF CRITICALS BUT...
JUST LIKE YOU, I HAVE OTHER WAYS ...

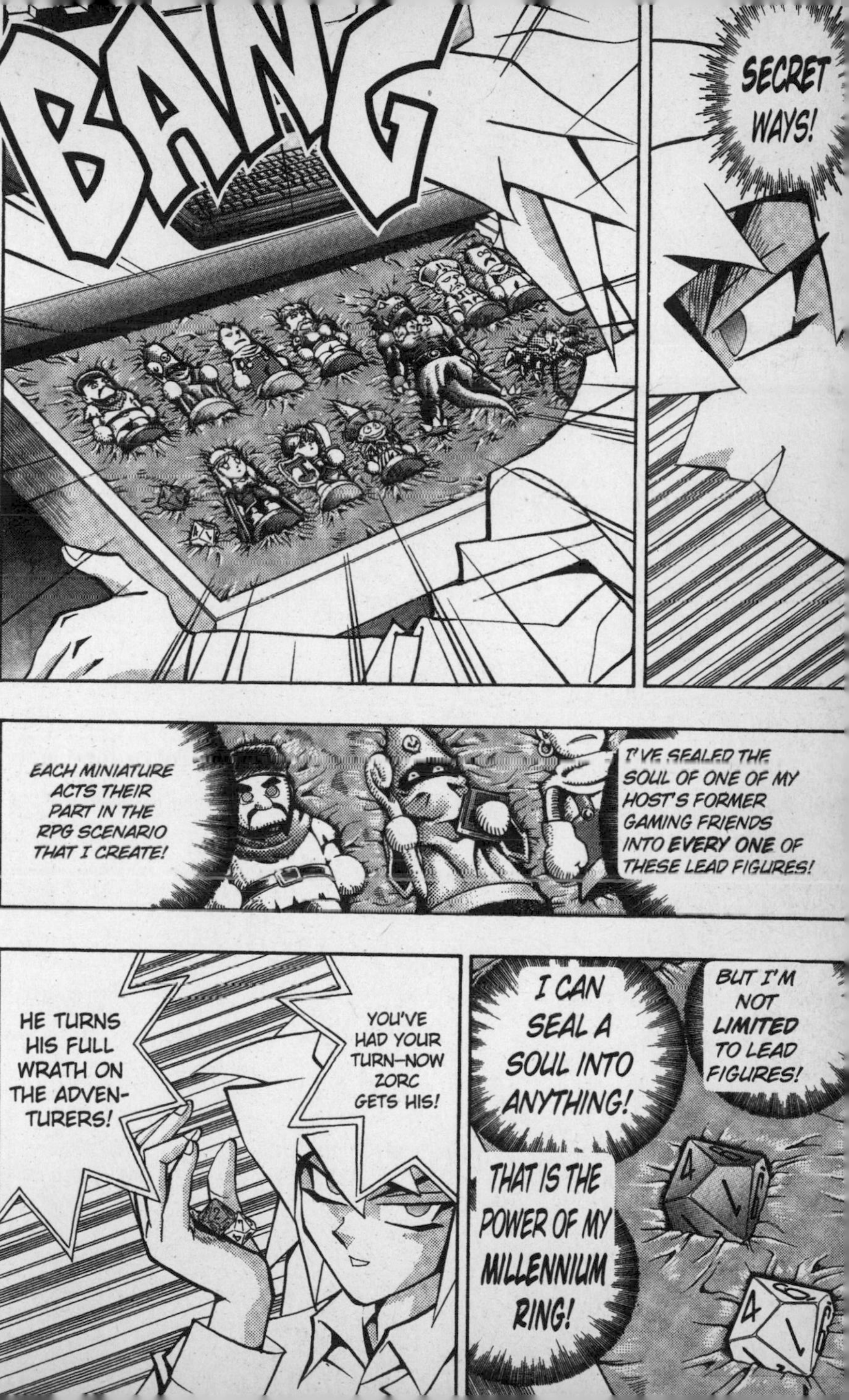
SECRET WAYS!
BANG
I'VE SEALED THE SOUL OF ONE OF MY HOST'S FORMER GAMING FRIENDS INTO **EVERY ONE** OF THESE LEAD FIGURES!
EACH MINIATURE ACTS THEIR PART IN THE RPG SCENARIO THAT I CREATE!
BUT I'M NOT **LIMITED** TO LEAD FIGURES!
I CAN SEAL A SOUL INTO ANYTHING!
THAT IS THE POWER OF MY MILLENNIUM RING!
YOU'VE HAD YOUR TURN—NOW ZORC GETS HIS!
HE TURNS HIS FULL WRATH ON THE ADVEN-TURERS!

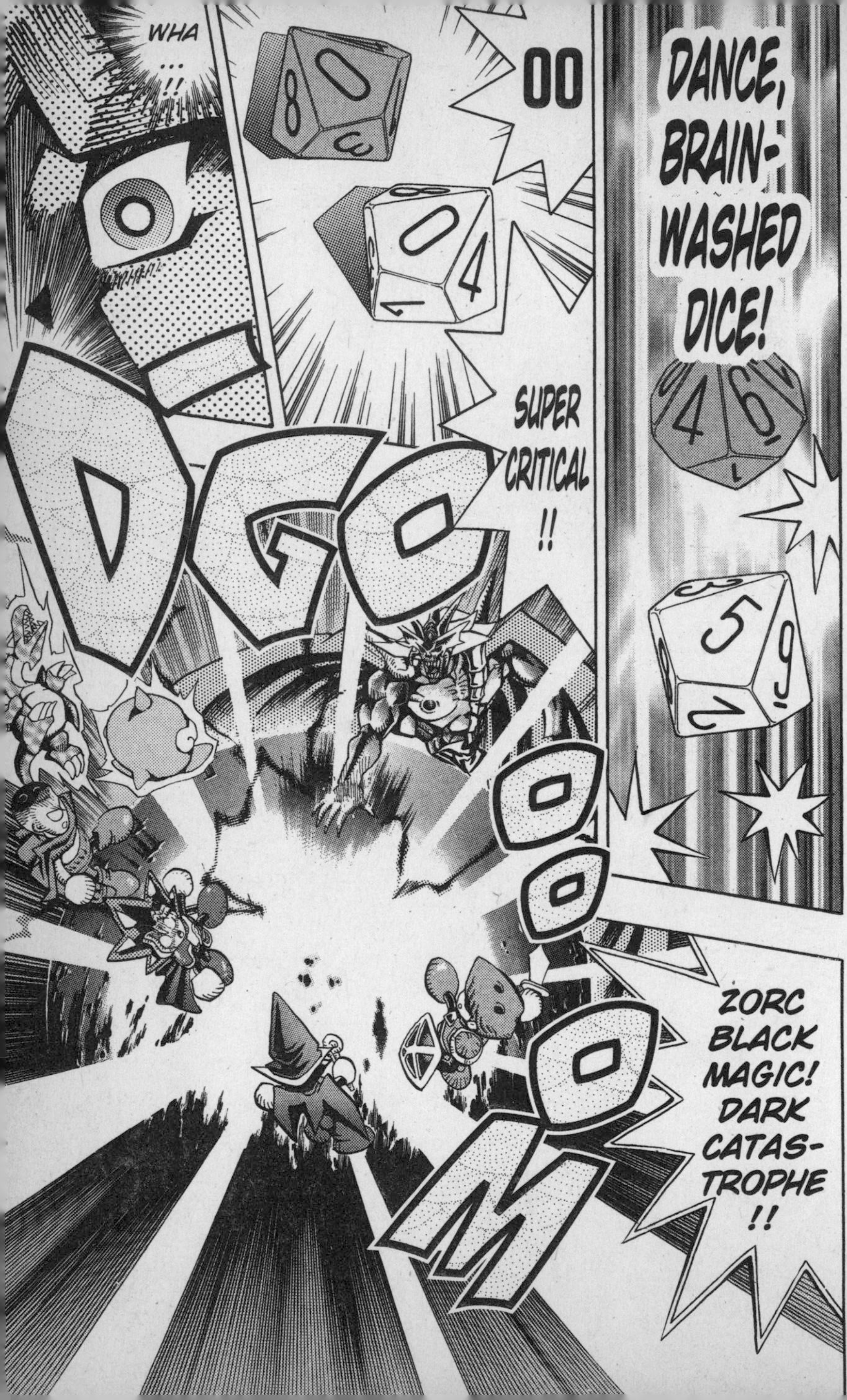
DANCE, BRAIN-WASHED DICE!
00
SUPER CRITICAL !!
WHA ... !!
DGOOOOM
ZORC BLACK MAGIC! DARK CATASTROPHE !!

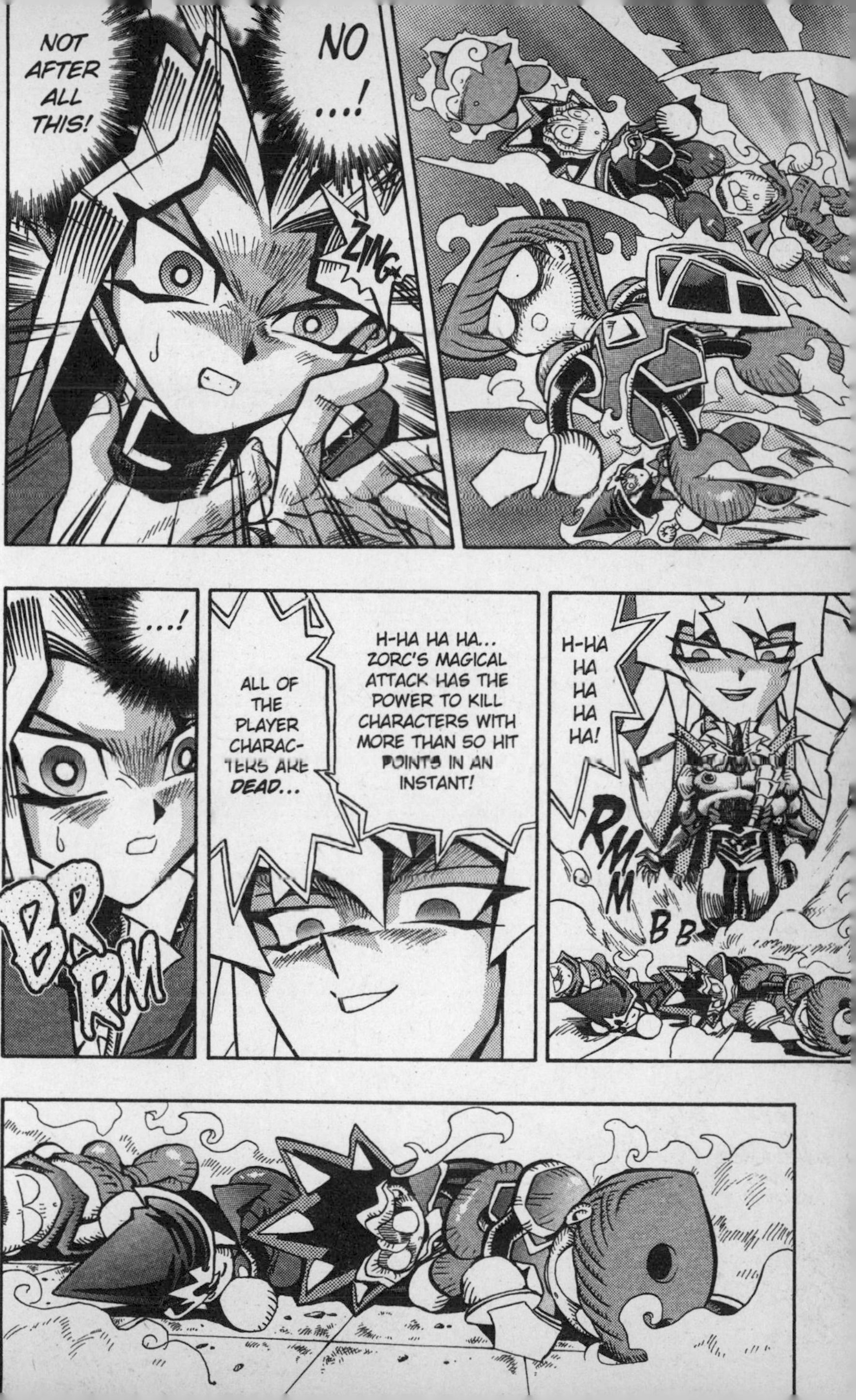
NO ...!
NOT AFTER ALL THIS!
ZING
H-HA HA HA HA HA HA!
RMMM
BB
H-HA HA HA... ZORC'S MAGICAL ATTACK HAS THE POWER TO KILL CHARACTERS WITH MORE THAN 50 HIT POINTS IN AN INSTANT!
ALL OF THE PLAYER CHARAC-TERS ARE DEAD...
...!
BBRM

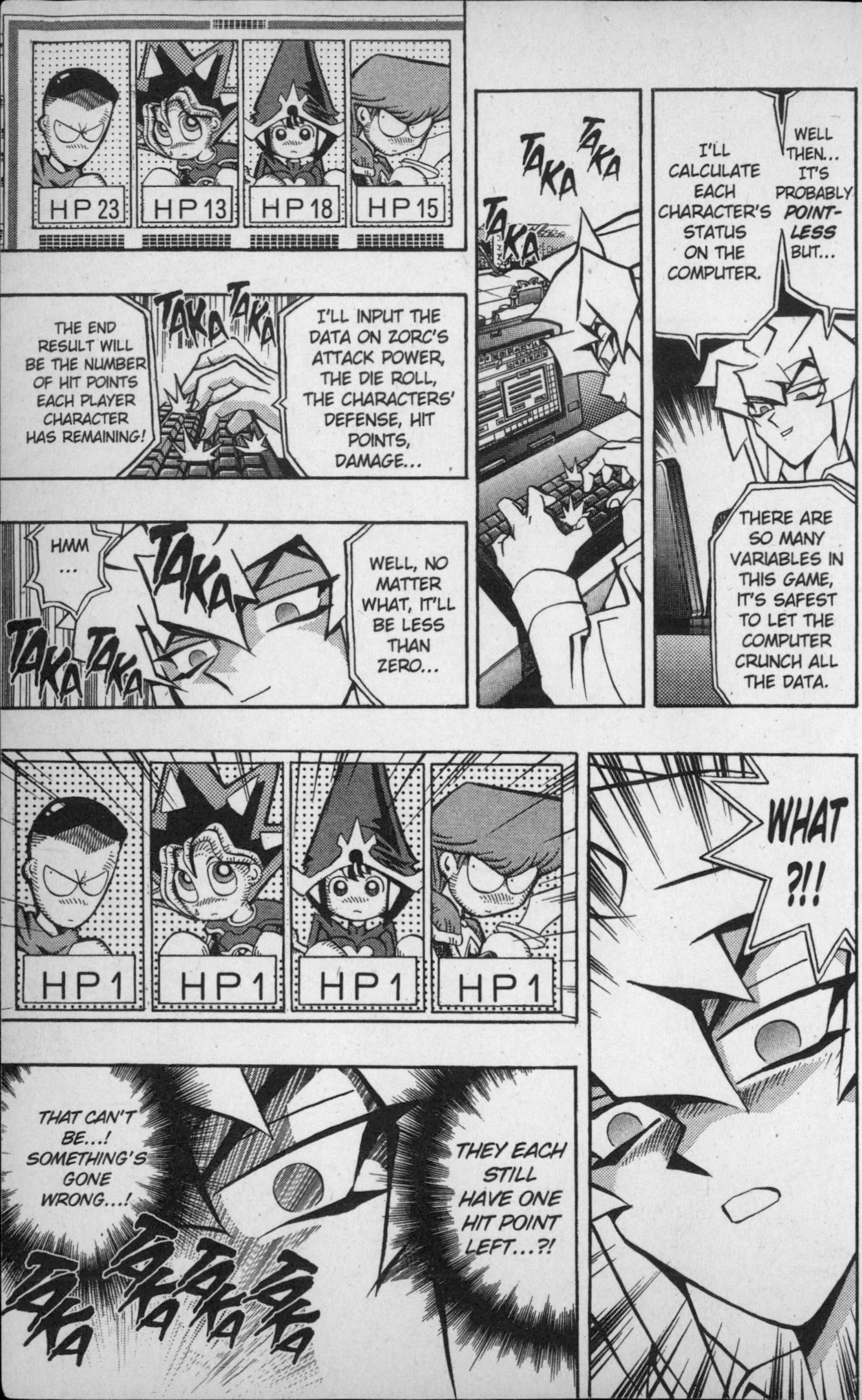
HP 23
HP 13
HP 18
HP 15
WELL THEN... IT'S PROBABLY POINTLESS BUT...
I'LL CALCULATE EACH CHARACTER'S STATUS ON THE COMPUTER.
THERE ARE SO MANY VARIABLES IN THIS GAME, IT'S SAFEST TO LET THE COMPUTER CRUNCH ALL THE DATA.
TAKA TAKA
TAKA
I'LL INPUT THE DATA ON ZORC'S ATTACK POWER, THE DIE ROLL, THE CHARACTERS' DEFENSE, HIT POINTS, DAMAGE...
TAKA TAKA
THE END RESULT WILL BE THE NUMBER OF HIT POINTS EACH PLAYER CHARACTER HAS REMAINING!
WELL, NO MATTER WHAT, IT'LL BE LESS THAN ZERO...
TAKA
HMM...
TAKA TAKA
WHAT?!!
HP 1
HP 1
HP 1
HP 1
THEY EACH STILL HAVE ONE HIT POINT LEFT...?!
THAT CAN'T BE...! SOMETHING'S GONE WRONG...!
TAKA TAKA TAKA TAKA

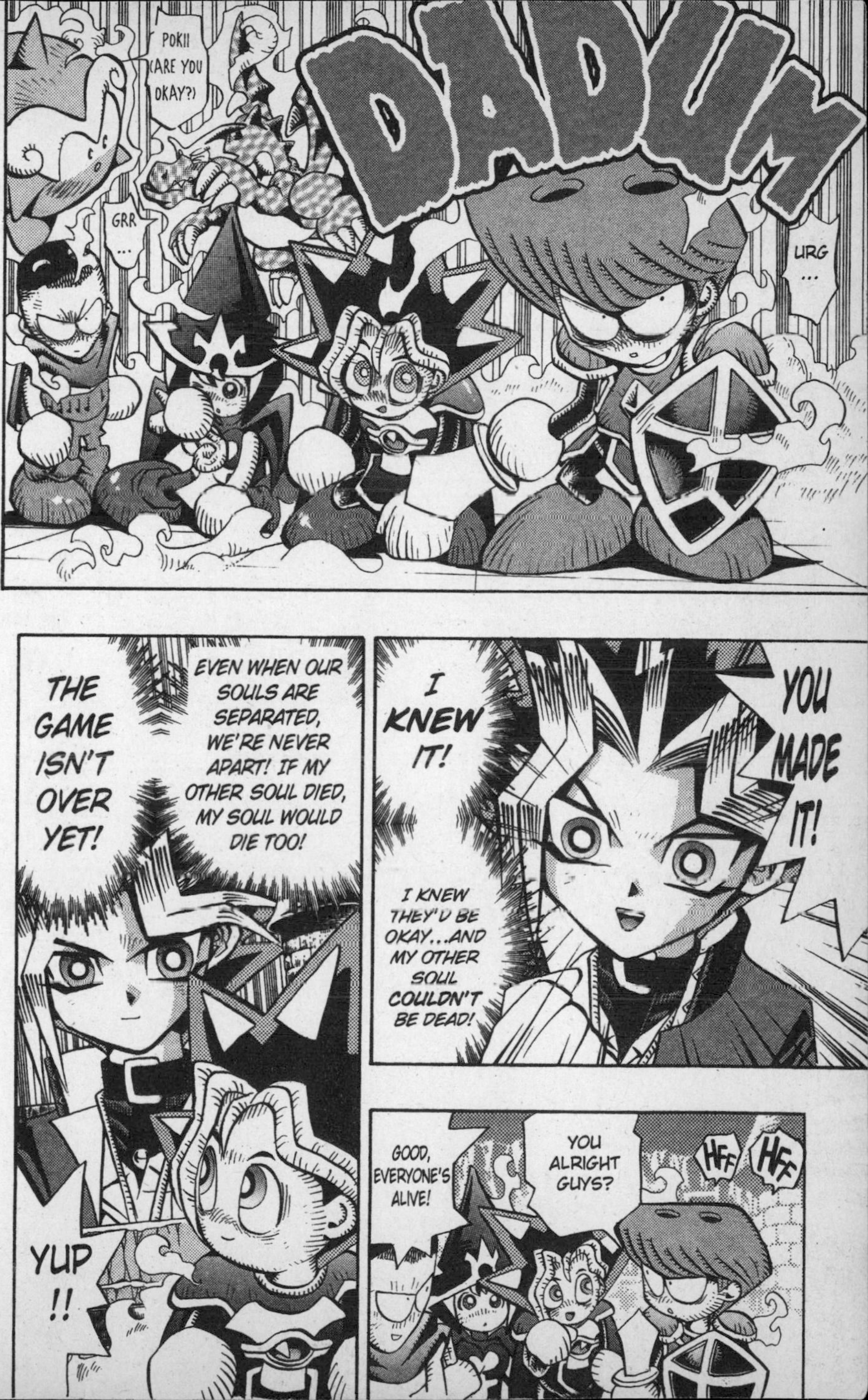
DADUM
URG...
POKII (ARE YOU OKAY?!)
GRR...
YOU MADE IT!
I KNEW IT!
I KNEW THEY'D BE OKAY...AND MY OTHER SOUL COULDN'T BE DEAD!
HFF HFF
YOU ALRIGHT GUYS?
GOOD, EVERYONE'S ALIVE!
EVEN WHEN OUR SOULS ARE SEPARATED, WE'RE NEVER APART! IF MY OTHER SOUL DIED, MY SOUL WOULD DIE TOO!
THE GAME ISN'T OVER YET!
YUP!!

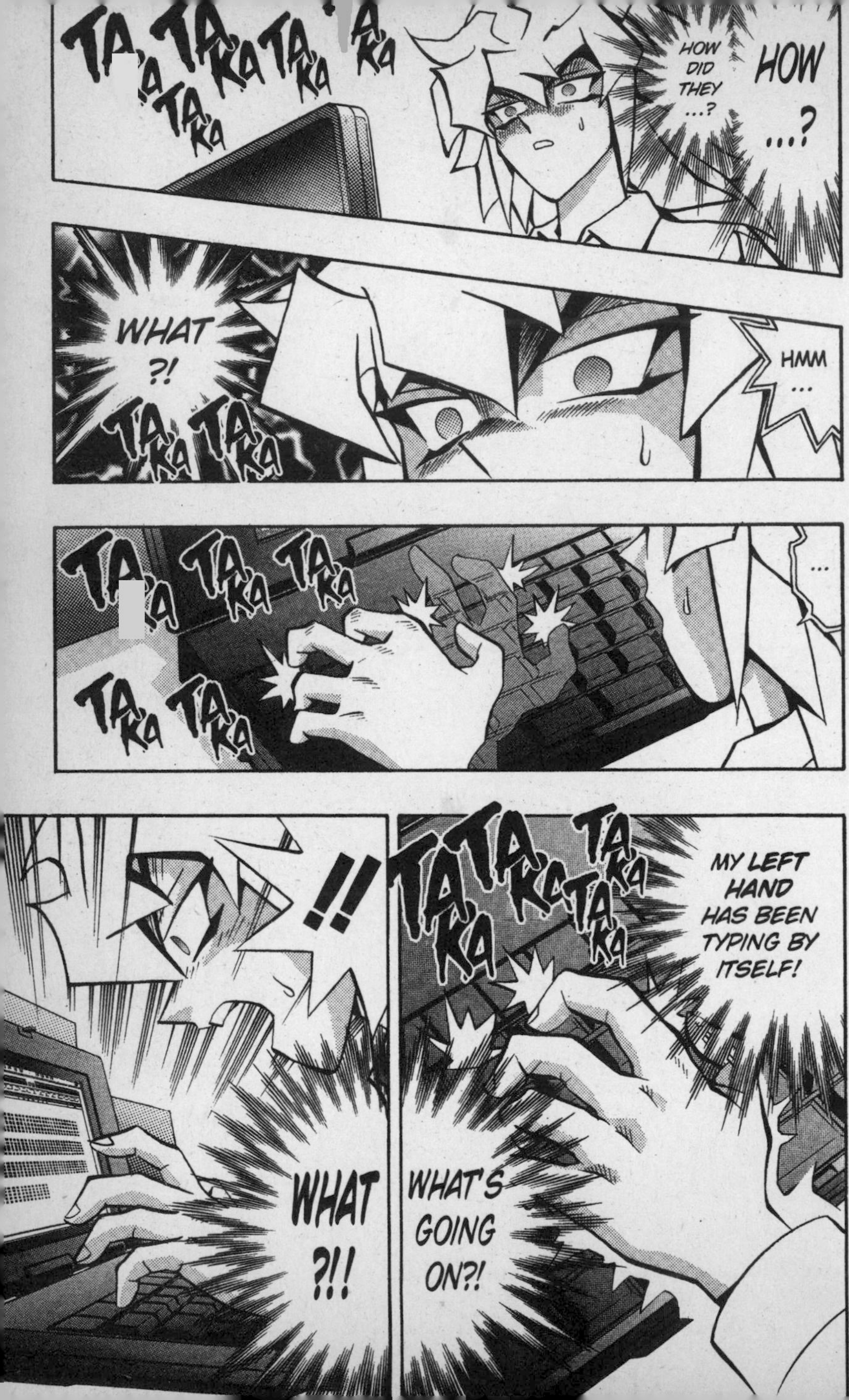
HOW ...?
HOW DID THEY ...?
TA KA TA KA TA KA TA KA TA KA
HMM ...
WHAT ?!
TA KA TA KA
...
TA KA TA KA TA KA
TA KA TA KA
MY LEFT HAND HAS BEEN TYPING BY ITSELF!
TA TA KA KA TA KA TA KA
WHAT'S GOING ON?!
!!
WHAT ?!!

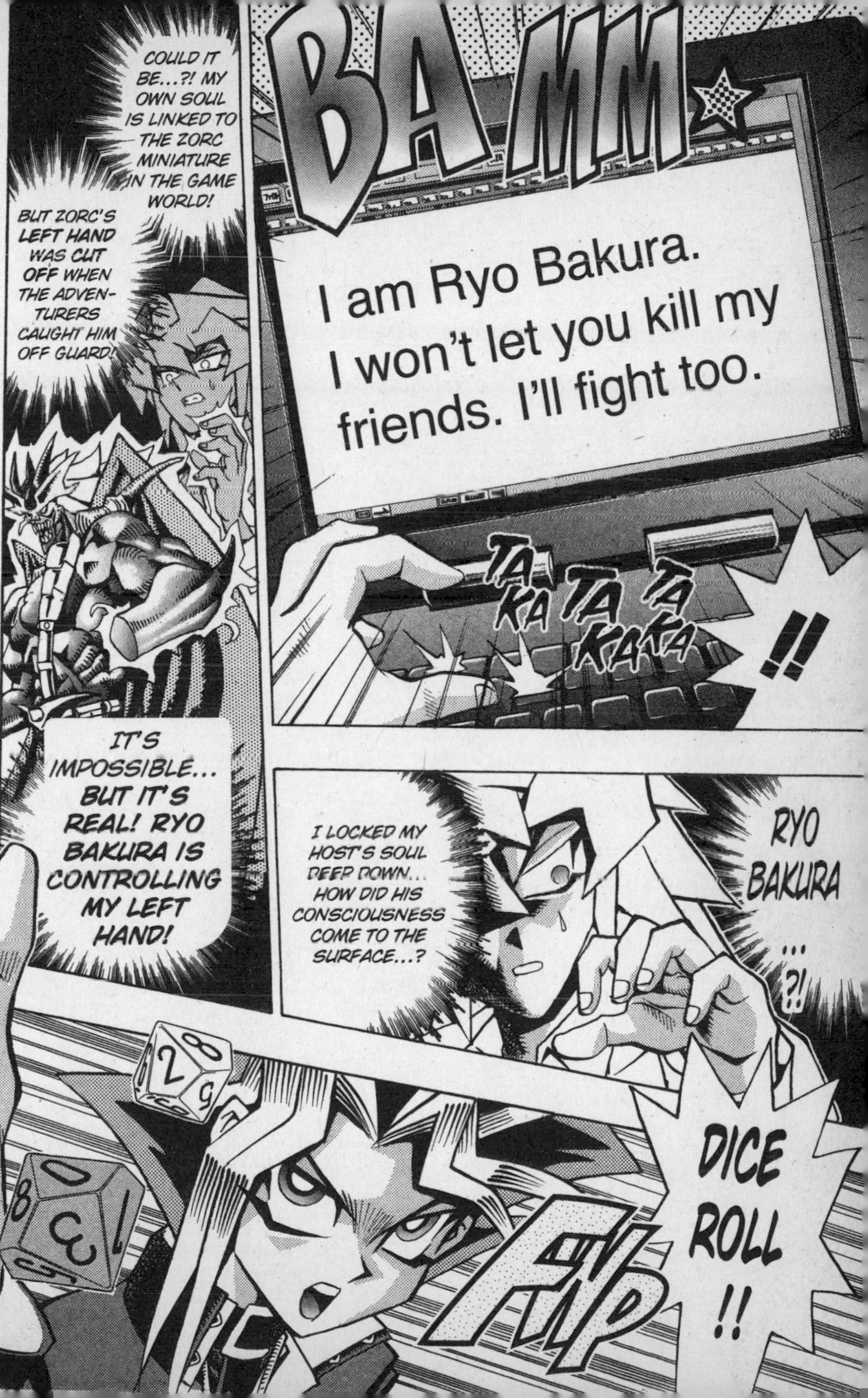
BAMM
I am Ryo Bakura.
I won't let you kill my friends. I'll fight too.
TAKA TAKA TAKA!!
RYO BAKURA...?!
I LOCKED MY HOST'S SOUL DEEP DOWN... HOW DID HIS CONSCIOUSNESS COME TO THE SURFACE...?
COULD IT BE...?! MY OWN SOUL IS LINKED TO THE ZORC MINIATURE IN THE GAME WORLD!
BUT ZORC'S LEFT HAND WAS CUT OFF WHEN THE ADVENTURERS CAUGHT HIM OFF GUARD!
IT'S IMPOSSIBLE... BUT IT'S REAL! RYO BAKURA IS CONTROLLING MY LEFT HAND!
DICE ROLL!!
FLIP

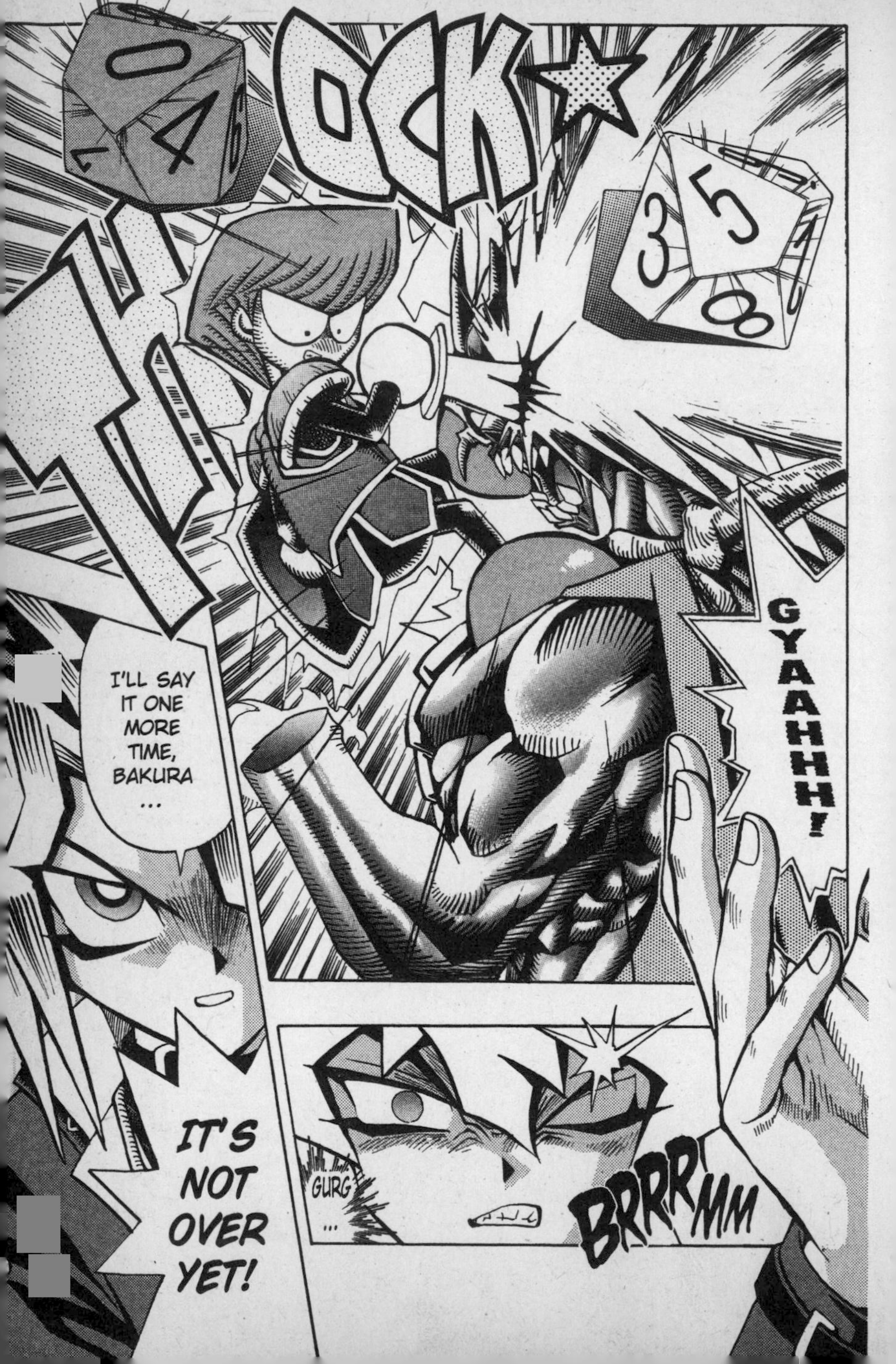

OCK☆
GYAAHHH!
GURG ...
BRRRMM
I'LL SAY IT ONE MORE TIME, BAKURA ...
IT'S NOT OVER YET!

Duel 57: Millennium Enemy 8: Fight! Fight!

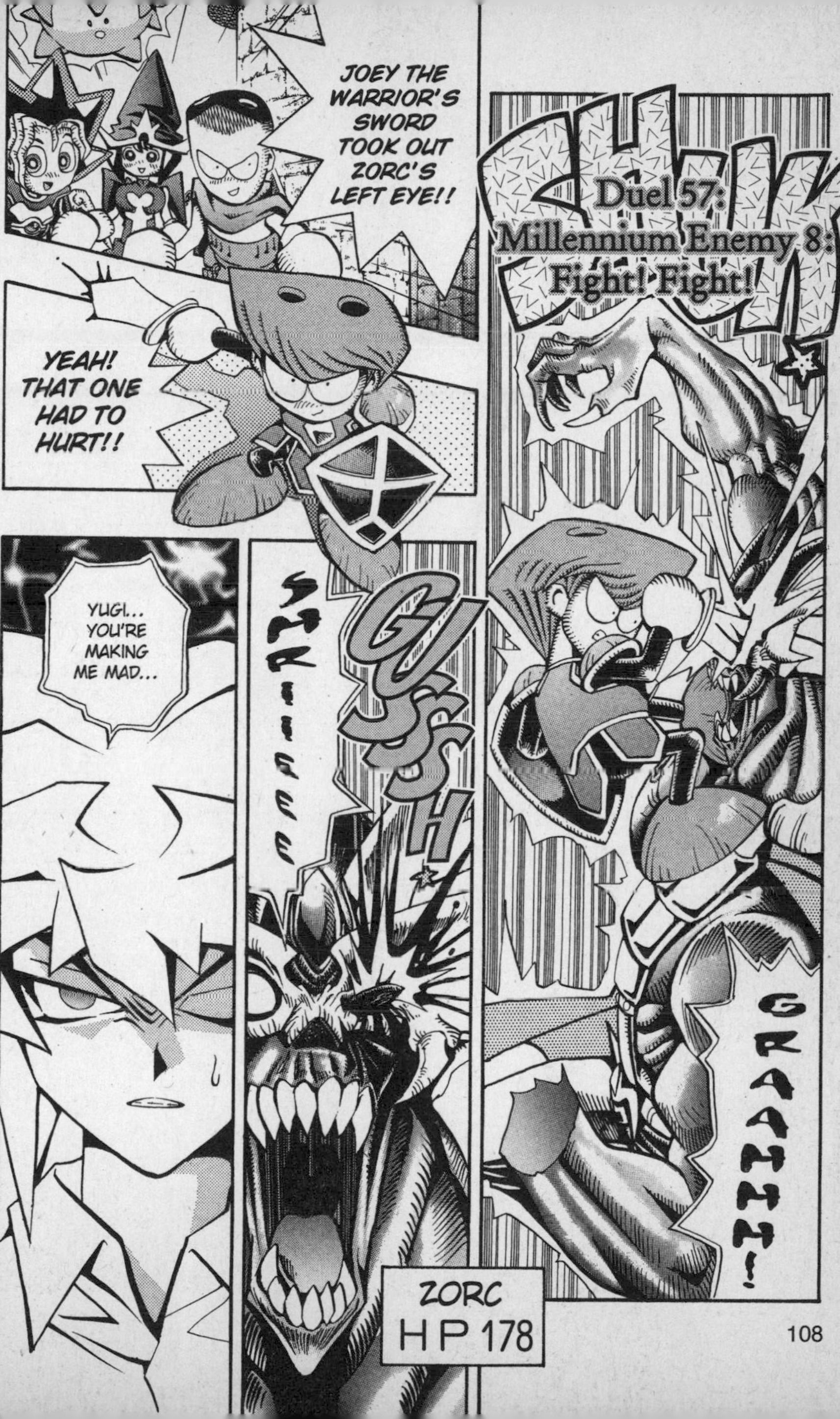
GRAAHHH!
JOEY THE WARRIOR'S SWORD TOOK OUT ZORC'S LEFT EYE!!
YEAH! THAT ONE HAD TO HURT!!
GUSH
ZORC
HP 178
YUGI... YOU'RE MAKING ME MAD...

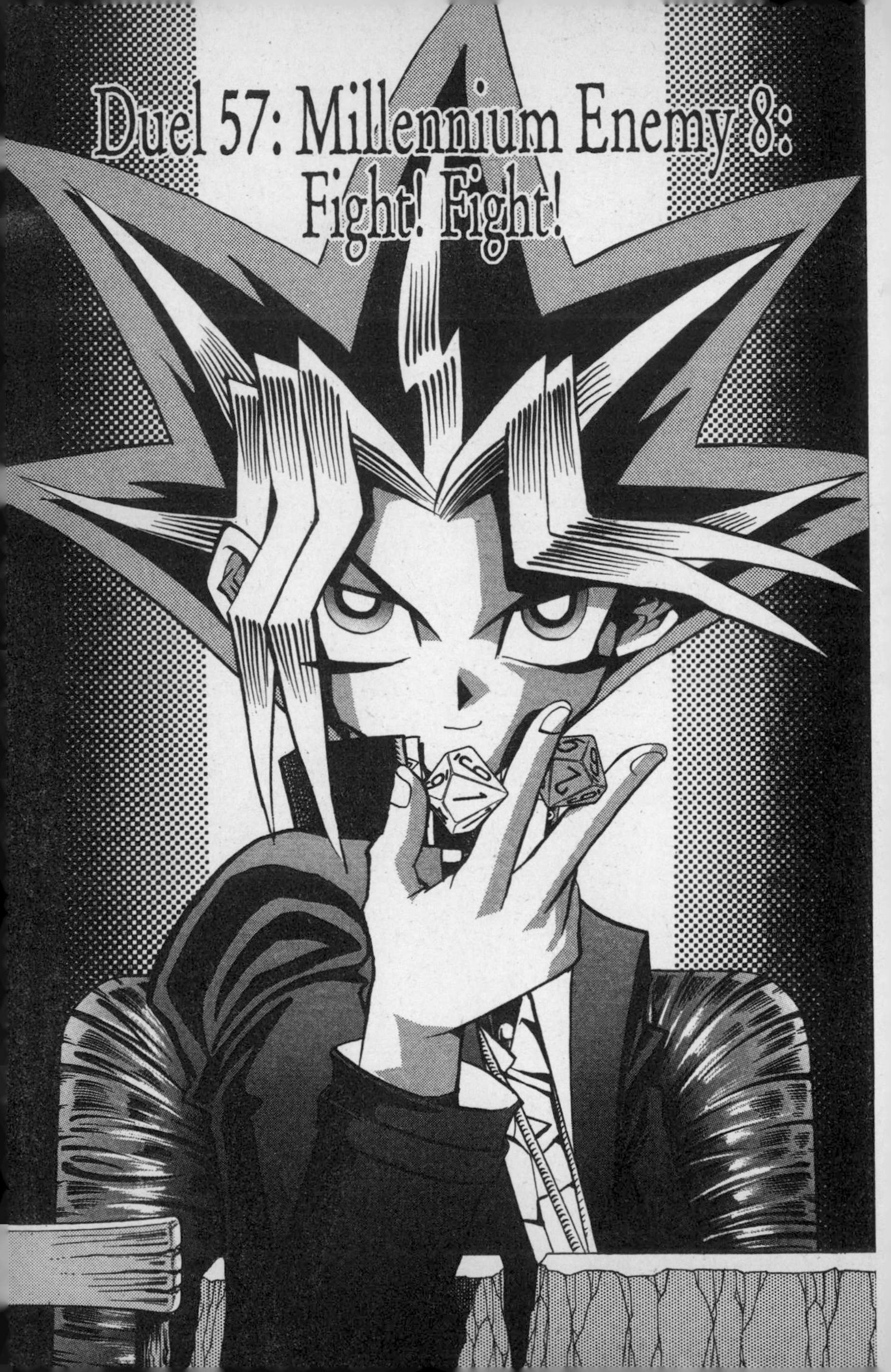
Duel 57: Millennium Enemy 8:
Fight! Fight!

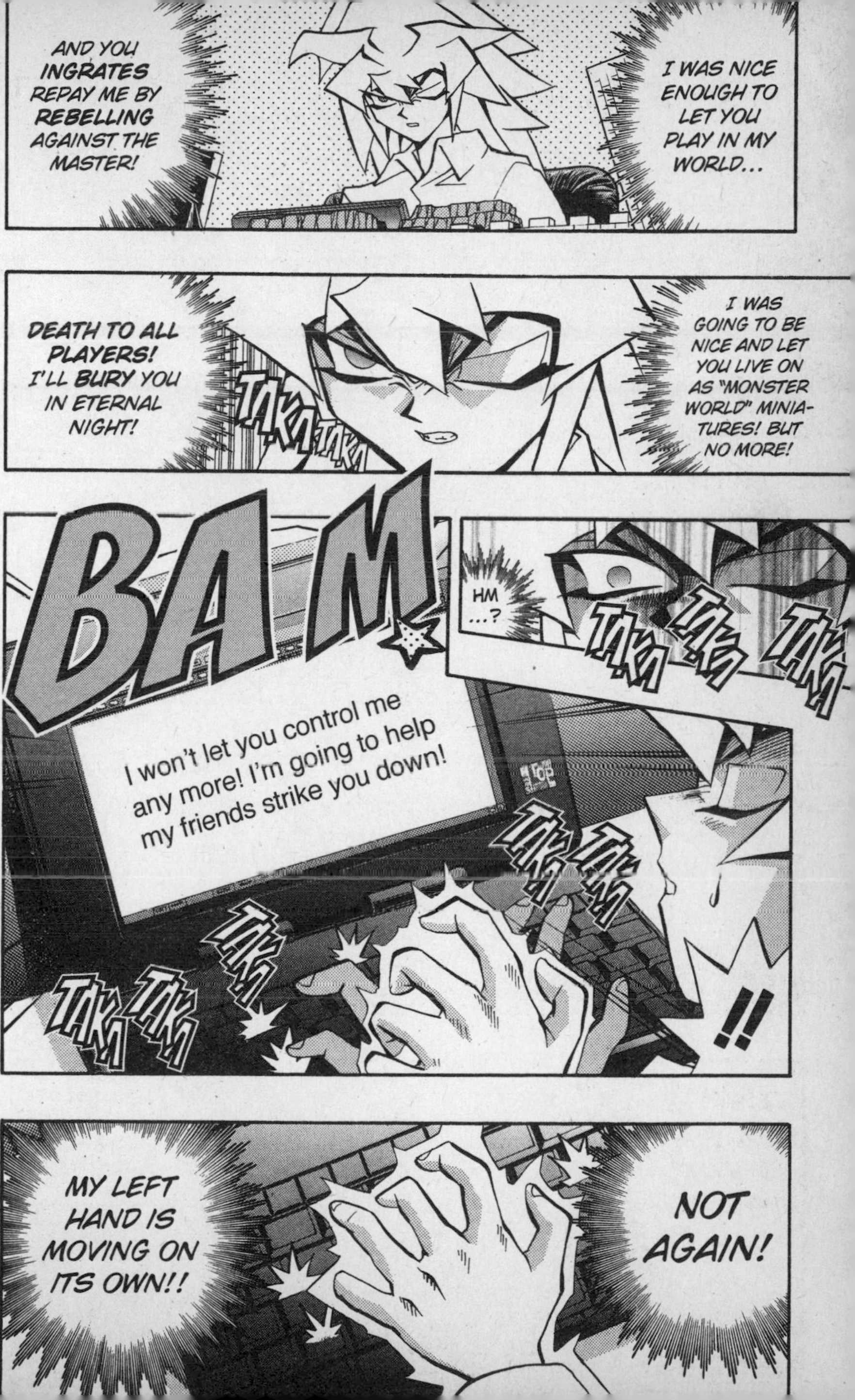
I WAS NICE ENOUGH TO LET YOU PLAY IN MY WORLD...
AND YOU INGRATES REPAY ME BY REBELLING AGAINST THE MASTER!
I WAS GOING TO BE NICE AND LET YOU LIVE ON AS "MONSTER WORLD" MINIATURES! BUT NO MORE!
TAKA TAKA
DEATH TO ALL PLAYERS! I'LL BURY YOU IN ETERNAL NIGHT!
HM ...?
TAKA TAKA TAKA
BAM
I won't let you control me any more! I'm going to help my friends strike you down!
TAKA TAKA TAKA TAKA TAKA
!!
NOT AGAIN!
MY LEFT HAND IS MOVING ON ITS OWN!!

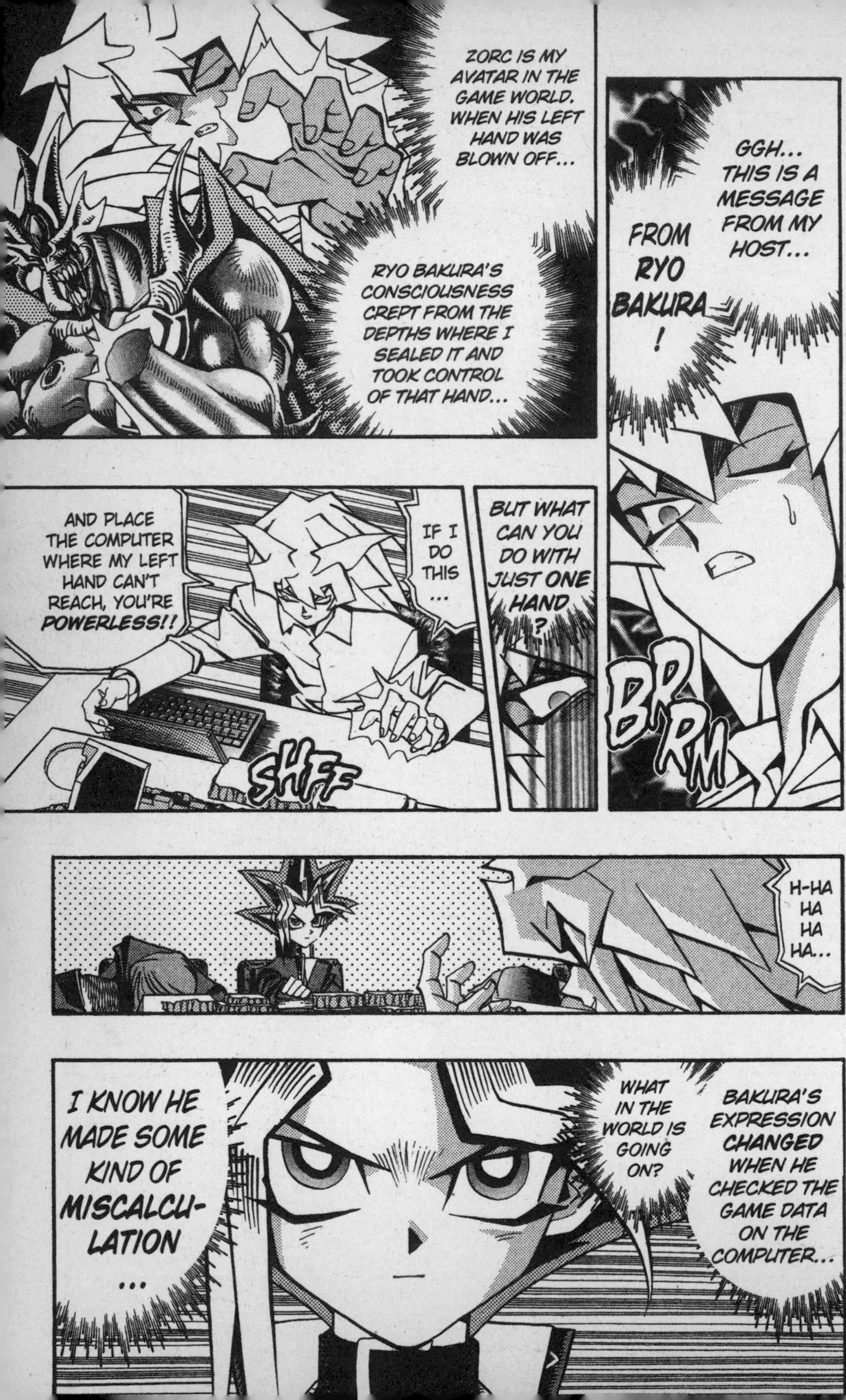

GGH... THIS IS A MESSAGE FROM MY HOST...
FROM RYO BAKURA!
BRRM
ZORC IS MY AVATAR IN THE GAME WORLD. WHEN HIS LEFT HAND WAS BLOWN OFF...
RYO BAKURA'S CONSCIOUSNESS CREPT FROM THE DEPTHS WHERE I SEALED IT AND TOOK CONTROL OF THAT HAND...
BUT WHAT CAN YOU DO WITH JUST ONE HAND?
IF I DO THIS...
AND PLACE THE COMPUTER WHERE MY LEFT HAND CAN'T REACH, YOU'RE POWERLESS!!
SHFF
H-HA HA HA HA...
BAKURA'S EXPRESSION CHANGED WHEN HE CHECKED THE GAME DATA ON THE COMPUTER...
WHAT IN THE WORLD IS GOING ON?
I KNOW HE MADE SOME KIND OF MISCALCULATION...

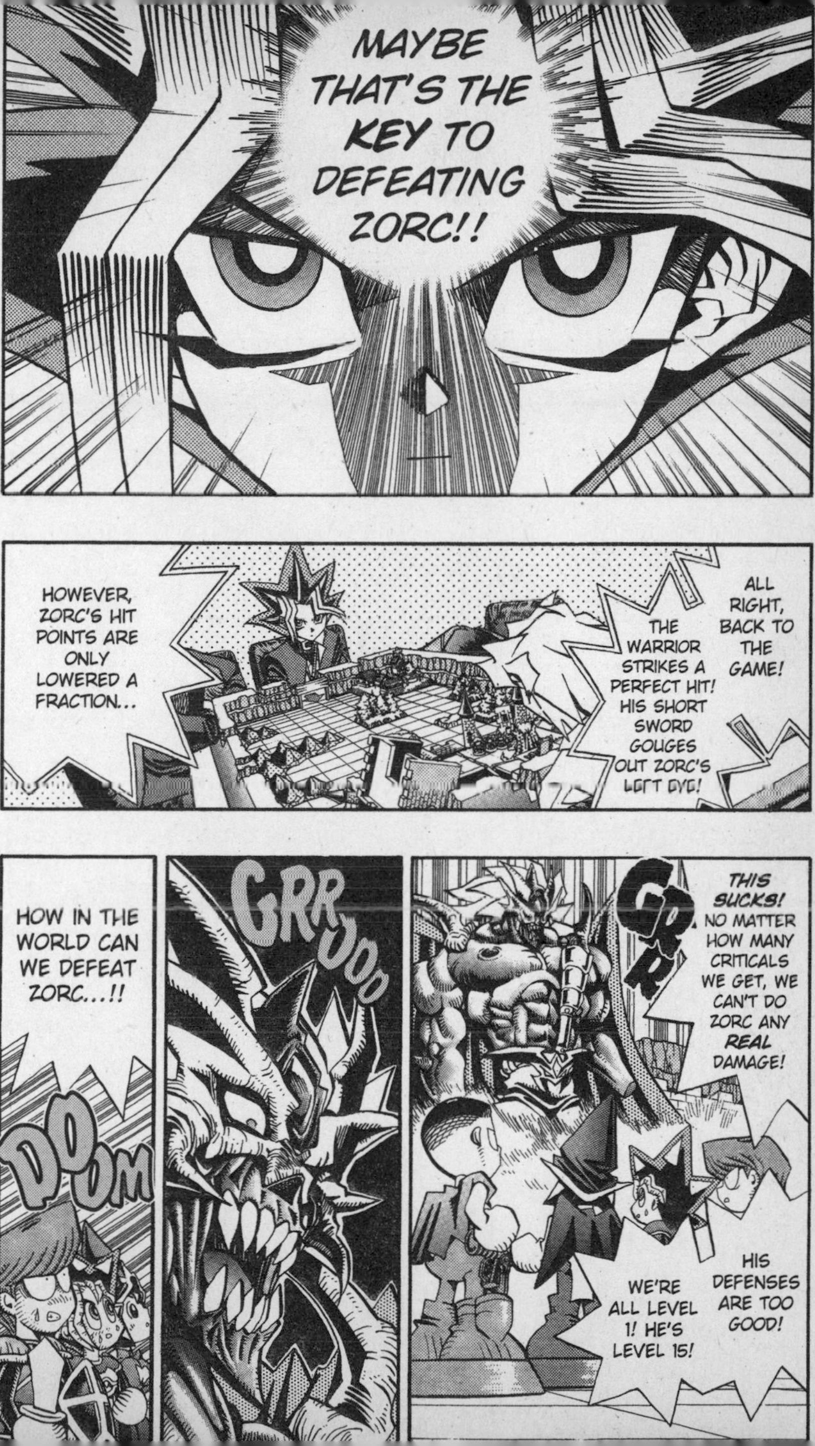
MAYBE THAT'S THE KEY TO DEFEATING ZORC!!
ALL RIGHT, BACK TO THE GAME!
THE WARRIOR STRIKES A PERFECT HIT! HIS SHORT SWORD GOUGES OUT ZORC'S LEFT EYE!
HOWEVER, ZORC'S HIT POINTS ARE ONLY LOWERED A FRACTION...
GRR
THIS SUCKS! NO MATTER HOW MANY CRITICALS WE GET, WE CAN'T DO ZORC ANY REAL DAMAGE!
HIS DEFENSES ARE TOO GOOD!
WE'RE ALL LEVEL 1! HE'S LEVEL 15!
GRROOO
HOW IN THE WORLD CAN WE DEFEAT ZORC...!!
DOOM

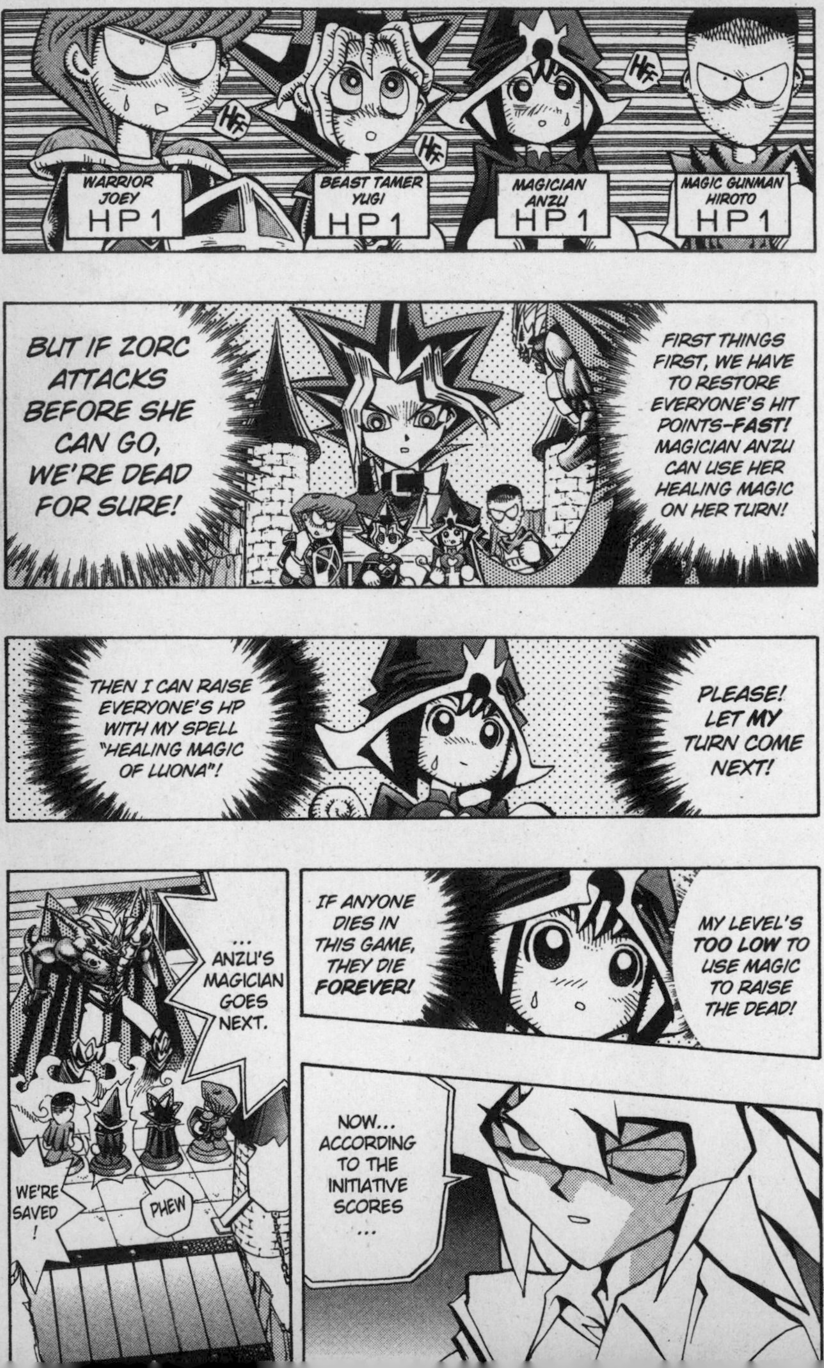
MAGIC GUNMAN HIROTO HP 1
HFF
MAGICIAN ANZU HP 1
HFF
HFF
BEAST TAMER YUGI HP 1
WARRIOR JOEY HP 1
FIRST THINGS FIRST, WE HAVE TO RESTORE EVERYONE'S HIT POINTS–FAST! MAGICIAN ANZU CAN USE HER HEALING MAGIC ON HER TURN!
BUT IF ZORC ATTACKS BEFORE SHE CAN GO, WE'RE DEAD FOR SURE!
PLEASE! LET MY TURN COME NEXT!
THEN I CAN RAISE EVERYONE'S HP WITH MY SPELL "HEALING MAGIC OF LUONA"!
MY LEVEL'S TOO LOW TO USE MAGIC TO RAISE THE DEAD!
IF ANYONE DIES IN THIS GAME, THEY DIE FOREVER!
NOW... ACCORDING TO THE INITIATIVE SCORES...
... ANZU'S MAGICIAN GOES NEXT.
PHEW
WE'RE SAVED!

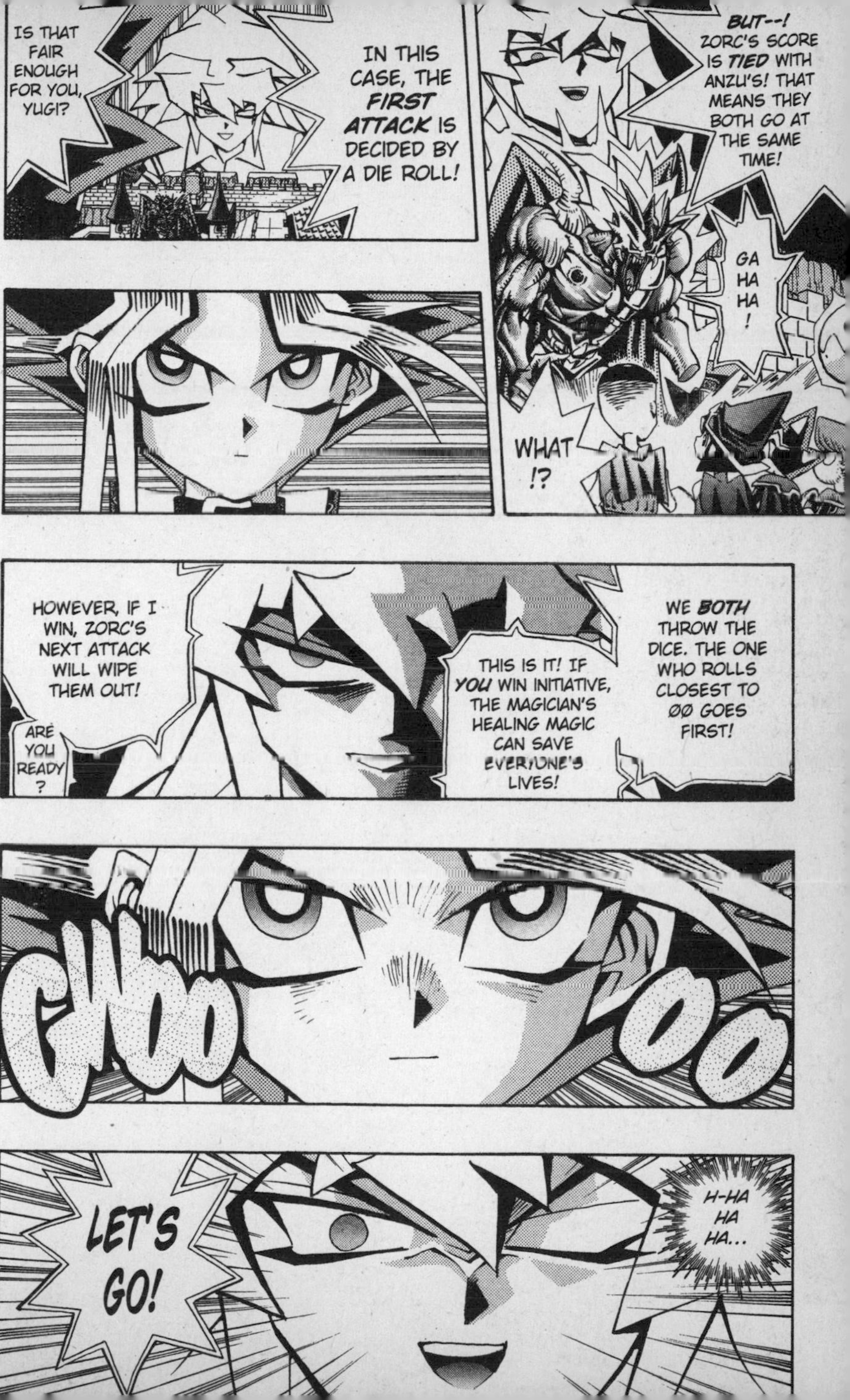
BUT--! ZORC'S SCORE IS TIED WITH ANZU'S! THAT MEANS THEY BOTH GO AT THE SAME TIME!
GA HA HA!
WHAT!?
IN THIS CASE, THE FIRST ATTACK IS DECIDED BY A DIE ROLL!
IS THAT FAIR ENOUGH FOR YOU, YUGI?
WE BOTH THROW THE DICE. THE ONE WHO ROLLS CLOSEST TO ØØ GOES FIRST!
THIS IS IT! IF YOU WIN INITIATIVE, THE MAGICIAN'S HEALING MAGIC CAN SAVE EVERYONE'S LIVES!
HOWEVER, IF I WIN, ZORC'S NEXT ATTACK WILL WIPE THEM OUT!
ARE YOU READY?
GWOOOO
H-HA HA HA...
LET'S GO!

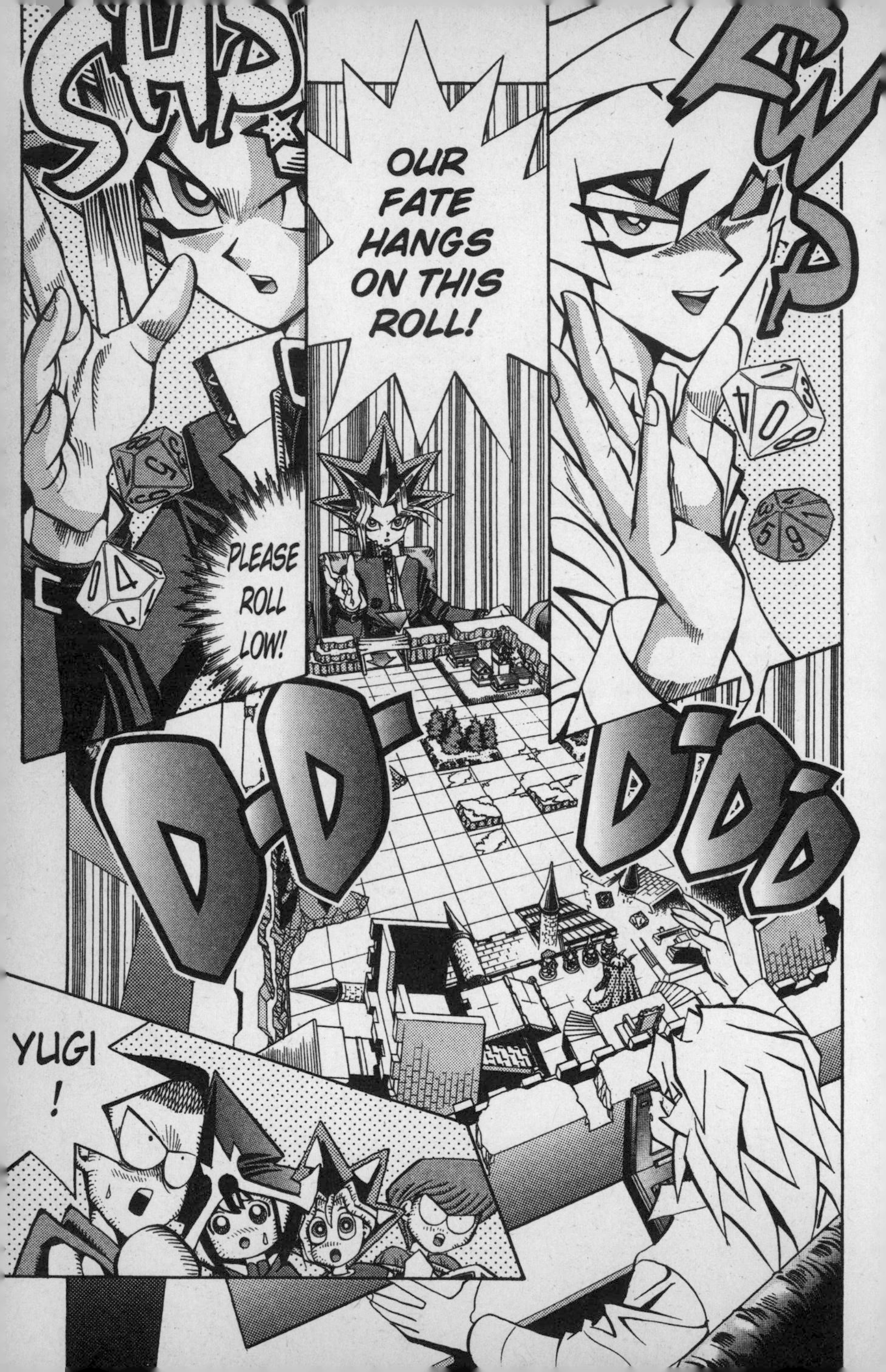
FWP
OUR FATE HANGS ON THIS ROLL!
SHP
PLEASE ROLL LOW!
YUGI!

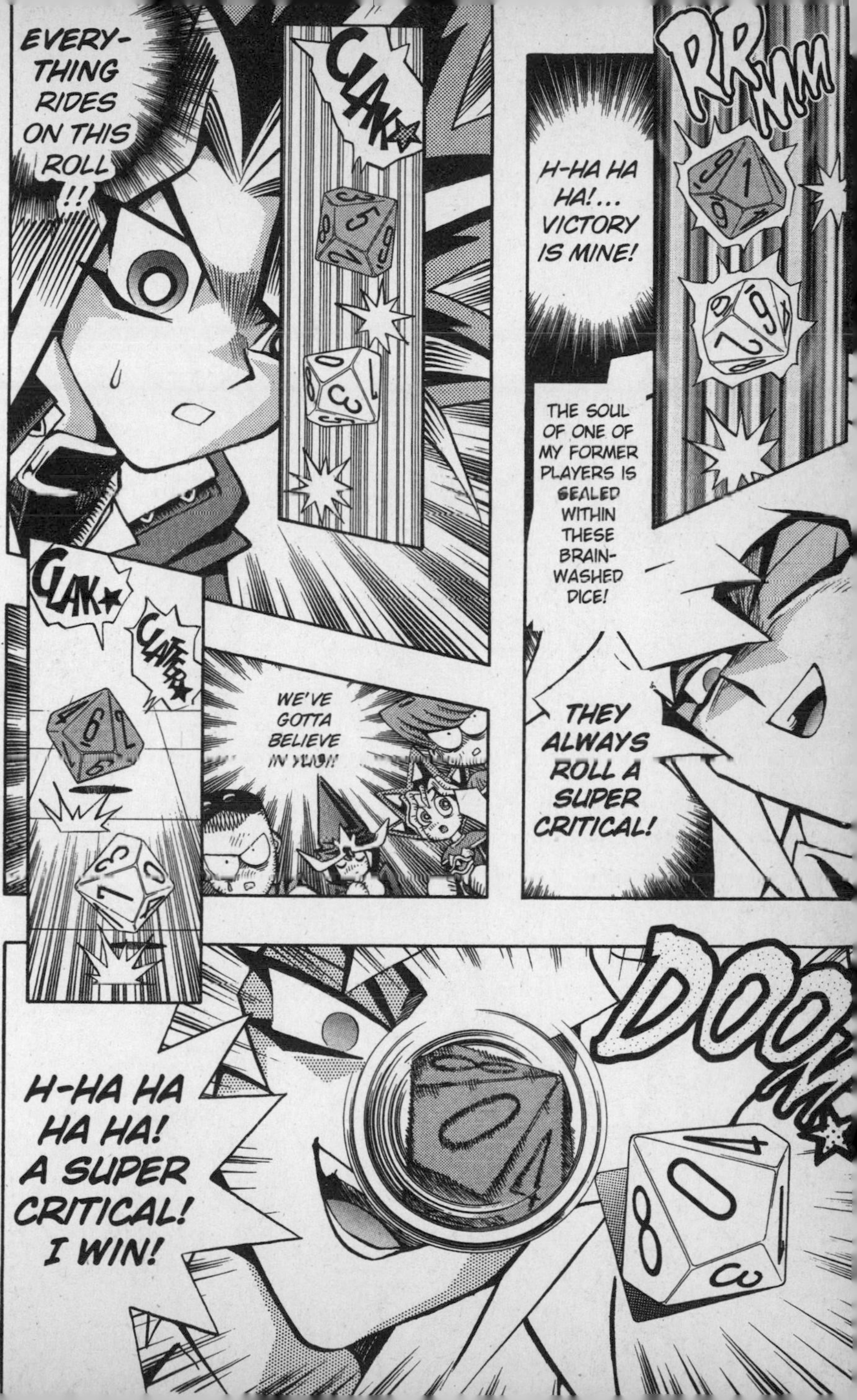
RRMM
H-HA HA HA!... VICTORY IS MINE!
CLAK★
EVERY-THING RIDES ON THIS ROLL!!
THE SOUL OF ONE OF MY FORMER PLAYERS IS SEALED WITHIN THESE BRAIN-WASHED DICE!
THEY ALWAYS ROLL A SUPER CRITICAL!
WE'VE GOTTA BELIEVE
CLAK★
CLATTER★
DOOM
H-HA HA HA HA! A SUPER CRITICAL! I WIN!

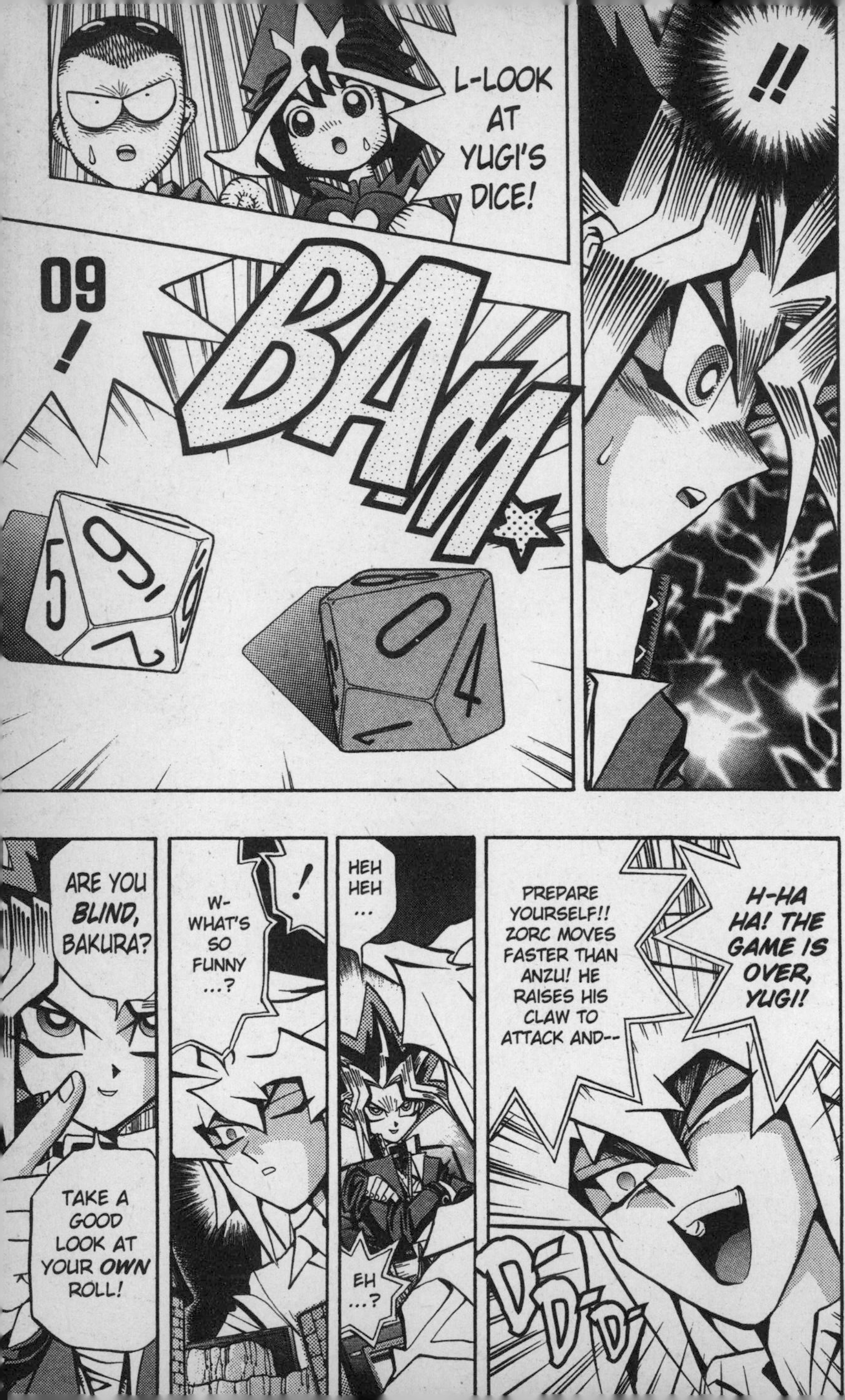
!!
L-LOOK AT YUGI'S DICE!
09 !
BAM
H-HA HA! THE GAME IS OVER, YUGI!
PREPARE YOURSELF!! ZORC MOVES FASTER THAN ANZU! HE RAISES HIS CLAW TO ATTACK AND--
D-D-D-
HEH HEH ...
EH ...?
!
W-WHAT'S SO FUNNY ...?
ARE YOU *BLIND*, BAKURA?
TAKE A GOOD LOOK AT YOUR *OWN* ROLL!

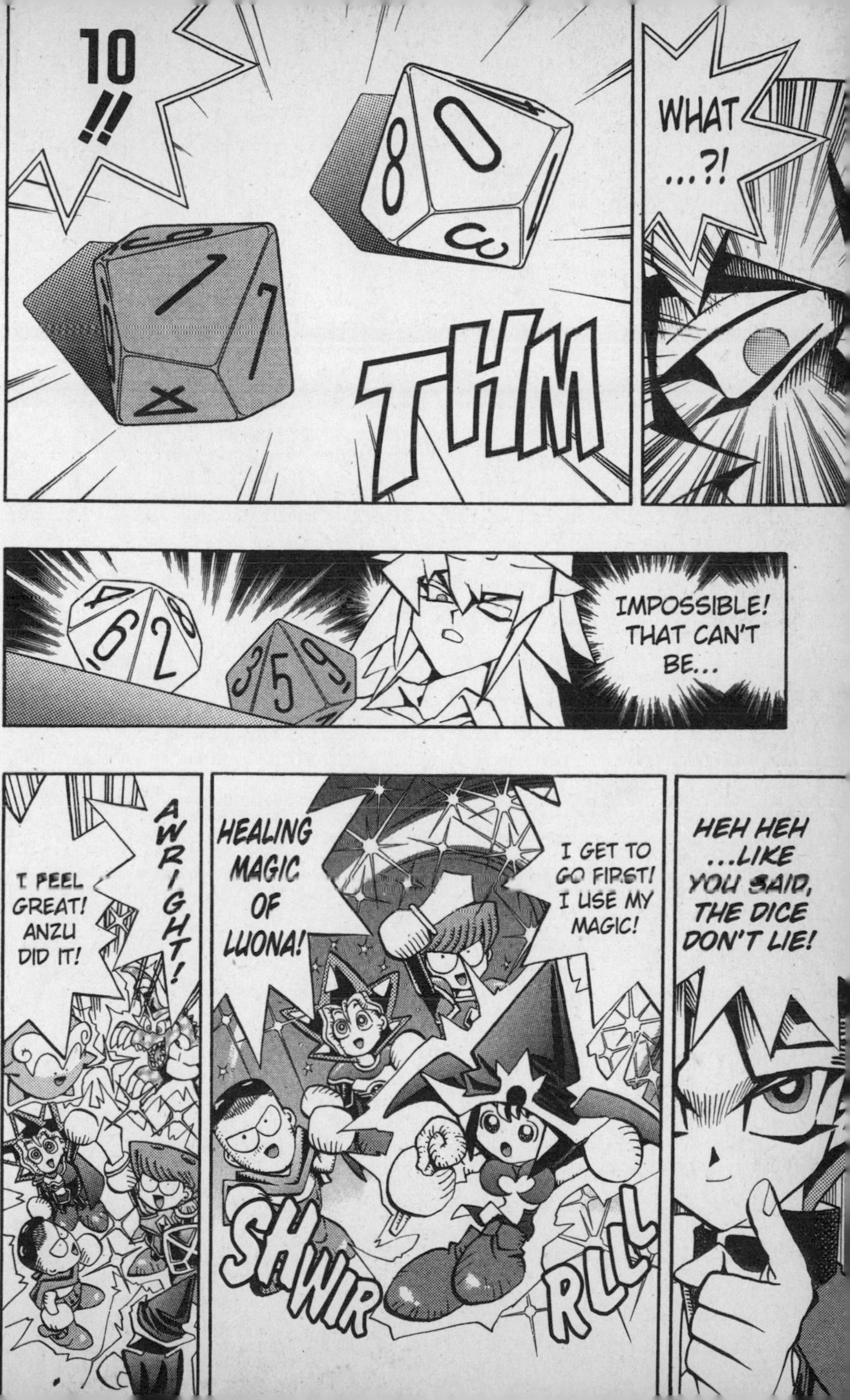
WHAT ...?!
10 !!
THM
IMPOSSIBLE! THAT CAN'T BE...
HEH HEH ...LIKE YOU SAID, THE DICE DON'T LIE!
I GET TO GO FIRST! I USE MY MAGIC!
HEALING MAGIC OF LUONA!
SHWIRRLLL
AWRIGHT!
I FEEL GREAT! ANZU DID IT!

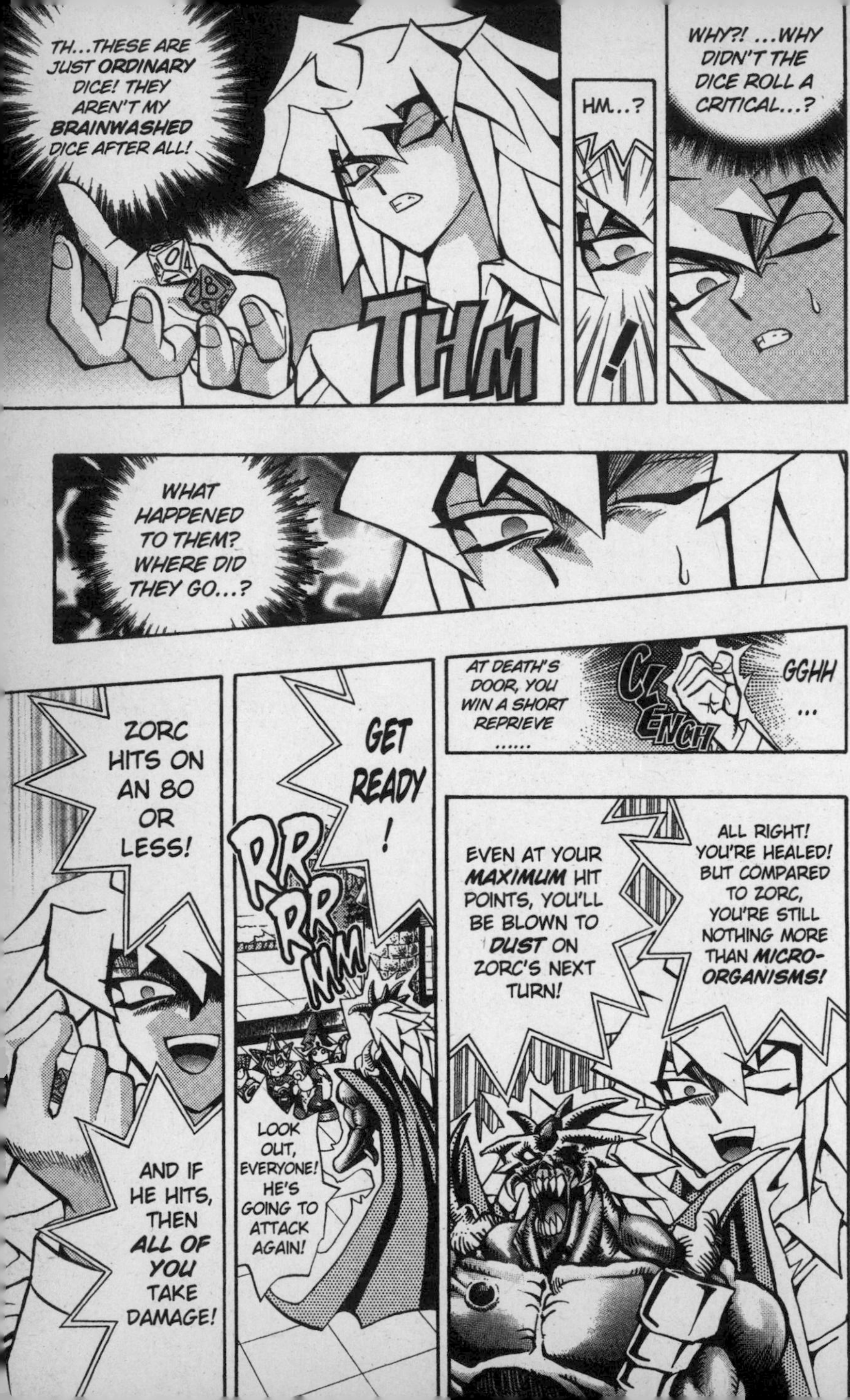
WHY?! ...WHY DIDN'T THE DICE ROLL A CRITICAL...?
HM...?
!
TH...THESE ARE JUST ORDINARY DICE! THEY AREN'T MY BRAINWASHED DICE AFTER ALL!
THM
WHAT HAPPENED TO THEM? WHERE DID THEY GO...?
GGHH...
CLENCH
AT DEATH'S DOOR, YOU WIN A SHORT REPRIEVE ......
ALL RIGHT! YOU'RE HEALED! BUT COMPARED TO ZORC, YOU'RE STILL NOTHING MORE THAN MICRO-ORGANISMS!
EVEN AT YOUR MAXIMUM HIT POINTS, YOU'LL BE BLOWN TO DUST ON ZORC'S NEXT TURN!
GET READY!
RRRRMM
LOOK OUT, EVERYONE! HE'S GOING TO ATTACK AGAIN!
ZORC HITS ON AN 80 OR LESS!
AND IF HE HITS, THEN ALL OF YOU TAKE DAMAGE!

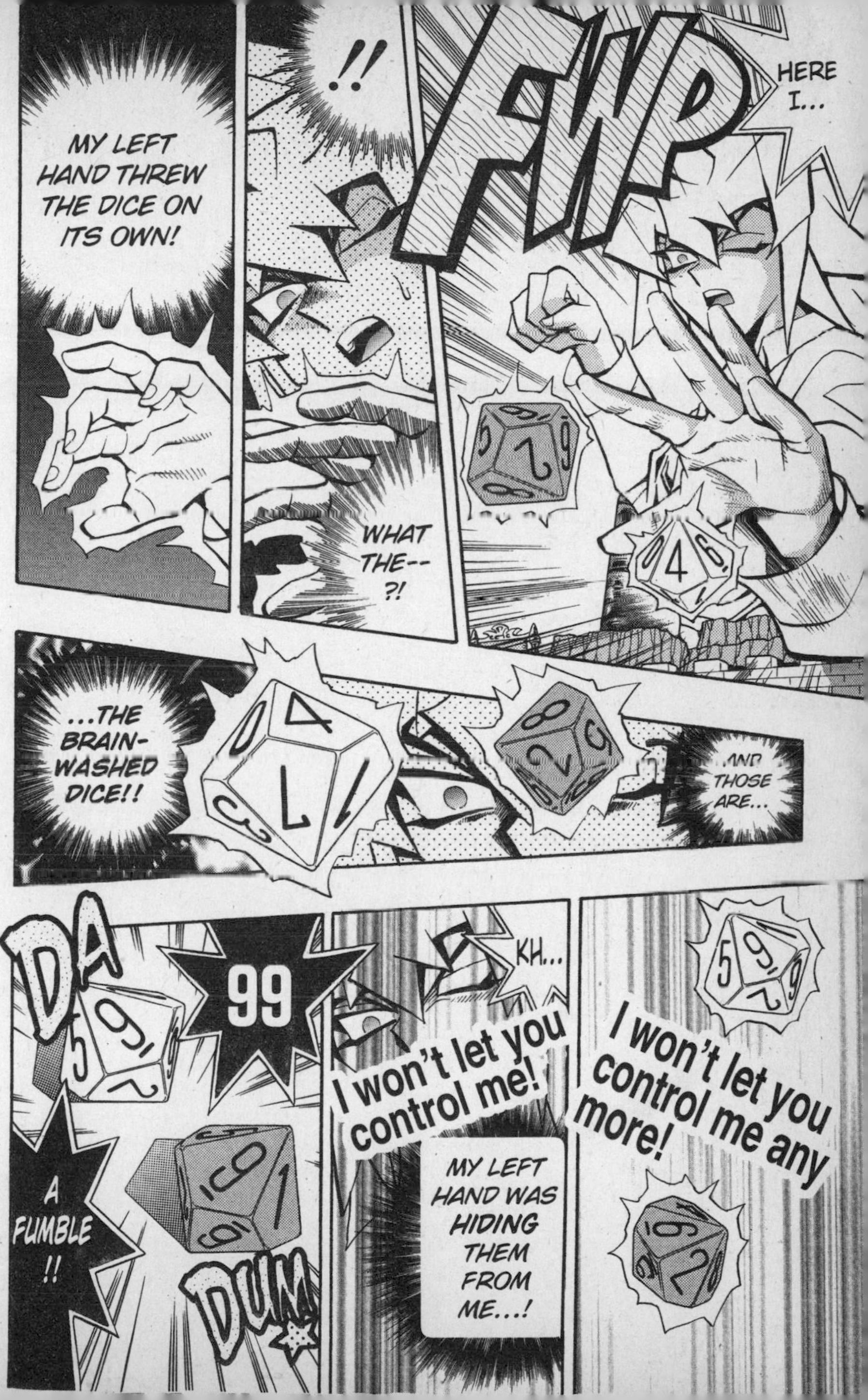
FWP
HERE I...
!!
WHAT THE--?!
MY LEFT HAND THREW THE DICE ON ITS OWN!
AND THOSE ARE...
...THE BRAIN-WASHED DICE!!
I won't let you control me any more!
KH...
I won't let you control me!
MY LEFT HAND WAS HIDING THEM FROM ME...!
DA
99
DUM
A FUMBLE!!

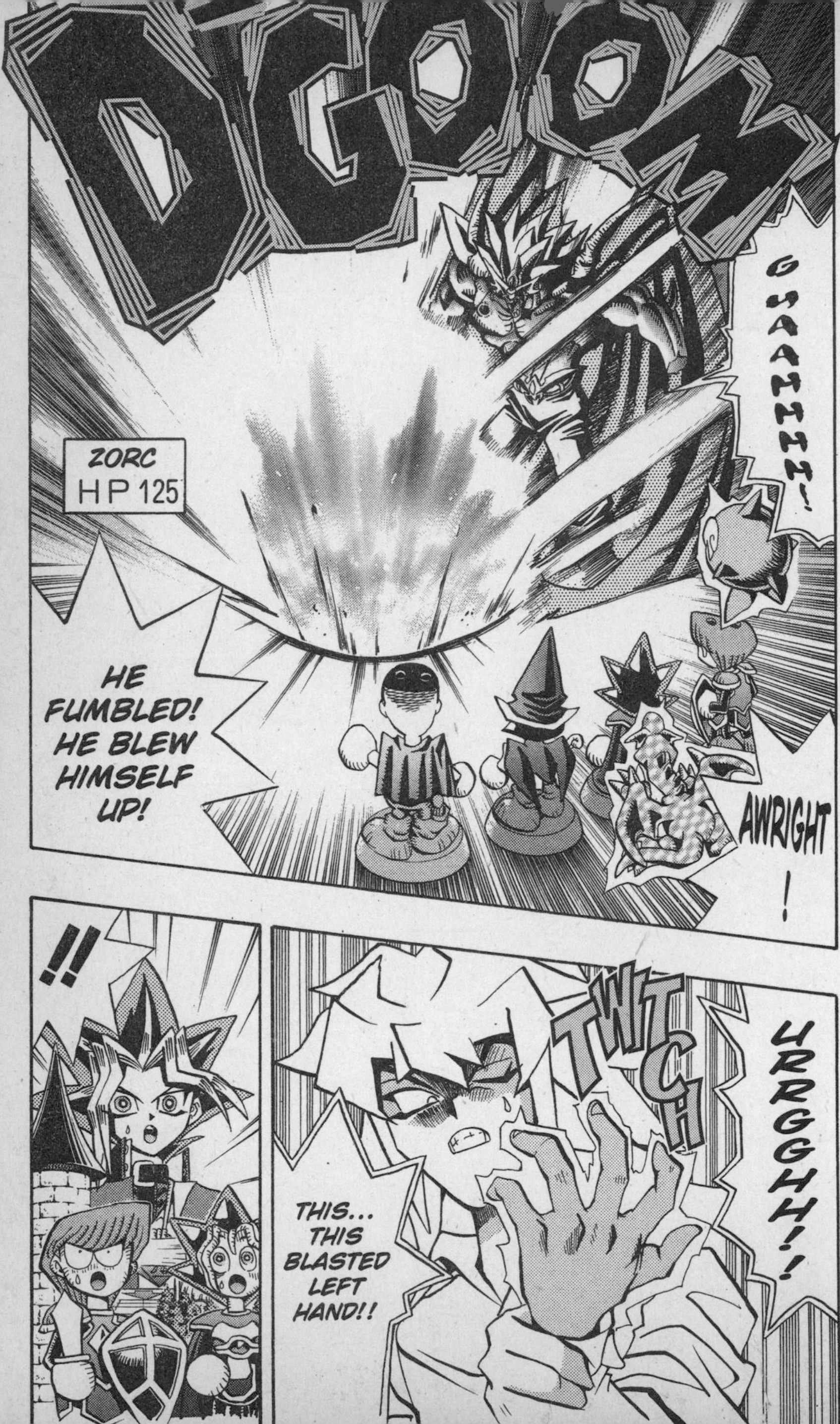
DGOOM
GUAAHHHH!
ZORC
HP 125
AWRIGHT!
HE FUMBLED! HE BLEW HIMSELF UP!
URRGGHH!!
TWITCH
THIS... THIS BLASTED LEFT HAND!!
!!

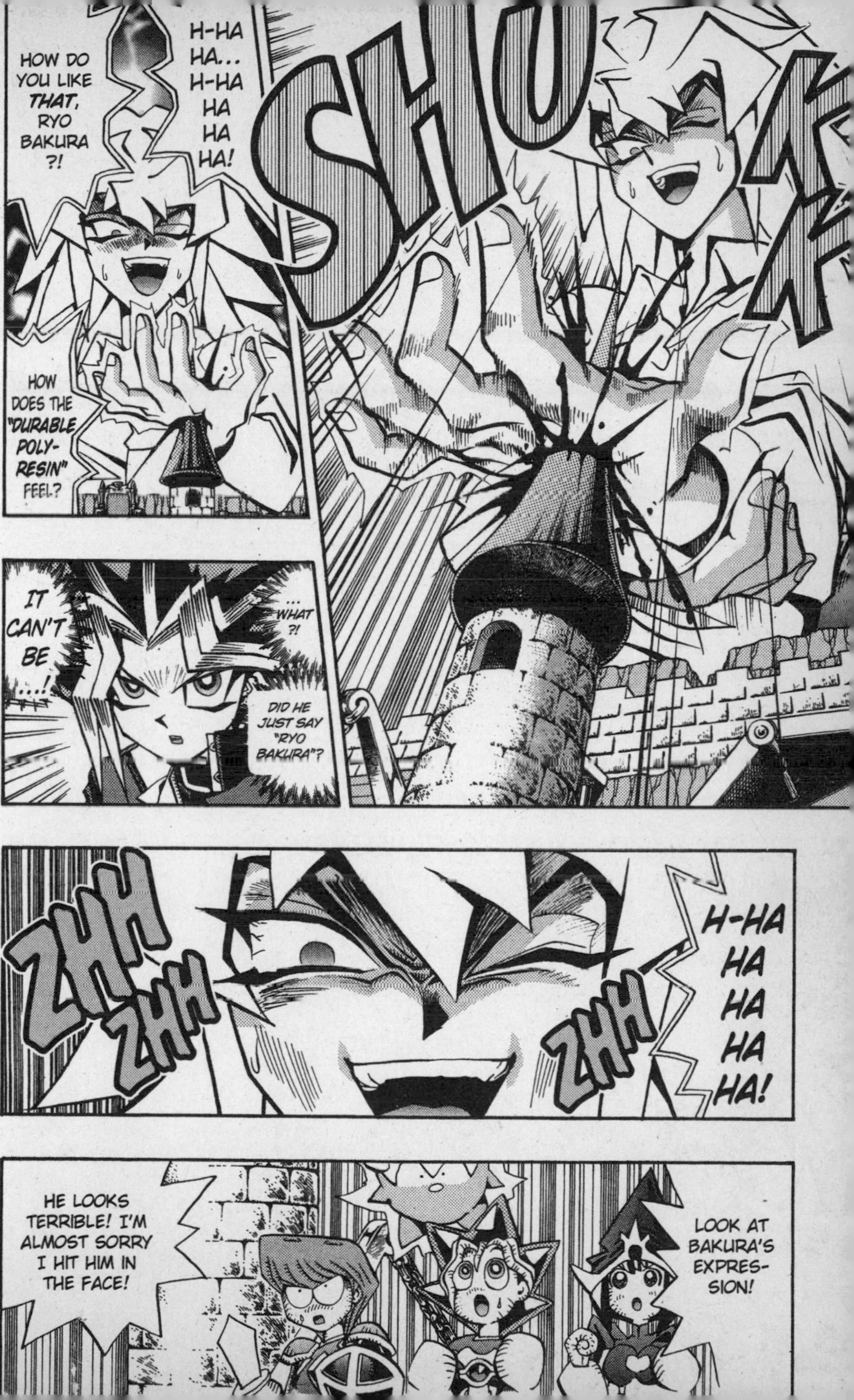
SHUKK
H-HA HA... H-HA HA HA HA!
HOW DO YOU LIKE THAT, RYO BAKURA?!
HOW DOES THE "DURABLE POLY-RESIN" FEEL?
...WHAT?!
IT CAN'T BE...!
DID HE JUST SAY "RYO BAKURA"?
H-HA HA HA HA HA!
ZHH
ZHH ZHH
LOOK AT BAKURA'S EXPRESSION!
HE LOOKS TERRIBLE! I'M ALMOST SORRY I HIT HIM IN THE FACE!

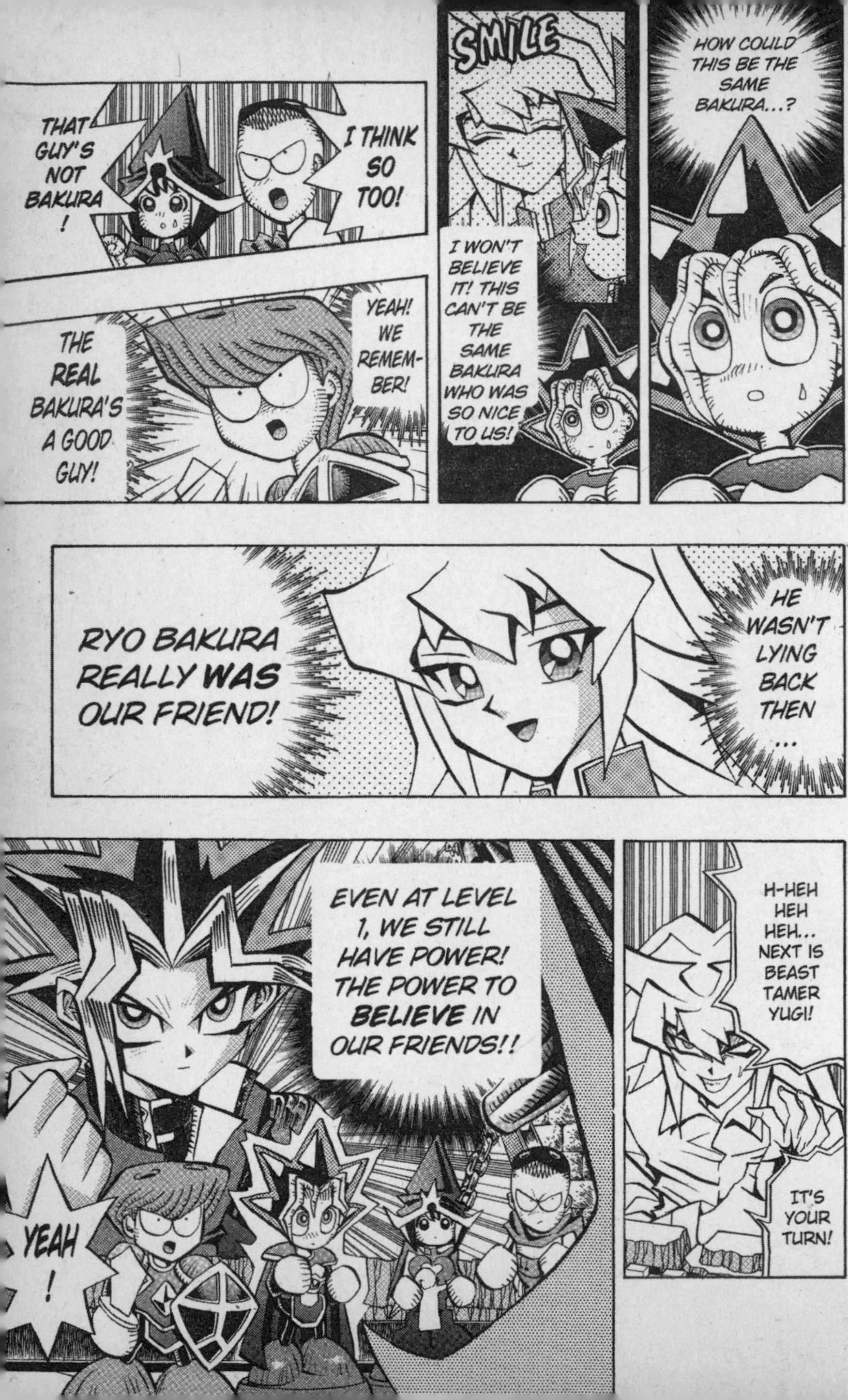
HOW COULD THIS BE THE SAME BAKURA...?
SMILE
I WON'T BELIEVE IT! THIS CAN'T BE THE SAME BAKURA WHO WAS SO NICE TO US!
I THINK SO TOO!
THAT GUY'S NOT BAKURA!
YEAH! WE REMEMBER!
THE REAL BAKURA'S A GOOD GUY!
HE WASN'T LYING BACK THEN...
RYO BAKURA REALLY **WAS** OUR FRIEND!
H-HEH HEH HEH... NEXT IS BEAST TAMER YUGI!
IT'S YOUR TURN!
EVEN AT LEVEL 1, WE STILL HAVE POWER! THE POWER TO **BELIEVE** IN OUR FRIENDS!!
YEAH!

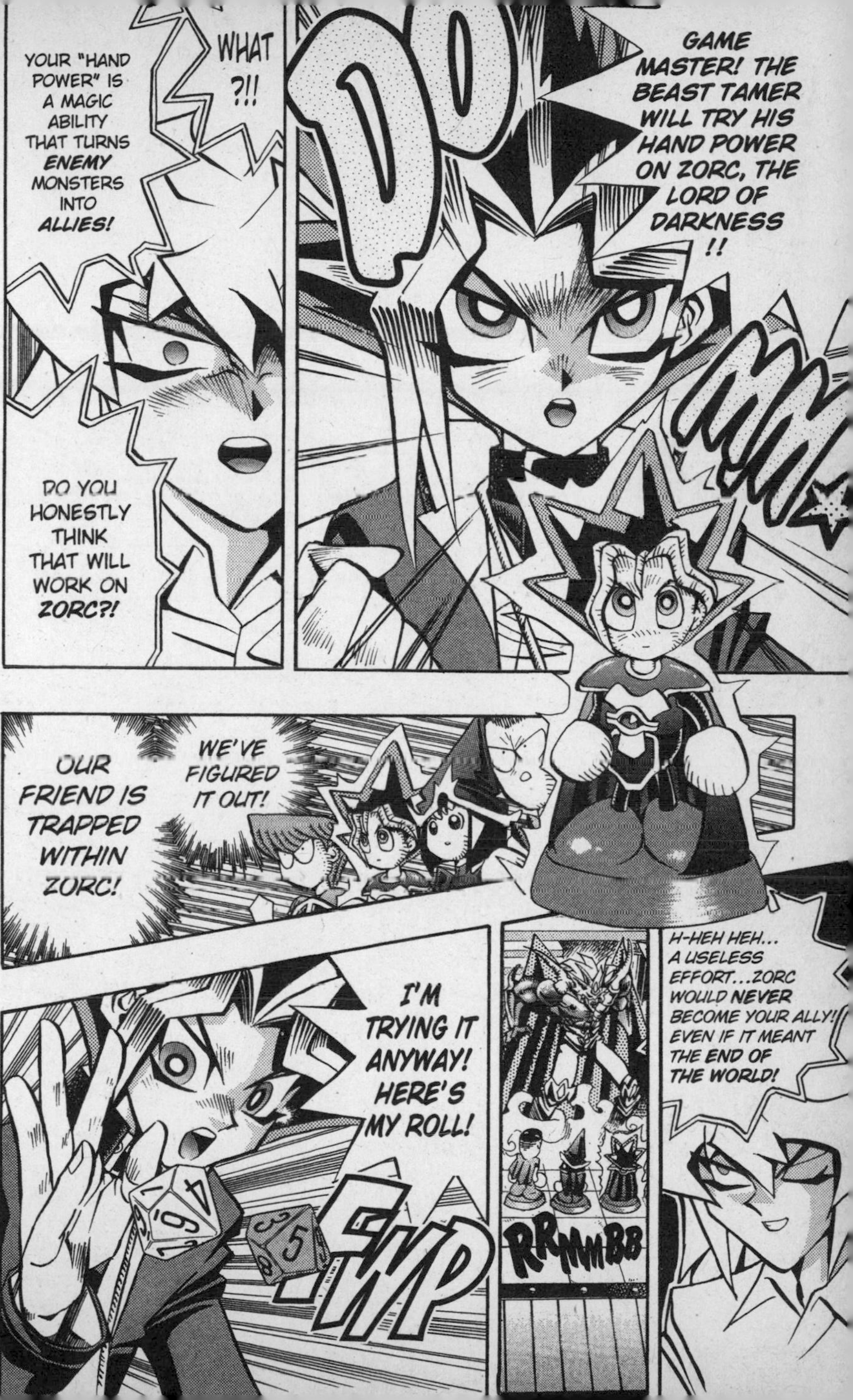
GAME MASTER! THE BEAST TAMER WILL TRY HIS HAND POWER ON ZORC, THE LORD OF DARKNESS !!
WHAT ?!!
YOUR "HAND POWER" IS A MAGIC ABILITY THAT TURNS ENEMY MONSTERS INTO ALLIES!
DO YOU HONESTLY THINK THAT WILL WORK ON ZORC?!
WE'VE FIGURED IT OUT!
OUR FRIEND IS TRAPPED WITHIN ZORC!
H-HEH HEH... A USELESS EFFORT...ZORC WOULD NEVER BECOME YOUR ALLY! EVEN IF IT MEANT THE END OF THE WORLD!
RRMMBB
I'M TRYING IT ANYWAY! HERE'S MY ROLL!

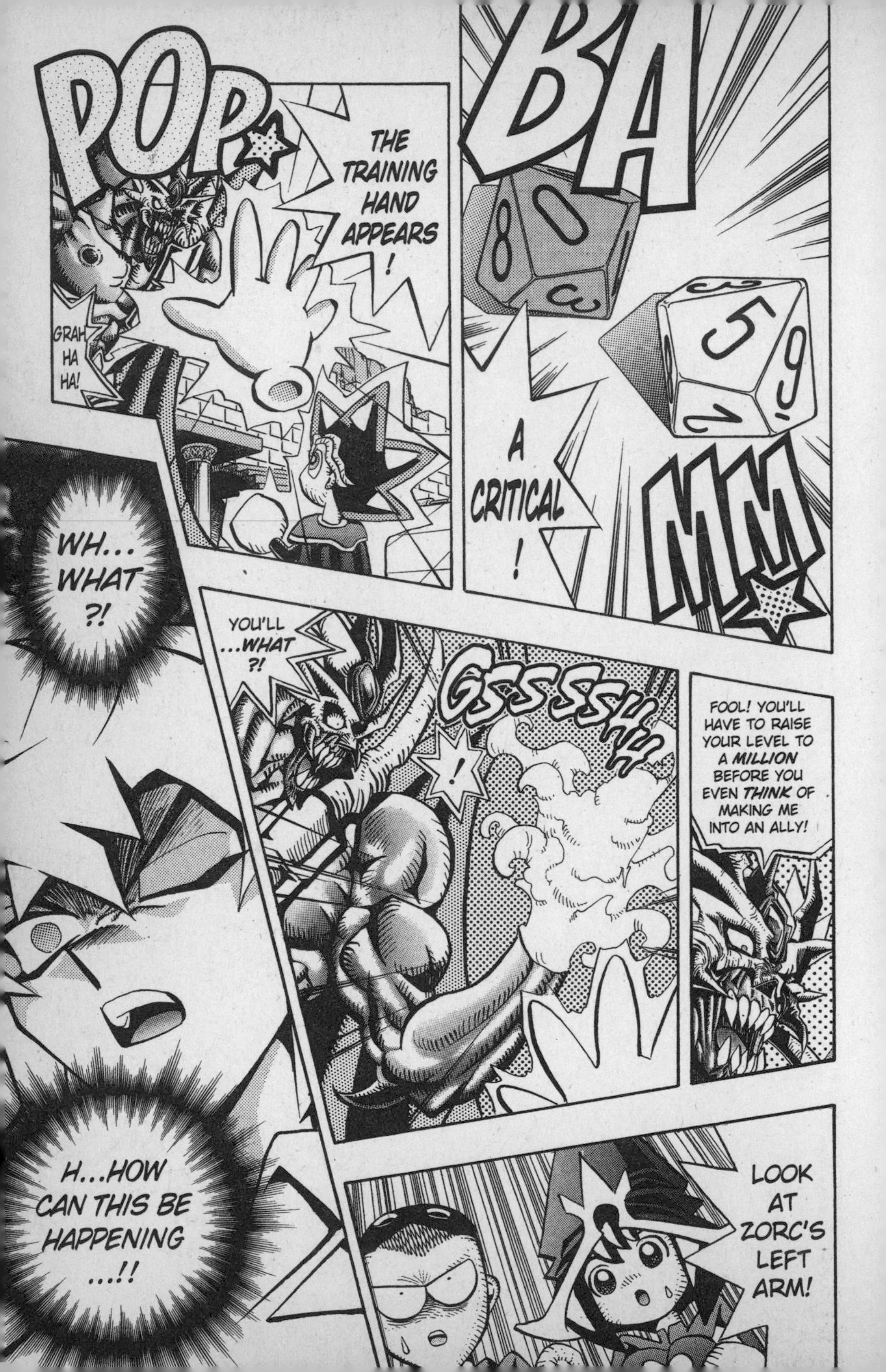
BA
A CRITICAL!
MM
POP
THE TRAINING HAND APPEARS!
GRAH HA HA!
FOOL! YOU'LL HAVE TO RAISE YOUR LEVEL TO A *MILLION* BEFORE YOU EVEN *THINK* OF MAKING ME INTO AN ALLY!
YOU'LL ...*WHAT* ?!
GSSSSH
!
LOOK AT ZORC'S LEFT ARM!
WH... WHAT ?!
H...HOW CAN THIS BE HAPPENING ...!!

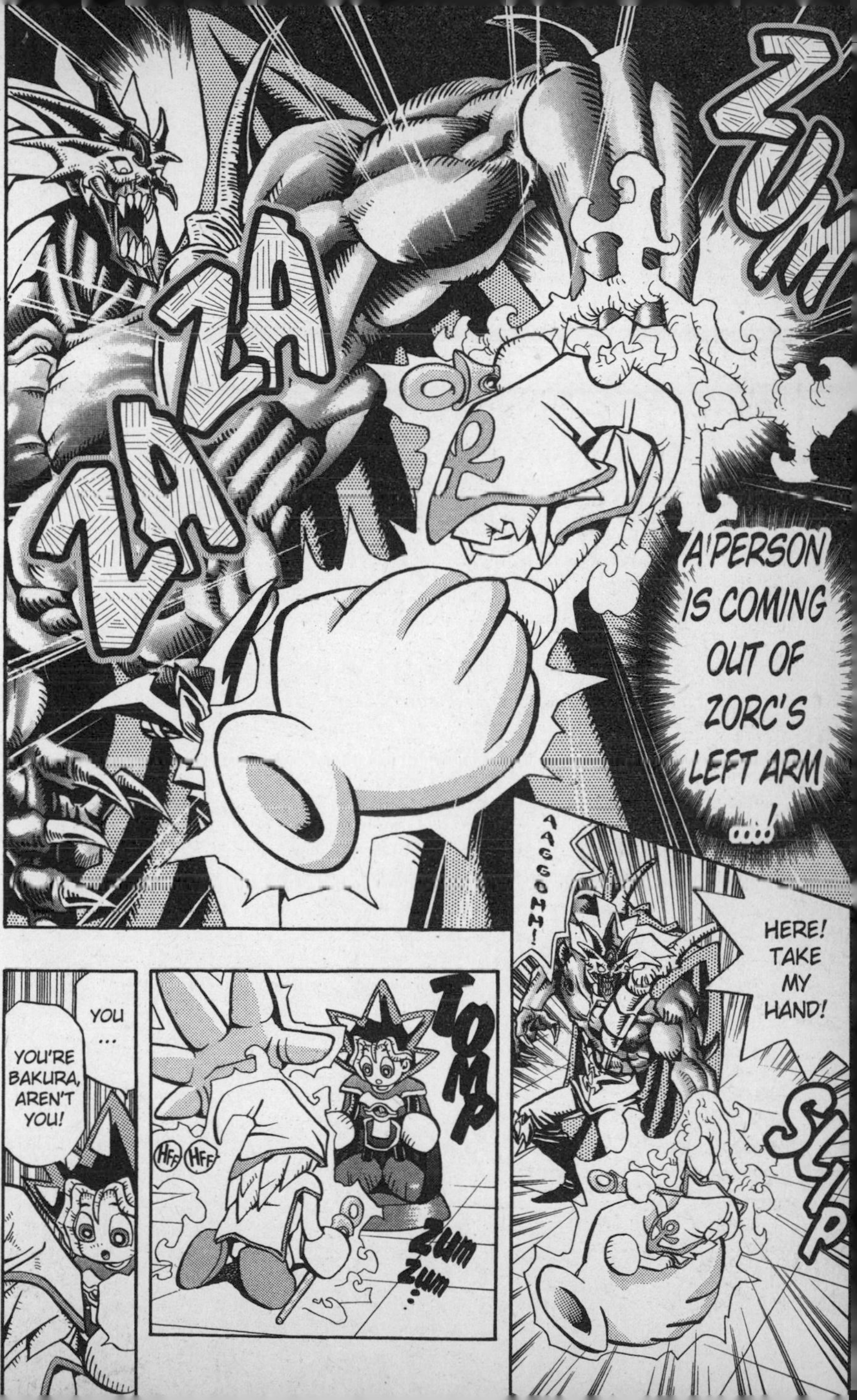
A PERSON IS COMING OUT OF ZORC'S LEFT ARM ...!
AAGGOHH!
HERE! TAKE MY HAND!
SLIP
TOMP
HFF HFF
ZUM ZUM...
YOU ...
YOU'RE BAKURA, AREN'T YOU!

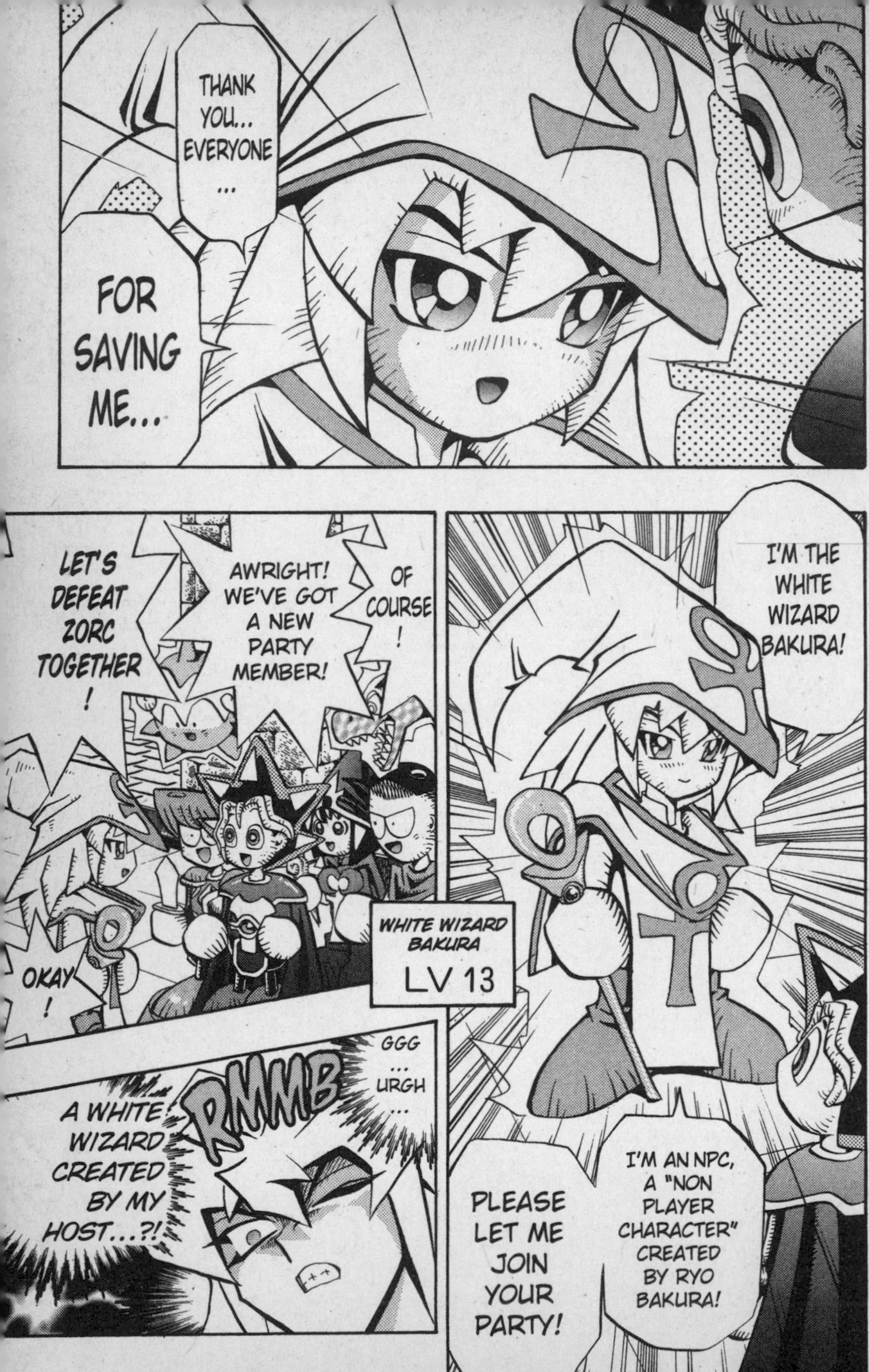
THANK YOU... EVERYONE ...
FOR SAVING ME...
I'M THE WHITE WIZARD BAKURA!
I'M AN NPC, A "NON PLAYER CHARACTER" CREATED BY RYO BAKURA!
PLEASE LET ME JOIN YOUR PARTY!
OF COURSE!
AWRIGHT! WE'VE GOT A NEW PARTY MEMBER!
LET'S DEFEAT ZORC TOGETHER!
WHITE WIZARD BAKURA
LV 13
OKAY!
GGG ... URGH ...
RMMB
A WHITE WIZARD CREATED BY MY HOST...?!

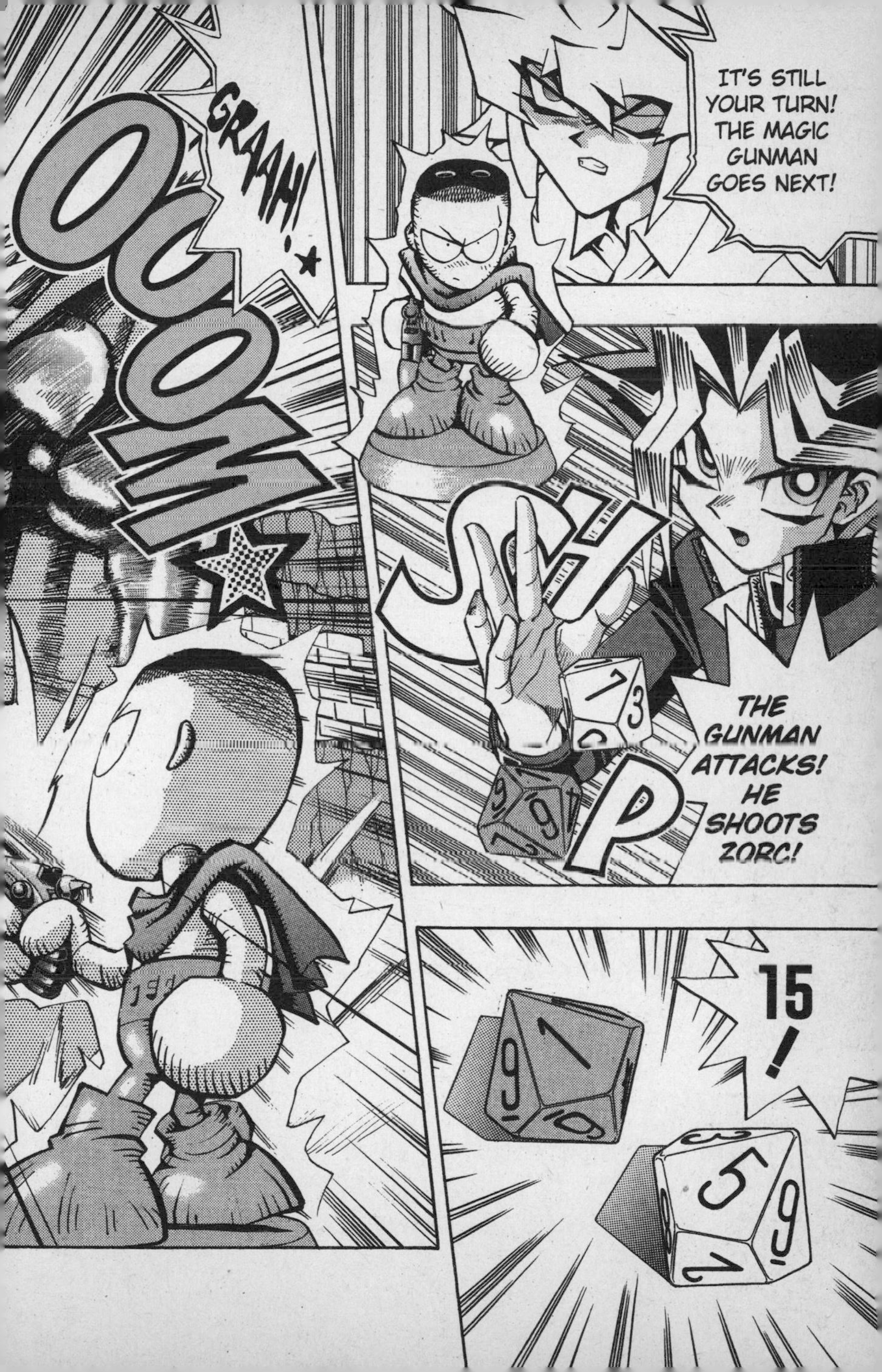
IT'S STILL YOUR TURN! THE MAGIC GUNMAN GOES NEXT!
THE GUNMAN ATTACKS! HE SHOOTS ZORC!
15!
GRAAAH!

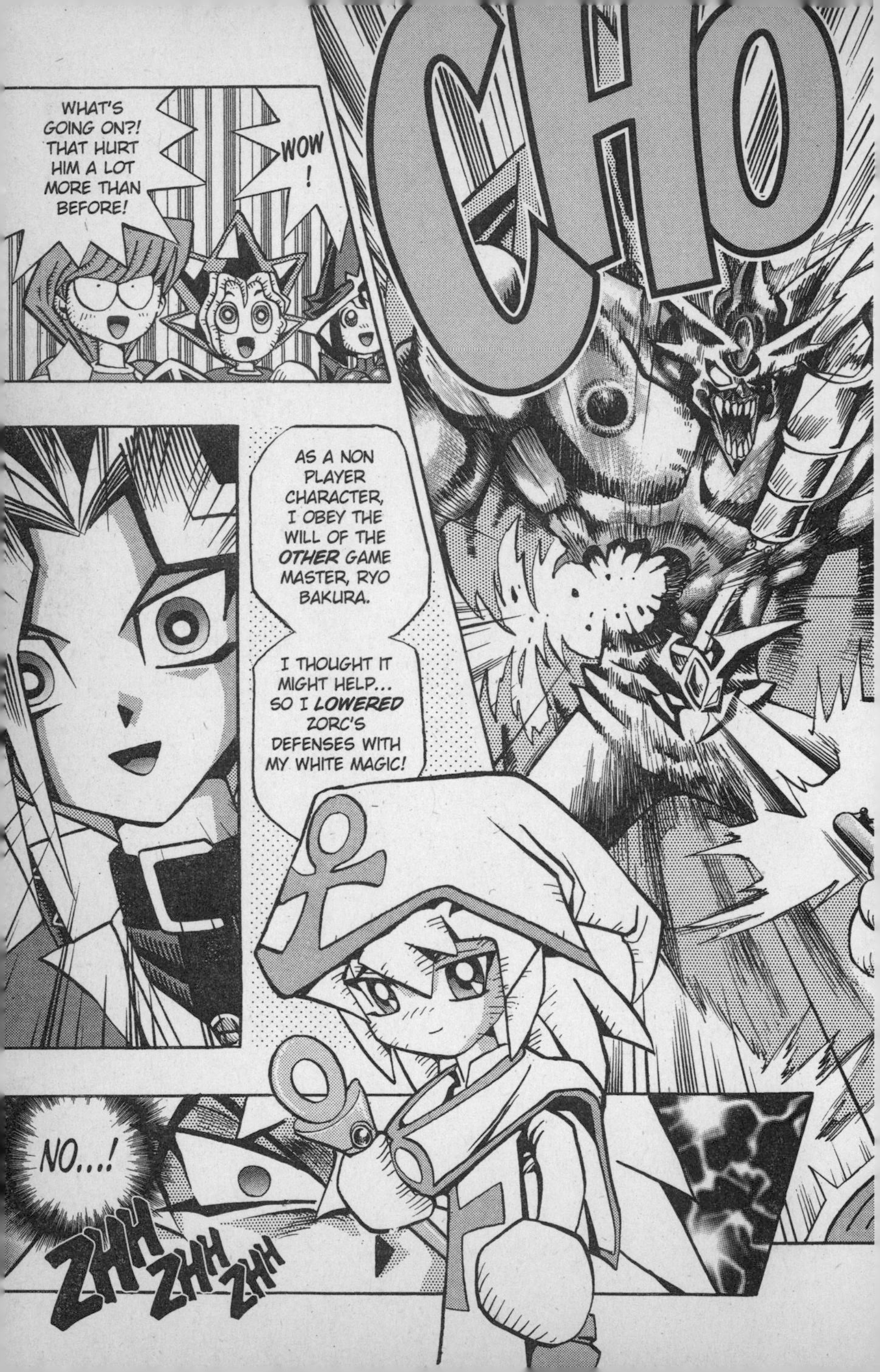
CHO
WOW!
WHAT'S GOING ON?! THAT HURT HIM A LOT MORE THAN BEFORE!
AS A NON PLAYER CHARACTER, I OBEY THE WILL OF THE **OTHER** GAME MASTER, RYO BAKURA.
I THOUGHT IT MIGHT HELP... SO I **LOWERED** ZORC'S DEFENSES WITH MY WHITE MAGIC!
NO...!
ZHH ZHH ZHH

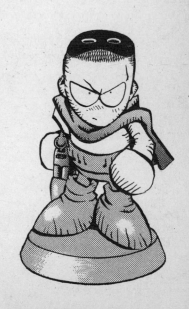

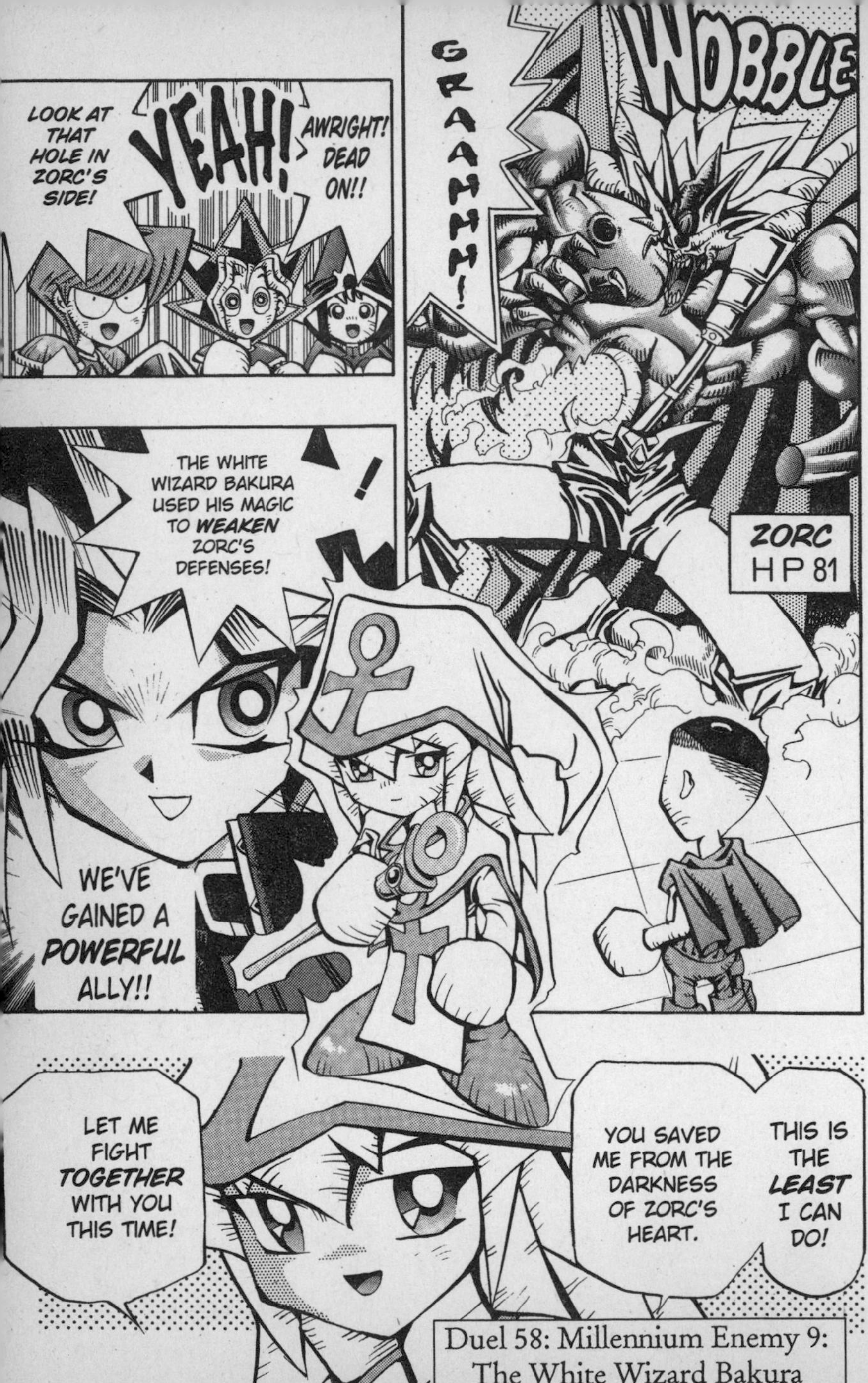
WOBBLE
GRAAHHH!
ZORC
HP 81
AWRIGHT! DEAD ON!!
YEAH!
LOOK AT THAT HOLE IN ZORC'S SIDE!
!
THE WHITE WIZARD BAKURA USED HIS MAGIC TO WEAKEN ZORC'S DEFENSES!
WE'VE GAINED A POWERFUL ALLY!!
YOU SAVED ME FROM THE DARKNESS OF ZORC'S HEART.
THIS IS THE LEAST I CAN DO!
LET ME FIGHT TOGETHER WITH YOU THIS TIME!

Duel 58: Millennium Enemy 9: The White Wizard Bakura

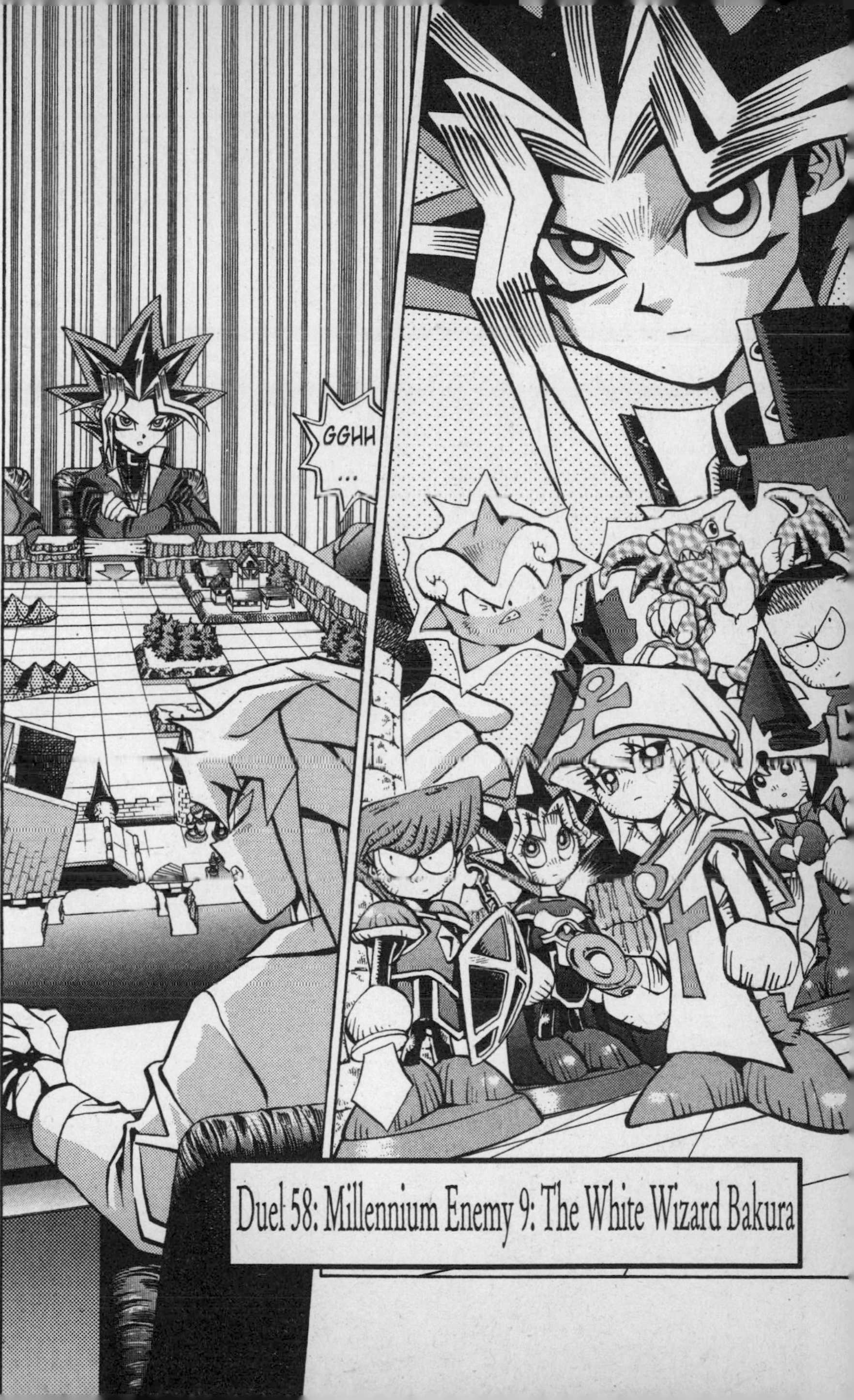
GGHH ...
Duel 58: Millennium Enemy 9: The White Wizard Bakura

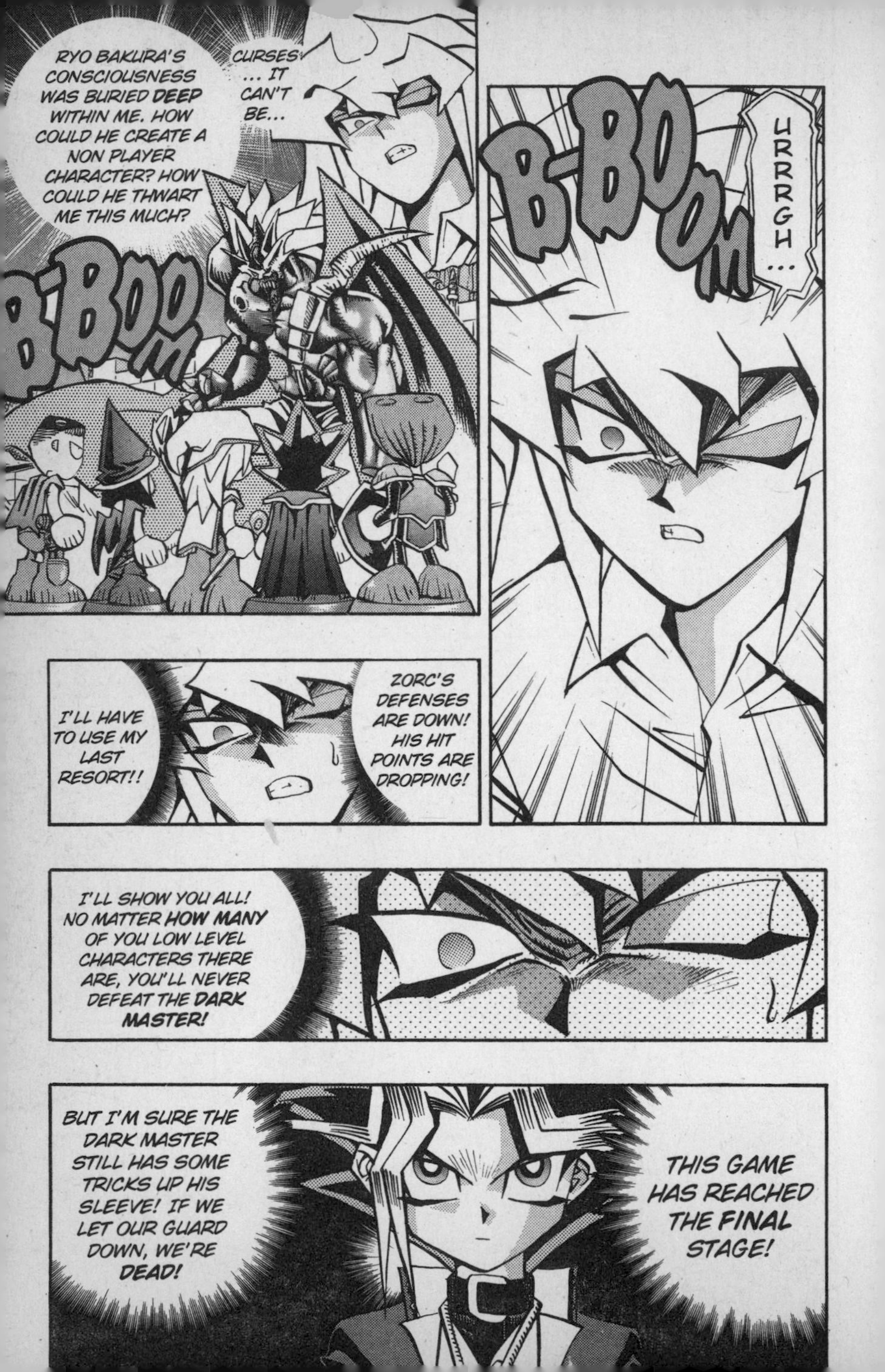
B-BOOM
URRRGH...
CURSES ... IT CAN'T BE...
RYO BAKURA'S CONSCIOUSNESS WAS BURIED DEEP WITHIN ME. HOW COULD HE CREATE A NON PLAYER CHARACTER? HOW COULD HE THWART ME THIS MUCH?
B-BOOM
ZORC'S DEFENSES ARE DOWN! HIS HIT POINTS ARE DROPPING!
I'LL HAVE TO USE MY LAST RESORT!!
I'LL SHOW YOU ALL! NO MATTER HOW MANY OF YOU LOW LEVEL CHARACTERS THERE ARE, YOU'LL NEVER DEFEAT THE DARK MASTER!
THIS GAME HAS REACHED THE FINAL STAGE!
BUT I'M SURE THE DARK MASTER STILL HAS SOME TRICKS UP HIS SLEEVE! IF WE LET OUR GUARD DOWN, WE'RE DEAD!

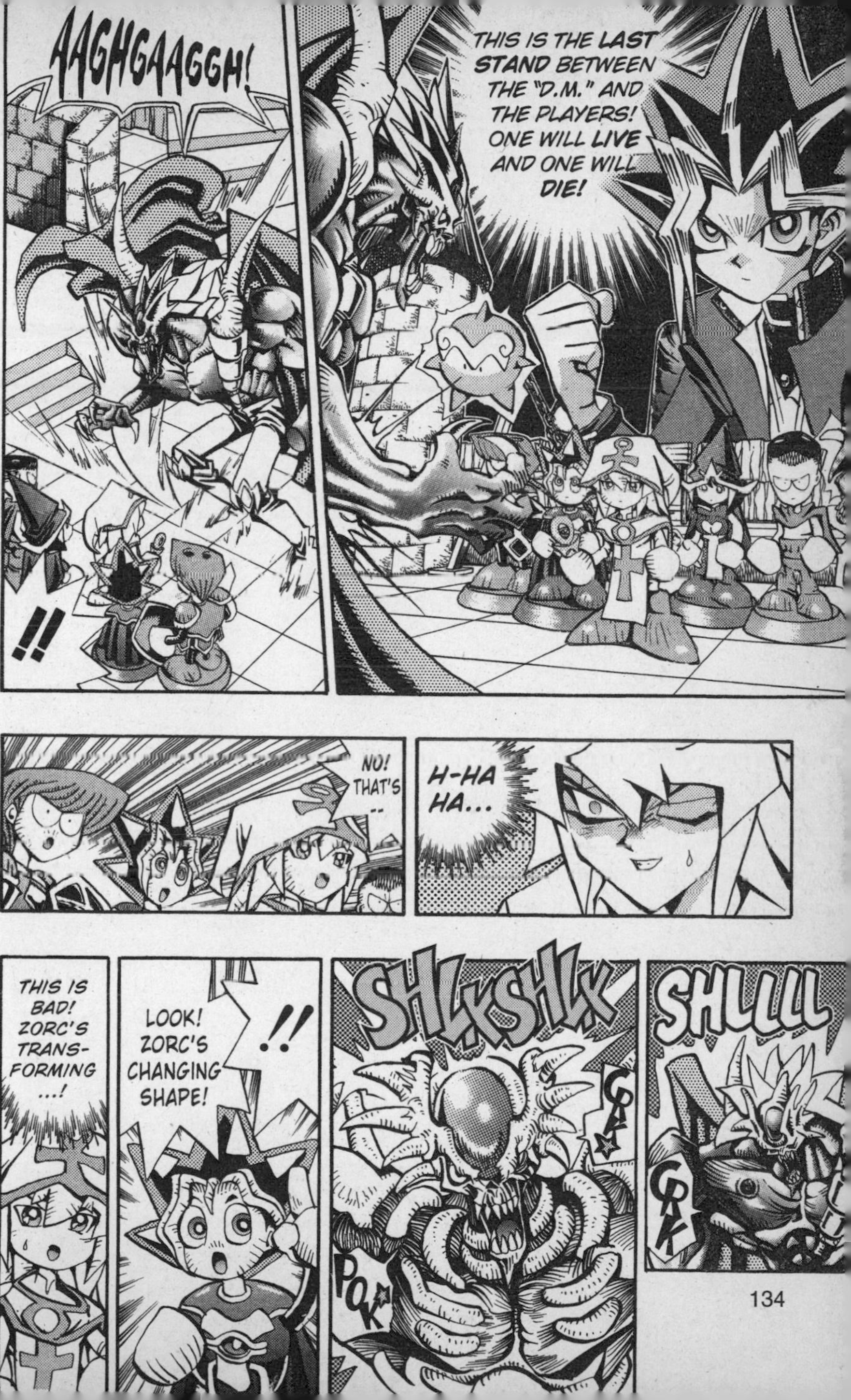
THIS IS THE LAST STAND BETWEEN THE "D.M." AND THE PLAYERS! ONE WILL LIVE AND ONE WILL DIE!
AAGHGAAAGGH!
!!
H-HA HA...
NO! THAT'S --
SHLLLL
GRK
SHLKSHLK
GRAK
POK
!!
LOOK! ZORC'S CHANGING SHAPE!
THIS IS BAD! ZORC'S TRANS-FORMING ...!

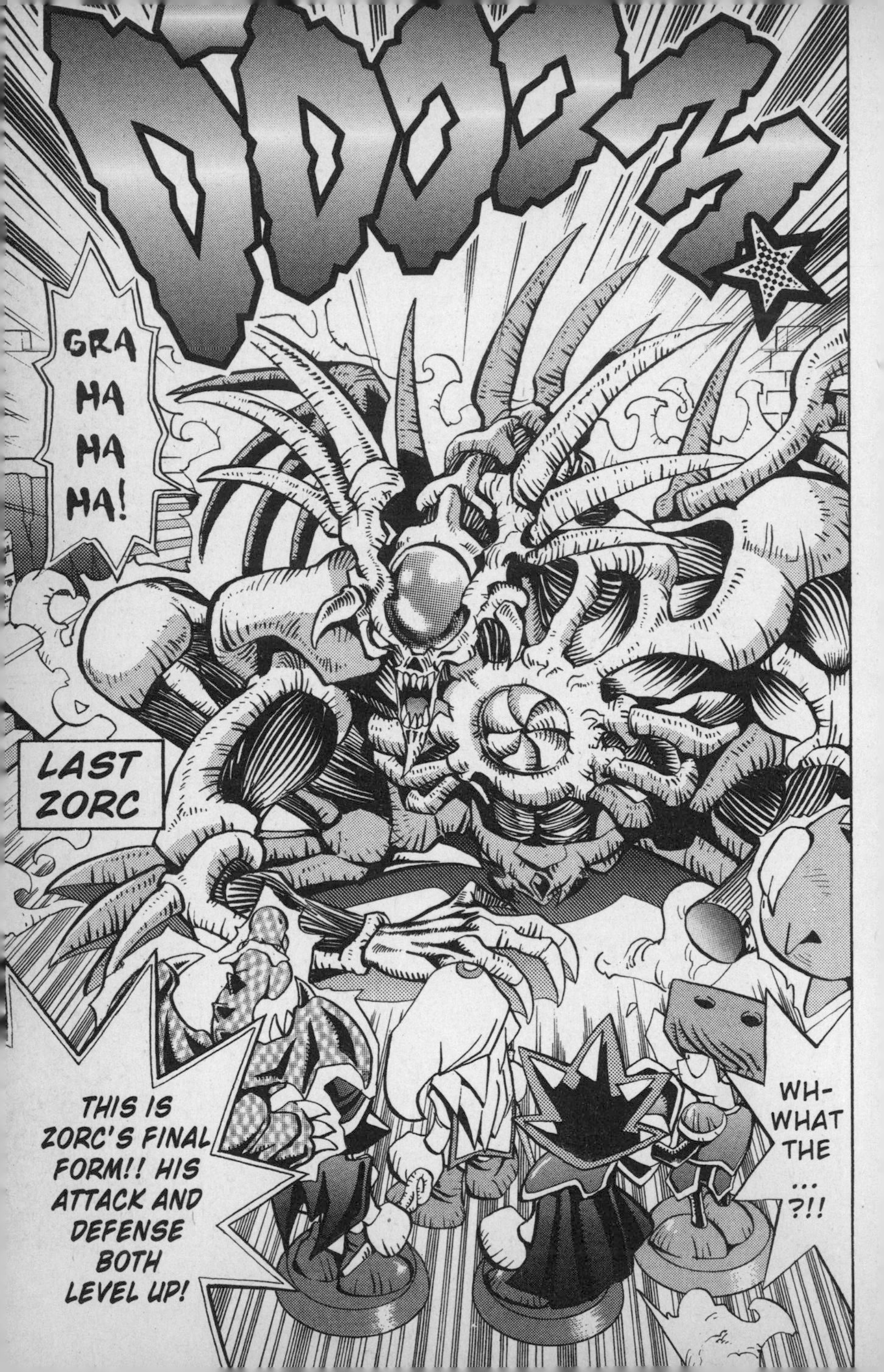
GRA HA HA HA!
LAST ZORC
WH-WHAT THE ...?!!
THIS IS ZORC'S FINAL FORM!! HIS ATTACK AND DEFENSE BOTH LEVEL UP!

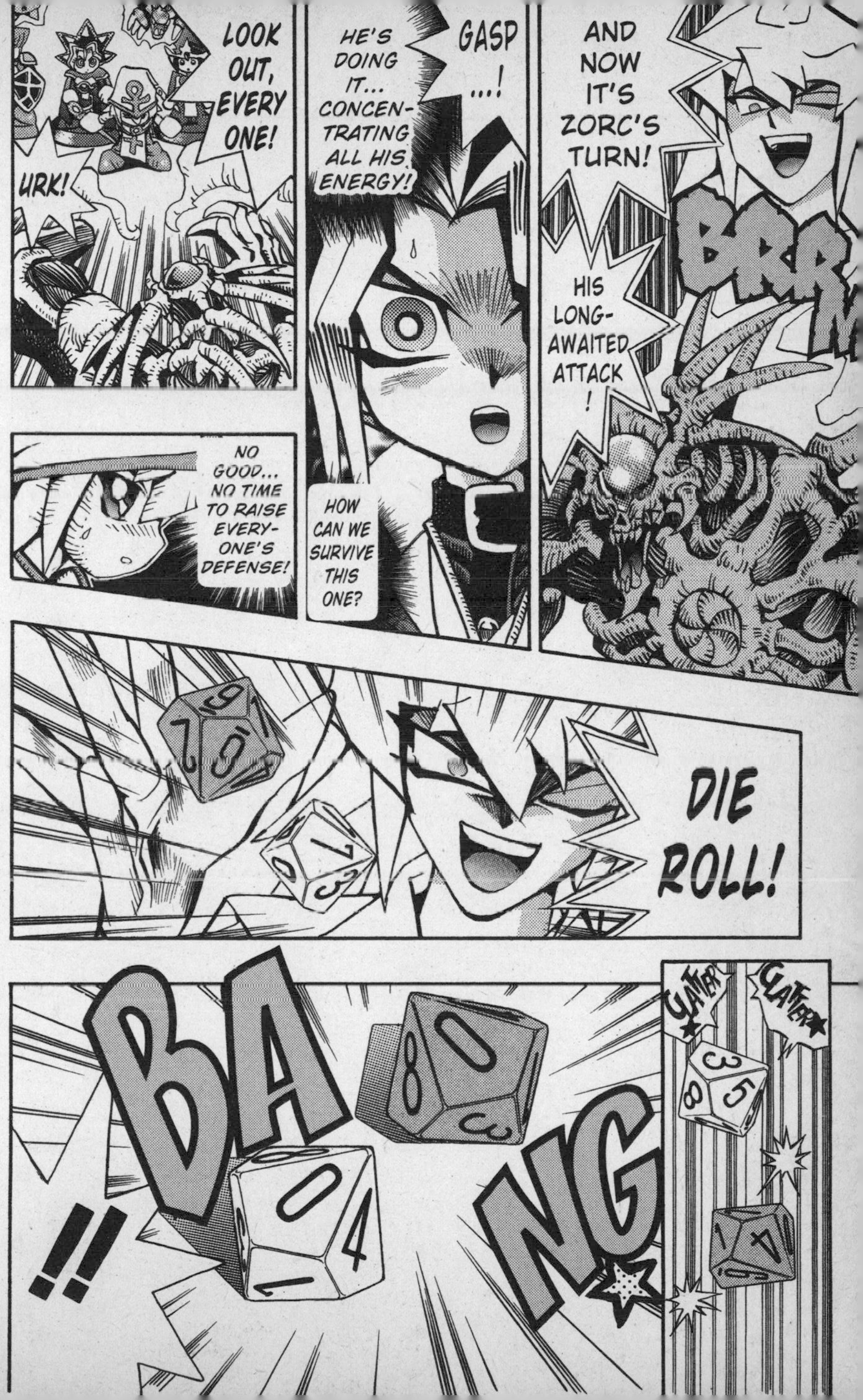
AND NOW IT'S ZORC'S TURN!
HIS LONG-AWAITED ATTACK!
GASP...!
HE'S DOING IT... CONCENTRATING ALL HIS ENERGY!
HOW CAN WE SURVIVE THIS ONE?
LOOK OUT, EVERY ONE!
URK!
NO GOOD... NO TIME TO RAISE EVERYONE'S DEFENSE!
DIE ROLL!
CLATTER★
CLATTER★
BANG!!

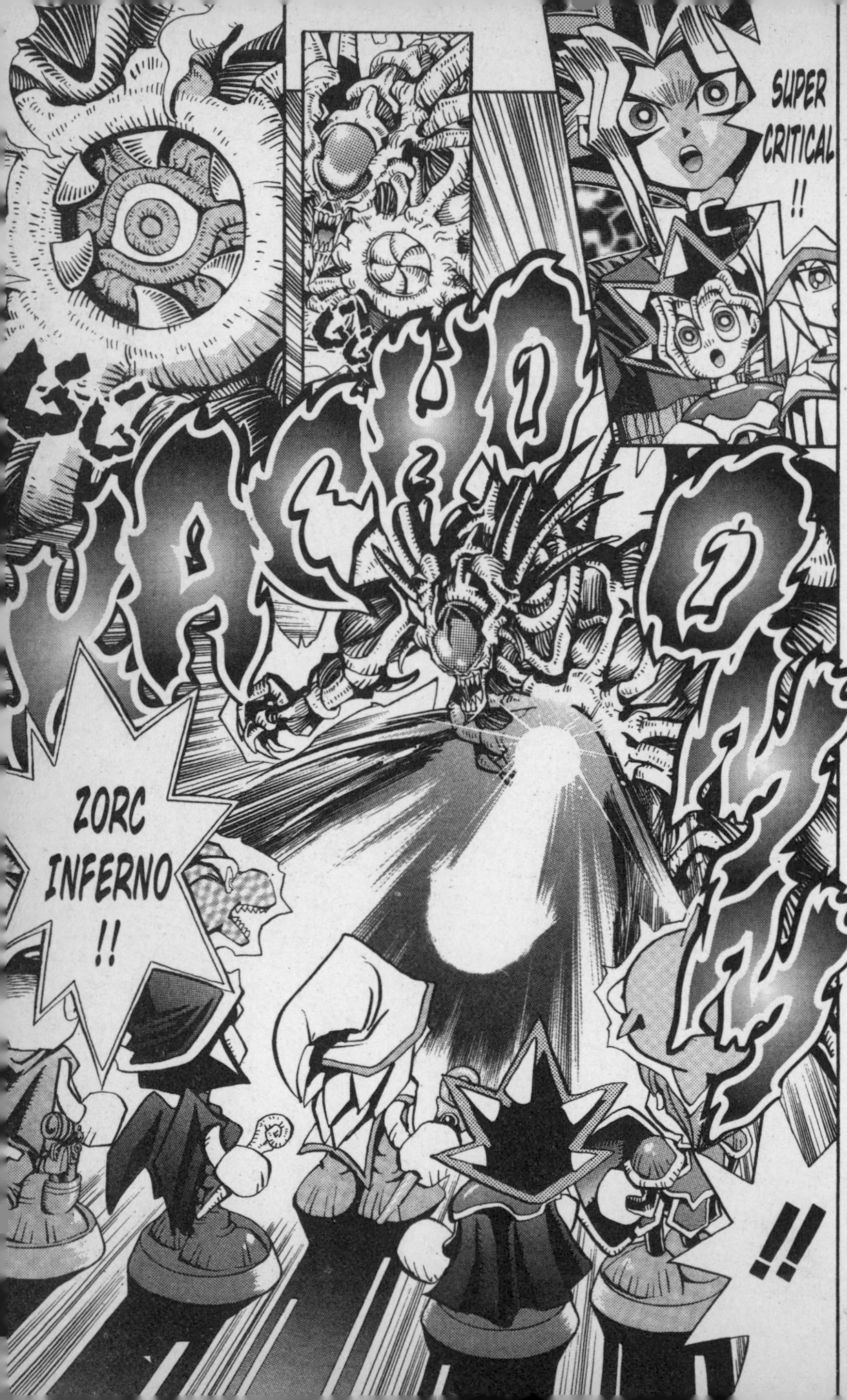
SUPER CRITICAL !!
ZORC INFERNO !!
!!

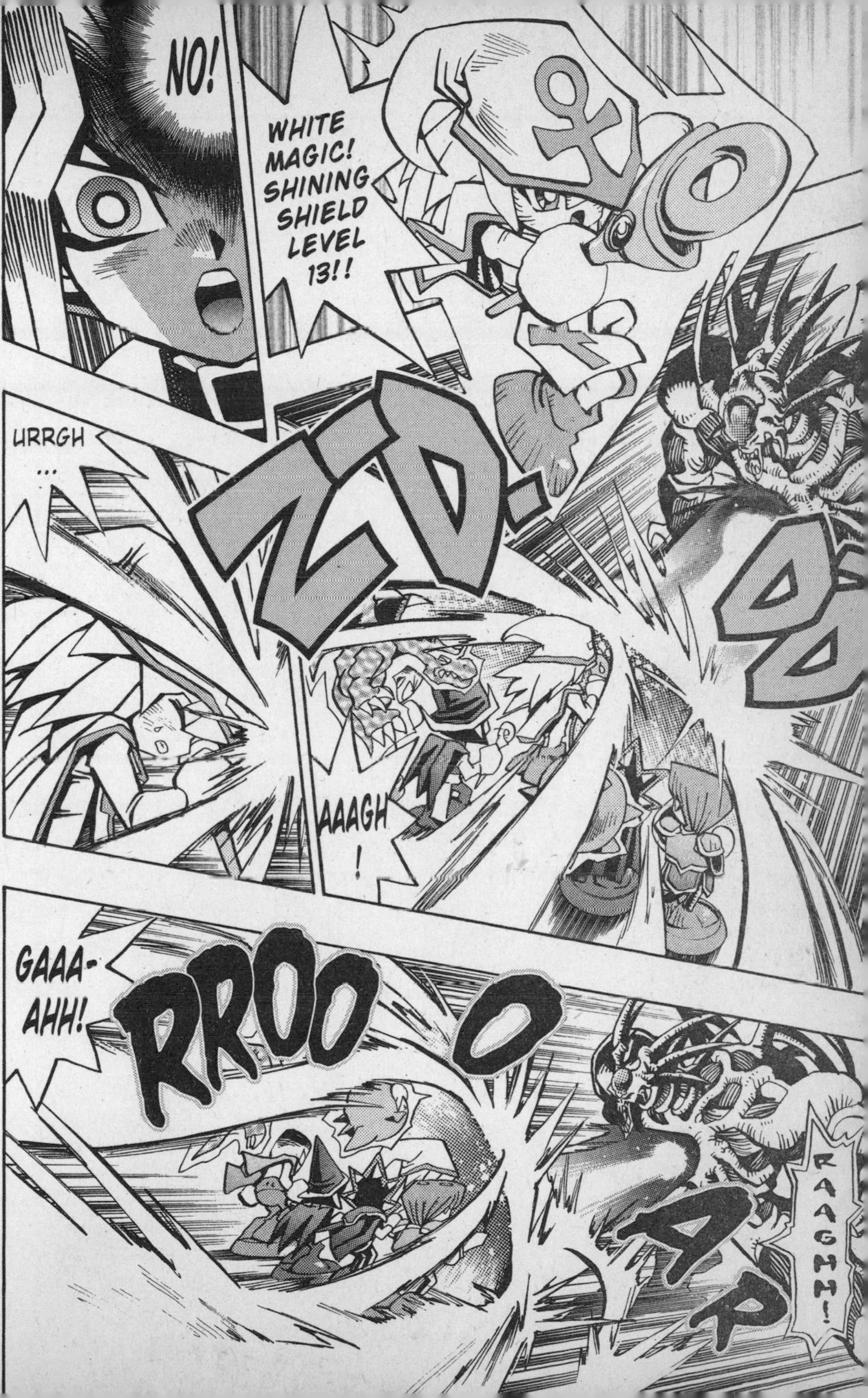
WHITE MAGIC! SHINING SHIELD LEVEL 13!!
NO!
ZD
DD
AAAGH!
URRGH ...
RAAGHH!
RROOOAR
GAAA-AHH!

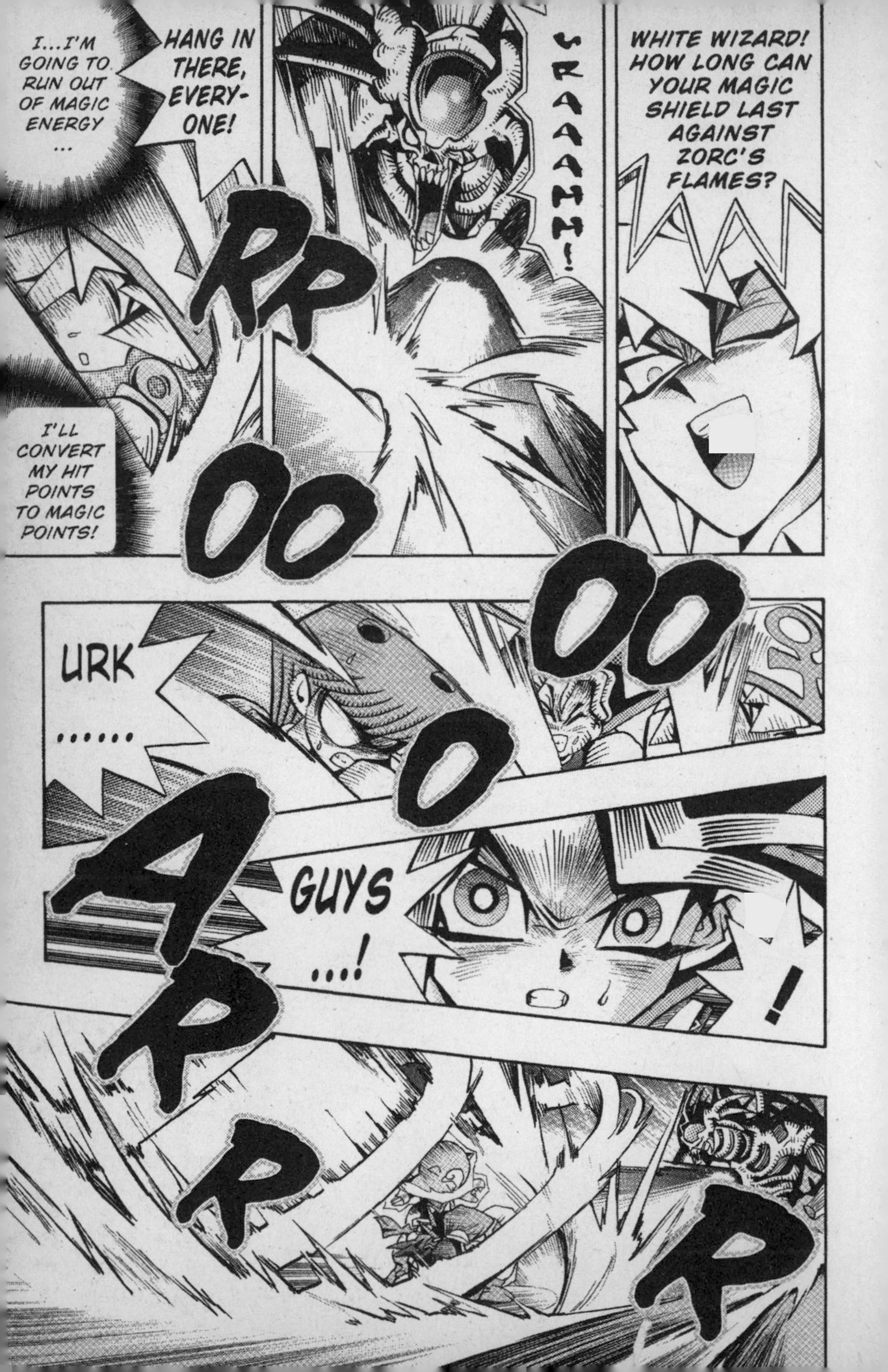

WHITE WIZARD! HOW LONG CAN YOUR MAGIC SHIELD LAST AGAINST ZORC'S FLAMES?
URAAAAHH!
HANG IN THERE, EVERY-ONE!
I...I'M GOING TO RUN OUT OF MAGIC ENERGY ...
I'LL CONVERT MY HIT POINTS TO MAGIC POINTS!
RROOOOOARRRR
URK ......
!
GUYS ...!

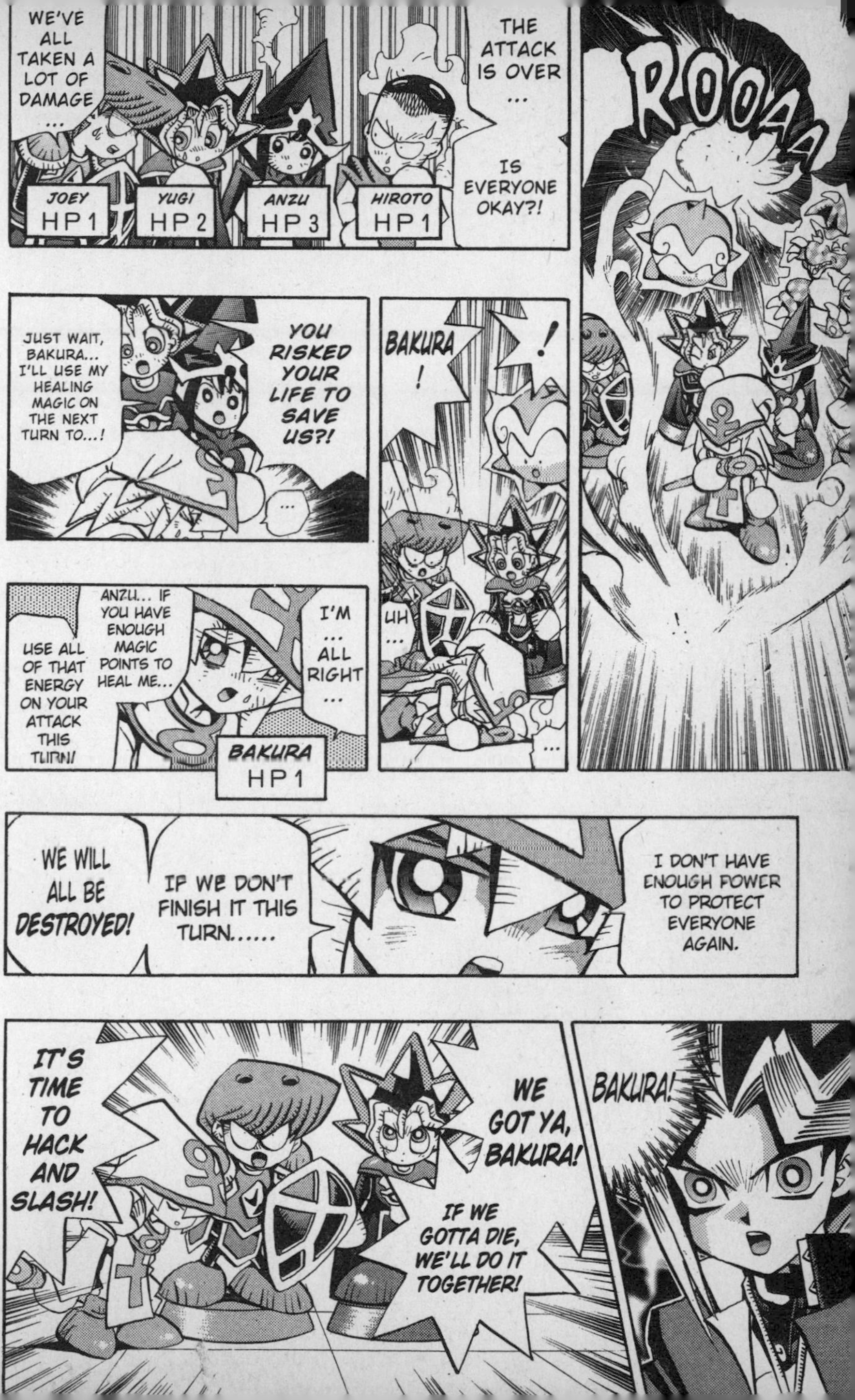
ROOAA
!
THE ATTACK IS OVER ...
IS EVERYONE OKAY?!
WE'VE ALL TAKEN A LOT OF DAMAGE ...
HIROTO HP 1
ANZU HP 3
YUGI HP 2
JOEY HP 1
!
BAKURA !
UH ...
...
YOU RISKED YOUR LIFE TO SAVE US?!
JUST WAIT, BAKURA... I'LL USE MY HEALING MAGIC ON THE NEXT TURN TO...!
...
I'M ... ALL RIGHT ...
ANZU... IF YOU HAVE ENOUGH MAGIC POINTS TO HEAL ME...
USE ALL OF THAT ENERGY ON YOUR ATTACK THIS TURN!
BAKURA HP 1
I DON'T HAVE ENOUGH POWER TO PROTECT EVERYONE AGAIN.
IF WE DON'T FINISH IT THIS TURN......
WE WILL ALL BE DESTROYED!
BAKURA!
WE GOT YA, BAKURA!
IF WE GOTTA DIE, WE'LL DO IT TOGETHER!
IT'S TIME TO HACK AND SLASH!

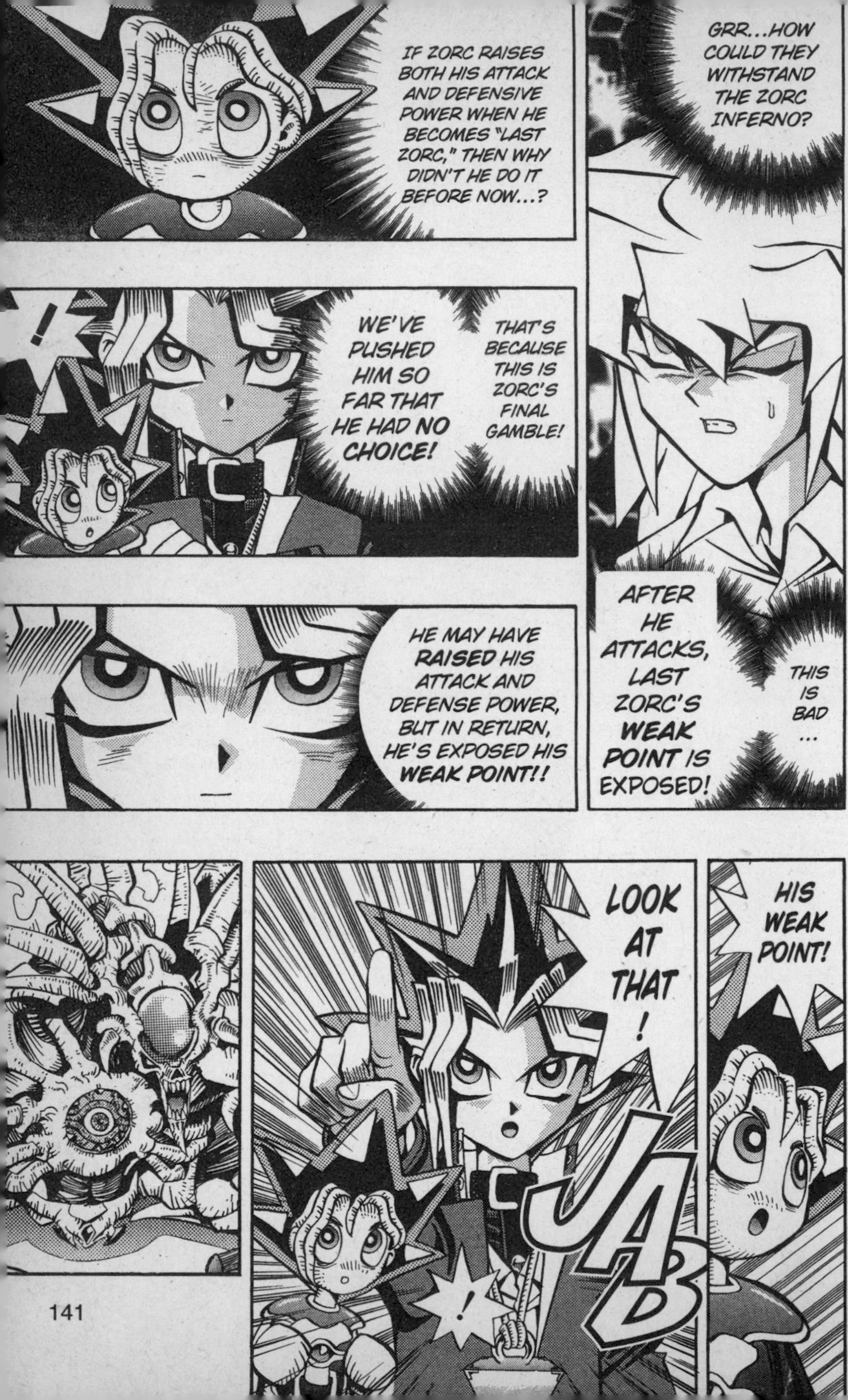
GRR...HOW COULD THEY WITHSTAND THE ZORC INFERNO?
IF ZORC RAISES BOTH HIS ATTACK AND DEFENSIVE POWER WHEN HE BECOMES "LAST ZORC," THEN WHY DIDN'T HE DO IT BEFORE NOW...?
THAT'S BECAUSE THIS IS ZORC'S FINAL GAMBLE!
WE'VE PUSHED HIM SO FAR THAT HE HAD NO CHOICE!
!
THIS IS BAD...
AFTER HE ATTACKS, LAST ZORC'S WEAK POINT IS EXPOSED!
HE MAY HAVE RAISED HIS ATTACK AND DEFENSE POWER, BUT IN RETURN, HE'S EXPOSED HIS WEAK POINT!!
HIS WEAK POINT!
LOOK AT THAT!
JAB
!

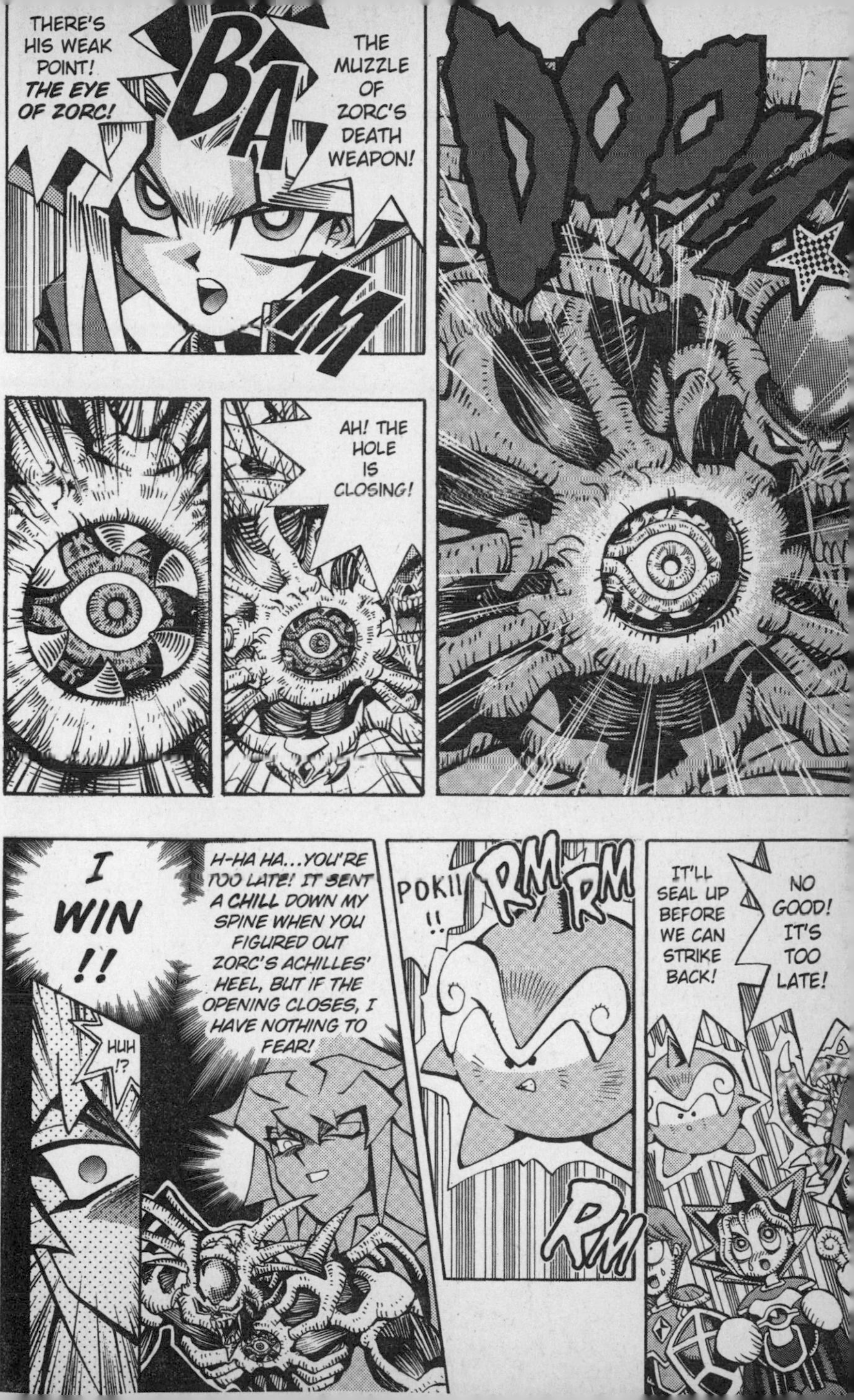
THE MUZZLE OF ZORC'S DEATH WEAPON!
THERE'S HIS WEAK POINT! *THE EYE OF ZORC!*
BAM
AH! THE HOLE IS CLOSING!
NO GOOD! IT'S TOO LATE!
IT'LL SEAL UP BEFORE WE CAN STRIKE BACK!
RM RM
POKII !!
RM
H-HA HA...YOU'RE TOO LATE! IT SENT A **CHILL** DOWN MY SPINE WHEN YOU FIGURED OUT ZORC'S ACHILLES' HEEL, BUT IF THE OPENING CLOSES, I HAVE NOTHING TO FEAR!
I WIN !!
HUH !?

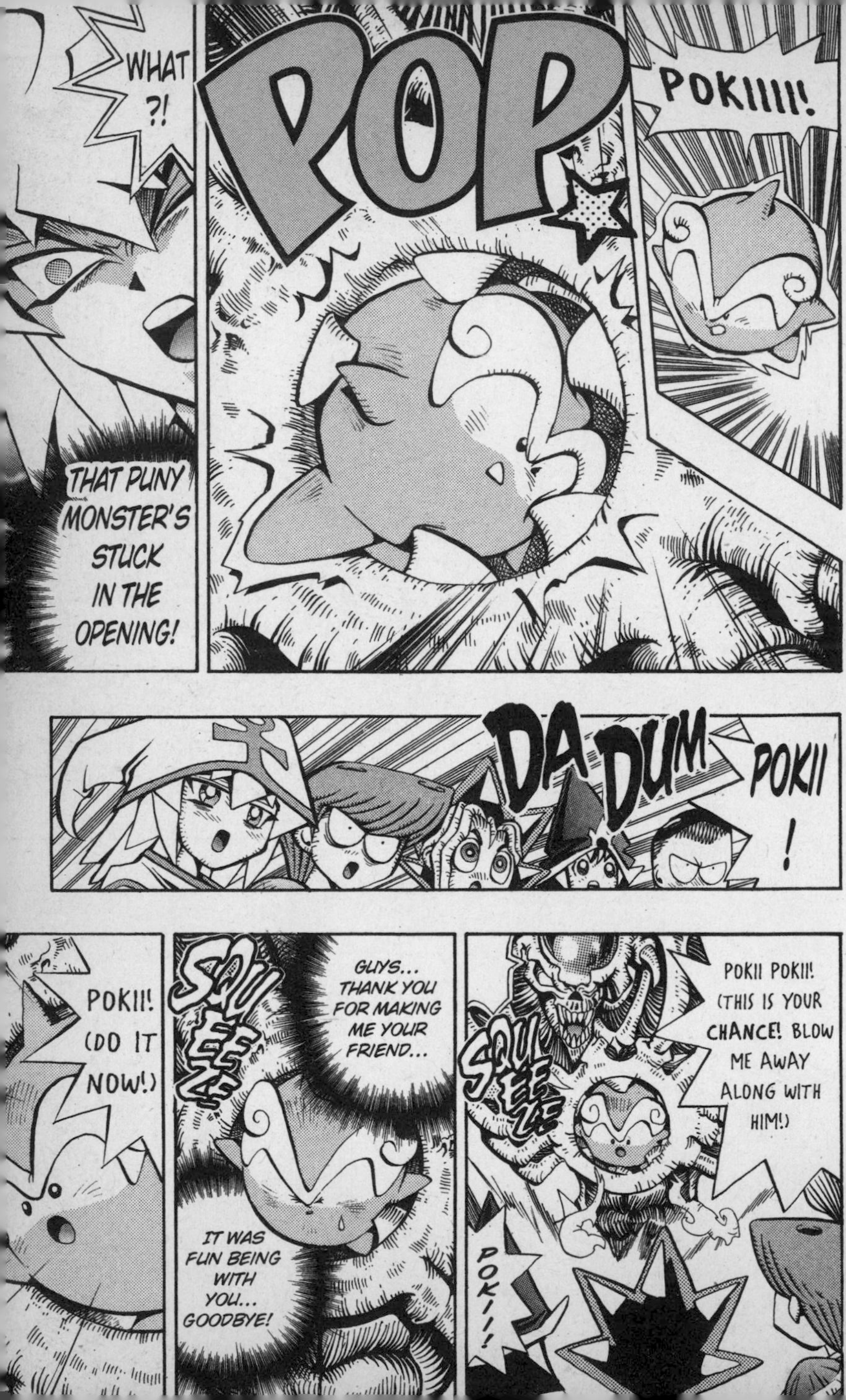
POKIIIII!
POP
WHAT ?!
THAT PUNY MONSTER'S STUCK IN THE OPENING!
POKII !
DA DUM
POKII POKII! (THIS IS YOUR CHANCE! BLOW ME AWAY ALONG WITH HIM!)
SQUEEZE
POKII!
SQUEEZE
GUYS... THANK YOU FOR MAKING ME YOUR FRIEND...
IT WAS FUN BEING WITH YOU... GOODBYE!
POKII! (DO IT NOW!)

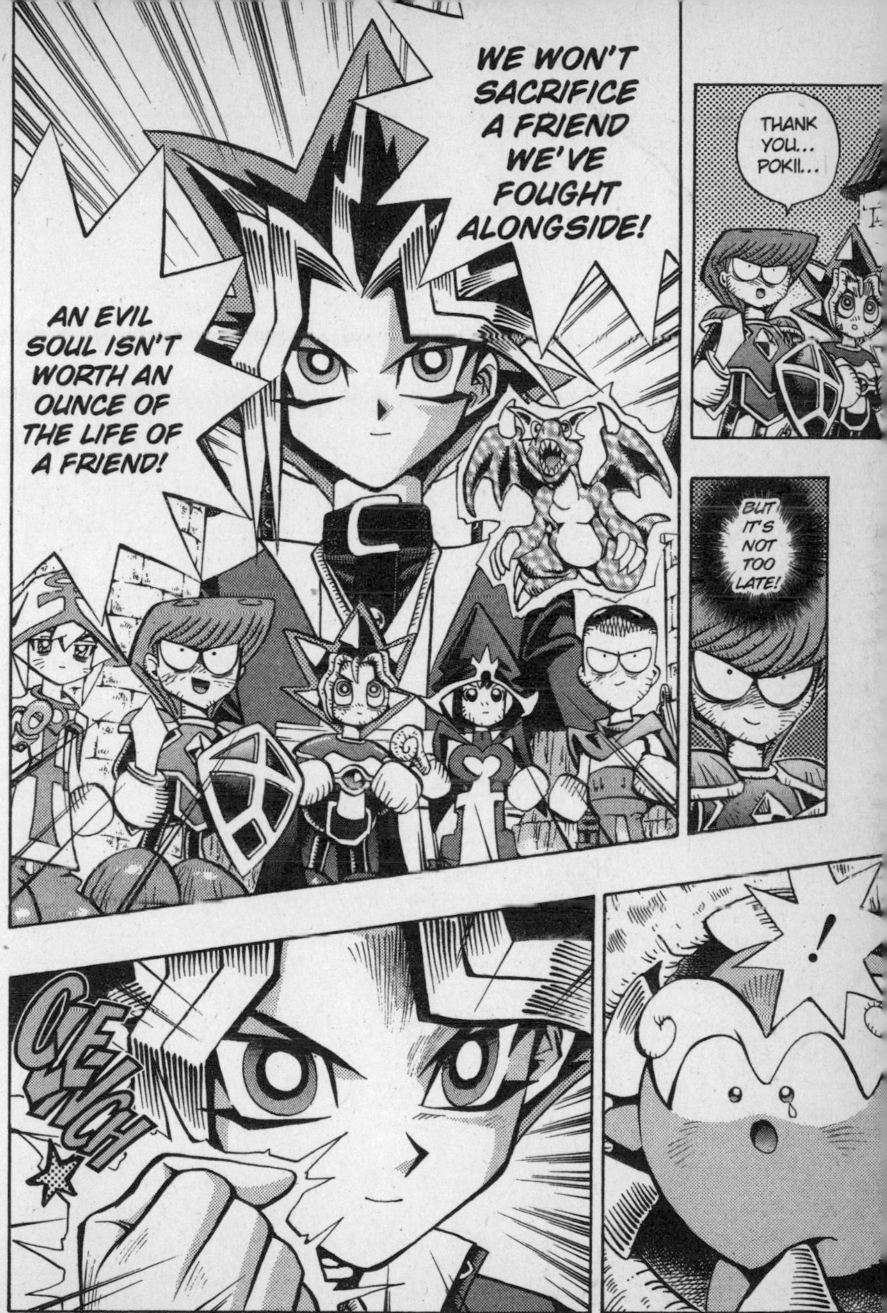
THANK YOU... POKII...
BUT IT'S NOT TOO LATE!
WE WON'T SACRIFICE A FRIEND WE'VE FOUGHT ALONGSIDE!
AN EVIL SOUL ISN'T WORTH AN OUNCE OF THE LIFE OF A FRIEND!
!
CLENCH

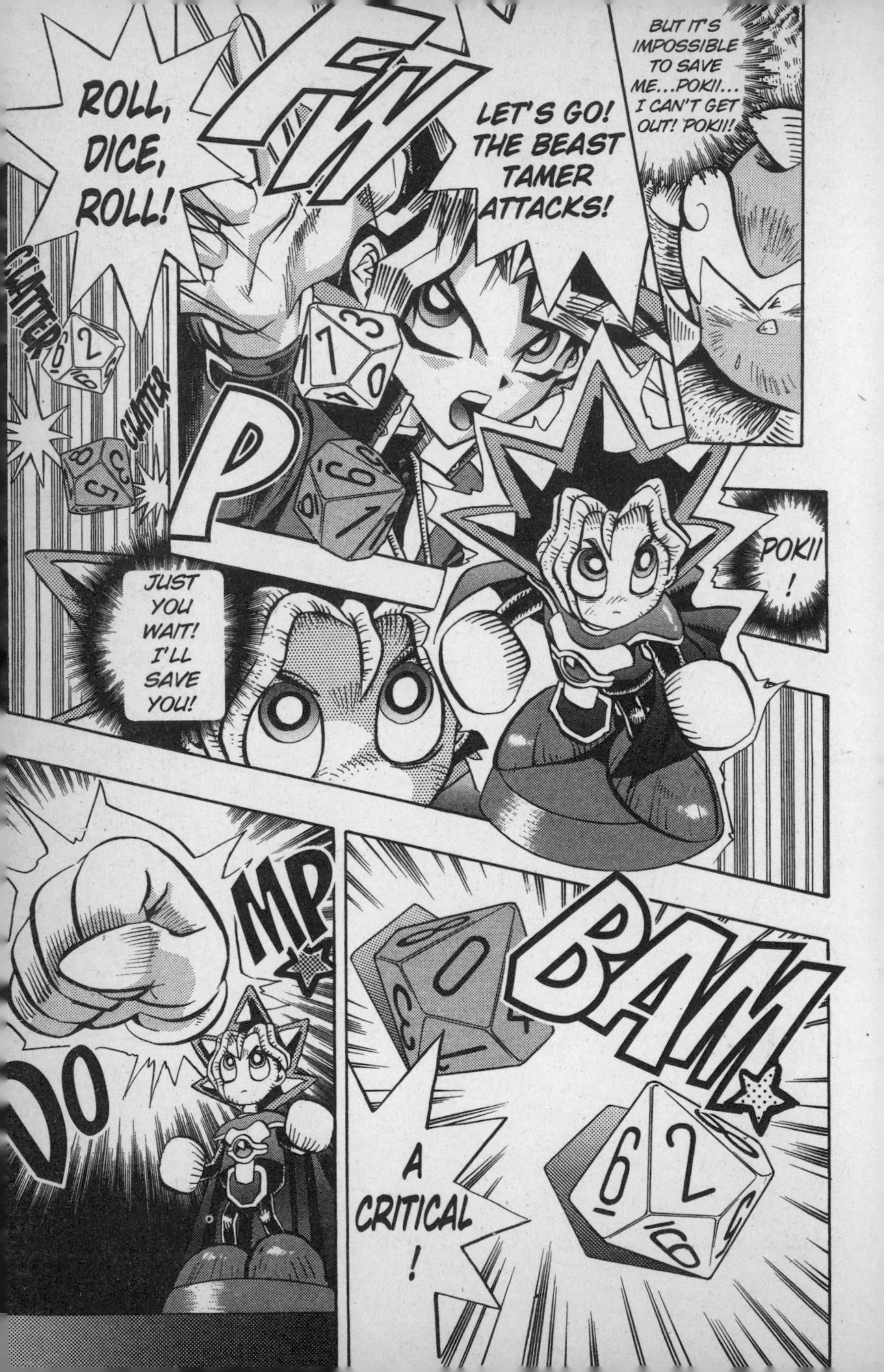
BUT IT'S IMPOSSIBLE TO SAVE ME...POKII... I CAN'T GET OUT! POKII!
LET'S GO! THE BEAST TAMER ATTACKS!
ROLL, DICE, ROLL!
CLATTER
CLATTER
POKII!
JUST YOU WAIT! I'LL SAVE YOU!
BAM
A CRITICAL!

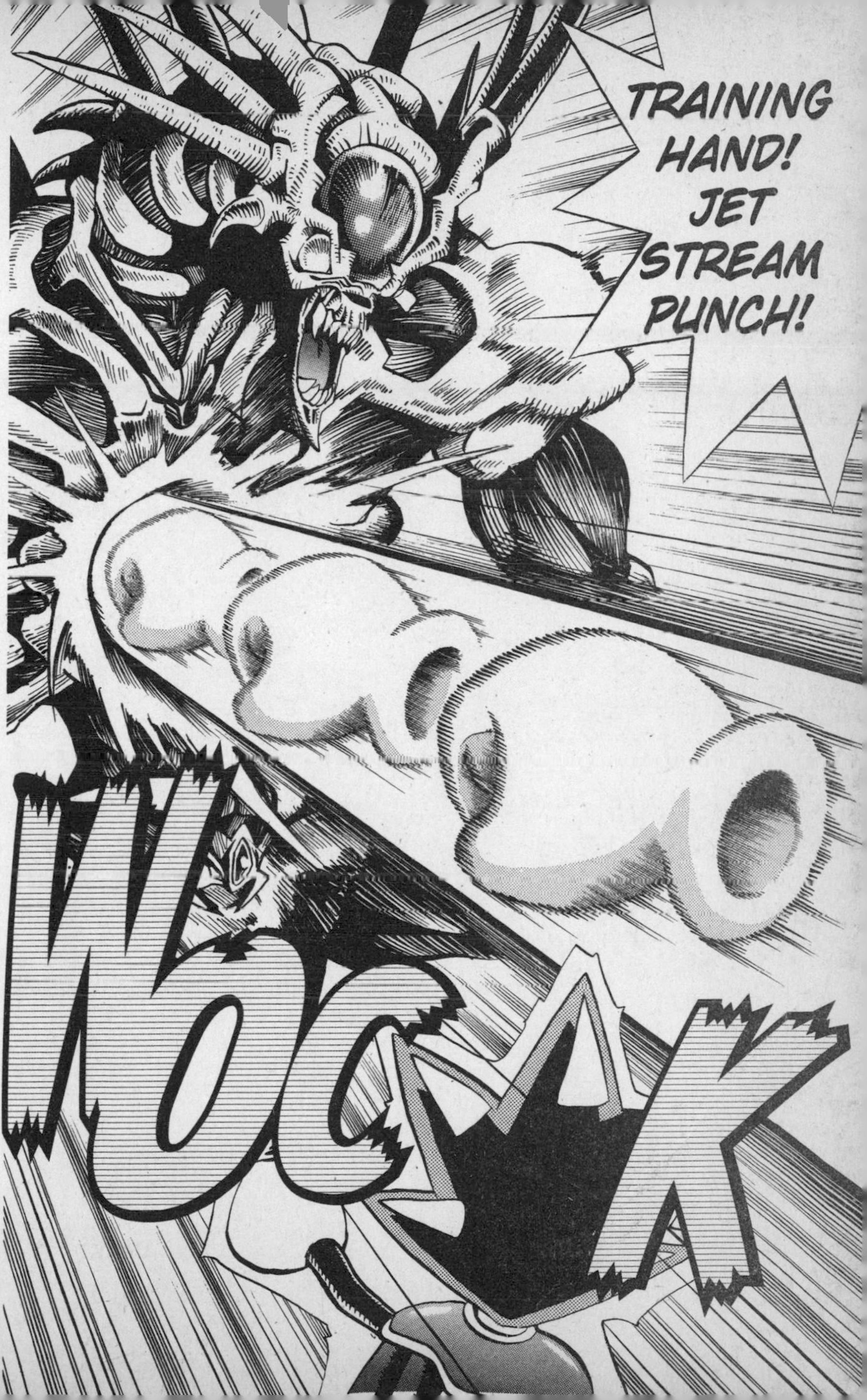
TRAINING HAND! JET STREAM PUNCH!
WOCK

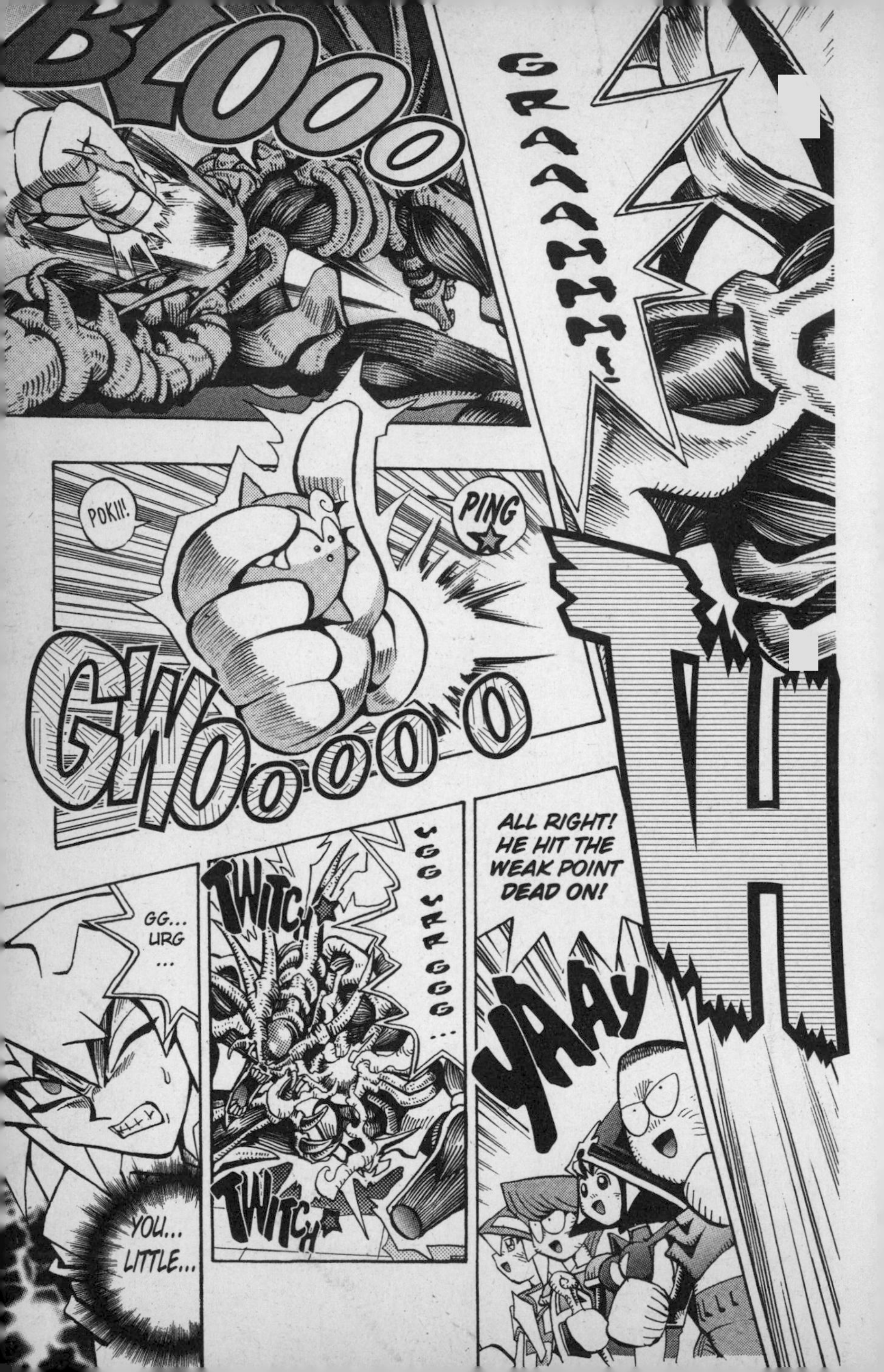
GRAAAHH!!
BLOOOO
POKII!
PING
GWOOOOOO
ALL RIGHT! HE HIT THE WEAK POINT DEAD ON!
YAAAY
TWITCH
UGG URR GGG...
TWITCH
GG... URG ...
YOU... LITTLE...

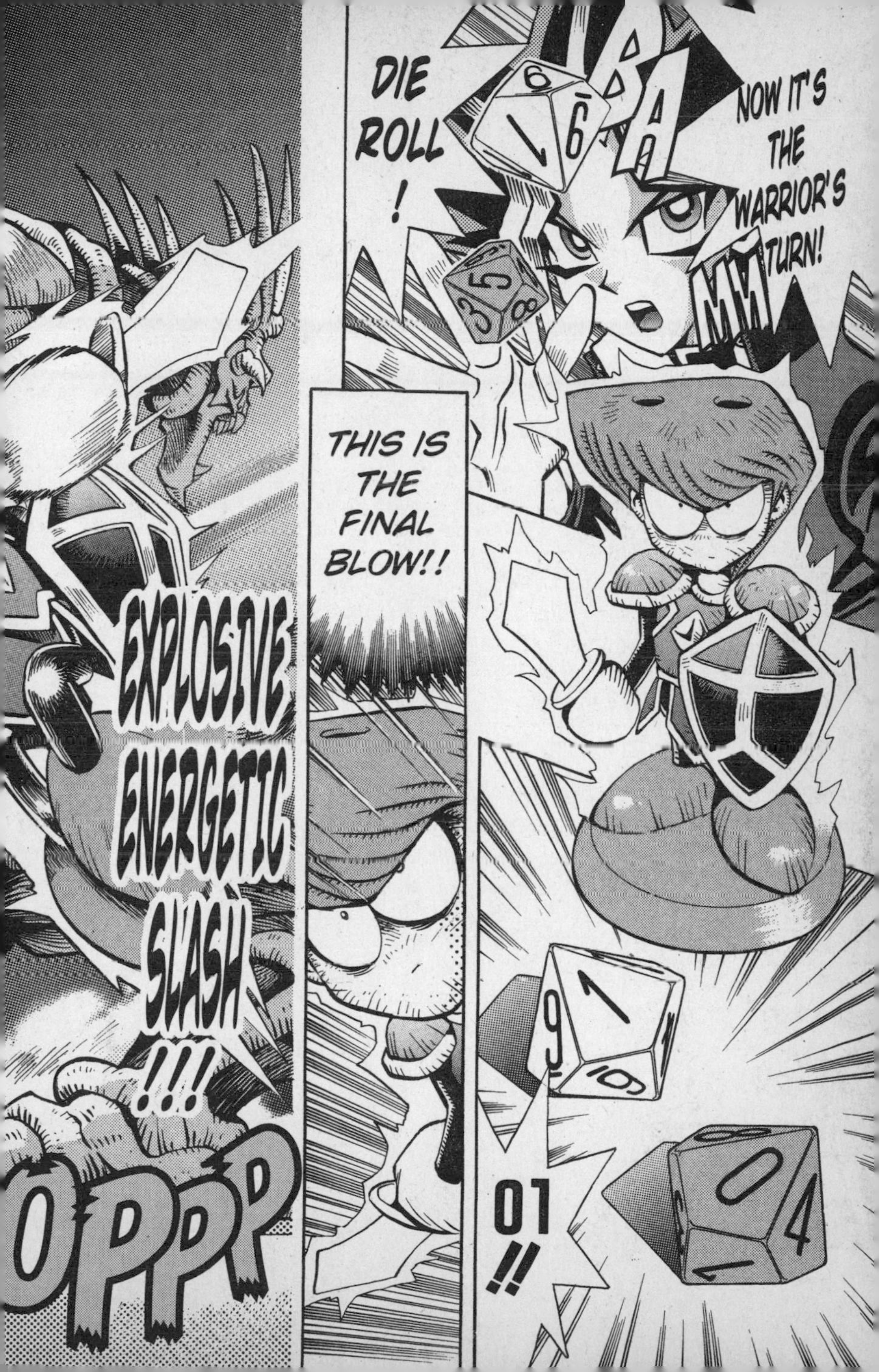
NOW IT'S THE WARRIOR'S TURN!
DIE ROLL!
01!!
THIS IS THE FINAL BLOW!!
EXPLOSIVE ENERGETIC SLASH!!!
OPPP

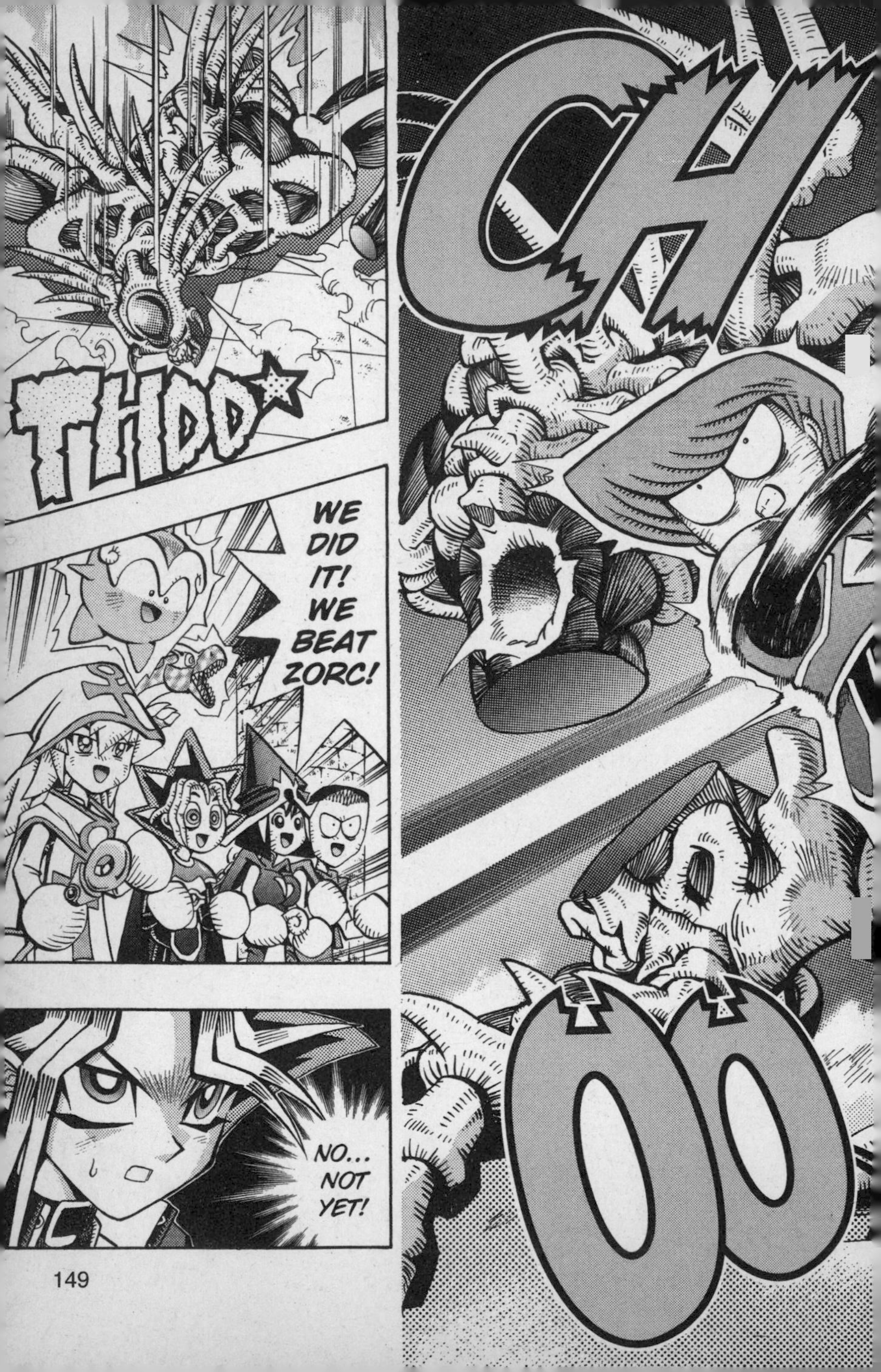
CH
OO
THDD
WE DID IT! WE BEAT ZORC!
NO... NOT YET!

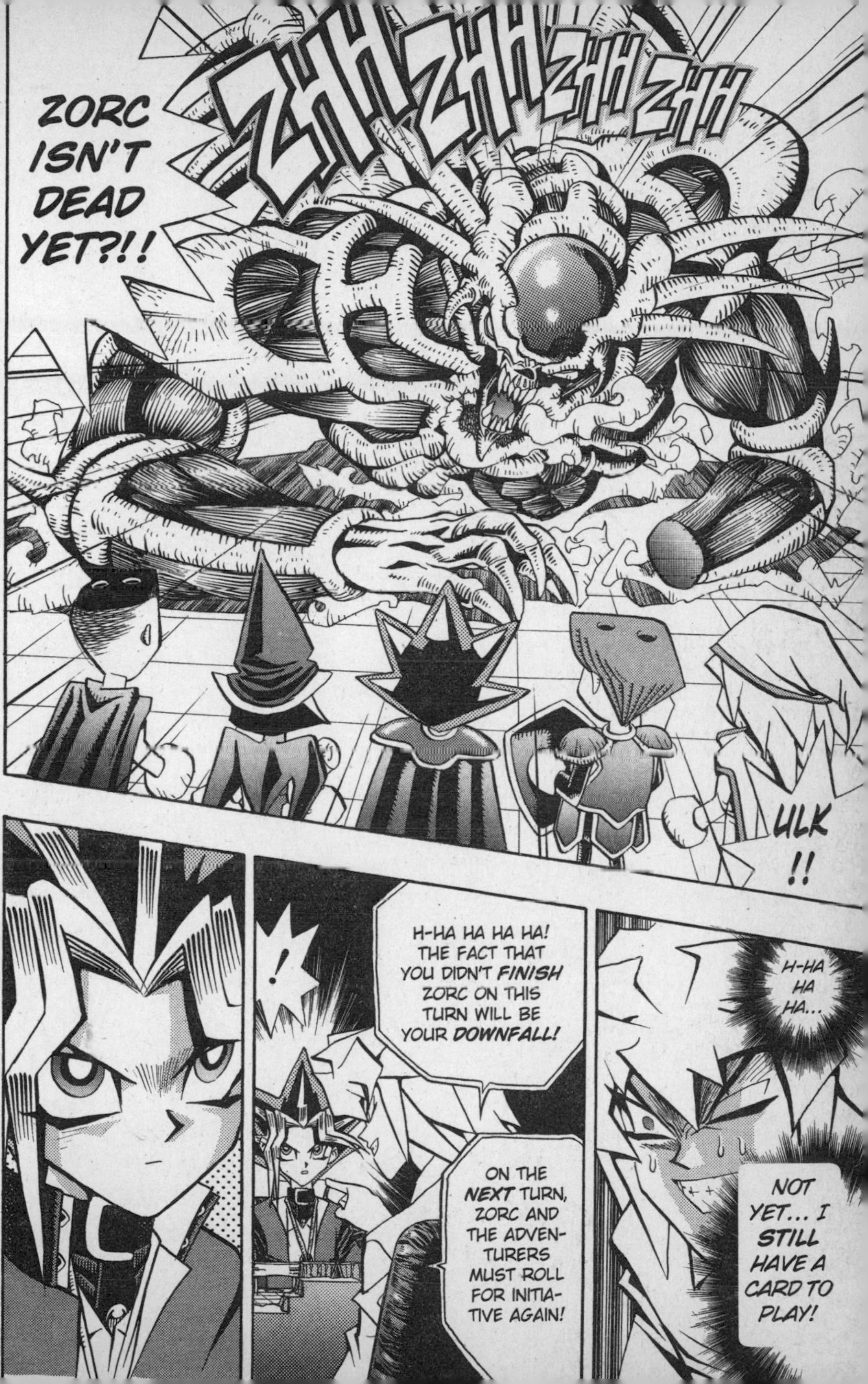
ZHH ZHH ZHH ZHH
ZORC ISN'T DEAD YET?!!
ULK !!
H-HA HA HA...
NOT YET... I *STILL* HAVE A CARD TO PLAY!
!
H-HA HA HA HA! THE FACT THAT YOU DIDN'T *FINISH* ZORC ON THIS TURN WILL BE YOUR *DOWNFALL!*
ON THE *NEXT* TURN, ZORC AND THE ADVEN-TURERS MUST ROLL FOR INITIA-TIVE AGAIN!

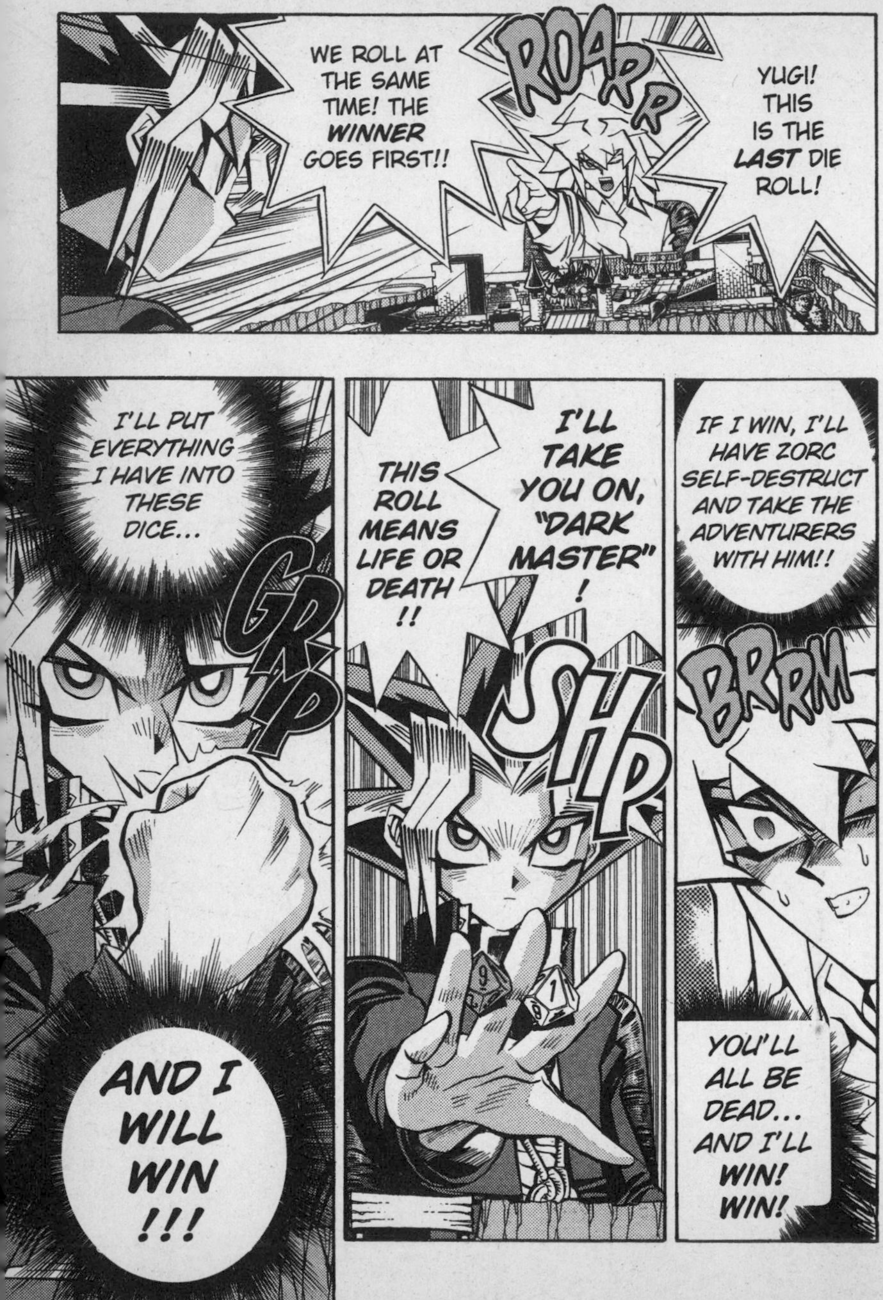
YUGI! THIS IS THE LAST DIE ROLL!
ROARR
WE ROLL AT THE SAME TIME! THE WINNER GOES FIRST!!
IF I WIN, I'LL HAVE ZORC SELF-DESTRUCT AND TAKE THE ADVENTURERS WITH HIM!!
BRRM
YOU'LL ALL BE DEAD... AND I'LL WIN! WIN!
I'LL TAKE YOU ON, "DARK MASTER"!
THIS ROLL MEANS LIFE OR DEATH!!
SHP
I'LL PUT EVERYTHING I HAVE INTO THESE DICE...
GRIP
AND I WILL WIN!!!

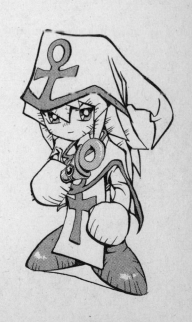

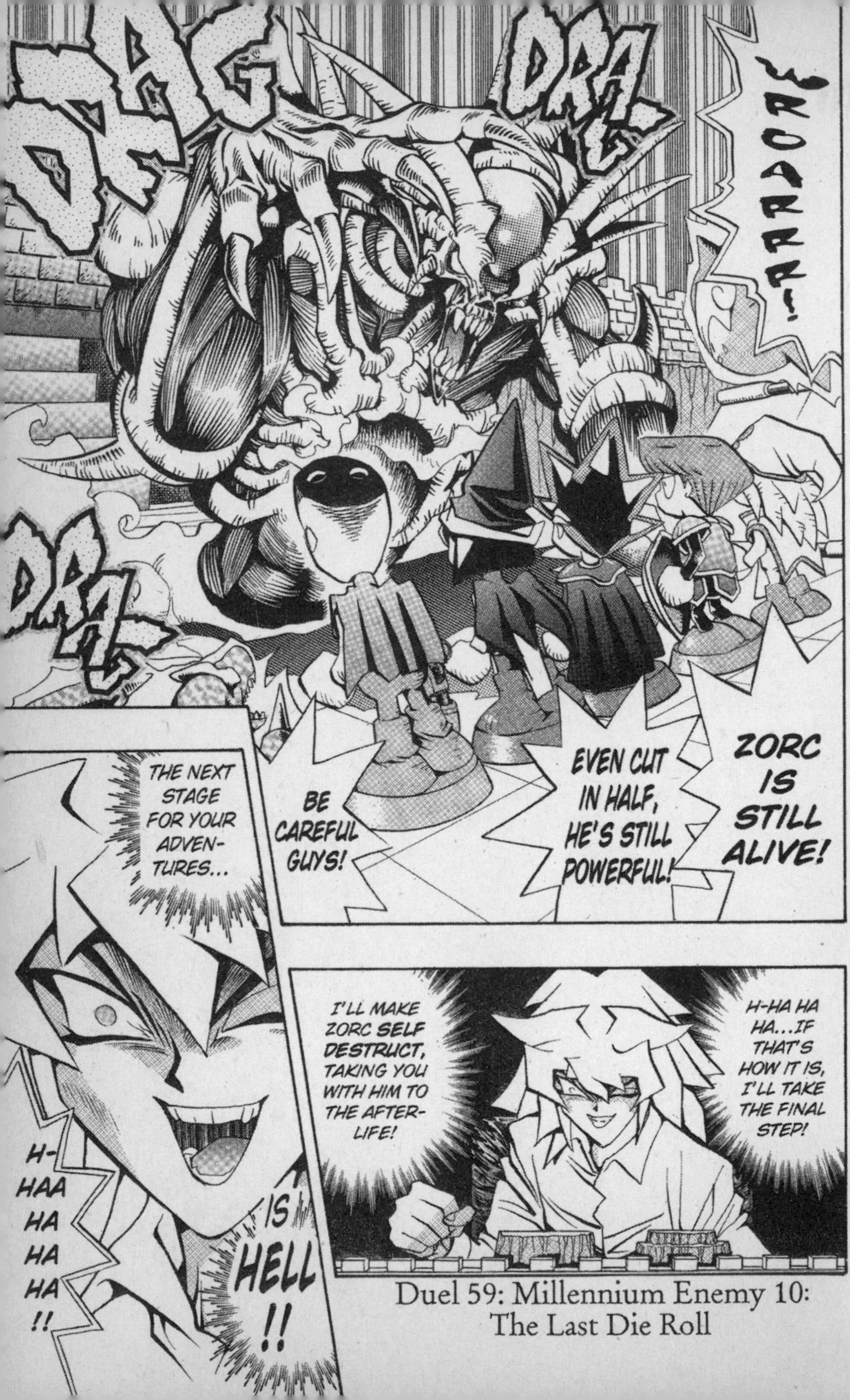
DRA
DRAG
DRA
ROARRR!
ZORC IS STILL ALIVE!
EVEN CUT IN HALF, HE'S STILL POWERFUL!
BE CAREFUL GUYS!
H-HA HA HA...IF THAT'S HOW IT IS, I'LL TAKE THE FINAL STEP!
I'LL MAKE ZORC SELF DESTRUCT, TAKING YOU WITH HIM TO THE AFTER-LIFE!
THE NEXT STAGE FOR YOUR ADVEN-TURES...
IS HELL!!
H-HAA HA HA HA!!
Duel 59: Millennium Enemy 10: The Last Die Roll

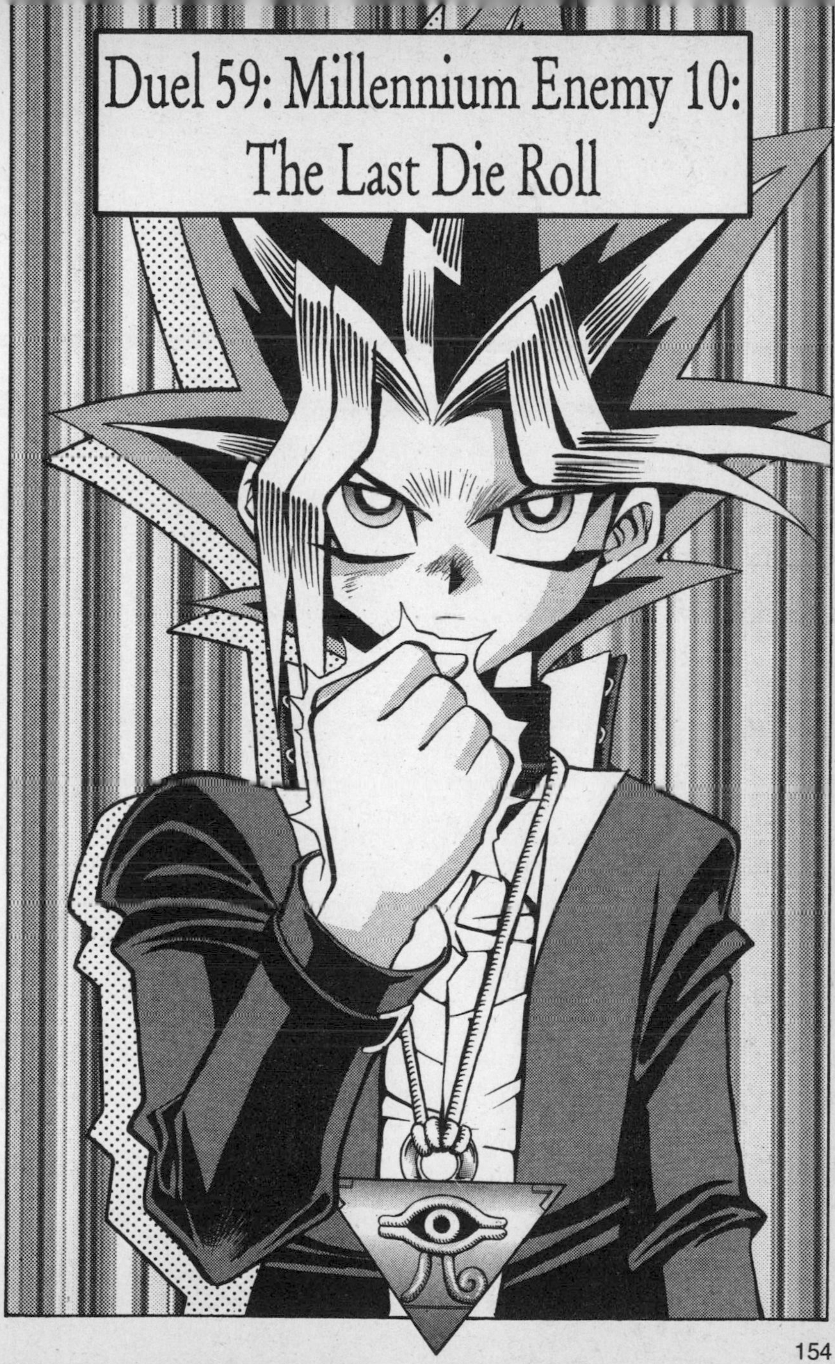
Duel 59: Millennium Enemy 10:
The Last Die Roll

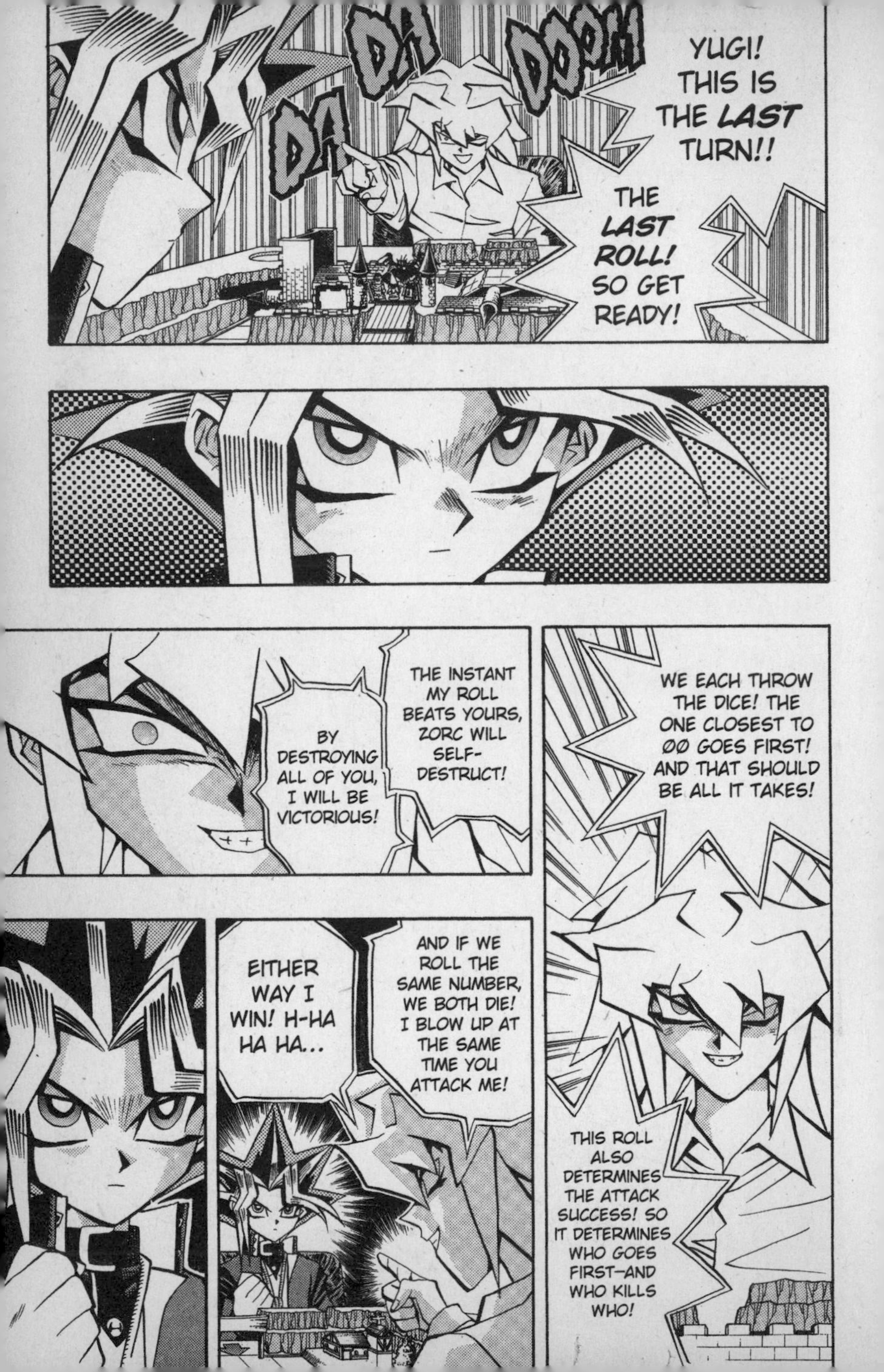
DA DA DOOM!!
YUGI! THIS IS THE LAST TURN!!
THE LAST ROLL! SO GET READY!
WE EACH THROW THE DICE! THE ONE CLOSEST TO ØØ GOES FIRST! AND THAT SHOULD BE ALL IT TAKES!
THIS ROLL ALSO DETERMINES THE ATTACK SUCCESS! SO IT DETERMINES WHO GOES FIRST—AND WHO KILLS WHO!
THE INSTANT MY ROLL BEATS YOURS, ZORC WILL SELF-DESTRUCT!
BY DESTROYING ALL OF YOU, I WILL BE VICTORIOUS!
AND IF WE ROLL THE SAME NUMBER, WE BOTH DIE! I BLOW UP AT THE SAME TIME YOU ATTACK ME!
EITHER WAY I WIN! H-HA HA HA...

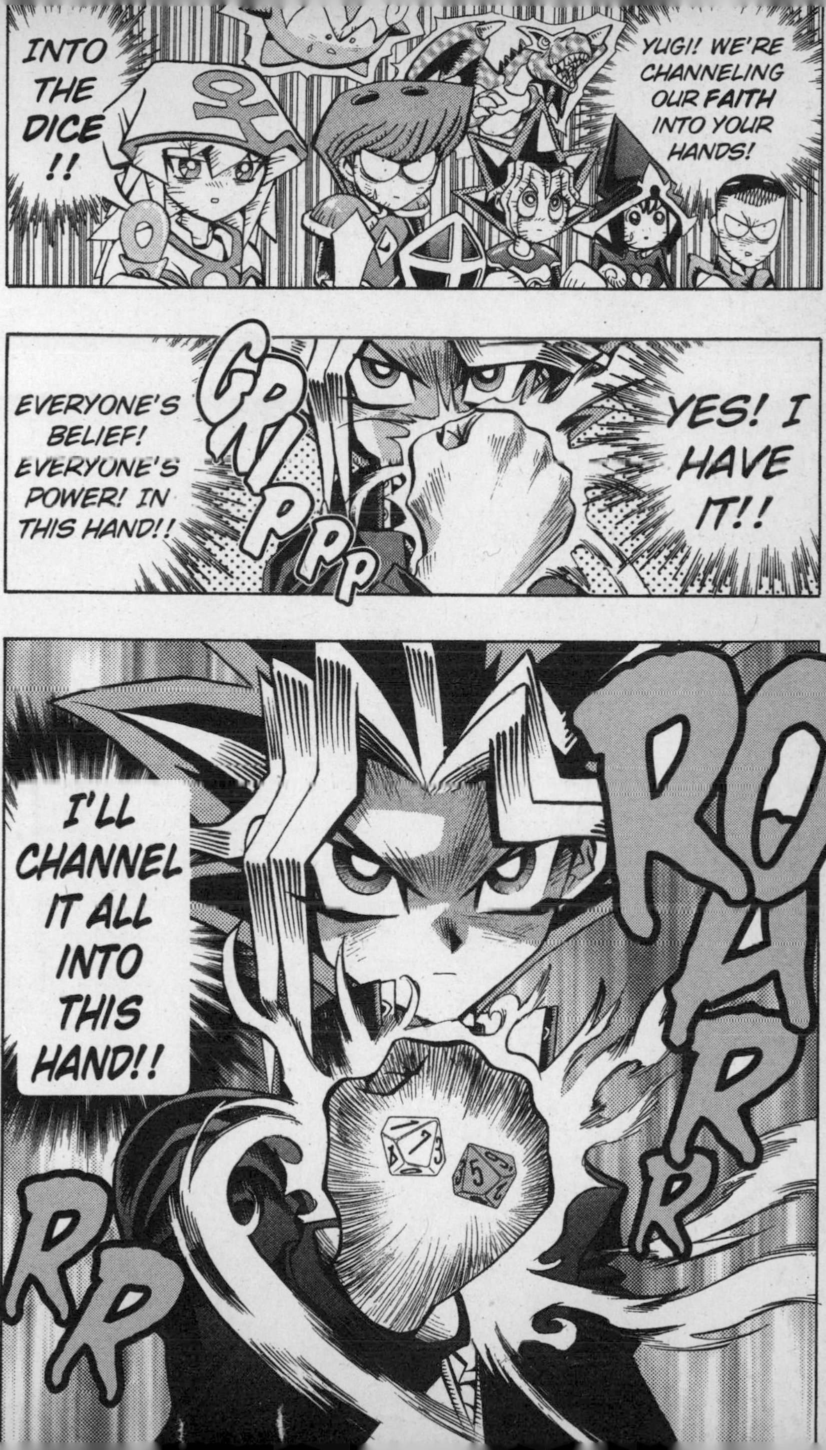
YUGI! WE'RE CHANNELING OUR FAITH INTO YOUR HANDS!
INTO THE DICE!!
YES! I HAVE IT!!
GRIPPP
EVERYONE'S BELIEF! EVERYONE'S POWER! IN THIS HAND!!
RORRR
I'LL CHANNEL IT ALL INTO THIS HAND!!
RR

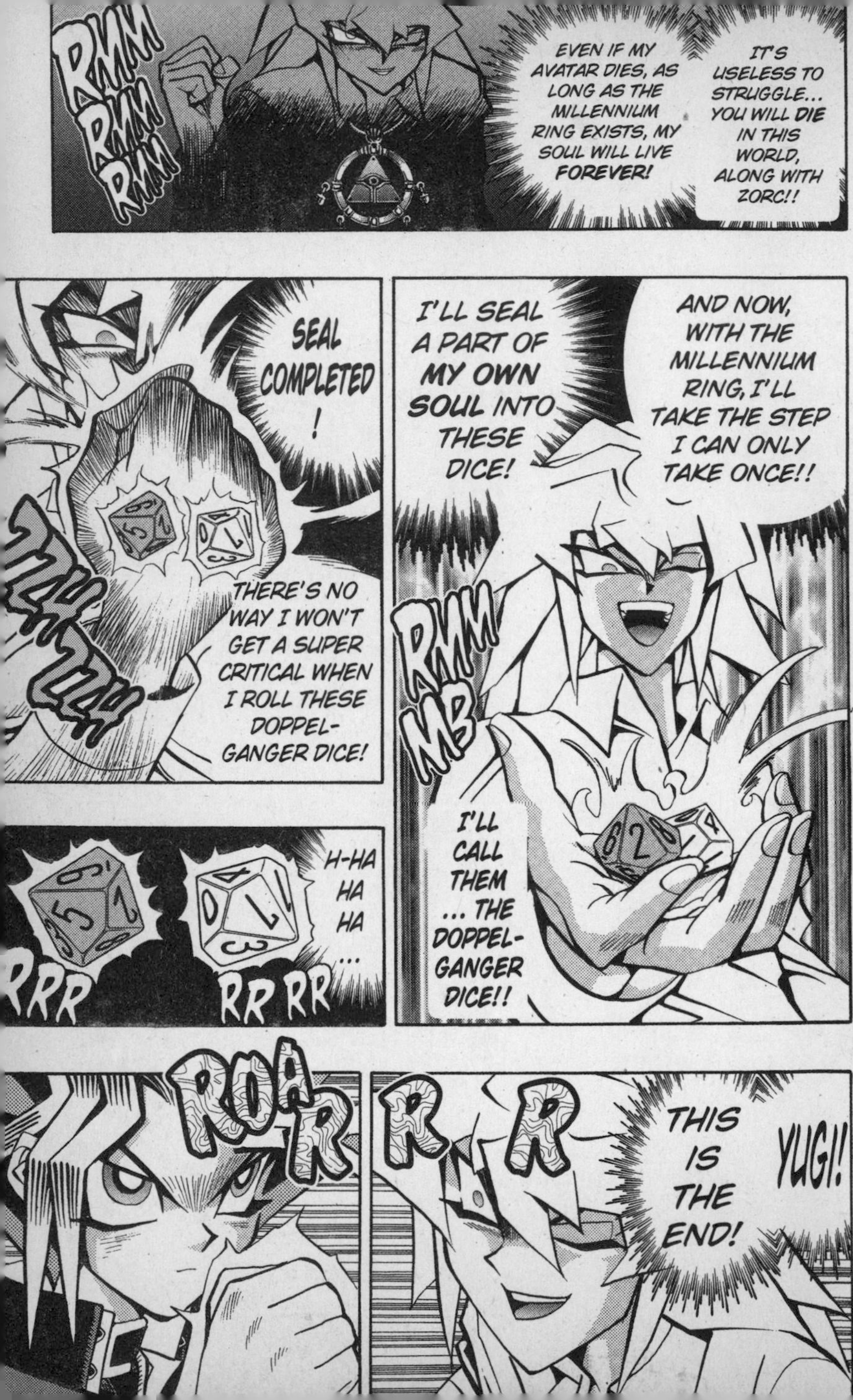
IT'S USELESS TO STRUGGLE... YOU WILL DIE IN THIS WORLD, ALONG WITH ZORC!!
EVEN IF MY AVATAR DIES, AS LONG AS THE MILLENNIUM RING EXISTS, MY SOUL WILL LIVE FOREVER!
RMM RMM RMM
AND NOW, WITH THE MILLENNIUM RING, I'LL TAKE THE STEP I CAN ONLY TAKE ONCE!!
I'LL SEAL A PART OF MY OWN SOUL INTO THESE DICE!
RMMMB
I'LL CALL THEM ... THE DOPPEL-GANGER DICE!!
SEAL COMPLETED!
THERE'S NO WAY I WON'T GET A SUPER CRITICAL WHEN I ROLL THESE DOPPEL-GANGER DICE!
H-HA HA HA...
RRR
RR RR
THIS IS THE END!
YUGI!
ROARR R R

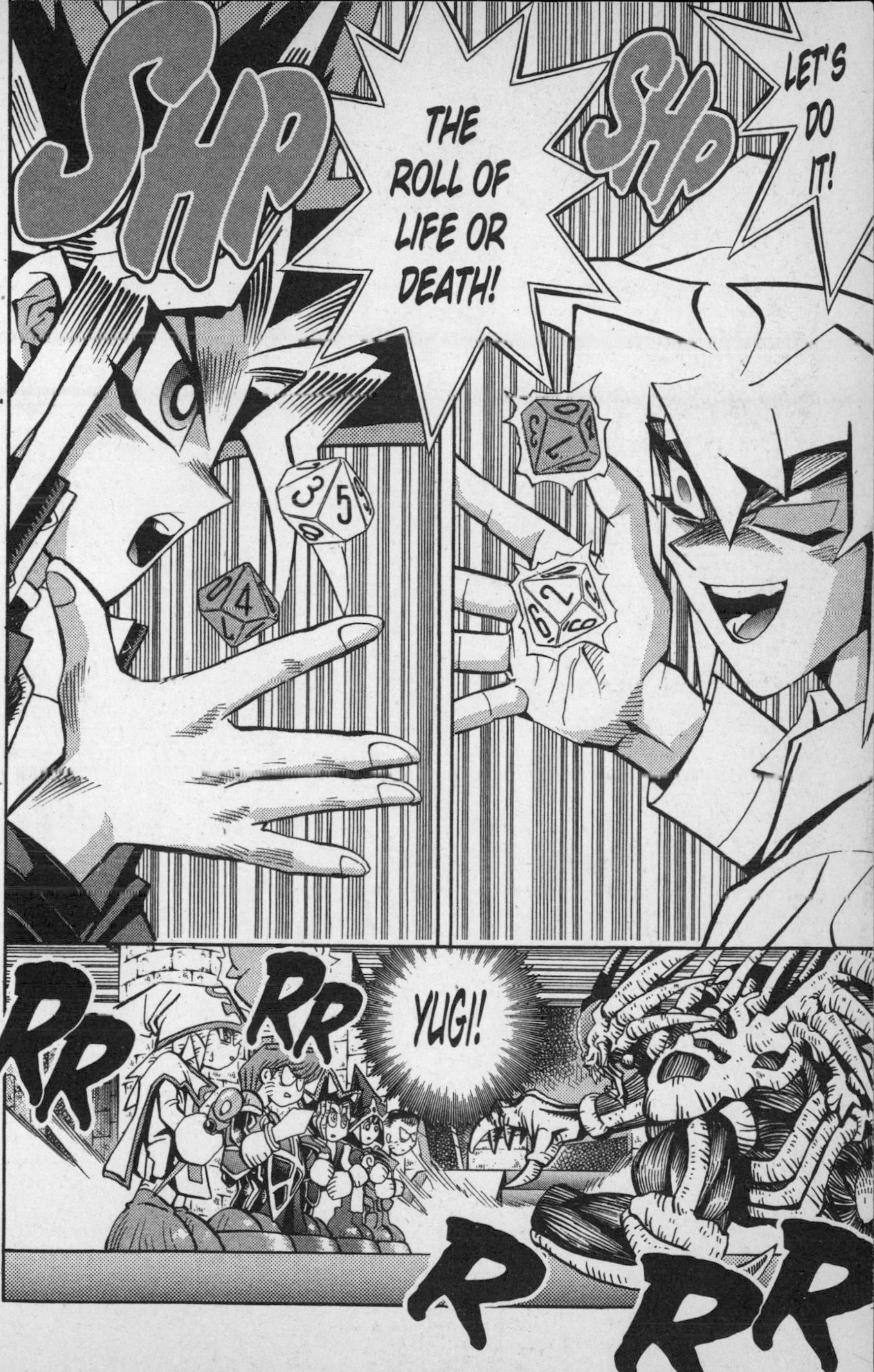
LET'S DO IT!
SHP
THE ROLL OF LIFE OR DEATH!
SHP
YUGI!
RR
RR
RR
R

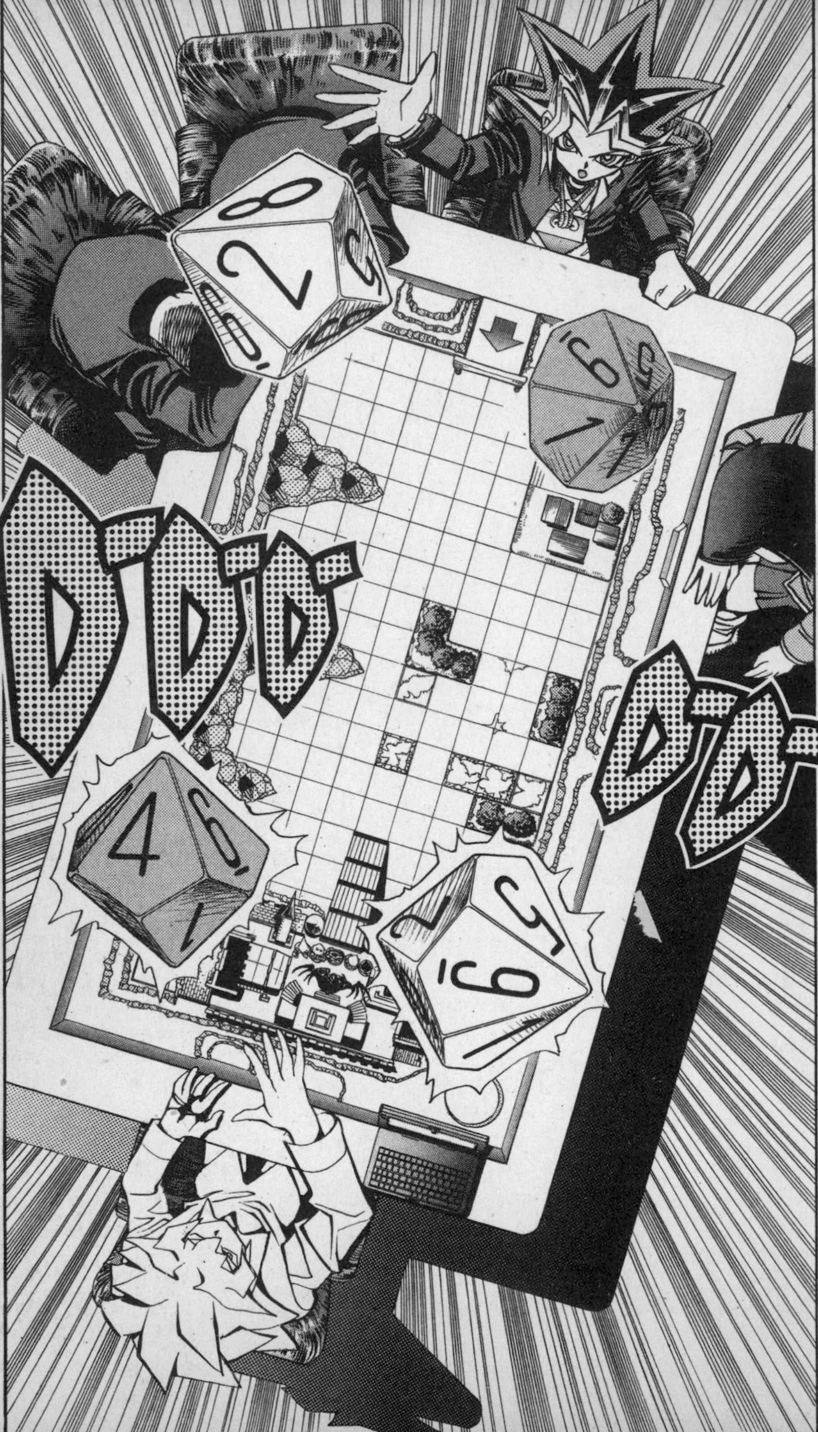
D'D'D'
D'D'

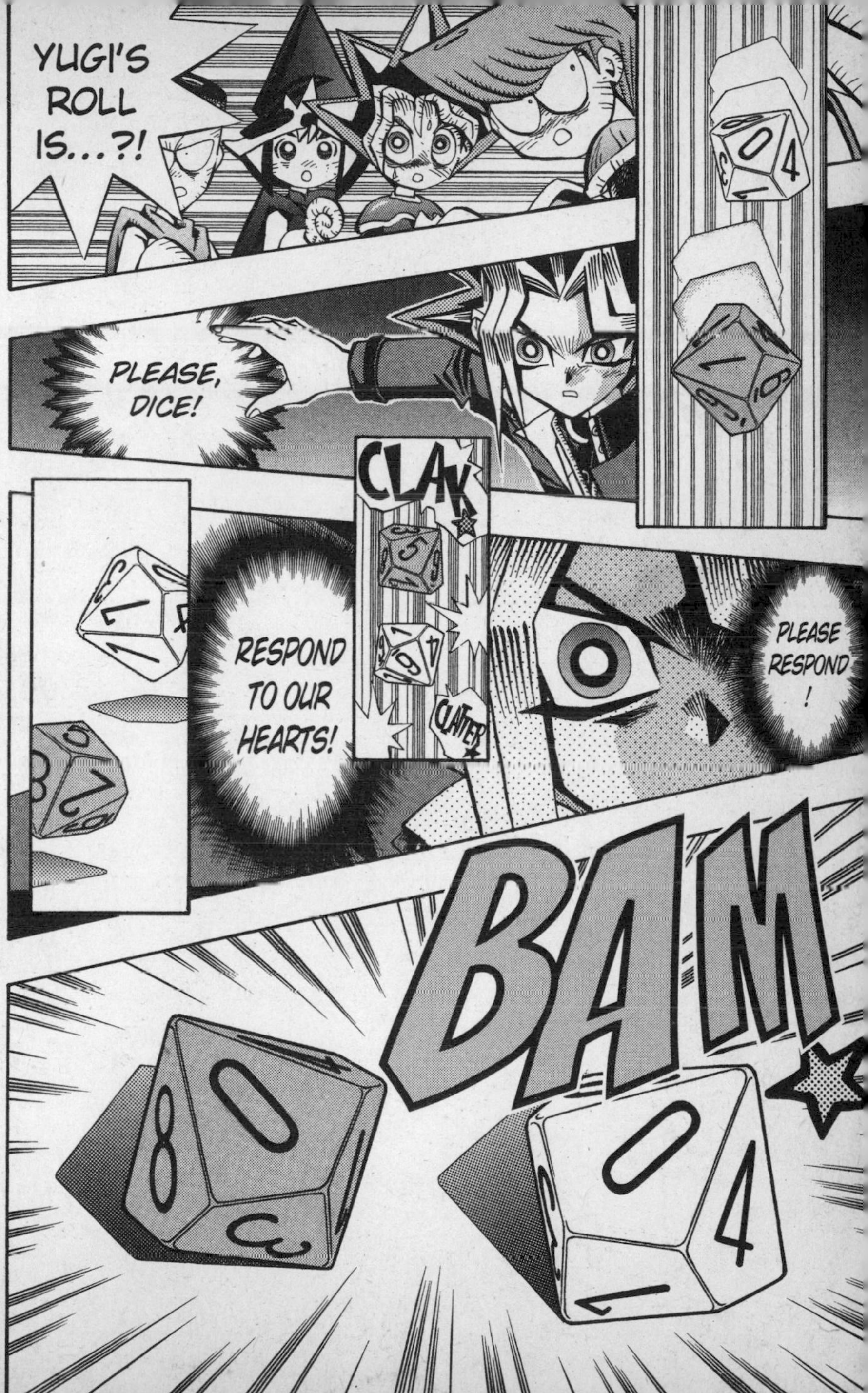
YUGI'S ROLL IS...?!
PLEASE, DICE!
PLEASE RESPOND!
CLAK
CLATTER
RESPOND TO OUR HEARTS!
BAM

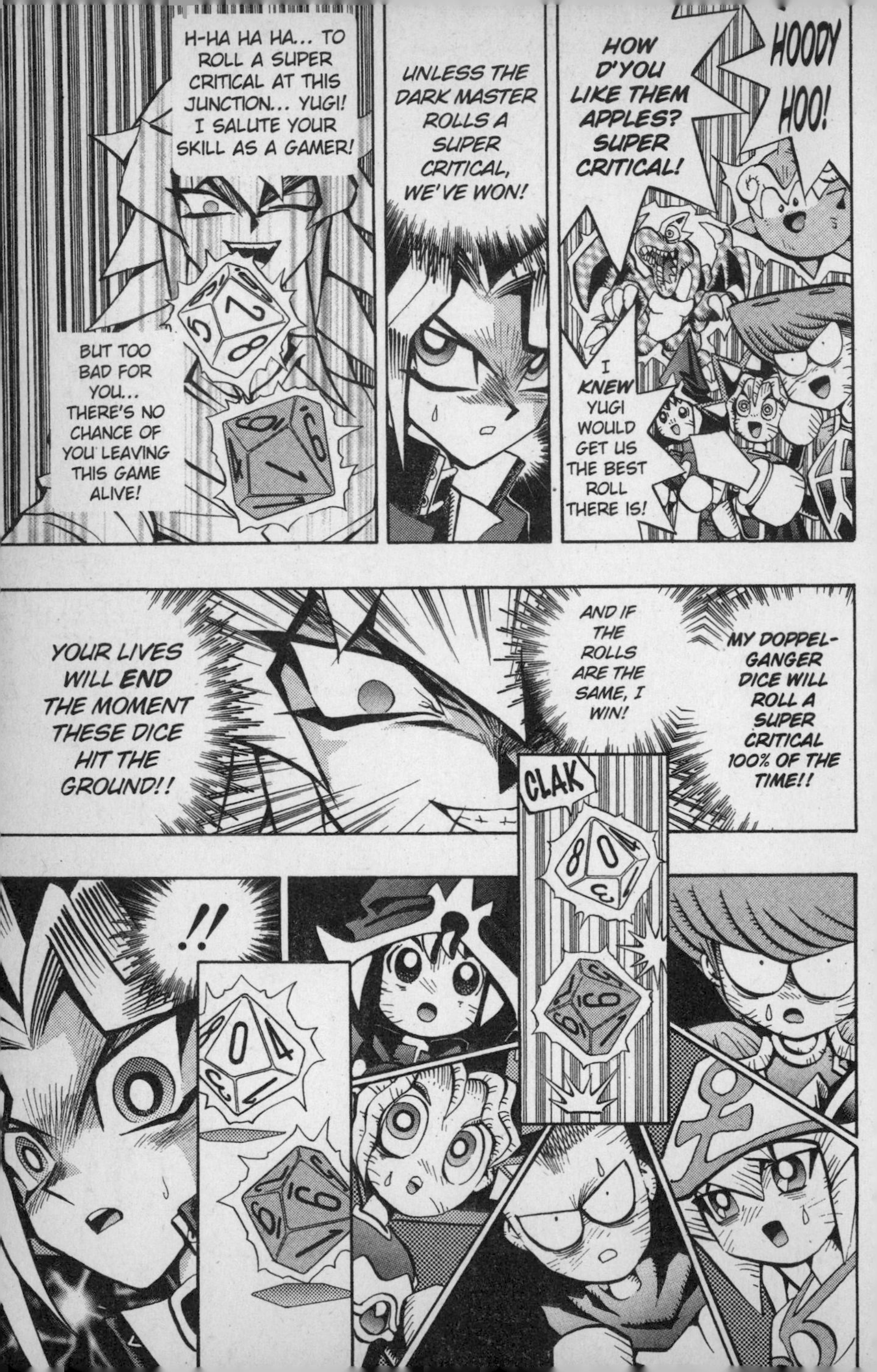
HOODY HOO!
HOW D'YOU LIKE THEM APPLES? SUPER CRITICAL!
I KNEW YUGI WOULD GET US THE BEST ROLL THERE IS!
UNLESS THE DARK MASTER ROLLS A SUPER CRITICAL, WE'VE WON!
H-HA HA HA... TO ROLL A SUPER CRITICAL AT THIS JUNCTION... YUGI! I SALUTE YOUR SKILL AS A GAMER!
BUT TOO BAD FOR YOU... THERE'S NO CHANCE OF YOU LEAVING THIS GAME ALIVE!
MY DOPPEL-GANGER DICE WILL ROLL A SUPER CRITICAL 100% OF THE TIME!!
AND IF THE ROLLS ARE THE SAME, I WIN!
YOUR LIVES WILL END THE MOMENT THESE DICE HIT THE GROUND!!
CLAK
!!

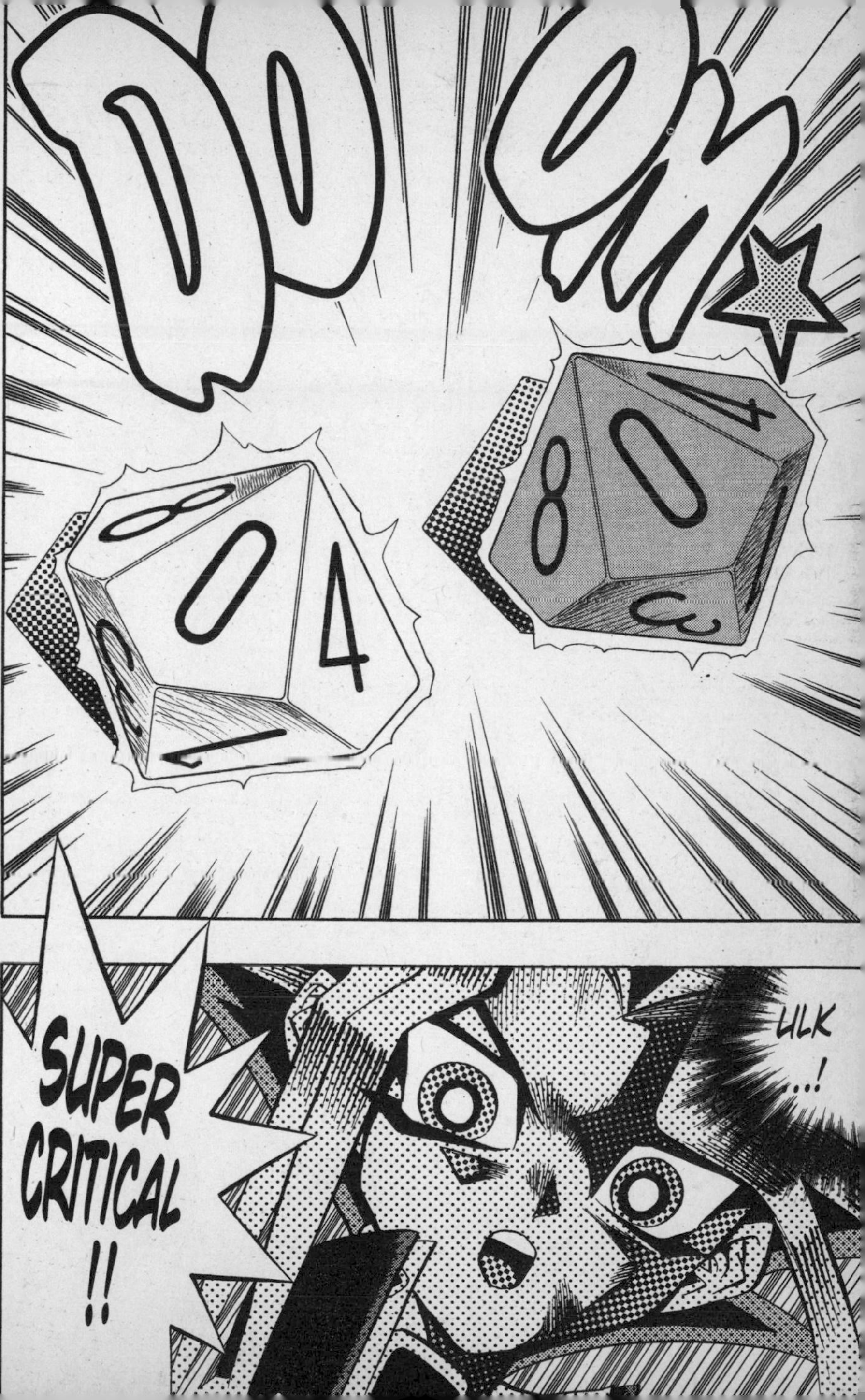

DOOM
ULK ...!
SUPER CRITICAL !!

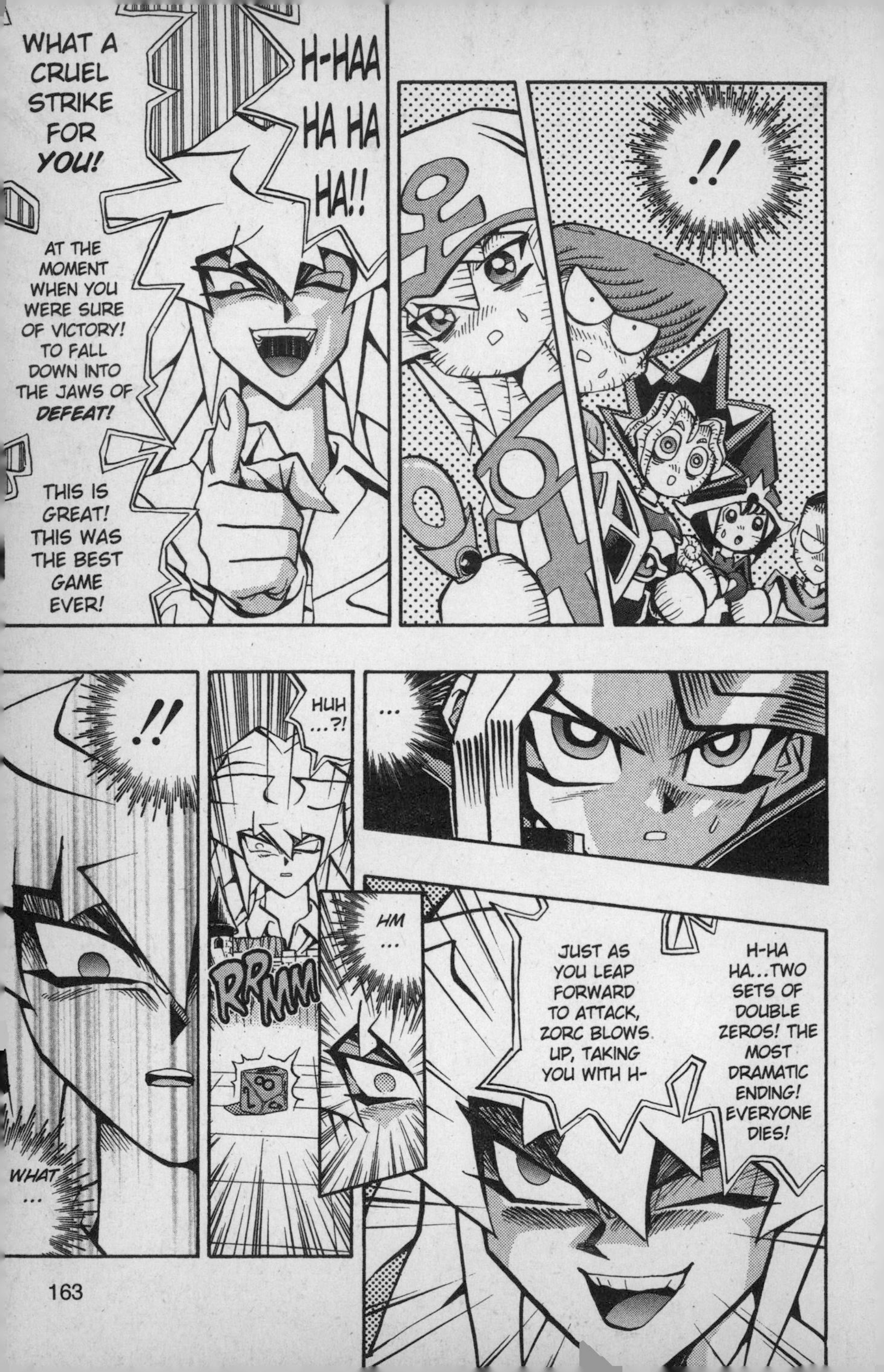
!!
H-HAA HA HA HA!!
WHAT A CRUEL STRIKE FOR *YOU!*
AT THE MOMENT WHEN YOU WERE SURE OF VICTORY! TO FALL DOWN INTO THE JAWS OF *DEFEAT!*
THIS IS GREAT! THIS WAS THE BEST GAME EVER!
...
H-HA HA...TWO SETS OF DOUBLE ZEROS! THE MOST DRAMATIC ENDING! EVERYONE DIES!
JUST AS YOU LEAP FORWARD TO ATTACK, ZORC BLOWS UP, TAKING YOU WITH H-
HM ...
HUH ...?!
RRMM
!!
WHAT ...

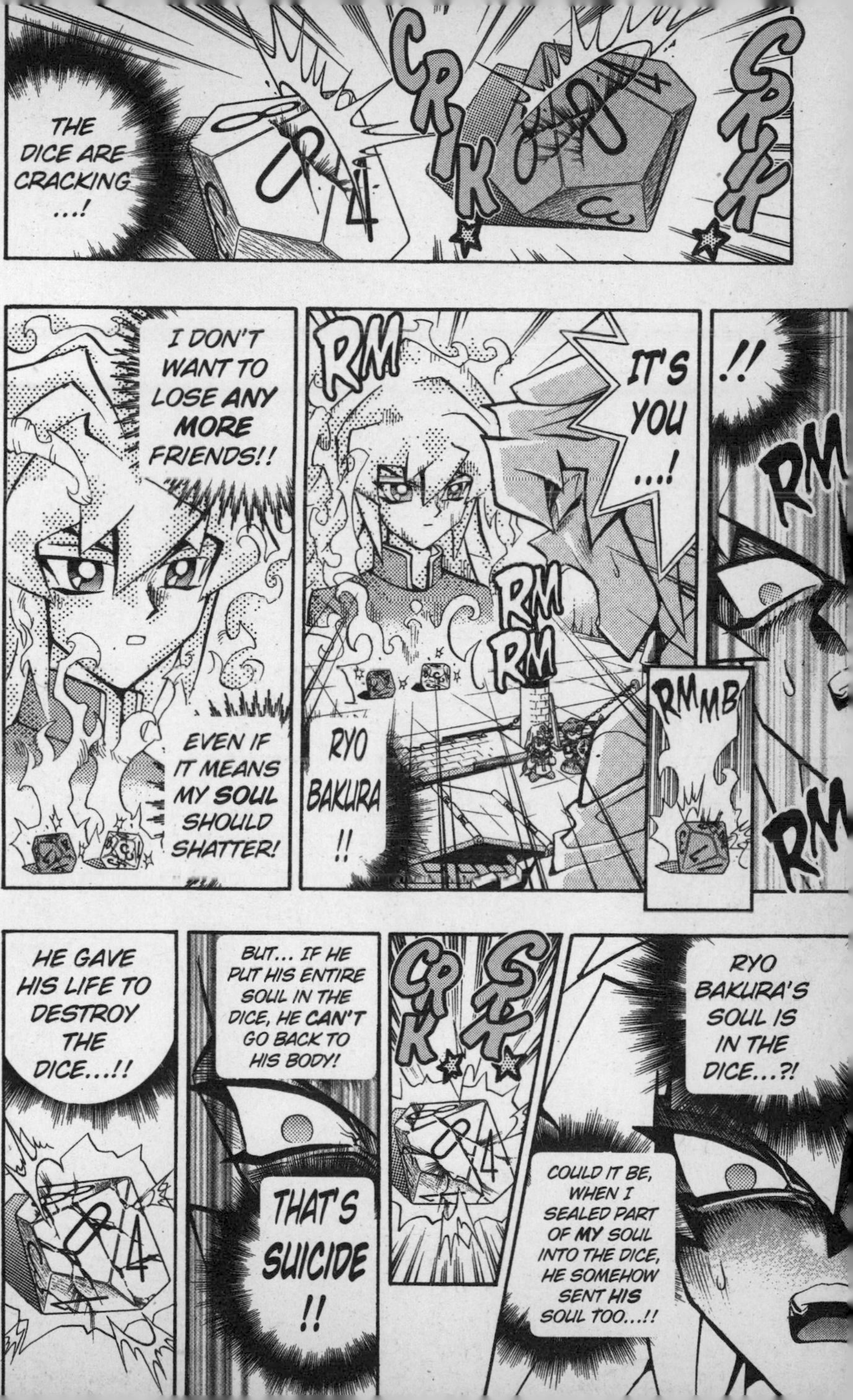
CRIK
CRIK
THE DICE ARE CRACKING...!
!!
RM
RM
IT'S YOU...!
RM
RM RM
RYO BAKURA!!
RMMB
I DON'T WANT TO LOSE ANY MORE FRIENDS!!
EVEN IF IT MEANS MY SOUL SHOULD SHATTER!
RYO BAKURA'S SOUL IS IN THE DICE...?!
COULD IT BE, WHEN I SEALED PART OF MY SOUL INTO THE DICE, HE SOMEHOW SENT HIS SOUL TOO...!!
CRIK
CRIK
BUT... IF HE PUT HIS ENTIRE SOUL IN THE DICE, HE CAN'T GO BACK TO HIS BODY!
THAT'S SUICIDE!!
HE GAVE HIS LIFE TO DESTROY THE DICE...!!

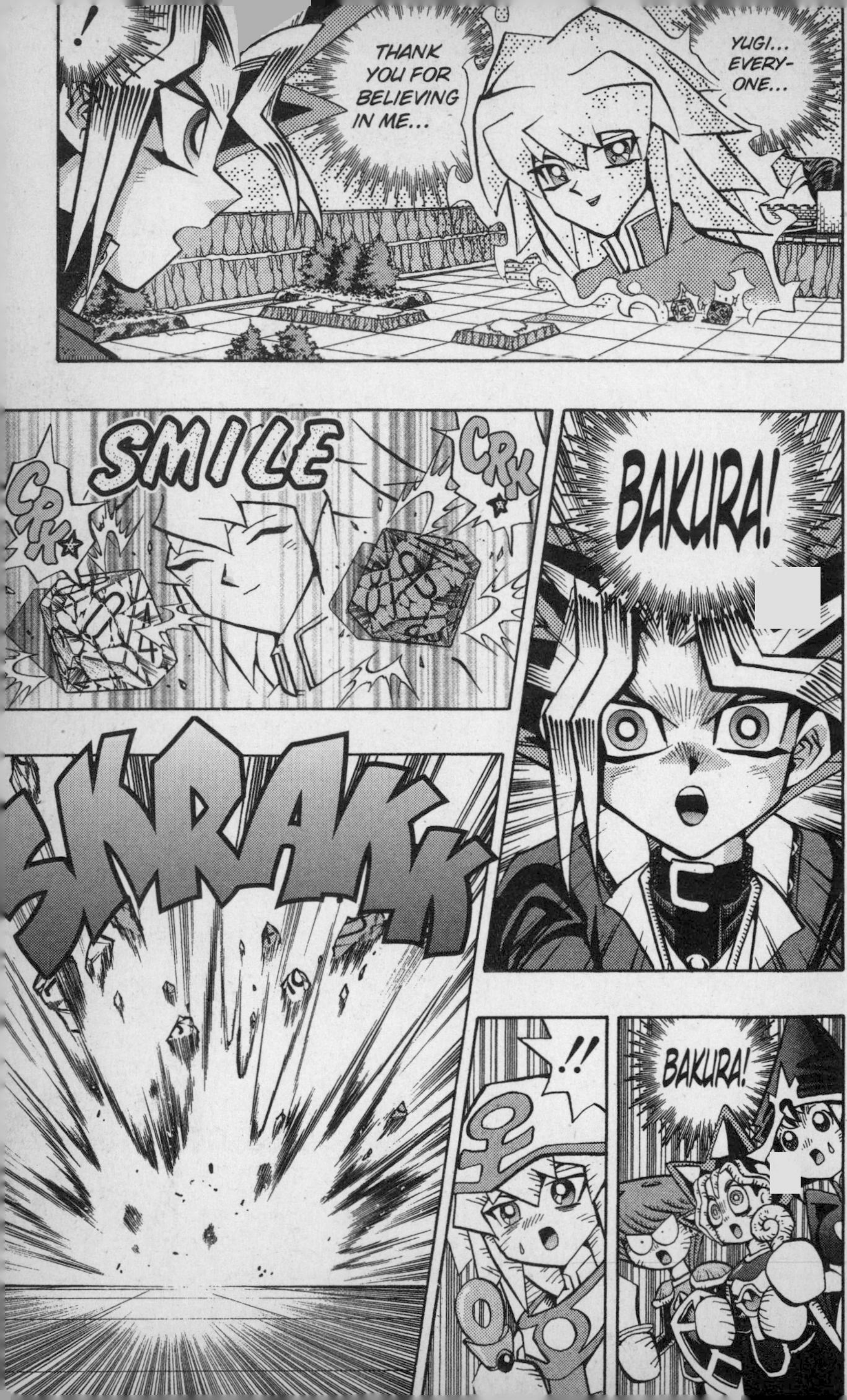
YUGI... EVERY-ONE...
THANK YOU FOR BELIEVING IN ME...
!
BAKURA!
CRK
SMILE
CRK
SHRAK
BAKURA!
!!

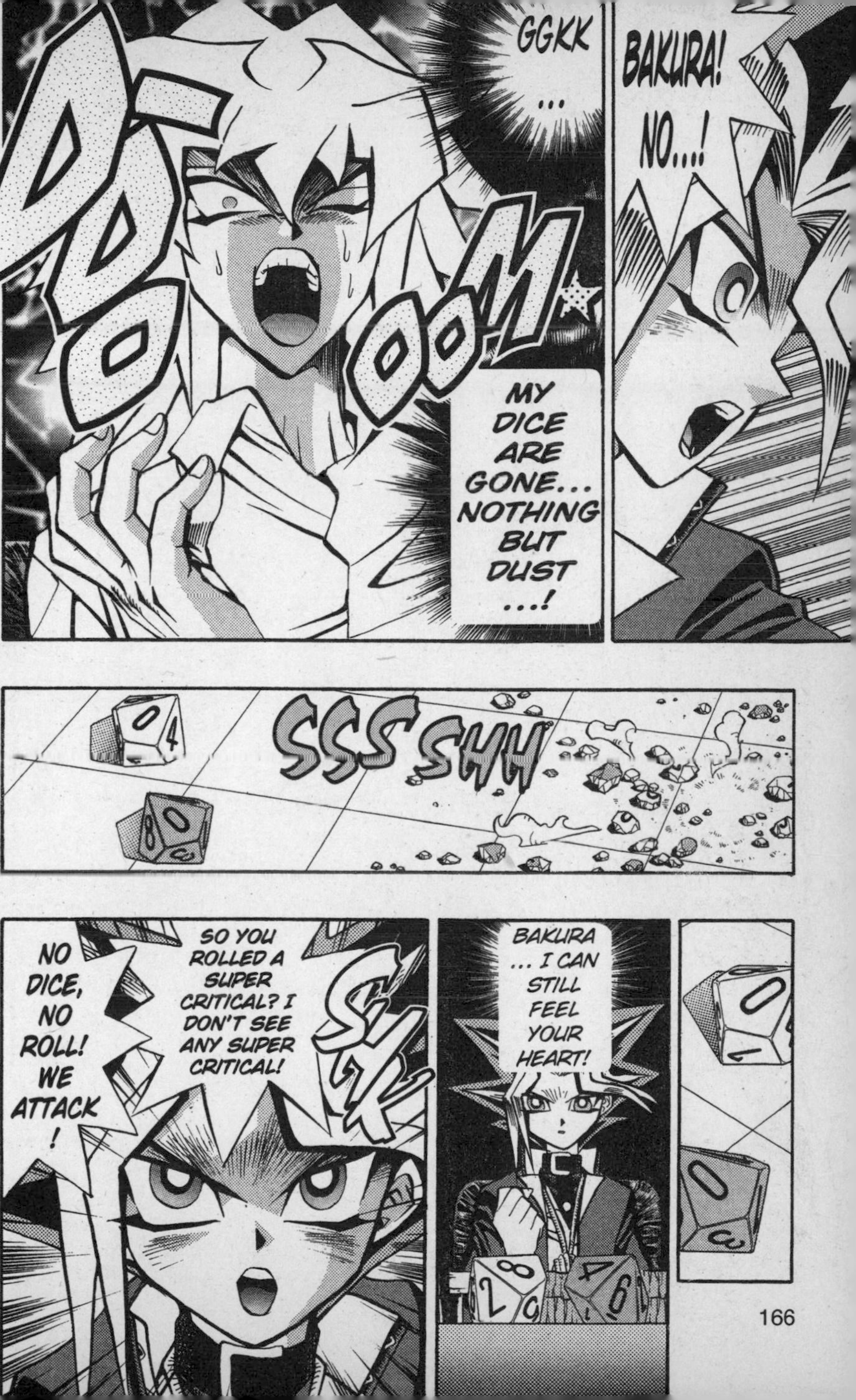
BAKURA! NO...!
GGKK ...
DOOOOM
MY DICE ARE GONE... NOTHING BUT DUST ...!
SSSSHH
BAKURA ... I CAN STILL FEEL YOUR HEART!
SK
SO YOU ROLLED A SUPER CRITICAL? I DON'T SEE ANY SUPER CRITICAL!
NO DICE, NO ROLL! WE ATTACK !

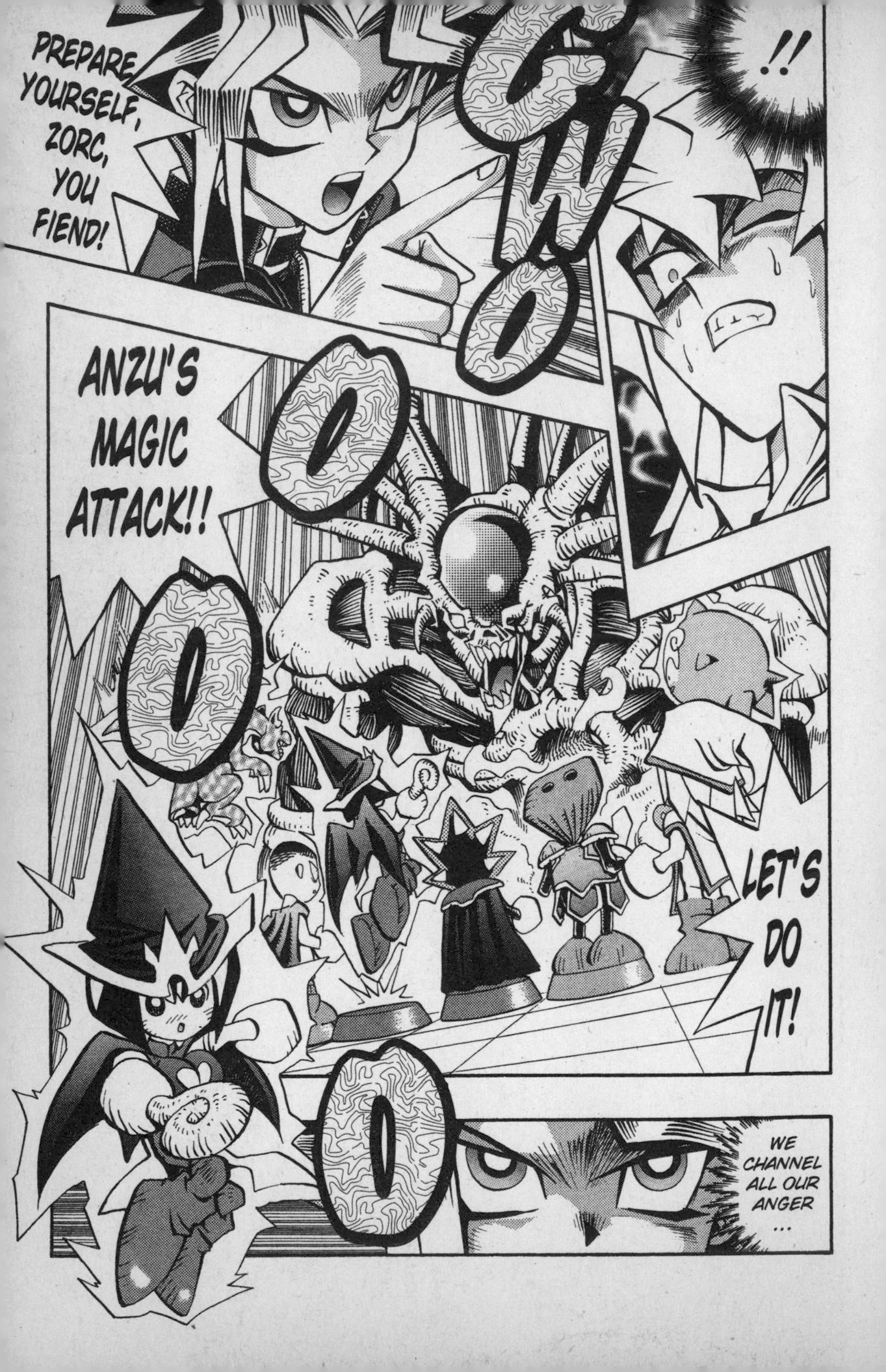
!!
PREPARE YOURSELF, ZORC, YOU FIEND!
LET'S DO IT!
ANZU'S MAGIC ATTACK!!
WE CHANNEL ALL OUR ANGER ...

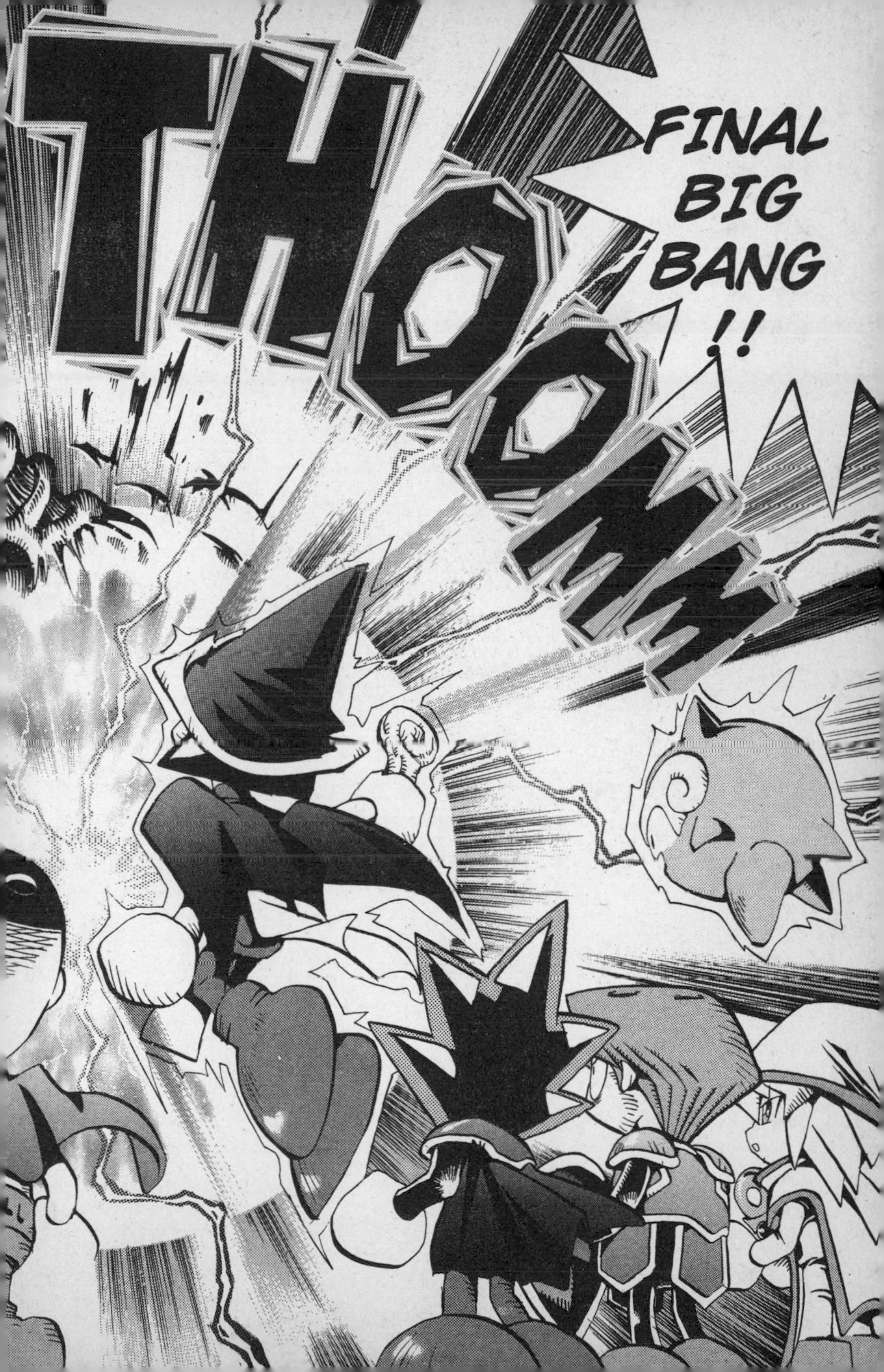
FINAL BIG BANG !!
THOOM

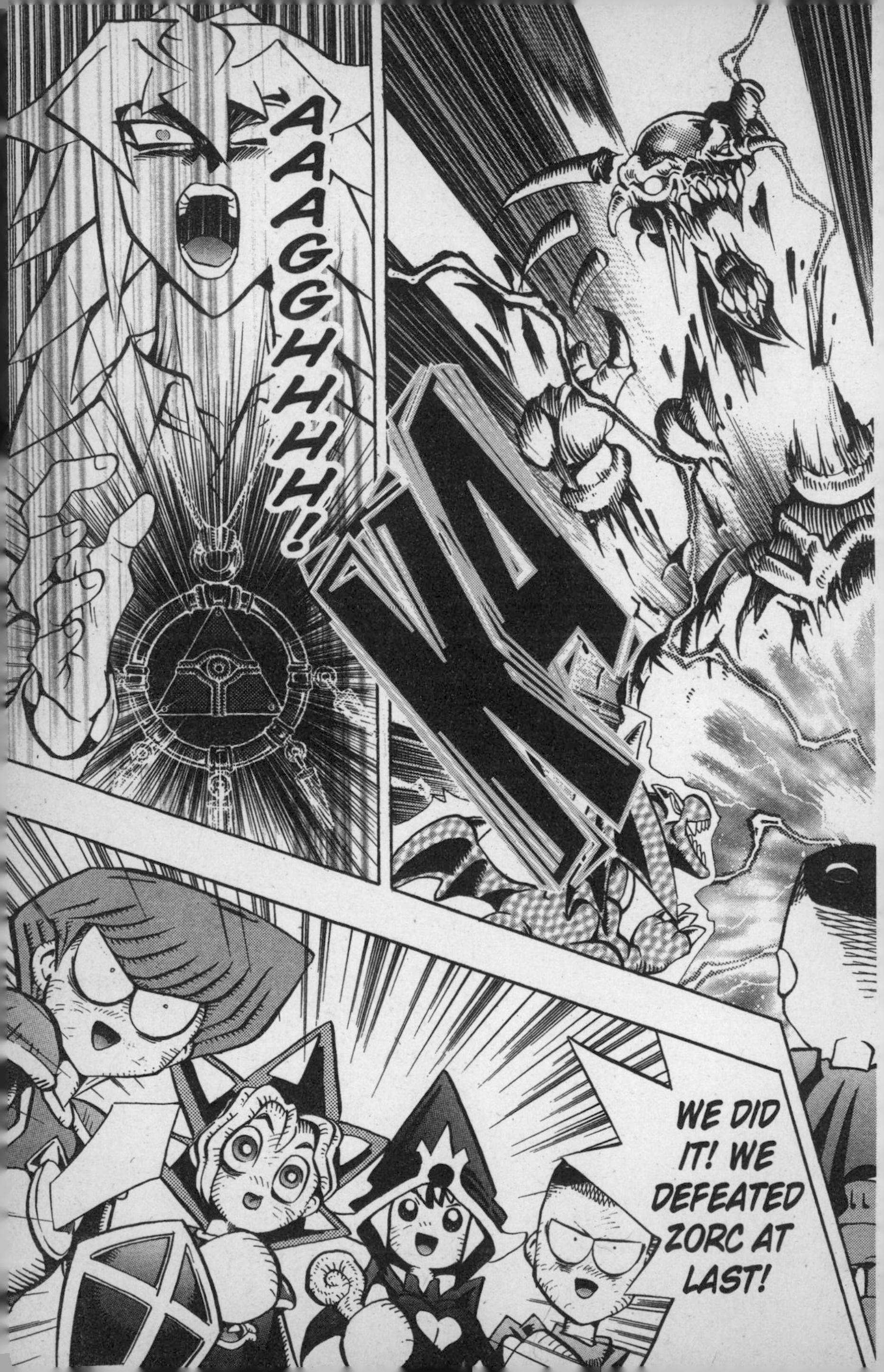
AAAAGGHHHHH!
WE DID IT! WE DEFEATED ZORC AT LAST!

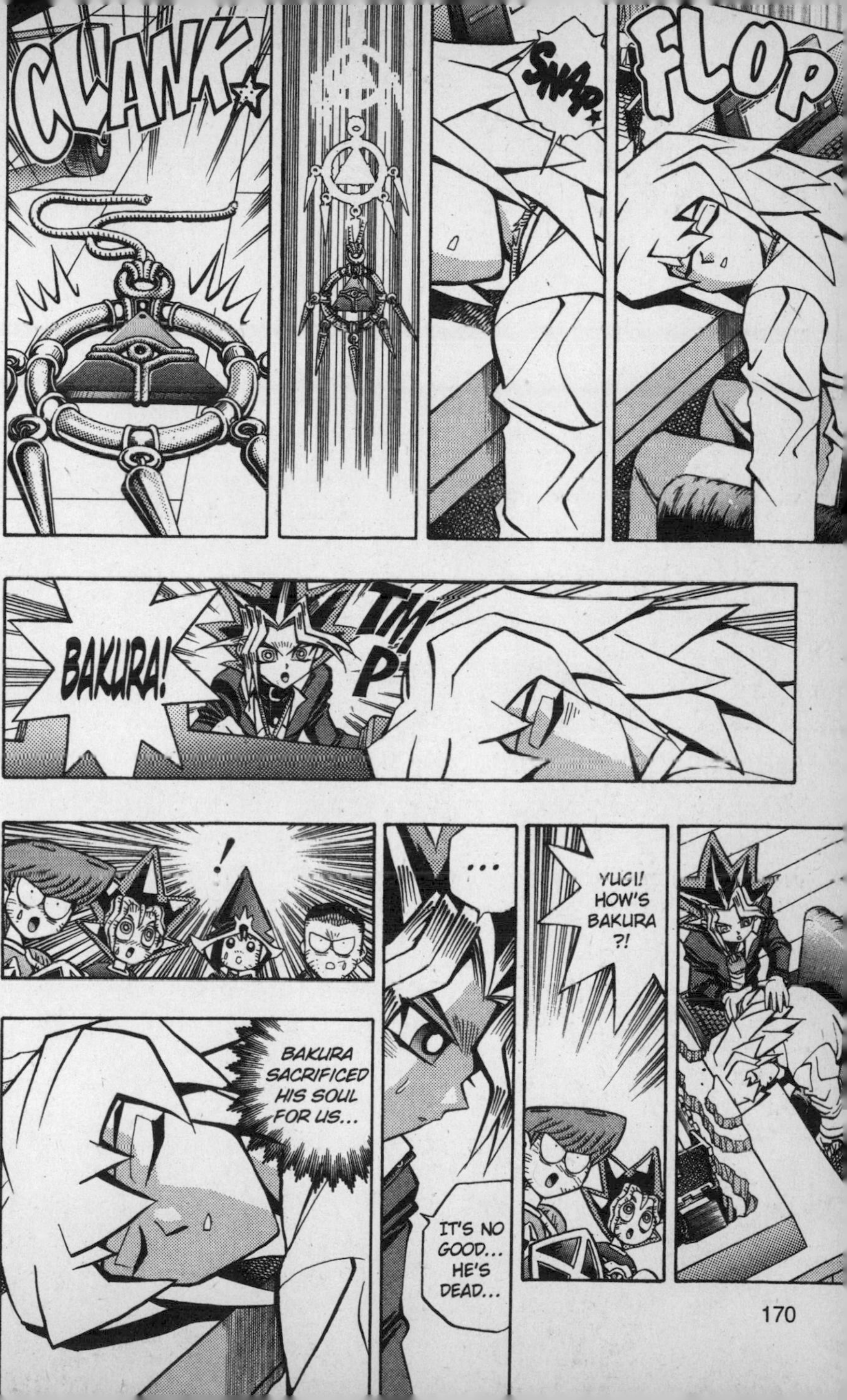
FLOP
SNAP
CLANK
TMP
BAKURA!
YUGI! HOW'S BAKURA ?!
...
IT'S NO GOOD... HE'S DEAD...
!
BAKURA SACRIFICED HIS SOUL FOR US...

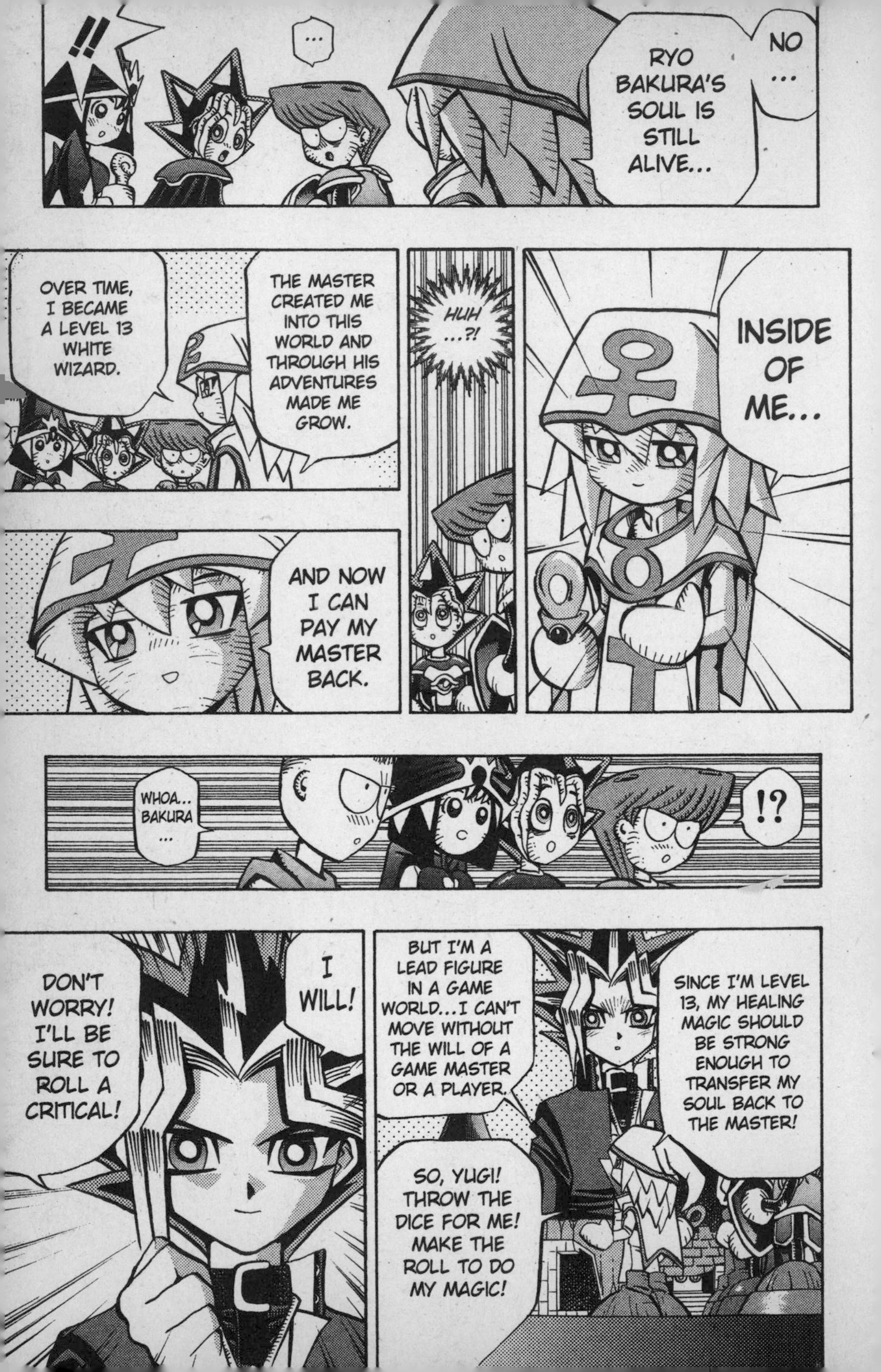
NO ...
RYO BAKURA'S SOUL IS STILL ALIVE...
...
!!
INSIDE OF ME...
HUH ...?!
THE MASTER CREATED ME INTO THIS WORLD AND THROUGH HIS ADVENTURES MADE ME GROW.
OVER TIME, I BECAME A LEVEL 13 WHITE WIZARD.
AND NOW I CAN PAY MY MASTER BACK.
!?
WHOA... BAKURA ...
SINCE I'M LEVEL 13, MY HEALING MAGIC SHOULD BE STRONG ENOUGH TO TRANSFER MY SOUL BACK TO THE MASTER!
BUT I'M A LEAD FIGURE IN A GAME WORLD...I CAN'T MOVE WITHOUT THE WILL OF A GAME MASTER OR A PLAYER.
SO, YUGI! THROW THE DICE FOR ME! MAKE THE ROLL TO DO MY MAGIC!
I WILL!
DON'T WORRY! I'LL BE SURE TO ROLL A CRITICAL!

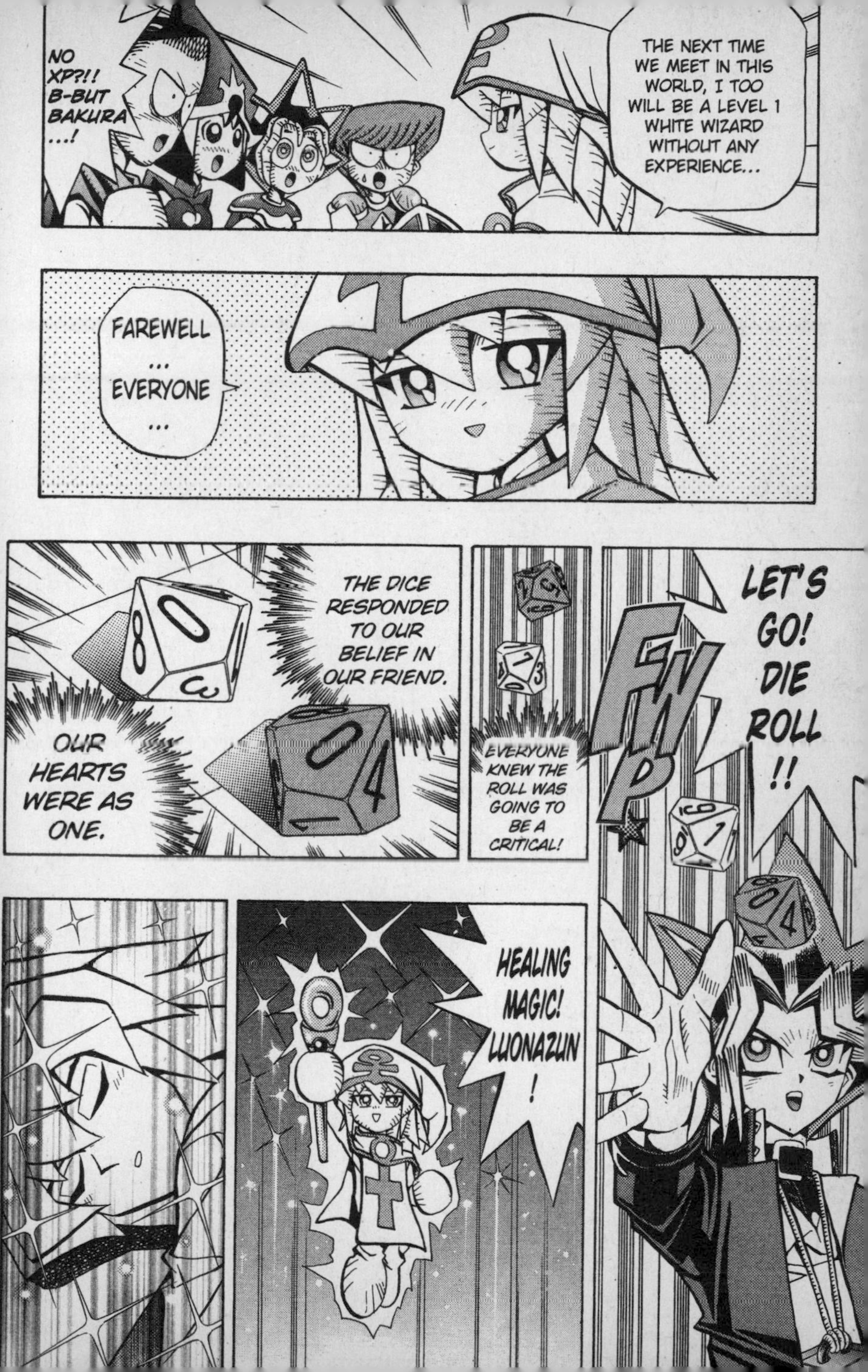
THE NEXT TIME WE MEET IN THIS WORLD, I TOO WILL BE A LEVEL 1 WHITE WIZARD WITHOUT ANY EXPERIENCE...
NO XP?!! B-BUT BAKURA ...!
FAREWELL ... EVERYONE ...
LET'S GO! DIE ROLL !!
FWIP
EVERYONE KNEW THE ROLL WAS GOING TO BE A CRITICAL!
THE DICE RESPONDED TO OUR BELIEF IN OUR FRIEND.
OUR HEARTS WERE AS ONE.
HEALING MAGIC! LUONAZUN !

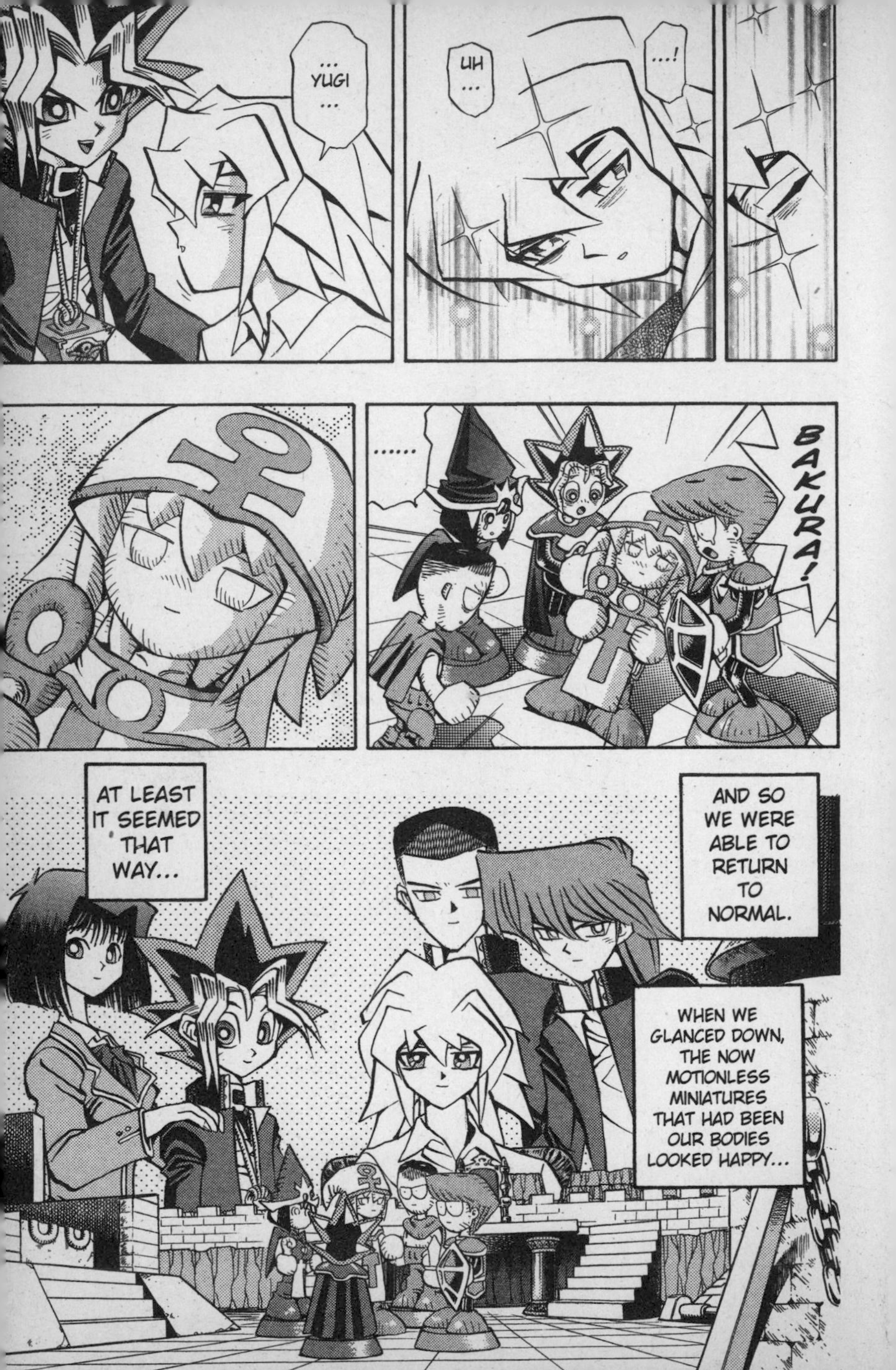
...!
UH ...
... YUGI ...
BAKURA!
......
AND SO WE WERE ABLE TO RETURN TO NORMAL.
WHEN WE GLANCED DOWN, THE NOW MOTIONLESS MINIATURES THAT HAD BEEN OUR BODIES LOOKED HAPPY...
AT LEAST IT SEEMED THAT WAY...

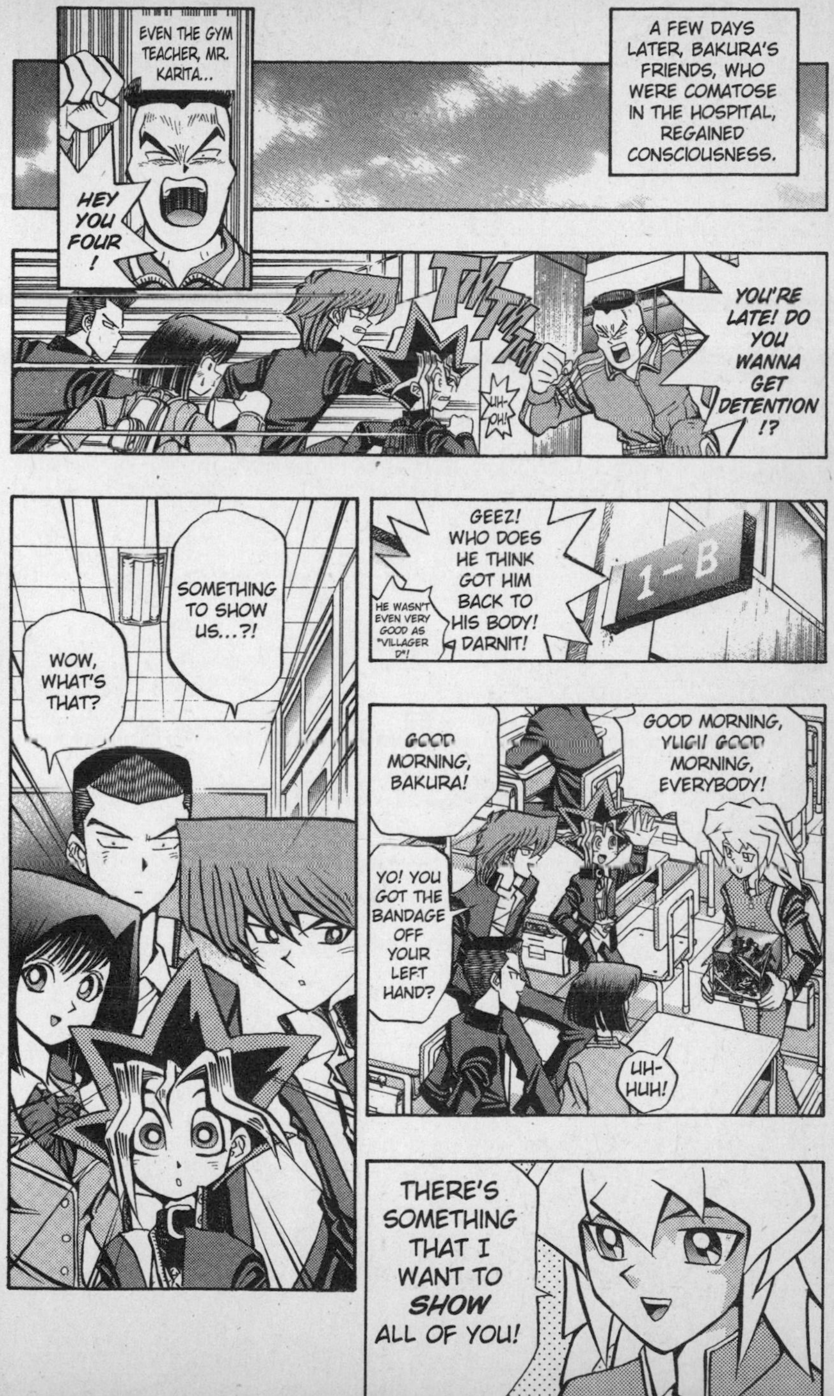
A FEW DAYS LATER, BAKURA'S FRIENDS, WHO WERE COMATOSE IN THE HOSPITAL, REGAINED CONSCIOUSNESS.
EVEN THE GYM TEACHER, MR. KARITA...
HEY YOU FOUR!
YOU'RE LATE! DO YOU WANNA GET DETENTION!?
UH-OH!
GEEZ! WHO DOES HE THINK GOT HIM BACK TO HIS BODY! DARNIT!
HE WASN'T EVEN VERY GOOD AS "VILLAGER D"!
1-B
GOOD MORNING, YUGI! GOOD MORNING, EVERYBODY!
GOOD MORNING, BAKURA!
YO! YOU GOT THE BANDAGE OFF YOUR LEFT HAND?
UH-HUH!
THERE'S SOMETHING THAT I WANT TO SHOW ALL OF YOU!
SOMETHING TO SHOW US...?!
WOW, WHAT'S THAT?

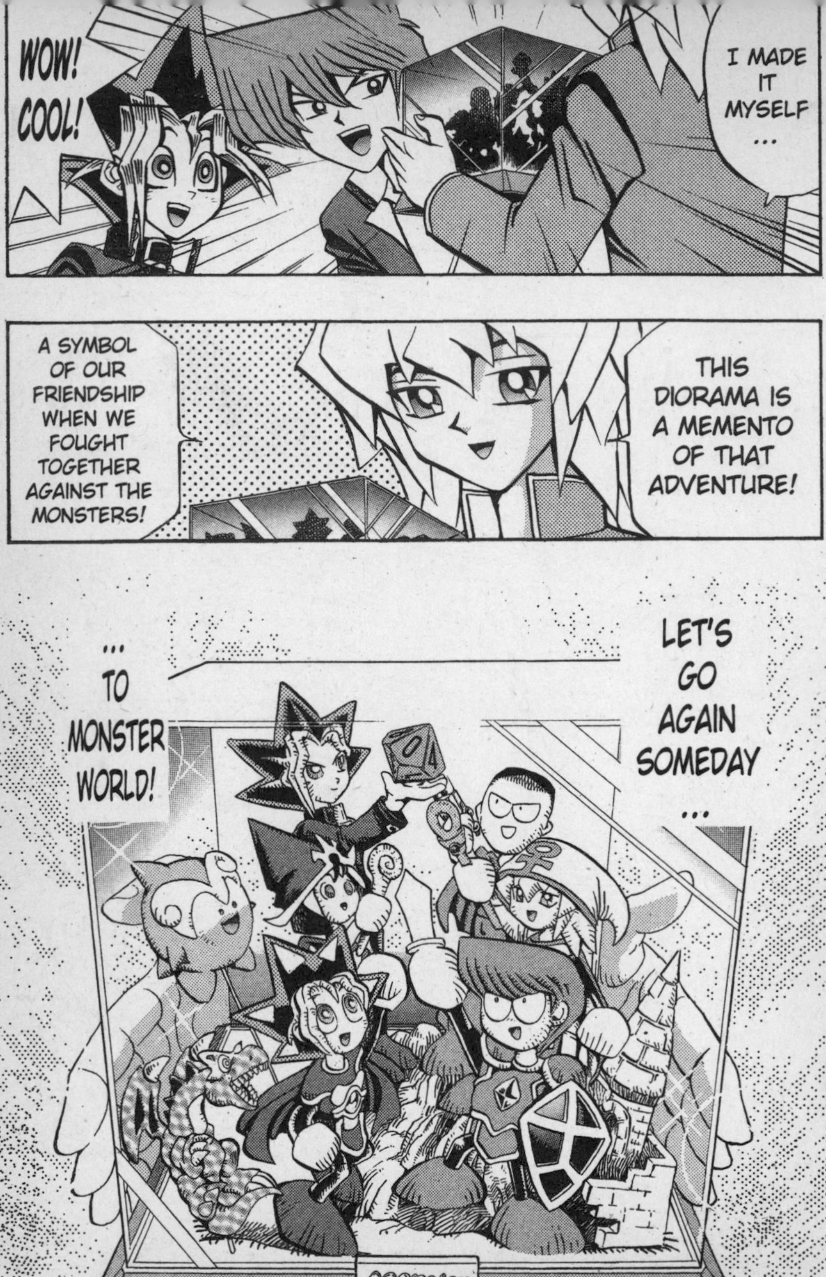
I MADE IT MYSELF ...
WOW! COOL!
THIS DIORAMA IS A MEMENTO OF THAT ADVENTURE!
A SYMBOL OF OUR FRIENDSHIP WHEN WE FOUGHT TOGETHER AGAINST THE MONSTERS!
LET'S GO AGAIN SOMEDAY ...
... TO MONSTER WORLD!
Monster World

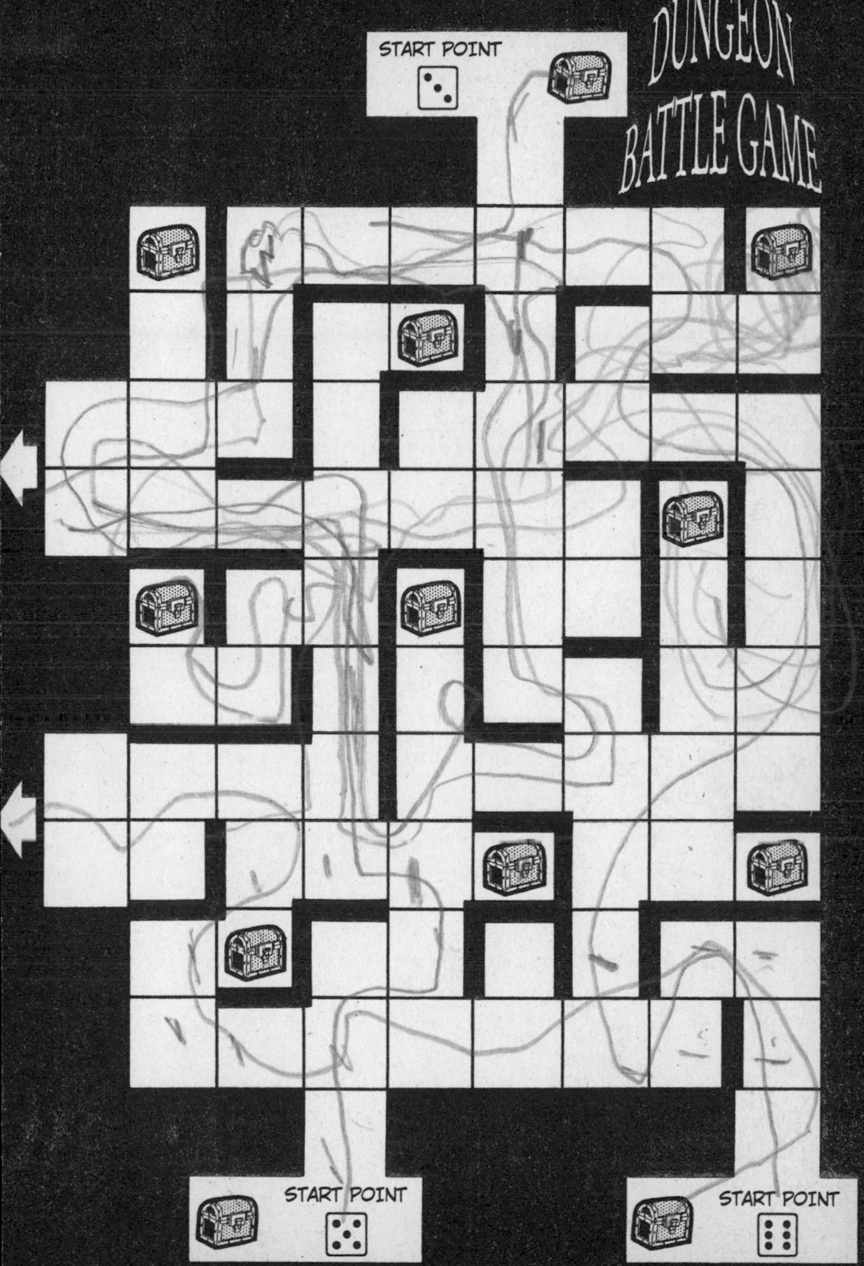
DUNGEON
BATTLE GAME
START POINT
START POINT
START POINT

TURN TO THE NEXT PAGE FOR THE RULES!

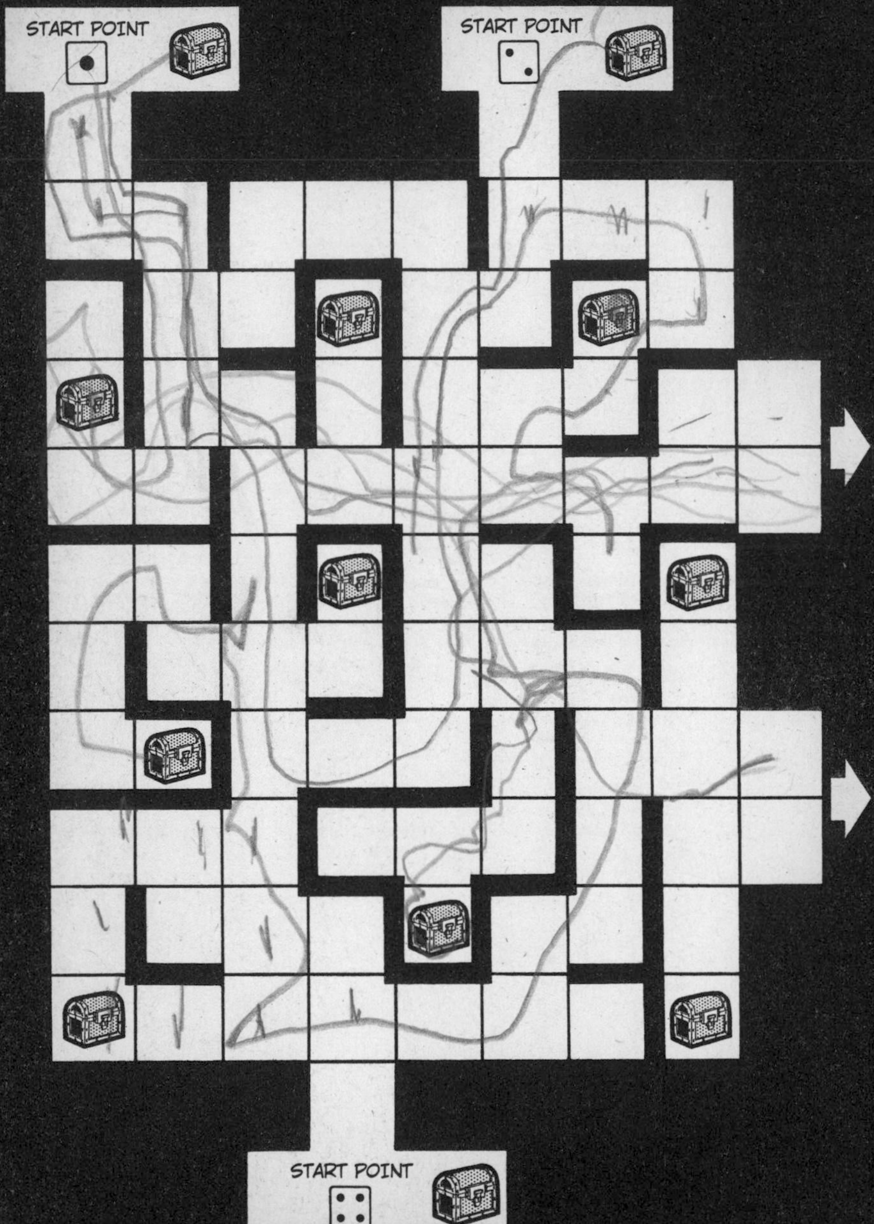
START POINT
START POINT
START POINT

DUNGEON BATTLE GAME

NUMBER OF PLAYERS: 2-4
WHAT YOU NEED: • FOUR SIX-SIDED DICE (TWO PAIRS OF TWO
DIFFERENT COLORS)
 • A GAME PIECE TO REPRESENT EACH PLAYER
 • A PHOTOCOPY OF PAGES 176-177 TO USE AS
A BOARD (AN ENLARGED PHOTOCOPY IS BEST)
 • PAPER, PENCIL AND CALCULATOR

HOW TO PLAY

• AT THE START OF THE GAME, EACH PLAYER ROLLS A SINGLE DIE. SHE THEN PLACES
HER PIECE ON THE "START POINT" FOR THAT NUMBER. (IF THE "START POINT" IS
ALREADY OCCUPIED, SHE MUST ROLL AGAIN.)
• AFTER THE PIECES ARE PLACED, CHARACTERS MOVE IN ORDER OF THEIR "START
POINT" NUMBER (GOING FROM 1 TO 6).
• EACH PLAYER STARTS WITH 300 LIFE POINTS (300P).
• ON YOUR TURN, YOU THROW A SINGLE DIE AND MOVE YOUR PIECE THAT MANY
SPACES (OR LESS, IF YOU WANT).
• WHEN YOU LAND ON A SPACE WITH A TREASURE CHEST, ROLL TWO DICE (ONE OF
EACH COLOR – CALL THEM "A" AND "B" FOR SHORT). THEN LOOK ON THE TABLE ON
PAGE 179 TO SEE WHAT WAS INSIDE.
• ON YOUR VERY FIRST TURN, ROLL THE "A" AND "B" DICE TO OPEN THE TREASURE
CHEST AT YOUR "START POINT"!
• A TREASURE CHEST CAN ONLY BE OPENED ONCE. AFTER IT HAS BEEN OPENED,
MARK IT AS "EMPTY" ON THE BOARD.

WINNING THE GAME

• THE POINT OF THE GAME IS TO GET ITEMS FROM TREASURE CHESTS AND USE THEM
TO DEFEAT THE OTHER PLAYERS! THE WINNER IS THE PLAYER WHO REDUCES ALL HIS
OPPONENTS' LIFE POINTS TO ZERO.
• THERE ARE TWO WAYS TO ATTACK OPPONENTS: *WEAPONS* OR *MAGIC ATTACKS.*
• *WEAPONS*: IF YOU FIND A WEAPON, LIKE "MASTER SWORD," YOU CAN ATTACK
OTHER PLAYERS BY STOPPING ON THE SAME SPACE AS THEM. (SEE THE RULES ON
THE NEXT PAGE.) YOU CAN ONLY ATTACK ANOTHER PLAYER ONCE PER TURN.
• *MAGIC ATTACKS*: SOME TREASURE CHEST ITEMS, LIKE "DEATH BALL", CAN HURT
OTHER PLAYERS FROM A DISTANCE. TO USE A MAGIC ATTACK ON YOUR TURN, THERE
MUST BE A STRAIGHT LINE BETWEEN YOU AND YOUR OPPONENT(S) WITH NO WALLS IN
THE WAY. IF THERE'S MORE THAN ONE OPPONENT IN A STRAIGHT LINE WITH NO WALLS
IN THE WAY, THE SAME MAGIC ATTACK DAMAGES *ALL OF THEM!* UNLIKE WEAPONS AND
SHIELDS, YOU CAN ONLY USE MAGIC ATTACKS ONCE, SO KEEP TRACK OF HOW MANY
YOU HAVE! YOU CAN ONLY USE A MAGIC ATTACK ONCE PER TURN.

WEAPONS & SHIELDS

• PLAYERS CAN ONLY USE ONE WEAPON AND ONE SHIELD AT A TIME. HOWEVER,
YOU CAN CARRY ONES YOU'RE NOT USING. KEEP TRACK OF EVERY WEAPON AND
SHIELD YOU FIND, BECAUSE SOME TREASURE CHESTS MAY MAKE YOU LOSE YOUR
BEST EQUIPMENT!
• IF YOU DON'T HAVE A WEAPON, YOU CAN STILL ATTACK OTHER PLAYERS WITH
YOUR BARE HANDS, BUT YOUR ATTACK STRENGTH IS ONLY (10A).

BATTLE SYSTEM

- "P" STANDS FOR THE PLAYERS' LIFE POINTS, "A" STANDS FOR THE WEAPONS' ATTACK STRENGTH, AND "D" STANDS FOR THE SHIELDS' DEFENSE POINTS.
- WHEN SOMEONE LANDS ON THE SAME SPACE AS SOMEONE ELSE AND WANTS TO FIGHT, BOTH PLAYERS ROLL ONE DIE. ONLY THE PLAYER WHO ROLLS HIGHER GETS TO ATTACK! (IF THE ROLLS ARE A TIE, THEY BOTH GET TO ATTACK, BUT THE DEFENDER GOES FIRST.) IF THE DEFENDER ROLLS A ⚅ THEY CAN CHOOSE TO RUN AWAY INSTEAD OF ATTACKING (ROLL A DIE AND MOVE THAT MANY SPACES AWAY, EVEN IF IT'S NOT THEIR TURN).
- THE ATTACKER ROLLS ONE DIE. MULTIPLY THE NUMBER BY THE WEAPON STRENGTH (A). THE DEFENDER LOSES THAT MANY LIFE POINTS!
- EXAMPLE: ⚁ X WEAPON 30A = 60P DAMAGE
- HOWEVER, IF THE DEFENDER IS WEARING A SHIELD, THE DAMAGE IS REDUCED BY THE SHIELD'S DEFENSE POINTS (D).
- EXAMPLE: OPPONENT'S ATTACK 200P - SHIELD 80D = 120P DAMAGE
- SHIELDS DON'T PROTECT AGAINST MAGIC ATTACKS.

TREASURE CHART

DIE B → / DIE A ↓	⚀	⚁	⚂	⚃	⚄	⚅
⚀	BLACK MAGIC "MEGIRA" MAGIC ATTACK: 200A	WHITE MAGIC "LLIONA" ADD 100P TO YOUR LIFE POINTS	GREAT SWORD WEAPON: 50A	DEATH BALL MAGIC ATTACK: 100A	STAFF WEAPON: 20A	CURSED TREASURE YOU PERMANENTLY LOSE YOUR BEST WEAPON AND SHIELD
⚁	BIG SHIELD SHIELD: 80D	MONSTER SCROLL "STRIPPER" A GENIE STEALS THE BEST WEAPON & SHIELD FROM ONE OPPONENT AND GIVES THEM TO YOU	WHITE MAGIC "LLIONA" ADD 200P TO YOUR LIFE POINTS	MASTER SHIELD SHIELD: 100D	FAIRY'S GIFT ADD 100P TO YOUR LIFE POINTS	LONG SWORD WEAPON: 40A
⚂	FAIRY'S GIFT ADD 200P TO YOUR LIFE POINTS	DEATH BALL MAGIC ATTACK: 100A	BLACK MAGIC "ZAP" ALL THE OTHER PLAYERS TAKE 100P DAMAGE (SHIELDS DON'T HELP)	FAIRY'S GIFT ADD 100P TO YOUR LIFE POINTS	IRON SHIELD SHIELD: 80D	WHITE MAGIC "LLIONA" ADD 100P TO YOUR LIFE POINTS
⚃	DEATH BALL MAGIC ATTACK: 100A	BATTLE AXE WEAPON: 40A	HERO'S SHIELD SHIELD: 80D	MONSTER SCROLL "GOGYAL" THE DEMONESS GOGYAL CAUSES 100P DAMAGE TO ANY ONE OPPONENT (SHIELDS DON'T HELP)	SPEAR WEAPON: 30A	GREAT SHIELD SHIELD: 100D
⚄	SABER WEAPON: 30A	BLACK MAGIC "FREEZE" ONE OF YOUR OPPONENTS LOSES HIS NEXT THREE TURNS	MASTER SWORD WEAPON: 50A	CURSED TREASURE YOU PERMANENTLY LOSE YOUR BEST WEAPON AND SHIELD	WHITE MAGIC "LLIONA" ADD 200P TO YOUR LIFE POINTS	DEATH BALL MAGIC ATTACK: 100A
⚅	BLACK MAGIC "GIDORA" MAGIC ATTACK: 100A	TRASH CAN LID SHIELD: 50D	FAIRY'S GIFT ADD 200P TO YOUR LIFE POINTS	HAMMER WEAPON: 20A	DEATH BALL MAGIC ATTACK: 100A	BLACK MAGIC "GANDA" MAGIC ATTACK: 200A

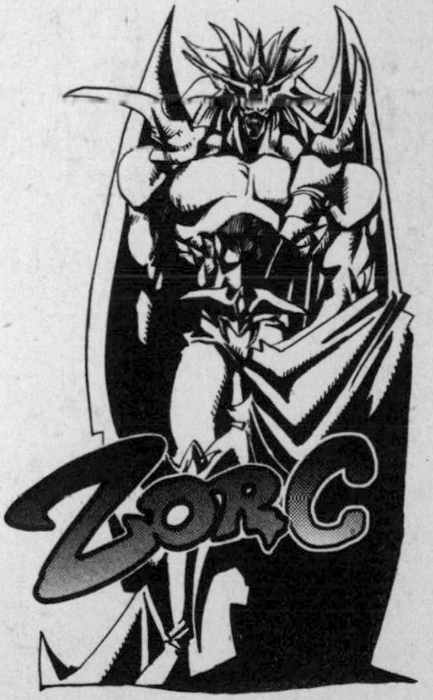
ZORC

IN THE NEXT VOLUME...

*A new **Yu-Gi-Oh!** series begins!*

Yu-Gi-Oh!: Duelist contains the original story behind the anime series, including scenes you never saw on TV! A mysterious videotape sends Yugi and his friends to Duelist Kingdom, the island home of super-rich American game designer Maximillion Pegasus. There, Yugi must compete with the world's greatest Duel Monsters players to win amazing riches... and discover the shocking secret behind the game!

COMING FEBRUARY 2005!

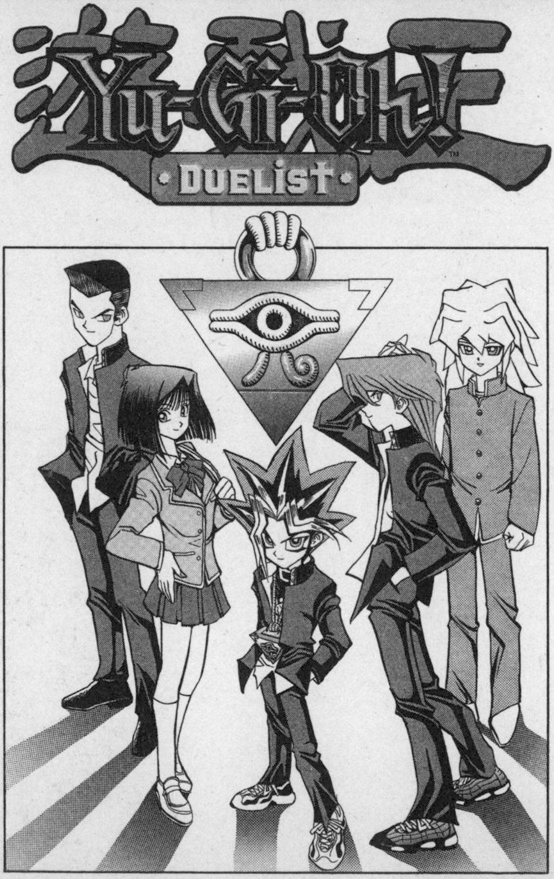
Yu-Gi-Oh!
DUELIST

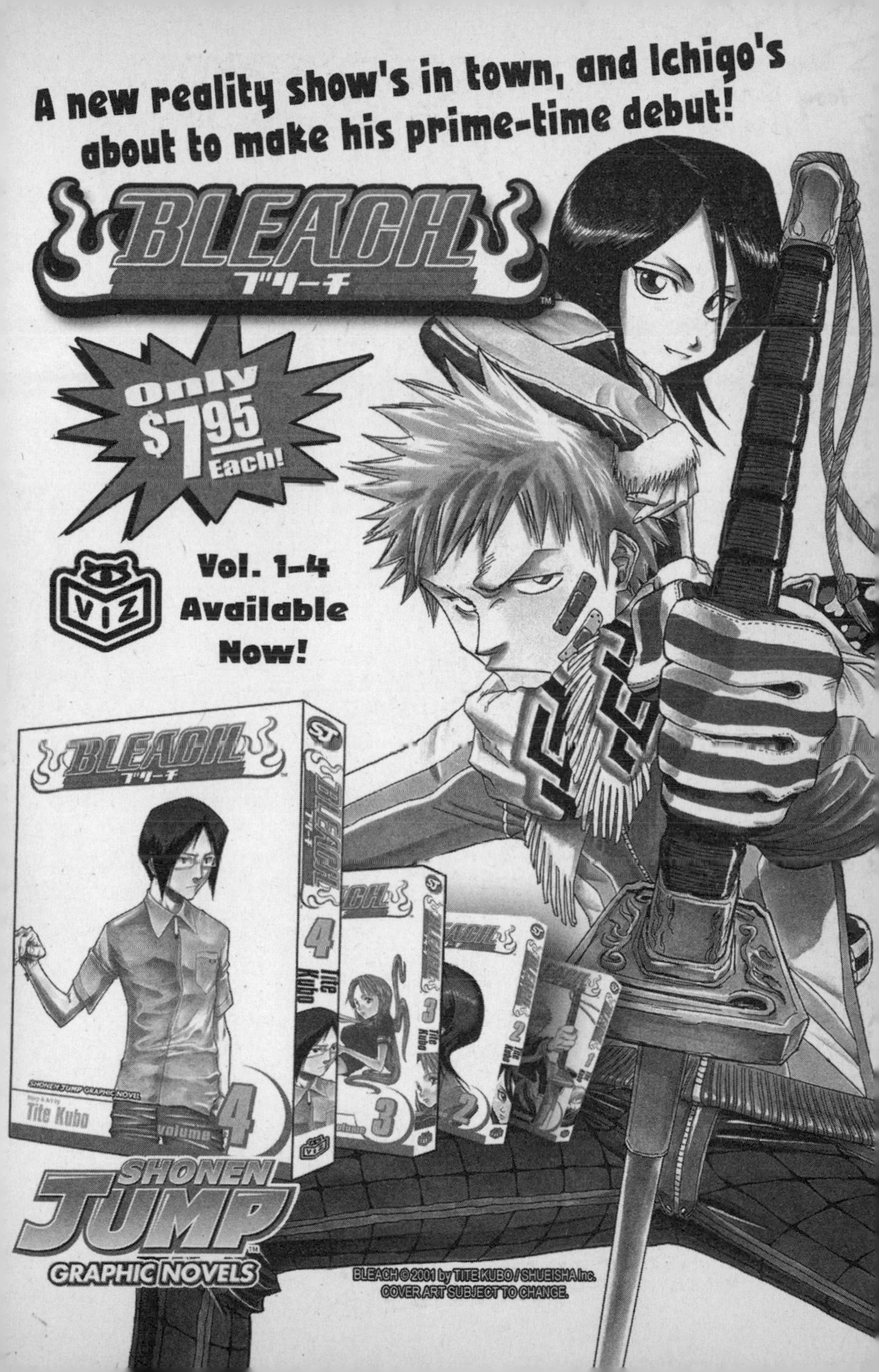
A new reality show's in town, and Ichigo's about to make his prime-time debut!
BLEACH
ブリーチ
Only $7.95 Each!
VIZ
Vol. 1-4 Available Now!
SHONEN JUMP GRAPHIC NOVELS
BLEACH © 2001 by TITE KUBO / SHUEISHA Inc.
COVER ART SUBJECT TO CHANGE.

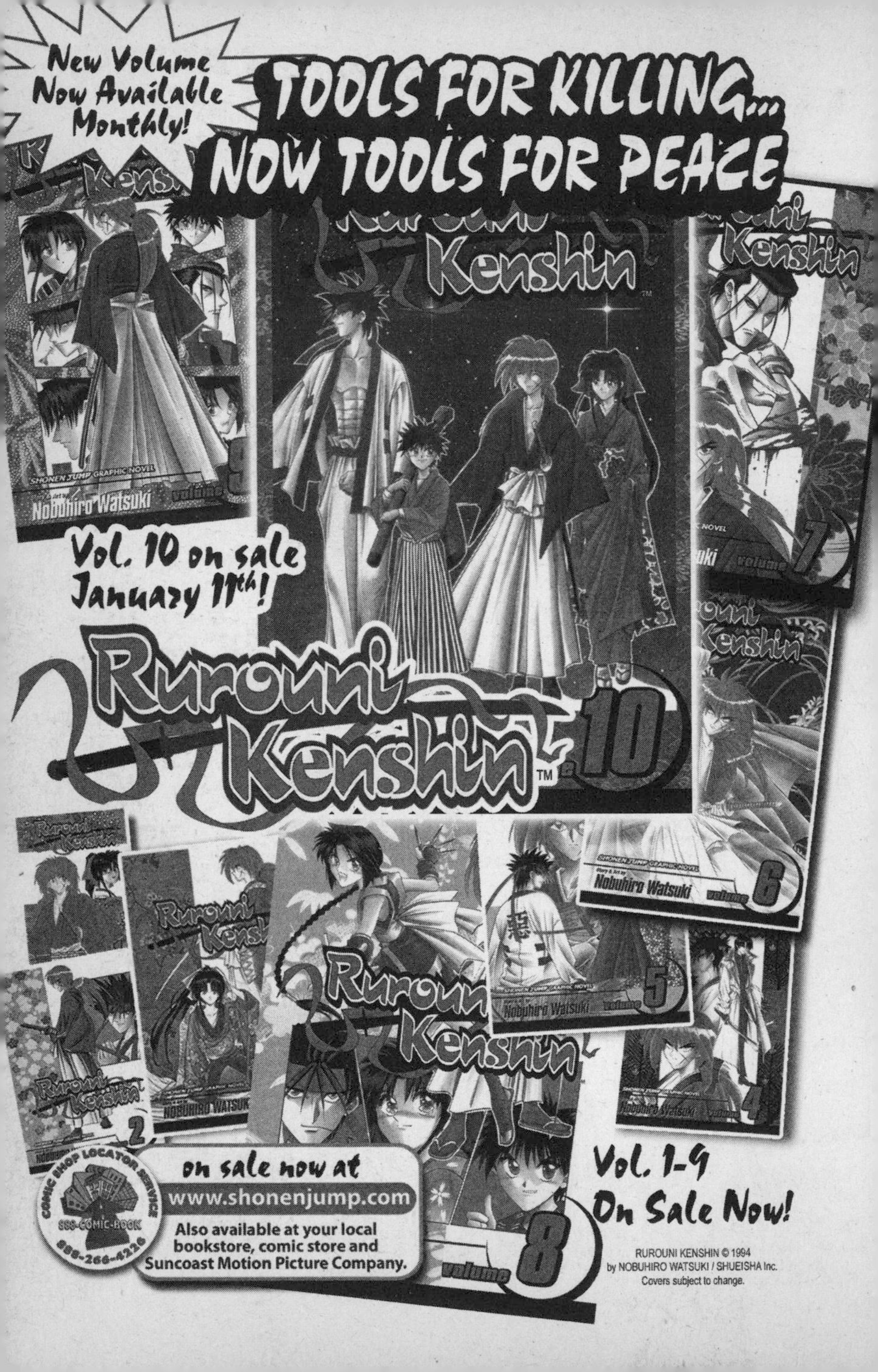
New Volume Now Available Monthly!
TOOLS FOR KILLING... NOW TOOLS FOR PEACE
Vol. 10 on sale January 11th!
Rurouni Kenshin™ 10
on sale now at
www.shonenjump.com
Also available at your local bookstore, comic store and Suncoast Motion Picture Company.
COMIC SHOP LOCATOR SERVICE
888-COMIC-BOOK
888-266-4226
Vol. 1-9 On Sale Now!
RUROUNI KENSHIN © 1994 by NOBUHIRO WATSUKI / SHUEISHA Inc.
Covers subject to change.

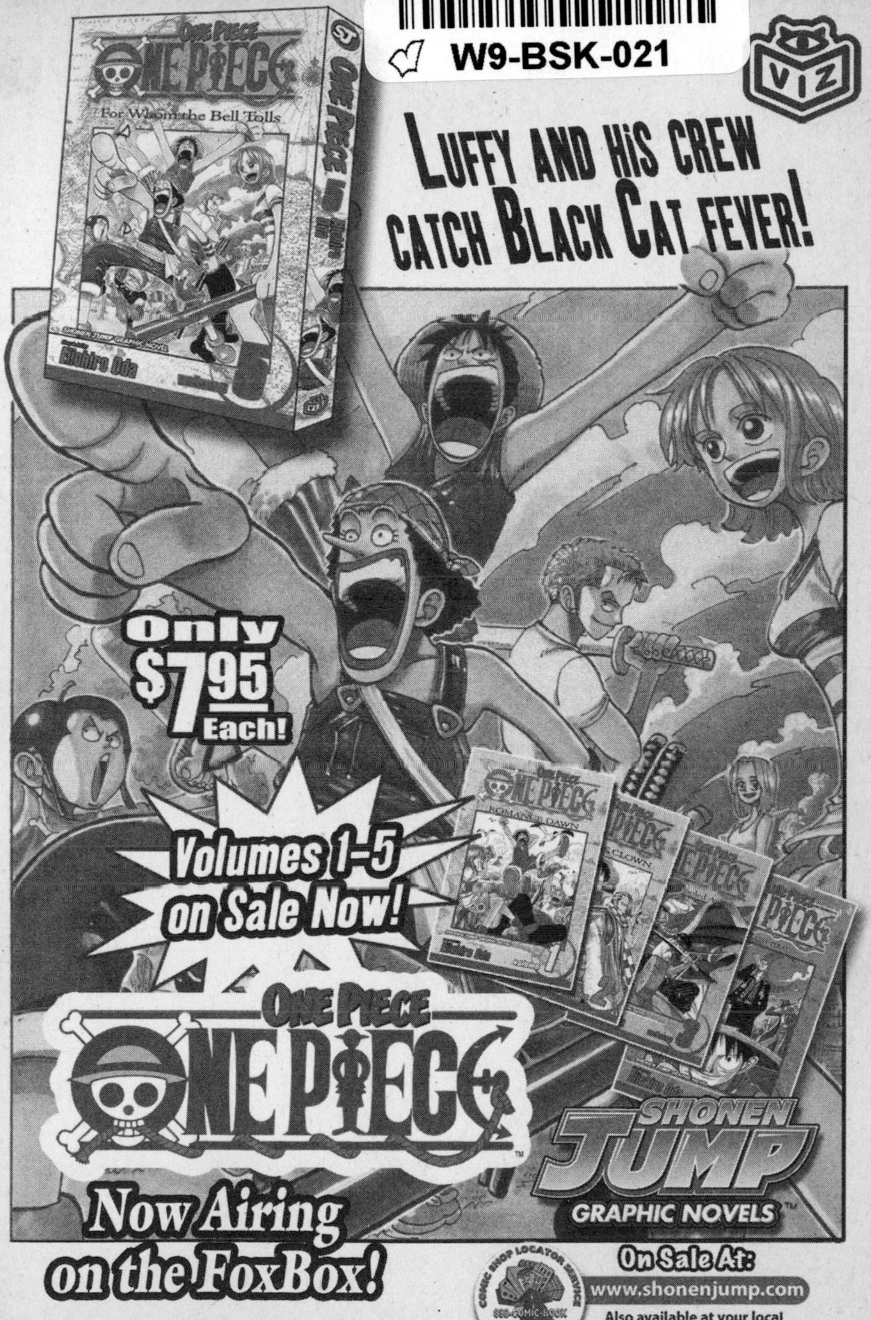

LUFFY AND HIS CREW
CATCH BLACK CAT FEVER!
ONE PIECE
For Whom the Bell Tolls
Only
$7.95
Each!
Volumes 1-5
on Sale Now!
ONE PIECE
SHONEN JUMP
GRAPHIC NOVELS™
Now Airing
on the FoxBox!
On Sale At:
www.shonenjump.com
Also available at your local
bookstore, comic store and
Suncoast Motion Picture Company.
COMIC SHOP LOCATOR SERVICE
888-COMIC-BOOK
888-266-4226